D1553565

The Unity of the Self

Representation and Mind
Hilary Putnam and Ned Block, editors

Representation and Reality
Hilary Putnam

Explaining Behavior: Reasons in a World of Causes
Fred Dretske

The Metaphysics of Meaning
Jerrold J. Katz

The Realistic Spirit: Wittgenstein, Philosophy, and the Mind
Cora Diamond

The Unity of the Self
Stephen L. White

The Unity of the Self

Stephen L. White

A Bradford Book
The MIT Press
Cambridge, Massachusetts
London, England

© 1991 Massachusetts Institute of Technology

All rights reserved. No part of this book may be reproduced in any form by any electronic or mechanical means (including photocopying, recording, or information storage and retrieval) without permission in writing from the publisher.

This book was set in Palatino by DEKR Corporation and was printed and bound in the United States of America.

Library of Congress Cataloging-in-Publication Data

White, Stephen L., 1948–
    The unity of the self / Stephen L. White.
        p.   cm. — (Representation and mind)
    "A Bradford book."
    Includes bibliographical references and index.
    ISBN 0-262-23162-X
    1. Philosophy of mind. 2. Self (Philosophy). 3. Identity (Psychology). 4. Ethics—Psychological aspects. I. Title. II. Series.
BD418.W45   1991   90-29869
126—dc20   CIP

To my mother and father

Contents

Preface

The order of these essays, with one exception, approximates both the sequence in which the arguments were developed and their increasing distance from the standard problems in the philosophy of mind. The first essays were in fact conceived as part of a functionalist account of content and qualia. The topic of qualia, however, leads naturally to the question of the nature of consciousness in general. And consciousness and self-consciousness raise problems beyond those raised by theories in the philosophy of mind or, indeed, by any nonnormative theory.

The accounts of consciousness compatible with functionalism characterize it in terms of relations between interacting subsystems of the psychological subject. But these homuncular analyses raise serious problems. For example, there seems to be no form of functional organization that could plausibly account for consciousness and that is unique to the subject as a whole. At the very least, any plausible theory of consciousness in homuncular terms will have the consequence that each of the two brain hemispheres is separately conscious. If, however, consciousness together with a high degree of conceptual sophistication is sufficient for personhood, then it is unclear how we can avoid the conclusion that there are at least two distinct persons and quite possibly many more in any normal human body. And this has the apparently absurd consequence that we would not be justified in destroying one hemisphere to save the person as a whole.

This is one example of the problem of explaining the unity of the homuncular subsystems of a single psychological subject. And it is a clear example of the way in which problems central to the philosophy of mind give rise to problems that belong more properly to moral psychology or even moral theory. Moreover, the usual theories of personal identity over time cannot easily be extended to address problems of this kind, and in any case they seem in need of serious revision. According to such theories, whether person A and person B existing at some later time are in fact the same person can depend only on the intrinsic features of A and B and the physical and psychological relations between them. But a number of examples suggest that this constraint, whose analogue regarding moral responsibility I call the intrinsic property constraint, cannot be met. Other factors including social norms and practices appear to be necessary to explain our responses in many cases where personal identity is at stake.

The problems regarding the unity of homuncular subsystems are especially acute where accounts of self-deception are concerned. The only plausible accounts of full-blown self-deception are humuncular analyses according to which it involves the manipulation of the beliefs of one of the subject's subsystems by another subsystem to whose operations the first system has no conscious access. And given the intrinsic similarities between this case and the case of deception by another, it is difficult to see how those who were self-deceived could be held responsible.

The account of responsibility required to deal with the problem of self-deception, however, involves more than simply rejecting the intrinsic property constraint. On the one hand, if social norms and practices provided the only justification of the punishment and blame that accompanies ascriptions of responsibility, then those who were punished or blamed would be scapegoats whose suffering was justified only by its contribution to the common social good. On the other hand, standard compatibilist accounts, which satisfy the intrinsic property constraints, are vulnerable to what I call the basic problem: Though there are senses in which we could have done other than what we did, there are also senses in which we could not. Why, then should we be punished on the basis of facts of the first kind rather than excused on the basis of the second kind of facts? It seems that no purely metaphysical account of responsibility, i.e., no account of the causal underpinnings of our actions that does not involve norms or values either implicitly or explicitly, will explain how the suffering entailed by ascriptions of responsibility and blame could be justified.

The solution to both these difficulties requires an account of internal justification according to which what one is justified in doing is necessarily connected with what one would be motivated to do, at least under ideal circumstances. The account I provide involves a justification of our practices of ascribing responsibility and blame that, because it appeals to the deepest commitments of those who are made to suffer, cannot be criticized for creating scapegoats. And since I argue that ascriptions of irrationality are a special case of ascriptions of blame, this approach yields an account of rationality as well.

This account of responsibility in terms of internalist justification is

applicable to the problematic cases of the unity of interacting subsystems. Thus it provides a way of handling both self-deception and the
problems of consciousness and self-consciousness. Moreover, the
basic problem applies to metaphysical accounts of personal identity
as well as metaphysical accounts of responsibility. Any account of
personal identity that is neither explicitly nor implicitly normative will
fail to answer the question how we are justified in making sacrifices
for those future persons that, according to the account, are our future
selves. Thus the account of internal justification has a role to play in
an account of the standard cases of personal identity as well.

In addition to its relevance to the standard cases, this account has
an important bearing on a question of unity over time that has not
been systematically discussed in the context of personal identity: the
question of one's ability to identify with future persons with whom
one is psychologically and physically continuous but who fail to share
one's conception of the good. This last form of unity—the unity of the
self across breaks in one's conception of the good—plays a crucial role
in the analysis of moral commitment. And the analysis of moral commitment is a central element in a range of controversies surrounding
the foundations of moral theory. In particular, it figures essentially in
the evaluation of contemporary formulations of utilitarianism and
contract theories.

The essays, then, involve reformulation of such issues as consciousness and self-consciousness, personal identity, self-deception, responsibility, and rationality in terms of the internal justification of certain
patterns of concern. Thus a significant number of issues from the
philosophy of mind and metaphysics are recast as, broadly speaking,
matters of moral psychology. If the essays serve no other purpose, I
hope they have the effect of moving the issues of moral psychology
somewhat closer to the center of contemporary philosophical concern.

These essays are intended to be self-contained, though in some
cases the arguments in the essays are qualified in the postscripts. Thus
there is some overlap among them in the exposition of the concepts
that are basic to the account of internal justification. The full account
of internal justification is developed in chapters 7 through 9 and in
the postscripts to chapters 8 and 9. It is summarized and extended in
chapter 10 and summarized and applied in chapter 11.

The essays have been shaped by discussions with a large number
of people, only some of whom are mentioned by name in the notes. I
am grateful to them for their comments and suggestions. I am especially grateful to Ned Block, Akeel Bilgrami, Norman Daniels, Daniel
Dennett, Brian Loar, William Lycan, Georges Rey, Amélie Rorty, Carol

Rovane, Stephen Schiffer, John Searle, and Peter Unger for their consistently acute criticisms and advice as the essays developed over the past ten years.

I am also grateful to Harry and Betty Stanton of The MIT Press for their advice and encouragement and to Joanna Poole and Alan Thwaits for their expertise and patience.

Finally, I owe a special debt to my wife, Judith Kahn, without whom this book, if it had come to exist at all, would have been the work of a very different author.

The Unity of the Self

Introduction

In discussing the problem of first-person self-reference, Roderick Chisholm poses the following question: "Is it possible that what I call my experience has *several* subjects? . . . Might not there be, for example, one person who is doing what I call my seeing and a second person who is doing what I call my hearing?" Chisholm concludes that "the answer lies in the fact of the unity of consciousness."[1] Contemporary research in the cognitive sciences, however, has made appeal to the unity of consciousness increasingly problematic. Therefore, I prefer to say that the answer reveals one aspect of the unity of the self.

This book is about what binds the self together and, equally important, what separates selves from one another. The self, as I use the term, is a subject of intentional states, such as beliefs and desires, as well as qualitative states, such as pains. And these intentional states must have certain contents if their subjects are to count as selves. Selves, we might say, are persons as they are represented to themselves from the first-person point of view. (I discuss the first-person point of view in chapter 6.) In addition, both the intentional states and the qualitative states must be appropriately integrated if the subject is to count as a person or self. What this integration involves is the subject of this study.

I shall be concerned with four primary sources of the unity of the self. The first two sources are discussed in section 1 of the introduction, the third in section 2, and the fourth in section 3. The first, the unity of practical reason, consists in the relations between our beliefs, desires, and actions in virtue of which our actions are largely rational, given our beliefs and desires. (The unity of theoretical reason—the relations between beliefs on the basis of which some count as reasonable, given others—can be treated in this context as a special case of the unity of practical reason.) In the absence of such unity, nothing we could count as a self would exist.

Self-knowledge, particularly privileged self-knowledge, provides a second source of unity. Not only do we have a great deal of knowledge regarding our own beliefs, desires, and qualitative states, but in some cases, it seems, our beliefs about ourselves could not be mistaken. The claim that one believes that one's experience is pleasant and that one is actually experiencing excruciating pain, if it is understood as the claim that one's belief is mistaken, seems unintelligible. Rather, it must be assumed that there is no single, unified subject that has both the sincere belief and a genuine experience of pain. But if this is the case, then our access to those qualitative experiences that are genuinely ours must in some sense be privileged. And something similar seems true for at least some of our own occurrent thoughts.

The third source of unity stems from those patterns of rational self-concern that are intimately tied both to the unity of the self over time and to the unity of the various subsystems of the mind that interact simultaneously. Self-identity over time is connected not only with our tendency to make special sacrifices for the benefit of our future selves but also with our willingness to take responsibility for our past selves. In addition, we take responsibility for the operations of some mental subsystems to whose activities we have no conscious access. In so doing, we make those operations integral to our self-conception.

The fourth source lies in the unity generated by unconditional, especially moral, commitments. This source, which is the foundation of our conception of the good, may reinforce one's unity as a self over time. By the same token, radical breaks in our conception of the good may undermine that unity. The implications that this has for moral commitment are particularly relevant to issues in contemporary moral theory.

1   The Metaphysics of the Self

In chapters 1 through 4, I offer a functionalist account of the first two sources of the unity of the self. (In characterizing functionalism as a metaphysical account, I am contrasting it with normative accounts that appeal to the content of the subject's particular commitments or desires or the particular norms or practices of the subject's society. I appeal to such normative considerations in explaining the third and fourth respects in which the self is unified.) According to this functionalist account, the unity of practical reason is a result of a priori constraints on the ascription of intentional states to a subject. On this account, what is essential to beliefs, desires, and intentions is the network of causal relations they bear to each other and to other internal states, perceptual inputs, and motor outputs. A belief has the content that it has as the result of two kinds of relations to other psychological states. The belief tends to arise as the result of certain kinds of evidential inputs and not others when the other beliefs that the subject holds are fixed. And it tends to bring about some actions rather than others when both the other beliefs and the desires of the subject are given. On this conception of belief, the task of radical interpretation, that is, the task of ascribing intentional states to a subject on the basis of its physical makeup, is subject to certain a priori constraints. These require that believers should be at least minimally rational, and this rationality guarantees the unity of practical reason.

Functionalism also provides a natural account of privileged self-knowledge. Just as there are a priori constraints that govern the relations between intentional states, there are also constraints that govern the relations between intentional states and qualitative states. The fact that it seems inconceivable that one should be in pain and believe on reflection that one is in a mildly pleasurable state is captured by the following a priori constraint. States that constitute pain and states that constitute the belief that one is in pain must overlap significantly in their dispositional makeup. And this constraint is sufficient to rule out the kind of dissociation between pain and pain belief that seems impossible to imagine.

Recent work on the content of belief, however, suggests that this content is not determined by the relation of beliefs to inputs, outputs, and other internal states. And this threatens to undermine the functionalist account of the unity of practical reason and self-knowledge. If two of our beliefs have the same content but we fail to recognize this fact, we may behave in ways whose rationality is difficult to explain. And if the contents of our beliefs depend on things to which we have no access, our knowledge of what we currently and occurrently believe will be open to question.

Practical rationality

That the contents of a subject's beliefs are not determined by that subject's internal functional states has been argued by Hilary Putnam and Tyler Burge. Putnam and Burge maintain that the contents of a subject's beliefs depend not only on the subject's psychology but also on the surrounding environment. For example, two subjects disposed to utter the same sentences containing the term 'water'—subjects who both describe what they refer to in the same way—may *mean* different things by using that term. If one subject's environment contains H_2O while the other's contains a different liquid with all the observable properties of water, then the first will have beliefs about water, while the second will not.

In chapter 1, I argue that this account of content fails to capture what functionally identical subjects have in common. I also argue that we can define a notion of content (narrow content) according to which the contents of a subject's beliefs depend solely on the subject's internal psychology. Very roughly, the narrow content of a subject's belief is a function from possible contexts of acquisition of the words in which the subject would express the belief to the proposition that the subject would express relative to those contexts. In this sense of 'content', the subject whose environment contains H_2O and the subject whose environment contains the liquid with the observable properties of water may express beliefs with the *same* content when they utter the words 'Water is wet'.

On this account, the narrow content of a belief is its truth-conditional potential. But such a characterization of narrow content has a serious limitation. Since the truth conditions of a belief make up its wide content, this approach defines the subject's own perspective (narrow content) only in terms of a perspective that is not the subject's own. In chapter 2, I argue that we can define narrow content independently of any reference to wide content. Suppose we assign sets of possible worlds to a subject in such a way as to capture not the wide content of the subject's beliefs but the world as the subject conceives it. This means, for example, that if the subject knows nothing about the difference between H_2O and the substance with the observable properties of water, then the set of possible worlds that defines the content of the subject's belief that would be expressed with the words 'Water is wet' should contain both the worlds at which H_2O is wet and the worlds at which the observably indistinguishable substance is wet.

But which possible worlds characterize the subject's conception of the way things are? I suggest, as a first approximation, that they are the worlds where the subject's actions are optimal, given his or her desires and opportunities for action. And here 'optimal' must be understood to mean *objectively* optimal; the subject's action is optimal just in case it is *in fact* the best action that subject could have chosen (given his or her desires) at the world in question. The appeal is to objective optimality because if we ignore such forms of irrationality as weakness of the will, all actions are *subjectively* optimal; that is, they all maximize the satisfaction of the subject's desires relative to the subject's beliefs. In contrast, at most possible worlds, even if none of the subject's actions are irrational, many will fail to be *objectively* optimal because some of the subject's beliefs will be false. And at worlds where the subject's actions *are* objectively optimal, this will normally be because all the subject's beliefs are true. Thus the worlds where the subject's actions are objectively optimal have a special claim to represent the subject's conception of the world. Let us call the worlds that represent this conception the subject's *notional worlds*. Then although the characterization in terms of objective optimality is in fact too simple to capture the concept of a notional world, I argue in chapter 2 that it provides the basis for a more complex definition that does. And content defined in terms of notional worlds is narrow content.

The fact that narrow content is necessary to capture the subject's own perspective has left some unconvinced that such a notion satisfies a legitimate need. On the account I have proposed, however, the ascription of narrow content is an essential element of the process of radical interpretation whereby the representational properties of a subject's intentional states are determined on the basis of that subject's physical properties. I argue that the a priori constraints that govern this process and thereby ensure the subject's minimal rationality apply to narrow content. Since this is the case and since what it is for a subject to have beliefs is defined by the constraints on radical interpretation, a subject's having beliefs with narrow content is fundamental to his or her having beliefs at all.

Privileged self-knowledge
The possibility of an account of narrow content removes the obstacle posed by theories of broad content to a functionalist account of our privileged self-knowledge of our occurrent beliefs. Such privileged knowledge, when it exists, will be knowledge of narrow content. And by imposing appropriate a priori constraints on the ascription of beliefs, functionalist theories can guarantee, contrary to what is usually assumed, that we have privileged knowledge of our conscious sensations as well. If the dispositions that underlie our being in pain must overlap to a very considerable extent the ones that underlie our believing that we are, then it will be impossible for us to think calmly and reflectively that we are in a mildly pleasurable state when we are actually consciously experiencing excruciating pain.

In chapters 3 and 4, however, I argue for a stronger claim. Nonfunctionalist theories cannot explain our access to our own pains, either because the explanation of that access requires reference to properties for which the theories in question provide no account, or because these theories cannot explain how such access could be privileged. Suppose that 'pain' picked out not a functional state but a neurophysiological state. We might imagine, for example, that pains are states in which our C fibers fire. Since there is no a priori connection between our being in pain and our C fibers firing, pain must have some feature (other than its being a C fiber firing) that, in our own cases and in ordinary contexts, enables us to recognize it as pain. (Compare this to the case of water. Since there is no a priori connection between a liquid's being water and its being H_2O, there will be some feature or features other than its being H_2O in virtue of which we can recognize it as water. In the case of water these will be its ordinary observable properties. However, the feature by which we recognize pain as pain is simply its being a state in which some part of us hurts.) And just as there is no a priori connection between a state's being a pain and its being a C fiber firing, so there is no *a priori* connection between its being a pain and its having *any* physical property. (For any such property, the discovery that pains had that property would be empirical.) Thus no reference to a physical property alone could explain how in ordinary contexts we succeed in recognizing our pains. Indeed, since there is no a priori connection between a state's being pain and its being any kind of state of a mental substance, reference to mental properties, as these are defined by substance dualism, provides no better explanation.

Suppose, then, that a theory explains a state's being a pain by reference to some property of that state and that there is no a priori connection between that property and the features we use in recognizing our own pains. We can conclude that the theory provides no account of our access to those pains. The argument for this conclusion I refer to in chapter 3 as the *property dualism argument*. Functionalist theories avoid this conclusion because it is plausible to claim that there *is* an a priori connection between a state's being a pain and its being a state with certain functional properties. These include under normal conditions its being a state that we desire should end, that shifts our attention toward the goal of relieving it, that is associated with the threat of bodily injury, and so forth. This connection is not one we could fail to make and still be competent in our use of the term 'pain'. Thus, according to functionalist theories, our normal access to our own pains is via the same property in virtue of which they are pains, the property that corresponds to their best functional or topic-neutral characterization.

There is one other conception of the mental, however, to which the property dualism argument does not apply. According to this conception, mental facts are not facts about an objective entity (that is, one that enters into causal relations with other objective entities and thus one that could be investigated in principle from a number of different points of view). Rather, mental facts are subjective facts, accessible in principle only to a single subject. On this view, the subjective and objective realms are complete in themselves, and each is perfectly self-contained; all causal interactions take place within the objective realm, and any such interaction between the two realms is ruled out on conceptual grounds.[2]

This conception of the mental according to which the mind is not in the world but is transcendental is not open to the property dualism argument. According to this view, there is nothing to a state's being a pain besides the subjective experience whose character we learn from our own case. This subjective experience, of which we are directly aware, is independent of any objective facts whatsoever and is accessible to each subject in principle only from his or her own first-person perspective. Since it cannot plausibly be claimed that we could imagine being in such a state without being in pain, the property dualism argument provides no objection to accounts of this kind.

I argue in chapter 4, however, that such accounts of qualitative states are open to another objection. Transcendental accounts of qualitative states, unless they are held in conjunction with a transcendental account of belief, cannot explain the fact that our access to our own pains is privileged. Given that the subjective and objective realms are each complete in themselves and cannot influence one another, there is no way in which the facts in one realm could determine the facts in the other. Thus if we had a transcendental account of qualia and a nontranscendental account of belief, there is no way in which the facts about belief could fix the qualitative facts. There is no way, for example, in which the fact that one *believes* that one is in pain could guarantee that one *is* in pain.

These objections do not apply, of course, to a theory that combines a transcendental account of qualia with a transcendental account of belief. But I argue in chapter 4 that no transcendental account of belief can succeed in explaining how subjective facts can fix the content of a proposition. Thus no transcendental theory of belief could explain how our beliefs have the propositional content they do. And in the absence of such a theory, the transcendental theory of qualia is unlikely to find wide support.

The normative turn

In chapters 1 through 4 my aim is not to provide a systematic and positive functionalist account of content and qualia. Rather, I argue that the most serious objections to such an account fail. And any functionalist account of content and qualia in turn provides certain metaphysical resources by reference to which the various kinds of unity that the self exhibits can be explained. These include, in addition to the a priori constraints on the relations between mental states, the relations of access by which subsystems of the mind exchange information. Such access relations are determined by facts like the following: that information is shared between the two brain hemispheres, that semantic information to which one is not attending and of which one is not consciously aware may influence one's interpretation of semantic information to which one does attend, that in cases of self-deception one seems to engage in actions motivated by information one would sincerely deny having, and so forth. Phenomena of this sort have led to theories in cognitive psychology that postulate the interaction of a number of separate subsystems, each of which has its own sources of information and its own dispositions and strategies. And these theories are well captured by homuncular models of the mind according to which such subsystems are the subjects of beliefs and desires and thus are intentional systems in their own right.

Where the explanation of the first two sources of the unity of the self are concerned, these resources seem adequate, as we have seen. But this is not true for the third source of unity. In the case of the unity of the various subsystems of the subject, the identity of the subject over time, and the subject's responsibility for his or her actions, access relations among subsystems and a priori constraints on the coexistence of mental states leave some of the most salient facts unexplained. First, as I point out in chapter 6, the most plausible theories of consciousness compatible with functionalism entail that a number of sophisticated subsystems of a normal human subject, including the two brain hemispheres, are separately conscious. And if this is the case, then Chisholm's question of how we know that there is not one person who does our seeing and another who does our hearing is difficult to avoid. A second problem, as I argue in chapters 5 and 7, is that neither our pretheoretical intuitions regarding personal identity nor our intuitions about moral responsibility, including our responsibility for the activities of some of our unconscious subsystems, have an explanation in terms of intrinsic psychological relations. Thus personal identity and responsibility will not be explained in purely functional terms. And there is a third and more general problem. Even if our ascriptions of responsibility did mirror intrinsic relations of psychological access, how could this justify punishment if the naturalistic and largely deterministic picture presupposed by functionalist theories is accurate? The same problem arises for the account of personal identity. Suppose that our pretheoretical intuitions about identity did perfectly mirror relations of psychological access; for example, suppose that they mirrored relations of psychological continuity. We can still ask what justifies our special concern for those future person stages with whom we are continuous in this sense.

The temptation at this point is to abandon not only functionalism but also the underlying assumption that the facts of philosophical and moral psychology are a part of the domain of the natural sciences. It is tempting to claim, for example, that none of the metaphysical resources compatible with naturalism are adequate to answer such questions as, Given that a future person stage will be psychologically and physically continuous with me now, will it be *me?* And such a claim would provide another opening for those who would introduce a category of subjective facts that are independent of the objective facts with which the natural sciences are concerned.

If the arguments in chapters 3 and 4 are correct, however, abandoning the functionalist and naturalist perspective is not an option open to us. The appeal of functionalism in the context of privileged self-knowledge is not simply that it requires no metaphysical commitments beyond those sanctioned by the natural sciences. It is that no functionalist account of privileged access could be adequate. And this claim is argued specifically with reference to the kinds of transcendental theories that our difficulties in explaining the third type of unity of the self might tempt us to adopt.

The alternative is to abandon the assumption that there is a metaphysical solution to the problems of identity and responsibility. Instead of treating these as metaphysical questions, we should treat them as normative questions about the best way of justifying those patterns of concern we exhibit for our past, present, and future selves. Such an approach is not entailed, of course, by a functionalist theory of mind. A functionalist might hold, for example, that personal identity is a matter of psychological continuity, and responsibility a matter of our actions' depending on our choices. Suppose, however, that we are committed to justifying those patterns of special concern that seem intimately connected with our concepts of identity and responsibility. And assume that we want the advantages of a functionalist account of the first two sources of the unity of the self. Then the normative approach to identity and responsibility is not only natural but apparently unavoidable. Thus in the remainder of the introduction I shall explore the implications of such an approach to these issues.

2   The Moral Psychology of the Self

It is natural to suppose that there is some intimate connection between the questions in category (1) and the questions in categories (2) and (3).

> 1. Is person *A* the same person as person *B* (where *B* exists at a later time than *A*)? Does *A* survive as *B*?
> 2. Do benefits to *B* compensate for comparable losses to *A*? Do they compensate *A*? Would *A* be rationally motivated to make significant sacrifices to provide comparably significant benefits to

B? Would *A* be rational in fearing the negative experiences suffered by *B*? Would *B* be rational in feeling grief for the losses of *A*?

3. Is *B* responsible for the actions of *A*? Is *A* responsible for the actions of *B*? Would *B* be rationally motivated to acquiesce in punishment or blame for the actions of *A*? Would *A* be rationally motivated to make whatever sacrifices were necessary to exercise responsibility over the future actions of *B*?

I assume, for example, that whereas *A*'s lossess at one time may be compensated by gains to *A* at a later time, *A*'s losses cannot be compensated by gains to *B* (where *B* is neither *A* at some later time nor a survivor of *A*).[3] This is surely in part because the assumption is supported by another natural assumption: that gains to *B* cannot (in general) compensate for losses to *A* *from A's point of view*. And this latter assumption is difficult to deny. Moreover, this assumption is implicit in most recent discussions of personal identity. Similar intuitions surround the relation between questions of identity and questions of responsibility. It is natural to assume that people are responsible only for the actions they themselves have performed.

That there is an intimate relation between the facts about personal identity and about our being justified in making sacrifices for the future and in taking responsibility for the past is unlikely to be challenged. But that they are related in this way does not indicate which kinds of facts, if either, are basic. According to most contemporary theories, it is the facts about personal identity that ground the facts about the justifiability of our making sacrifices for the future and of our taking responsibility for the past. According to these theories, we are justified in making sacrifices for the future when (but, of course, not only when) that future is our *own*. And we are justified in taking responsibility for those past actions we have performed *ourselves*. For theorists who make this assumption, the facts about personal identity require an independent characterization. Such characterizations have typically appealed to nonnormative facts, such as those about psychological continuity or physical continuity or both, that can be established independently of any facts about how we are justified in behaving in relation to past or future persons.

Whatever their details, such theories of personal identity face a problem. As we have seen, it is difficult to explain how a nonnormative theory—one that makes no appeal either explicitly or implicitly to values or norms—can explain why we *should* make provisions or take responsibility for persons with whom we are psychologically or physically continuous. Both those who appeal to psychological continuity in explaining personal identity and those who appeal to physical continuity assume the work is done when we have a theory that predicts the choices we are disposed to make under a wide range of circumstances relevant to our survival. The assumption is that what is required is a theory that predicts, for example, whether we would make a sacrifice for a future person A or a future person B, where A and B differ in their physical and psychological relations to us. But even given such a theory, the question would still arise as to why we were justified in making that sacrifice. Let us call this problem for any nonnormative theory that predicts our patterns of concern the *basic problem*. Since this problem arises most clearly in the case of moral responsibility, I shall first consider the problem in that context. I shall then consider how the treatment of moral responsibility that addresses that problem can be applied to the problem of personal identity.

Responsibility and rationality
The accounts of personal identity in terms of psychological or physical continuity are vulnerable, as we have seen, to the basic problem. And a completely analogous difficulty arises when we consider responsibility. What justifies the suffering entailed by our being blamed and punished for our past actions? Compatibilist accounts of responsibility hold that we may be responsible for what we have done, even if our actions are completely determined. Most such accounts suggest that we are responsible because there is a sense (or there are senses) in which we could have performed actions other than those we performed. But given that our actions were fixed by the state of the world centuries before we were born, together with the laws of nature, there are equally obvious senses in which we could *not* have done other than what we did. What justifies our being made to suffer because in one sense we could have done otherwise, rather than our being excused because there are other senses in which, quite obviously, we could not? The attempt to answer normative questions of this kind by appeal to nonnormative facts will necessarily fail to explain how those facts justify our practices regarding responsibility and blame. I shall call compatibilist accounts according to which the suffering involved in ascriptions of responsibility and blame is justified by appeal to nonnormative facts versions of *indirect compatibilism*. Indirect compatibilism, then, provides no solution to the basic problem. (In chapters 7 and 9, I raise a different problem for indirect accounts of moral responsibility, which involves the claim that such accounts face a dilemma. However, the basic problem, which is not presented until chapter 8, is both simpler and more fundamental. Thus in sketching

the argument of chapter 7, I am helping myself to a formulation that depends in part on the later chapter.)

The task, then, is to find an alternative account of responsibility according to which the suffering involved in ascriptions of responsibility and blame is justified directly, that is, without reference to such nonnormative claims as the claim that our actions could have been other than they were. I shall call such an account a version of *direct compatibilism*. A direct compatibilist account of responsibility, if it is to be complete, must specify how the suffering entailed by punishment and blame is to be justified. Existing versions of direct compatibilism appeal to utilitarian considerations. I argue that such a form of justification is inappropriate because it involves the sacrifice of those who are made to suffer in the pursuit of higher aggregate utility. And I argue (in chapter 11) that recent defenses of utilitarianism do not answer this objection.

As an alternative, I offer an internalist form of justification according to which what we are justified in doing is necessarily connected with our actual motivational makeup (see chapters 7 through 11). This account of internalist justification is couched in terms of a relation of support among a subject's noninstrumental desires. The fundamental intuition, which requires significant qualification, is that we are justified in acting on a desire just in case it is one we would keep if we could change any of our desires at will. I refer to the set of desires we would keep under these circumstances as our *ideal reflective equilibrium* (IRE). And what determines whether some particular desire is part of our IRE is the degree of support it receives from our other desires. Thus there are important analogies between this account of the justification of action and coherentist accounts of the justification of belief.

Direct compatibilism, when it is coupled with an account of internal justification, avoids both the basic problem and the objections raised by an appeal to utilitarian considerations. But our being internally justified in acquiescing in our own punishment and blame (and in that of others) will provide a justification of our social practices regarding responsibility only if our acquiescence, in virtue of being internally justified, is *rational*. In other words, internal justification as analyzed in terms of ideal reflective equilibria will be of interest only if it constitutes *rational* justification.

It may be objected, however, that on the account I am proposing we may be internally justified in doing what is clearly irrational. Consider the person who is future-Tuesday-indifferent. Such a person prefers to accept great pain that will be experienced on future Tuesdays rather than suffer the slightest discomfort on any other day. And this person would trade very intense pleasures available on future Tuesdays for the mildest pleasures available at other times of the week. Such a preference, it might be maintained, is irrational, whether or not it is supported in the subject's ideal reflective equilibrium. And since there is no reason why such a preference could not be supported in IRE, it seems to follow that rationality requires more than internal justification.

As I argue in chapter 9, however, the ascription of irrationality to a subject is itself a form of blame. As such it raises the same problem that ascriptions of blame raise in the context of moral responsibility. There is a straightforward sense in which we always do the best we can under the circumstances in which we act. Whenever there is a temptation to describe one of our decisions as suboptimal, given our own goals and information, this suboptimality will always have some explanation. For example, the decision may have been made under time constraints or under pressure, our computational resources may have been inadequate to produce an optimal decision, and so forth. And when this explanation is added to the description of our circumstances, the decision will be optimal in the light of the revised description. Thus it is unclear how we could be justified in accepting the blame implicit in ascriptions of irrationality. Such ascriptions, in other words, raise another version of the basic problem.

The solution to the basic problem for ascriptions of irrationality is the same as the solution for ascriptions of responsibility and blame. We will not be justified in acquiescing in blame for decisions that involve no false beliefs and no faulty inferences when the decisions are motivated by desires in IRE. Given that the motivating desires are in IRE, there will be nothing in our motivational makeup that would justify such acquiescence. But, as I argue in the case of moral responsibility, we will be justified in acquiescing in blame for some actions stemming from desires out of IRE. This assimilation of the problem raised by ascriptions of irrationality to the problem raised by ascriptions of responsibility provides a solution to the basic problem as it applies to irrationality. And it is difficult to see how an approach not modeled on the internalist direct compatibilist account of moral responsibility could do so.

This approach to rationality also has the consequence that actions motivated by desires in IRE are not irrational. This means in particular that future-Tuesday-indifference need not involve any irrationality. The claim, then, that internal justification is not sufficient for rationality is open to one of two objections. Either the claim is unsupported by any explicit account of rationality, or it is supported by an account that cannot provide a solution to the basic problem.

Personal identity

There is an analogue, where personal identity is concerned, to the internalist direct compatibilist approach to responsibility. Instead of attempting to justify our dispositions to accept responsibility for the actions of persons who existed in the past and to make sacrifices for persons who will exist in the future by reference to the nonnormative relations those persons bear to us, we can justify those dispositions directly. That is, we can provide them with an internalist justification by appealing to the relations of support between the desires on which the dispositions are based and our other desires and commitments.

In chapter 5, I examine the puzzle cases to which appeal is frequently made in testing theories of the identity of persons over time. I argue that a careful analysis of these cases shows that personal identity (or, more accurately, survival) depends on more than the intrinsic features of the subjects in question; it also depends on the social norms and practices of the subjects' society. And subjects who have internalized different sets of norms will be justified in expressing their concern for the future and their willingness to take responsibility for the past in very different ways.

The approach to personal identity that takes the justification of our special concern regarding past and future persons as basic provides an explanation of these results. If, as this approach suggests, the justification of our special concern depends on a wide range of other desires and commitments, then the fact that our intuitions regarding identity depend on our assumptions regarding social norms and practices is exactly the result we should have been prepared to find.

Self-deception and weakness of the will

Although the problems associated with the unity of the self over time are more familiar, the synchronic unity of the self raises equally serious difficulties. These difficulties become especially acute when we consider homuncular models, which depict the mind as a set of interacting subsystems. In such models each subsystem is represented as having its own intentional states, including sophisticated beliefs, goals, and strategies, and as having only limited access to the intentional states of the other subsystems. While models of this kind make the synchronic unity of the self especially problematic, they are well entrenched in contemporary cognitive psychology. Moreover, they are necessary to the explanation of self-deception, whose pervasiveness is difficult to deny. Thus we cannot ignore the possibility that such models undermine our assumption that the self exhibits a synchronic as well as a diachronic unity.

Consider first self-deception. Only a homuncular model, it seems, could make sense of the following possibility: that we should make ourselves believe a proposition that we continue to believe is false and that we should purposely avoid new evidence that would force the falsity of that belief upon us. Such a description is coherent only if we suppose that the self is divided into two subsystems, one of which manipulates the beliefs of the other without the latter's being conscious of the process. The description is coherent, in other words, only if we assimilate self-deception to other deception. But this analysis raises a difficult problem of its own. If we assimilate self-deception to other deception, how can we be justified in holding people responsible for self-deception when they are not responsible for being deceived by others?

The solution to this problem depends on the internalist direct compatibilist theory of responsibility sketched in response to the basic problem. We can be rationally justified in acquiescing in the ascription of responsibility and blame even if we are blamed for the activities of a subsystem to which we have no conscious access. First, this is not ruled out by the intrinsic similarity between self-deception and other deception. The distinction we make between different cases where responsibility is concerned need not depend solely on their intrinsic features. (This is analogous to the claim that distinctions regarding personal identity may depend on the social circumstances as well as the intrinsic properties of the subjects involved.) Second, there are several reasons why we might be justified in acquiescing in such an ascription of responsibility. We may, for example, be motivated to do so by the desire for a sphere in which we are autonomous and in which our authority is unquestioned. Moreover, we may be in a better position to take precautions against self-deception than against many forms of deception by others.

In addition to providing an account of self-deception, the internalist direct compatibilist account of moral responsibility answers a fundamental question about weakness of the will. This is the question how we distinguish actions that are merely weak-willed and for which we are responsible from actions that are genuinely compulsive and for which our responsibility is at least significantly diminished. In both cases we act on desires that are badly supported by our other desires and commitments. Our pretheoretical assumption is that in the case of weak-willed actions, we could have done other than we did. And this assumption ordinarily carries with it the claim that our being blamed for having performed those actions is justifiable. But to appeal to the claim that we can be blamed for our actions because they could have been other than they were would be to abandon the advantages of direct compatibilism.

Imagine, however, that there were no distinction between actions that are weak-willed and actions that we are genuinely compelled to perform. Then we could never be punished or blamed for being weak-willed. But in this case, those whose basic desires were in line with the norms of their society (that is, whose best supported desires were the desires not to harm others without justification, not to lie, not to steal, etc.) could not be blamed, whatever their actual behavior turned out to be. For subjects in these circumstances, the threat of punishment or blame for antisocial actions they might commit would have no deterrent effect. The responsibility for the control of their behavior, in such a situation, would rest with society as a whole. However, since this control could not involve punishment or blame, it would almost certainly take the form of medical or psychotherapeutic intervention aimed at preventing the harm that such antisocial actions would cause. There would then be no sphere of behavior for which those subjects who could not be blamed bore the ultimate responsibility. Therefore, they could claim no sphere in which they were the final authorities. And it is not difficult to imagine that those who desire autonomy might find such a social arrangement unattractive. Thus a desire for autonomy could justify our accepting responsibility on internalist grounds for weak-willed as well as self-deceptive behavior.

Consciousness and self-consciousness
A second problem concerning the unity of homuncular systems is raised by accounts of the nature of consciousness. The most plausible accounts compatible with functionalism equate consciousness with the integration of the outputs of a number of perceptual modules (assumed to be relatively independent of each other in their operations) and the outputs of some number of other subsystems to produce a unified and complex mental representation. Consciousness, then, according to these accounts, is a matter of the relations of access between homuncular systems, together with the sophistication and complexity of the representations those systems process.

The difficulty with this model of consciousness is that the functional specification—that we have a system that integrates in a single complex representation the outputs of a set of subsystems that operate independently of each other—is, for any given human subject, very probably not uniquely realized. On the contrary, this type of functional organization is almost certainly realized in a wide variety of different subsystems of the mind and at a wide variety of different levels. This will be the case even if we confine our consideration to the most sophisticated subsystems—systems to which we can attribute complex beliefs, goals, and strategies. Thus, as we have seen, accounts of this kind have the consequence that the consciousness of the person as a whole does not exhaust the consciousness associated with the physical system of which the person consists. Rather, it is a consequence of such accounts that many of the person's most sophisticated subsystems are themselves fully and separately conscious.

These accounts of consciousness that are currently under consideration do not, of course, exhaust the range of physicalist and functionalist theories that might be offered. But even if we deliberately attempt to tailor a physicalist or functionalist theory to avoid the unintuitive consequences of the current accounts, the attempt is bound to fail in view of the relation between the two brain hemispheres. In the first place, any plausible functional or physical characterization of consciousness that applies to one of the two hemispheres will apply to the other. Second, the two hemispheres are *separately* conscious; though they share roughly the same set of beliefs, these beliefs are separately tokened in each hemisphere. It would therefore be possible to render either of the two hemispheres unconscious without interrupting the conscious experiences of the other.

If fully and separately conscious subjects, each of whom possesses the conceptual sophistication necessary for personhood, are different persons, then our two brain hemispheres are not parts of a single person but are each persons in their own rights. But this conclusion would have very bizarre consequences. We might be unjustified, for example, in removing (and thereby destroying) one hemisphere in order to save what we would normally regard as the person, since this would be an instance of killing one person to save another. And since the destruction of one of a person's brain hemispheres to save the person does not seem unjustified, there must be something seriously wrong with one of our previous assumptions about the self.

In chapter 6, I argue that there is nothing wrong with an account of consciousness according to which it has an explanation in either physicalist or functionalist terms. This claim is supported by the analysis of content and qualia in chapters 3 and 4, in which I argue against the alternatives to functionalist accounts. Given a functionalist account of qualia as well as of content, it is not clear what room is left for an antifunctionalist account of consciousness. Is it really possible to suppose that someone might have all the intentional *and qualitative* states we have and still lack consciousness? The mistake, rather, is in the assumption that consciousness has any direct bearing on either personhood or the self.

I argue in chapter 6 that it is not consciousness but self-consciousness that has a significant bearing on these two notions. Personhood and selfhood are not simply a matter of the consciousness of the subject under consideration. They are a matter instead of self-consciousness as it is constituted by a certain characteristic pattern of concern. And I argue that none of our most sophisticated subsystems, including the two brain hemispheres, are separately *self*-conscious. Moreover, the type of argument that leads to this conclusion has a great deal in common with the arguments that support my accounts of personal identity and responsibility. Like those arguments, the argument that it is self-consciousness that bears on personhood proceeds not from metaphysical considerations but from an examination of the patterns of concern that are rationally justified when one system is an integrated part of another.

3   *The Self and Moral Theory*

There is an important qualification to the coherentist account of the relation of support among desires and of internal justification. Let us define an *unconditional desire* as one such that the state of affairs for which it is the desire is one we want now to be realized in the future, whether the desire for that state continues in the future or not. We want now, for example, to continue in the future to treat others honestly, even if in the future we no longer wish to do so. Unconditional desires thus defined introduce a noncoherentist element into the account of support among desires; that is, they play a foundational role relative to conditional desires. If an unconditional desire fails to cohere with a conditional desire, a subject will always choose, if possible, to eliminate the conditional desire. This is because, whether a desire is conditional or unconditional, eliminating it will ordinarily decrease the likelihood that it will be satisfied. But from the perspective of the subject who contemplates eliminating a desire, this fact can be discounted if the desire to be eliminated is conditional. If the desire is conditional, there is nothing to choose between a future in which it is satisfied and one in which it no longer exists. By definition, however, an unconditional desire is one for which this is not the case. Therefore, from the perspective of the subject making the choice, choosing to eliminate an unconditional desire in favor of a conditional desire always involves a serious loss, whereas making the opposite choice does not. Thus in cases of conflict it is the conditional desire that the subject will be motivated to eliminate.

The analysis of internal justification in terms of relations of support among conditional and unconditional desires (together with the anal-

ysis of rationality that I propose in chapter 9) has the following consequence. It is not necessarily the case that if we are rational, we will
be concerned about the welfare of any future person who is psychologically and physically continuous with us, regardless of that person's
conception of the good. We may instead be committed to our own
conception of the good on the basis of our unconditional desires, and
we may be prepared to withdraw our concern from any future extension of ourselves who lacks this conception.

This analysis of unconditional desires explains the possibility of
moral commitment in the following way. Given the existence of unconditional desires, we need not be prepared to change our motivational makeup simply because doing so would produce desires that
are more likely to be satisfied than our present ones. And not only
may we be unprepared to make such changes in our motivational
makeup, we may be rationally motivated to resist such changes if we
anticipate that they will be induced by external circumstances. Moreover, if such an externally induced change is unavoidable, we need
not be rationally motivated to make sacrifices for the future person
with whom we will be physically and psychologically continuous. We
may be rationally motivated instead to withdraw any special concern
we would have for that future person.

Moral commitment and contract theories
This analysis of moral commitment provides the basis for arguments
against what are currently the two most influential approaches to
ethical theory: contract theories and consequentialism. The following
argument applies to the particular kind of contract theory put forward
by Rawls. Rawls claims that the principles of justice are ones we would
choose in creating a social contract if we lacked the information to pick
principles biased in our favor. But any theory that appeals to a hypothetical contract is open to the objection that what we would agree to
under hypothetical conditions has no bearing on our actual motives
or commitments. In order to guarantee that what we would decide
behind a veil of ignorance is relevant to our actual behavior, Rawls
appeals to what is, in effect, an internalized counterpart of the veil.
Rawls argues that we should (rationally) support those institutions by
which we would be best served not only given our actual conception
of the good but also in the light of all the radically different conceptions
that we might come to have in the future. This means that whatever
our moral commitments are now, we should (rationally) be willing
now to take out what amounts to insurance on all of our possible
future selves (or future extensions), even at the expense of our actual
moral commitments. But even if we are fully rational, we need not be

willing to make such a sacrifice. And we cannot assume behind the veil of ignorance that we would do so.

Rawls's assumption that we are prepared to make this kind of sacrifice is based on his claim that we have a highest-order interest in rationality. Suppose we recognize now that in the future we may believe that some conception of the good is superior to the one we presently hold. Rawls's claim is that we are rationally motivated now to arrange that if such a state of affairs were realized, we would be in a position to pursue the new conception. But construed literally, the idea of a highest-order interest, like the idea of a highest-order desire, makes little sense. For a desire of any order, we could have a higher-order desire that the first desire be frustrated. Moreover, there is no sense to be made of the notion of a highest-order commitment to rationality by reference to the coherentist account of commitment in terms of conditional and unconditional desires. Certain conceptions of the good, for example, a religious fundamentalist conception and a secular conception, may be so radically different that no empirical evidence could establish the superiority of one over the other. And if one of a pair of such conceptions of the good were held unconditionally, one could not be rationally motivated (from the perspective of the conception one held) to make sacrifices to ensure the satisfaction of one's desires should one come to hold the other conception. But now suppose that one is behind the veil of ignorance and one is contemplating the possibility that when the veil is lifted, one will discover that one's conception of the good is a theocratic one. One will then realize that when the veil is lifted, one will not be willing to support a liberal, secular state merely because one might be converted (in spite of one's best efforts to prevent the process from occurring) to a secular conception of the good.

Although this argument applies to Rawls's particular type of contract theory, Rawls's strategy of internalizing the veil of ignorance must be made to work if contract theories are to avoid the charge that hypothetical contracts are irrelevant. If this strategy fails, as I argue it does, the problem is one for which contract theories have no solution. I conclude, then, that certain of the communitarian objections to contract theories are correct.

Moral commitment and consequentialism
The issues of moral commitment and the conative structure of the self arise again in connection with consequentialist moral theories. Two sorts of criticisms of consequentialism in general and utilitarianism in particular have led proponents to reassess the relations between the prescriptions of the theories and the moral psychology of the subjects

to which they apply. Utilitarians, it is alleged, cannot do justice to our commitment to the rights of individuals. Let us call this an *external objection*, since it appeals to moral intuitions whose source is pretheoretical and hence outside utilitarian theory. It is also claimed that utilitarianism is sometimes self-defeating, that is, that there are circumstances in which subjects who are disposed to do what utilitarianism requires make a smaller contribution to aggregate utility than they could have made had they not been so disposed. Let us call this an *internal objection*, since there is no appeal to moral considerations of a nonutilitarian sort.

Utilitarians have replied by invoking indirect forms of utilitarianism, according to which what are assessed for their contribution to aggregate utility need not be actions; sets of rules or types of motivational makeup, for example, may be assessed instead. In addition, utilitarians have denied that utilitarianism must be construed as a decision procedure. They have claimed that utilitarianism is best construed as a criterion of morally correct action. Utilitarianism need not, according to this interpretation, provide the terms in which agents assess their alternatives and choose the actions they intend to perform. Utilitarianism may require that agents refrain from thinking like utilitarians and that they assess their alternatives from an antiutilitarian and indeed anticonsequentialist perspective.

Like Rawls's attempt to internalize the veil of ignorance in the psychology of the individual agent, these replies by utilitarians depend on assumptions in moral psychology that are never made fully explicit. Consider first the appeal to rule utilitarianism as a way of answering the objection that utilitarianism condones rights violations. Assume that there are some possible circumstances in which violating an individual's rights would have the best consequences. Assume, however, that the set of rules prescribed by rule utilitarianism, that is, the set of rules that if followed generally would yield the best consequences, would never permit such a violation. If we ignore the dimension of moral psychology, this might seem to answer the first objection to utilitarianism. But now imagine someone whose deepest commitment is to promoting the greatest possible aggregate utility. And consider what could motivate that person to follow the set of rules endorsed by rule utilitarianism when the action they prescribed was not the one prescribed by act utilitarianism, i.e., when it was not the action in that person's actual circumstances that would make the greatest contribution to aggregate utility. A commitment to rule utilitarianism is not an opaque barrier between the agent and the desires that motivated that commitment in the first place. As long as the desire to maximize aggregate utility remains, it will, in the absence of any further assumptions about the agent's psychology, render the commitment to rule utilitarianism ineffective. The same argument applies to the appeal to rule utilitarianism to deal with the problem of utilitarian self-defeat.

Both motive utilitarianism (and other forms of indirect utilitarianism) and the approach that distinguishes between utilitarianism as a decision procedure and utilitarianism as a criterion of morally correct action impose constraints on the psychology of moral agents, as well as on the actions chosen. Thus they are both relevant to the problem at hand. Even those utilitarians who adopt one of these approaches, however, have failed to pursue the implications of their psychological assumptions. If we are to refrain from thinking like a utilitarian or to act on nonutilitarian or antiutilitarian motives, there are two possibilities. The first is that we act on the basis of a disposition to perform actions contrary to our deepest moral commitments. The alternative is that our deepest moral commitments are themselves antiutilitarian. Given these alternatives, the utilitarian faces a dilemma. If the disposition to respect the rights of others is not a genuine moral commitment, then in cases where the stakes are high, the means to override this disposition will almost certainly be available. And we will be motivated to adopt these means by our underlying commitment to utilitarianism. Suppose, on the other hand, that the commitment to rights is a genuine moral commitment. Then it is unclear how the fact that a commitment to an antiutilitarian morality might be required on utilitarian grounds could vindicate utilitarianism.

Proponents of utilitarianism may answer this objection by an appeal to moral realism. It may be argued that utilitarianism can be true even if we are not disposed to act on utilitarian grounds. But this reply leads to a second dilemma for utilitarians. If a moral theory can be true independently of whether the actions that it prescribes are internally justified for the community to which it applies, then the truth of the theory is a merely anthropological fact. And such facts lack the significance that the truth of a moral theory is ordinarily assumed to have.

If the appeal to realism is to avoid this objection, it must be claimed that a moral commitment to utilitarianism is justified for us or that the majority of people in our community are converging in that direction. For those who take this line, the original internal and external objections to utilitarianism have to be met head on rather than by appeal to the possibility of adopting utilitarianism in an indirect form. It would have to be claimed, for example, that our deepest commitments are utilitarian in nature and that our pretheoretical intuitions that seem to favor rights are merely vestigial. It would also have to be claimed that the circumstances in which utilitarianism is self-defeating are too unlikely and of too little significance to undermine our commitment.

In chapter 11, I argue that given the best explanation of our moral commitments, it is highly unlikely that we are utilitarians in IRE or that we will converge to utilitarianism as our empirical beliefs about the world become more sophisticated. It is a consequence of this analysis of moral commitment that if we have a genuine commitment to a rights-based morality, we would not be rationally motivated to abandon that commitment merely to produce a higher aggregate utility.

PART I
Content

Chapter 1
Partial Character and the Language of Thought

Hilary Putnam has argued in a number of articles that a speaker's psychology fails to determine the content of his beliefs.[1] In a recent series of papers Stephen Stich and Tyler Burge have extended Putnam's suggestions, and in so doing, have raised what may be among the most serious problems for a functionalist theory of belief.[2] These problems concern the possibility of correlating beliefs and functional states, given some assumptions, widely held by causal theorists of reference, about the individuation of beliefs. In the first section I shall examine the arguments advanced by Burge and Stich and discuss some of the difficulties that their own positions raise. In section 2, I shall consider two plausible strategies for countering their arguments, each of which, as I shall go on to argue, is ultimately unsatisfactory. In section 3, I propose a more adequate response in defense of functionalism, which is based on the concepts of partial character and context of acquisition. I shall then show in section 4 that the concept of partial character is of interest quite apart from its role in a defense of functionalism and that it plays a part in the analysis of meaning change as well as in our understanding of the notion of a language of thought.

1   Autonomous Psychology and Belief-Desire Explanation

In "Autonomous Psychology and the Belief-Desire Thesis," Stich argues that a tension exists between the following two principles:

> *The Principle of psychological autonomy*   The properties and relations to be invoked in an explanatory psychological theory must be supervenient upon the *current, internal physical* properties and relations of organisms (i.e., just those properties that an organism shares with all of its replicas).

Pacific Philosophical Quarterly 63 (1982): 347–365. Copyright 1982 by the University of Southern California. Reprinted with permission.

The Belief-Desire Thesis   (a) Human action is, at least in part, caused by, and explained in terms of, beliefs and desires. (b) Singular causal statements connecting particular beliefs and desires and actions are true in virtue of being subsumed by laws of a psychological theory which specify nomological relations among beliefs, desires, and action.[3]

In other words, a singular causal statement connecting a belief and an action is subsumed, according to the belief-desire thesis, by a law of a psychological theory that mentions beliefs and desires, not by a law of a physical theory that mentions only physical states, some of which are type or token identical with the beliefs and desires in question.

Stich claims that if the autonomy principle is accepted, then there will be a large number of belief properties that could not play a role in an explanatory psychological theory, i.e., there will be a large number of belief properties that will not satisfy the belief-desire thesis.[4] This claim is based on his assumption that a sufficient condition for the nonidentity of two belief properties is that tokens of them differ in truth value. His claim is supported by a number of examples in which an individual has a belief that is true, while the corresponding belief of a physical replica is false. Stich concludes that the individual instantiates a belief property different from the one the replica instantiates and that in view of this difference the principle of psychological autonomy forces the conclusion that the belief property instantiated by the individual is not a property that could figure in an explanatory psychological theory. In other words, no such belief will be subsumed by the laws of an explanatory psychological theory. But since our belief in the possibility of such a psychological theory rests on our expectation that beliefs of the sort cited in the examples *do* play a role in the explanation of human action, the examples are held to undermine our belief in the possibility of such a theory.

Stich's first example involves indexical beliefs. Stich imagines that a duplicate of himself, in which he is replicated atom for atom, has been created in the last five minutes. Both he and his replica share the belief that would be appropriately expressed by the sentence 'I have tasted a Chateau d'Yquem '62.' But since his belief is true and his replica's is not, the belief property that he instantiates is not a property shared by all his replicas and thus, by the principle of psychological autonomy, not one that could figure in an explanatory psychological theory. Since the same argument applies to beliefs involving other indexicals, such as 'here' and 'now', indexical beliefs will not occur in the relevant sort of psychological explanation.

Stich's other examples support the same form of argument, adding further classes of beliefs that will not figure in psychological explanation. Like indexical beliefs, beliefs involving natural kind terms and proper names can be eliminated from the domain of psychological theory. Following Putnam, we can imagine a planet, called Twin Earth, that is an almost exact physical replica of Earth and on which there is an almost exact physical replica of each individual.[5] Twin Earth differs from Earth only in the fact that the natural kind that has all the obvious properties of water and fills the oceans, lakes and resevoirs is not H_2O but a substance whose formula we may abbreviate XYZ. Putnam's claim is that the expression 'water', as used by our Twin Earth doubles, refers to XYZ, not to H_2O. Given this assumption, had our ancestors believed that lizards dissolved in water, their beliefs would have been false, while the beliefs that their Twin Earth doubles would have expressed in the same words might have been true—lizards might have dissolved in XYZ. Hence beliefs involving natural kind terms, because of the way such terms pick out their referents, are barred from psychology. A similar argument rules out beliefs involving proper names.

Since Stich's arguments are not explicitly directed at functionalism, it will be useful to pause long enough to make the antifunctionalist implications explicit. I am taking functionalism as the thesis that intentional predicates like 'X believes that p' are definable in terms of functional predicates that are themselves defined in terms of the relations between inputs, internal states, and outputs of a system. There are, of course, different versions of functionalism, and the differences will have a bearing on what counts as a functional predicate, but in this context the differences need not concern us. Stich's argument that certain classes of beliefs could not figure in psychological explanations is equally an argument that these beliefs could not have logically necessary and sufficient conditions in terms of functional states. Since one's physical replicas do share all of one's functional states and fail to share many of one's belief states, many different belief states will correspond to the same functional state; hence necessary and sufficient conditions for these belief states could not be given in functional terms. Moreover, the differences between one's own beliefs and the beliefs of one's physical replicas could not get a functional explanation.

Clearly these arguments do not count against all possible versions of functionalism. In particular, we might consider an eliminative version of functionalism according to which functional predicates replace rather than define intentional predicates. Stich in fact gives some indication that he would favor such a theory. Functional properties do satisfy the principle of psychological autonomy, and in many central cases, belief properties do not. Hence in the construction of an explanatory psychological theory it is the belief properties that Stich would have us abandon.[6]

Where Putnam was concerned with the role of the physical environment in determining the meanings of the expressions of a subject, Burge in "Individualism and the Mental" is concerned with the role of the social environment. Burge proposes a thought experiment with parallels to the Twin Earth example that is designed to show that speakers who are functionally and physically indistinguishable may entertain different beliefs, not as a result of proximity to different natural kinds, but as a result of membership in different linguistic communities.

In the first step of the thought experiment Burge imagines a subject whose understanding of the concept of arthritis is incomplete. The subject fails to realize that arthritis is specifically a condition of the joints. Although he has a number of true beliefs about arthritis, for example, that he has had arthritis for years, that his arthritis in his wrists and fingers is more painful than his arthritis in his ankles, that stiffening joints is a symptom of arthritis, that certain sorts of aches are characteristic of arthritis, and so forth, he has, in addition to these true beliefs, the false belief that he has arthritis of the thigh.

In the second step of the experiment Burge has us imagine a counterfactual situation in which the speaker remains unchanged, at least physically, while we replace his community with one in which the word 'arthritis' is used to cover various rheumatoid ailments, the one in the subject's thigh as well as the genuinely arthritic conditions.

In the third step Burge asks us to concede that the subject in the actual situation and his alternate self in the counterfactual situation have different beliefs, even though they may have been physically indistinguishable throughout their lives. Burge points out that it is hard to see how the subject's alternate self could have acquired the concept of arthritis and that the concept of arthritis and the concept that was acquired by the subject's alternate self are not even extensionally equivalent. This is because the subject's belief that he would express by saying 'I have arthritis of the thigh' is false, whereas the belief that his alternate self would express in the same way is true. Hence, according to Burge, the subject's alternate self does not have the belief that he has had arthritis for many years, that stiffening of the joints is a symptom of arthritis, and so forth, even though he does have beliefs that he would express in exactly these words—the same words in which the subject himself would express the beliefs in question.

The implications of this example for functionalism are the same as those of Stich's examples, and Burge makes the antifunctionalist consequences explicit. Since the subject and his alternate self share all the same functional states and they do not have the same beliefs, functional states do not explain belief. But although Burge's example complements Stich's, Burge and Stich draw radically different conclusions. Stich, faced with the incompatibility of the principle of psychological autonomy and the belief-desire thesis, at least insofar as the latter is held to apply to the full range of our belief ascriptions, opts to drop the belief-desire thesis. Burge, faced with the same choice, chooses to drop the principle of psychological autonomy. Stich's reason for preferring the principle of psychological autonomy is that functional states explain behavior at least under its physical description and that, for the purposes of psychological explanation, this is precisely what we want. Burge, on the other hand, is anxious to emphasize the influence of the social on the mental, as well as to preserve our ordinary forms of belief-desire explanations.

Unlike Burge and Stich, I find the prospect of choosing one of these principles over the other an unattractive one. It is a particularly unpalatable choice for functionalists committed to the idea that functional states explain, in some sense, our ordinary belief-desire ascriptions. In the next section I shall examine two ways of trying to reconcile the two theses. Although we will see that they are ultimately unsatisfactory, they will shed some light on another more satisfactory method.

2   Stereotypes and Qualitative Predicates

Since the problems that Burge and Stich raise for an autonomous belief-desire psychology are direct applications and extensions of Putnam's claims about reference, the obvious place to look for an answer to these difficulties would be in Putnam's own discussion of meaning and belief. Putnam describes the meaning of a natural-kind term in terms of its normal form of description:[7]

> My proposal is that the normal form description of the meaning of a word should be a finite sequence, or 'vector', whose components should certainly include the following (it might be desirable to have other types of components as well): (1) the syntactic markers that apply to the word, e.g. 'noun'; (2) the semantic markers that apply to the word, e.g. 'animal', 'period of time'; (3) a description of the additional features of the stereotype if any; (4) a description of the extension.

The following convention is a part of this proposal: the components of the vector all represent a hypothesis about the individual speaker's competence, *except the extension*. Thus the normal form description for 'water' might be, in part:

Syntactic Markers	Semantic Markers	Stereotype	Extension
mass noun, concrete;	natural kind; liquid;	colorless; transparent; tasteless; thirst-quenching; etc.	H_2O (give or take impurities)

This proposal is an attempt to separate the social and the physical contribution to meaning, which is represented in the fourth column, from the individual's contributions, represented in the first three columns. As a representation of meaning, however, this hovers uneasily between two distinct paradigms. Intensions—functions from possible worlds to extensions—determine what is meant without any reference to the rules or recognitional capacities that would give the function psychological reality. The function from possible worlds to truth values associated with 'snow is white', for example, determines a set of worlds whose only common feature is that snow is white in those worlds, thereby fixing the meaning of the sentence. The conception of meaning that corresponds to intensions, therefore, does not supply a rule, applicable in an indefinite number of circumstances, that would allow us to determine whether in those circumstances snow was in fact white. Hence the conception of meaning that *does* correspond to such a rule or recognitional capacity provides a distinct and independent paradigm.

According to Putnam, 'water' picks out H_2O with respect to every possible world. Hence the difference between specifying the intension of 'water' and specifying H_2O is merely the difference between a constant function and the value of that constant function—a difference that can be safely ignored. Thus Putnam's representation of the meaning of 'water' falls under the paradigm associated with intensions. Putnam makes some concession as well, however, to recognitional capacity in his inclusion of the stereotype associated with 'water.' The stereotype does not, of course, fix the referent of 'water' as H_2O, but this is in line with Putnam's contention that what is in the head (the rule or the stereotype) does not fix reference. Still, there are a number of problems that suggest that Putnam has underestimated the extent to which what is in the head *does* contribute to the determination of the referent.

First, there is more to what is in the head than is represented in Putnam's stereotypes. Speakers of the language must have a general commitment to use the language in the same way it is used in the community, and these commitments will be represented by the intentions with which speakers engage in linguistic activity. These intentions (or at least some important aspects of them) will be in the head in Putnam's sense and will help determine the extensions of the speakers' concepts.

Second, words like 'elm' and 'beech', which figure prominently in Putnam's examples, must be the exception rather than the rule—at least among the words speakers commonly use. A speaker's working vocabulary could not be made up solely, or even largely, of words that have what we might call a thin stereotype, i.e., a stereotype that does not determine a recognitional capacity that would allow the subject to discriminate typical examples of the concept in question, at least under favorable conditions. If a speaker's working vocabulary were made up of such words, it would be an uninterpreted language as far as he was concerned, and we would cease to regard him as a speaker of that language. We may tolerate speakers who cannot tell elms from beeches, but speakers who cannot associate even such common words as 'chair' with certain typical examples identified by ostension in their environment will not ordinarily count as speakers of English. And notice that such a person is still in a much stronger position than the one who cannot *tell* elms from beeches, since this latter person not only has not associated 'elm' with some class of objects but also lacks a recognitional capacity capable of discriminating typical members of the class under any even roughly coextensional concepts. That is, like the person who cannot distinguish identical twins, he has not recognized those features that make elms and beeches discriminable. Thin stereotypes work because of the division of linguistic labor, but for every meaningful expression, some members of the community, the experts, must have thick stereotypes if the expressions are to have an appropriate connection with the world. Moreover, every member of the speech community must have *some* thick stereotypes if he or she is to be capable of communication with the experts.

Third, Putnam never really addresses the problem of semantic compositionality, that is, the problem of how the truth conditions (or whatever properties of sentences come to play the theoretical role ordinarily reserved for truth conditions in a theory of meaning) of complex sentences are generated from their simpler components. Putnam does mention that a speaker may have synonymous terms in his vocabulary that he does not recognize as synonyms, e.g., a bilingual speaker may associate the same stereotype and extension with '*buche*' as with 'beech' and believe that this tree is a beech (it has a name plate on it) without believing it is a *buche* (he is agnostic on this question). In dealing with this case, Putnam introduces the notion of a representation under which the speaker believes a proposition, so that the speaker is said to believe the proposition that this is a beech under one representation and not under another. This is just to say, presumably, that the truth conditions of some belief sentences depend, in addition to their dependence on the truth conditions of the embedded proposition, on the way in which the believer represents the proposition to himself. Thus,

(1) Oscar believes that this is a beech

will be true and

(2) Oscar believes that this is a *buche*

will be false, even though

(3) This is a beech

and

(4) This is a *buche*

express the same proposition. Putnam seems to be suggesting that at least certain important features of the respective logical forms are represented by

(5) Believes [Oscar, P, R_1],

(6) Believes [Oscar, P, R_2],

where P is the proposition expressed by (3) and (4) and R_1 is the representation under which Oscar believes it and R_2 the representation under which he is agnostic. Thus we can say again that the extensions of some of a speaker's utterances, such as

(7) I believe this is a beech

and

(8) I believe this is a *buche*,

depend on more than his thin stereotypes. But Putnam says very little about the relation between stereotypes and representations.

Finally, another aspect of meaning that is, in one clear sense, in the head, and that helps determine the extensions of our concepts is the set of dispositions that govern the similarity judgments we make in novel situations. Here too the concepts that an individual possesses are not completely settled by what is in *his* head, but neither are they settled by experts. The boundaries of predicates such as 'is red' or 'is funny' are settled at least partly by the extralinguistic dispositions to make similarity judgments of a majority of the speech community.

What is being criticized is the lack of an adequate theory of the way in which what is in the head contributes to the determination of meaning and reference. Putnam does provide a way of separating the individual and external components of meaning, but he provides no mechanism for the connection between the internal component of the meaning of a linguistic expression and the extension. The best indication of this is the fact that we can imagine people with precisely the internal components of meaning postulated by Putnam and living in a world with precisely the natural kinds that our world has but who have concepts with different extensions (and therefore, in Putnam's sense, different meanings). In the first place, a group of people who had vocabularies composed of only those words for which we have, according to Putnam, thin stereotypes would probably not count as speakers of a language at all—even if the group consisted of quasi experts who did associate detailed definitions couched in terms of other words in the vocabulary with a selected subset of the words. Similarly, a group of people who had different dispositions regarding similarity judgments would associate different intensions and extensions with many of their words, even if they shared all of our thin stereotypes. Furthermore, people who lacked our linguistic intentions to use words in accordance with the use of the community and the experts would also lack many of our extensions.

The upshot of this is that a theory that effected a division of the internal and external components of meaning without these defects would clearly be welcome. In fact, Putnam's remarks on the indexicality of terms like 'water' suggest a different approach to the internal and external contributions to meaning. "Now then, we have maintained that indexicality extends beyond the *obviously* indexical words and morphemes (e.g. the tenses of verbs). Our theory can be summarized as saying that words like 'water' have an unnoticed indexical component: 'water' is stuff that bears a certain similarity relation to the water *around here*."[8] The idea that this remark suggests (but does not endorse) would take Putnam's own characterization of water, "stuff that bears a certain similarity relation to the water *around here*," as the basis of a theory, which we might call the indexical-description theory of meaning. The meaning of 'water' would be characterized by descriptive terms, for example, 'whatever is wet, fills the lakes, comes out of the faucets, etc.', which would pick out water in the actual world and which, together with the explicit indexical 'here', would insure that 'water' as used by us functions rigidly to denote, in every possible world, H_2O. 'Water' as used on Twin Earth will have a different meaning, at least in the sense that it will denote XYZ in any possible world.

The indexical-description theory is an attempt to address simultaneously two problems. The first problem is just the problem of effecting the division of internal and external components of meaning already mentioned. This is accomplished by isolating the semantic differences between speakers on Earth and their Twin Earth counterparts in the explicitly indexical portions of their respective languages and locating the semantic similarities in the descriptive portions of those languages. The second problem involves accounting for the determination of the speaker's extensions by the internal components of meaning, and this is handled by invoking the descriptions under which the speaker apprehends the referents of his expressions while permitting the description to contain explicit indexicals to account for rigid designations and "circular" descriptions to allow for cases in which the speaker succeeds in referring even without access to a noncircular description that individuates the object of reference.

Not only does this theory purport to solve both problems; it seems to provide the two problems with a common solution supported by two kinds of considerations. First, consideration of what the physical duplicates share semantically suggests that even if they associate *different* extensions with words such as 'water', this must be in virtue of sharing predicates with which they do associate the same intensions and extensions, e.g., 'wet', 'thirst-quenching', etc. Call such predicates the autonomous predicates. Their intensions and extensions do not depend on environmental facts that could vary from one physical duplicate to another; hence they must be applicable on the basis of features that are fully manifest to each subject. The intuition is that what is in the head determines the intensions and extensions of the autonomous predicates, and these, together with explicit indexicals, determine the intensions and extensions of other predicates and singular terms. Thus by providing relatively rich descriptions in terms of autonomous predicates and explicit indexicals, the theory provides a means by which what is in the head determines (together with the external contributions) the intensions and extensions. Second, the theory eliminates the earlier counterexamples (e.g., the example of the "speakers" whose language is uninterpreted), specifies the semantic properties that the functional duplicates share, and provides a plausible approach to semantic compositionality, since we allow the descriptions to function as the meanings of singular terms and not only as a means of fixing their referents.

In spite of these advantages, advocates of such an approach face a difficult dilemma. Either there is no reason to believe in the existence of the autonomous predicates postulated, or they will turn out to be essentially private and therefore inappropriate candidates for the role specified for them by the theory. The argument for this contention is quite straightforward. Unless the autonomous predicates are themselves capable of acquiring different intensions and extensions in different physical environments, their stability will be purchased at the cost of making them inappropriate vehicles of intersubjective communication. Take 'is wet'. Though apparently qualitative, wetness on Twin Earth might well be a property not of liquids but of quantities of very small solid particles that slide by one another easily. Thus the substances that exhibit the macro properties of liquids on earth are on Twin Earth more like quantities of very fine sand or graphite particles. Even if we move toward predicates like 'looks red to me', the same problem arises. Situations in which earthlings would be confident in saying that an object looked red to them might be situations in which the object was in fact invisible but emitted ultrasonic sound waves that produced subliminally, by hypnotic suggestion, the image of a red object with the features of the actual object.

In the case of 'looks red to me' the difficulty is engendered in part by certain features of the word 'looks', but the word 'red' raises equally serious problems. Imagine a case in which a physical duplicate of a normal speaker of English lives in a community in which the word 'red' is applied to a wider band of the spectrum than it is among speakers of English. In such a case, if Burge is right, the duplicate's concept of red would not be ours, and even the retreat to 'seems red to me' could not produce an autonomous predicate in the sense defined above. Apparently only the complete retreat to pure sense data, assuming that such a retreat is intelligible, could rule out such difficulties, and such a retreat seems to preclude the straightforward explication of our communicative abilities that the indexical-description theory was intended to produce.

These arguments do not prove, nor is it necessary to argue, that no version of the indexical-description theory is viable. They do show that none of the *usual* strategies for effecting a division of our vocabulary (or of the concepts definable in terms of our vocabulary) into qualitative and nonqualitative concepts will succeed and thus that there is no very compelling reason to believe in the existence of autonomous concepts. Thus a theory that does not presuppose the possibility of such a division would be a far more attractive solution to the problem of separating the individual and external contributions to the intensions and extensions of a speaker's concepts.

3   *Partial Character*

I have claimed that the indexical-description theory attempts to separate the individual and external contributions to the intensions and extensions of a speaker's expressions by dividing the speaker's vocabulary. Explicit indexicals are the locus of both the individual and external contributions, autonomous predicates are the locus of the individual contributions, and other terms, singular and general, have senses that are identical with the senses of descriptions made up of autonomous predicates and explicit indexicals.

The alternative approach that I want to suggest does not locate the indexical component, and thereby the external contribution, in a subset of the speaker's vocabulary but spreads both the individual and the external contributions over the entire vocabulary. The result is that each word or concept contains both an indexical and an autonomous component. Since this is true of the explicit indexicals on the indexical-description theory, we will need a counterpart to the distinction, which is recognized regarding explicit indexicals, between those aspects of meaning shared by all speakers and those aspects that vary with the differences in the speaker's circumstances.

The clearest characterization of these different aspects of indexicals is found in David Kaplan's distinction between content and character.[9] Kaplan's characterization depends on distinguishing *circumstances* at which an utterance may be evaluated and *contexts* in which an utterance may be used. Since I intend to draw a distinction that Kaplan does not make, I shall speak instead of contexts of evaluation and contexts of utterance.

Kaplan's distinction between context and character is clearest in the cases of sentences like

(9) I am not speaking now.

Clearly, (9) is false whenever it is uttered, but it is not *necessarily* false. On any occasion on which it is uttered, the speaker might not have uttered it. Thus there must be possible worlds in which it is true. Finding these worlds could not require, of course, that we look for situations in which someone uttering the sentence is not speaking. Instead, we take an utterance of the sentence in some context of utterance, fix the speaker, and look at the cotemporal activities of that person in other possible worlds or contexts of evaluation. Those in which he is not speaking are the worlds in which the sentence is true relative to the context of utterance chosen.

The choice of a context of utterance determines a function from contexts of evaluation to truth values. Kaplan calls such a function a content. Ordinarily it is called an intension, and this is the term I shall use throughout the paper. 'Content' will be used only in a strictly pretheoretical sense. Since there is nothing special about the actual context of utterance, we need another function from contexts of utterance to intensions, i.e., a function from contexts to a function from contexts to truth values. Kaplan calls such a function the character of an utterance, and in this case I shall adopt his terminology.[10]

For Kaplan, a variable character (i.e., a nonconstant function from contexts of utterance to intensions) is associated with indexical expressions, such as 'I', 'now', 'you', and so forth. Nonindexicals have a constant character, since their intension is a constant function of their context of utterance; every context of utterance is mapped onto the same intension. The character of complex expressions is a function of the character of their constituent components.

Putnam's claim, supported by the Twin Earth example, amounts to the thesis that the intension and the extension of even such ostensibly nonindexical words as 'water' (or, more accurately, utterances of those words) vary according to the context in which the word was acquired. But any proposal to define a function from the contexts of acquisition of words to the characters associated with the words, by analogy with the function from contexts of utterance to intensions, faces the difficulty that nothing will distinguish the words except their physical shape. Whereas 'I' retains its reference to the speaker in any context of utterance, if we allow the context of acquisition to vary, and this includes the training involved in the use of the word, 'red' could mean anything from *green* to *garrulous*. Thus the words will have no fixed significance that remains invariant from one context of acquisition to another analogous to the character that 'I' retains in different contexts of utterance.

Rather than allowing the contexts of acquisition of a word to vary at random, I propose to look at that subset of the set of possible contexts of acquisition in which speakers who have acquired the word in question are (or are "sufficiently close" to being functional duplicates. Let us define the partial character of a word W as follows:

> A *possible context of acquisition* is an ordered pair consisting of a possible world and a functional state token that exists in that world. We say that the possible world is *centered on* the token. (Intuitively, the possible world fixes the causal history and the causal environment of the token.)

> Two possible contexts of acquisition are *functionally equivalent* if and only if they are centered on functional states that are type identical (or "sufficiently close").

A possible context of acquisition CA = ⟨the actual world, functional state token S⟩ is a *context of acquisition of a word type W* if and only if S is the functional state token underlying a use of W. For CA = ⟨possible world PW, functional state token S⟩, CA is a *possible context of acquisition of a word type W* if and only if CA is functionally equivalent to a context of acquisition of W.

An *interpretation* of a word type W is an element of the set E of equivalence classes of possible contexts of acquisition of W generated by the relation of functional equivalence.

A possible context of acquisition CA = ⟨possible world PW, functional state token S⟩ of word type W *fixes the character of W as C* if and only if, given the causal relations between S and its social and physical environment in PW, a correct causal theory of reference entails that the character of W is C.

The *partial character* of a word type W relative to an interpretation I of W is a function F from I to the set of characters such that for CA ∈ I, F(CA) = the character C such that CA fixes the character of W as C.

The easiest way of seeing the definitions at work is by applying them to the Burge and Stich examples. Consider Stich's example in which he and his double both believe that they have tasted a Chateau d'Yquem '62. Stich's belief is true. His double, having been created in the past five minutes, has a false belief. Therefore, they have different beliefs in spite of being in the same functional state. The semantic property that Stich and his double share is that their sentences have the same character. Since their contexts of utterance (or more properly their contexts of occurrence) differ, however, the same character maps their utterances onto different intensions and in this case onto different extensions. It is clear, however, that in this kind of case and for the purposes of psychology, character is the relevant dimension along which beliefs are to be assessed. As John Perry has pointed out,[11] if Smith believes he is being attacked by a bear, and Jones shares this belief in the sense that his belief has the same intension as Smith's, then whereas Smith will curl up in a ball, Jones will run for help. If, on the other hand, Jones shares Smith's belief in the sense that his belief has the same character as Smith's, Jones will curl up in a ball as well. The same remarks apply to Stich's second case, involving implicit indexical references to a time and location.

It is in the case of proper names and natural-kind terms that the distinction between character and partial character comes into play.

Stich believes that Saul Kripke was born in Nebraska and Stich's double on Twin Earth has the same belief, though his belief is about Saul Kripke's double. Here we can say that though their beliefs differ in character, intension, and extension, they share the same partial character. If Stich had acquired his belief on Twin Earth in the normal way, then even expressed on Earth the belief would have been about Saul Kripke's double and would have been true at those possible worlds in which Saul Kripke's double is born in the Twin Earth counterpart of Nebraska. Stich's H_2O and XYZ example is handled by the same analysis, and Burge's arthritis example is also amenable to this kind of treatment. If Burge's counterfactual counterpart of his hypothetical user of the term 'arthritis' had acquired the word in a context like ours, then like the hypothetical speaker he would have had a false belief about arthritis and not a true belief about some more general rheumatoid condition.

It is possible, then, to concede to Burge and Stich that there is a clear sense in which functional duplicates do not have the same beliefs, and hence a clear sense in which a subject's functional states do not explain his beliefs. The crucial point is that there is an equally clear sense in which functional duplicates do share the same beliefs; they share the same partial characters. The burden of the rest of the paper will be to show that to share the same partial character *is* in one interesting sense to share the same belief. Moreover, I shall show that partial character is a notion of general theoretical interest quite apart from its role in the issues raised by Burge and Stich.

One criticism of this treatment, which will quickly occur to anyone sympathetic to either the Stich or Burge approach, would be the claim that the functional and/or physical similarity that, by hypothesis, the speakers share with their doubles has merely been renamed. Part of the answer to this criticism will come in the application of the notion of partial character. The first and most important point to be made, however, is this: partial character is a semantic notion and one that allows us to describe those respects in which functionally similar speakers share the same semantic properties. To this it might be objected that although there is a point to recording the semantic similarities of those speakers whose beliefs relate them to the same intensions, there is no corresponding point in attempting to catalogue the semantic similarities of speakers whose beliefs do not relate them to the same intensions (putting aside for the moment the case of explicit indexicals and characters). In the latter case, it might be maintained, no theoretical advantage is to be gained by postulating similarities over and above the functional similarities.

Let us call a theory of semantic content that has this implication a restrictive theory of semantic ascription. One strong motivation for ascribing semantic similarities over and above functional similarities stems from the problems presented by nondenoting terms for a causal theory of reference. The notion of partial character allows us to reconcile Kripke's claim that if fossils of a species similar to horses with a single horn were discovered they would not be unicorns with the obvious truth that not all nondenoting terms have the same meaning.[12] If Kripke is right, 'unicorn' and 'griffin' pick out the same extension at every possible world, the null set. Hence the possible world apparatus will not be sufficient to distinguish them in meaning, since they are both associated with the same intension. When we look at partial characters, however, the picture changes significantly. Consider a possible world in which creatures—call them U and G—satisfying the descriptions associated with 'unicorn' and 'griffin' exist, in which those of our ancestors who believed in unicorns and griffins have alternate selves who are functional (and physical) duplicates, and in which the beliefs of their alternate selves are in the right sort of causal contact with these creatures. In such a possible world—call it PW—a typical inhabitant will associate a different intension with 'unicorn' from the one which he associates with 'griffin'. But this means that his alternate self in the actual world will associate a different *partial character* with 'unicorn' from the one he associates with 'griffin', since for a believer of the myths in the actual world, the functional states associated with 'unicorn' and 'griffin'—call them S_1 and S_2—will be such that *if* he had acquired them in PW, his state S_1 *would* have been associated with the intension taking a possible world to the set of U's in that world, and his state S_2 would have been associated with the intension taking a possible world to the set of G's in that world.

Such cases of nondenoting terms have a natural generalization in the case of the brain in the vat. Suppose we imagine a brain that is a functional duplicate of a normal psychological subject and that is being fed completely fabricated sensory stimuli by a group of neurophysiologists. We then have a case in which the causal theory of reference provides no guidance in ascribing semantic content to the functional states in question but in which the subject's experience viewed from the inside is identical to that of a normal subject. Hence there ought to be the same utility in going beyond functional ascription to semantic ascriptions in the case of the brain in the vat as there is in the case of a normal subject, at least if our goal is an understanding of the brain's psychology or of the brain's "world." Partial character allows such a semantic characterization.

4   The Application of Partial Character

We have now seen that the concept of partial character is capable of performing the function for which it was designed. It provides a way of treating the semantic similarities between functional duplicates in diverse environments, reconciles autonomous psychology with the belief-desire thesis, and reconciles functionalism with the indexicality of many ordinary predicates. There are, moreover, less obvious contexts in which a slight generalization of the notion of partial character may be used to advantage. Consider Hartry Field's example of the term 'mass' in Newton's idiolect.[13] Newton believes many things of mass, and roughly speaking, according to Field, half are true of rest mass and half are true of relativistic mass. The principle of charity, which advises us to maximize the number of true beliefs of the subject whose language is being interpreted, provides no guidance here. Either translation will result in the same number of true beliefs. Nor could we maintain that in Newton's idiolect 'mass' lacked reference since, according to Field, so many of Newton's beliefs that were obviously true would turn out to be false. Field claims that it is genuinely indeterminate whether Newton's 'mass' referred to rest mass or relativistic mass.

As it stands, the notion of partial character is no help in this situation. Partial character maps contexts of acquisition onto characters that determine intensions. Hence partial character explains how what is in a speaker's head can determine different intensions in different contexts. Since Newton's meaning is indeterminate even after we have been *given* all the information about the context of acquisition, partial character has no immediate relevance.

Instead of taking partial character as a mapping (from contexts of acquisition to characters) that determines particular intensions when the characters are constant functions (as they are for nonindexicals), let partial character be a mapping from contexts of acquisition to sets of characters, each member of which (for nonindexicals) determines a single intension. Such a set of characters I shall call a *determined character set*. Hence the context of acquisition determines a set of intensions, which may or may not be a unit set. In other words, some contexts of acquisition narrow the meaning of a particular term down to a single intension and others do not. Newton's context of acquisition, because it led to his observation of both rest mass and relativistic mass, did not determine a single intension.

Field's solution to this problem has definite parallels with this treatment in terms of partial character. Field does not define partial denotation or signification, but intuitively, the idea is as follows. Certain considerations about a speaker's causal relations to extralinguistic objects and his dispositions to assent to sentences ordinarily allow us to say that his singular terms denote certain objects and that his predicates have certain significations (extensions). Sometimes, however, these considerations will fail to determine a unique object as the referent of a singular term or a unique set as the signification of a predicate. In such cases each of the objects or sets will be a partial denotation or signification of the term in question.

Field's references to the causal relation between the speaker and objects and his reference to the speaker's dispositions correspond *roughly* to my notion of the external and internal contributions to meaning, though Field does not consider that particular part of the external contribution made up of the dispositions and causal relations to extralinguistic reality of the other members of the speaker's community. Nor does Field dissociate the two contributions to meaning as I have, and hence he cannot show the variation in the meanings of words that corresponds to the variation in the context of acquisition while the functional makeup of the speaker is held constant. Furthermore, Field avoids possible world semantics by assigning extensions rather than intensions and does not distinguish intensions and character. Thus the analogue to Field's notions of partial denotation and partial significance is the idea that a given context of acquisition may only narrow the partial character of a term down to a set of intensions rather than to a unique intension.

Field's approach has come under criticism from those who believe that his presentation of the facts in the Newton case is faulty and that the actual cases of indeterminacy found in the history of science are of an entirely different sort. Philip Kitcher has recently offered a somewhat different analysis of the kinds of cases Field is concerned with and has suggested that his analysis does better justice to the actual cases in the history of science than Field's does.[14] As we have seen, Field associates a set of objects or a set of sets of objects with expression types. In Field's terminology the expression type partially signifies each object or set of objects. Kitcher, on the other hand, associates a set of initiating *events* with an expression type, i.e., events that initiate the use of a token of the expression type, and each initiating event is associated with a single object or extension. Thus, in general, each token of the expression type will be associated with only *one* object or set of objects. Only those token expressions whose utterance is related in the right way to more than one initiating event will be associated with more than one extension, and Kitcher seems to assume that these cases will prove the exception rather than the rule.

It seems clear that Kitcher and Field are operating with two distinct paradigms of the sort of indeterminacy of meaning that conceptual change in the history of science generates. Kitcher's paradigm is perhaps best understood in terms of the nonscientific example he provides. Kitcher imagines a famous and eccentric millionairess, Eustacia Evergreen, who, in an effort to secure a measure of privacy, hires an imposter to lead her public life in a new community. Residents of the community who had produced tokens of 'Eustacia Evergreen' as a causal result of newspaper reports will eventually come to produce such tokens as a causal result of contact with the imposter as well. Kitcher claims that those tokens that are the right sort of causal result of the newspaper reports will refer to Eustacia, that those that are the right sort of result of contact with the imposter will refer to the imposter, and that the reference of some tokens may be indeterminate. In general, however, Kitcher's assumption is that most (or many) tokens will be traced back to a single initiating event, which will involve one referent or the other but not both.

Field does not provide a nonscientific example of the sort of indeterminacy he has in mind, but the construction of one comparable to the Eustacia Evergreen example will help reveal the differences in the cases with which Field and Kitcher are concerned. Imagine a mountainous region in which all and only tall people are beautiful. The inhabitants of the region have only one word, 'beautiful', for the people who are both tall and beautiful. They also hold certain theoretical views about "beauty" based on a rudimentary theory of genetics; they believe that "beauty" is inherited from the mother's side of the family and that it skips a generation.

Now let us suppose that in fact height is inherited from the mother's side of the family and that beauty is ordinarily passed on from either side. However, at the altitudes these mountain dwellers inhabit, the mechanism whereby the father's side of the family passes on beauty is inhibited, and the net effect is that both height and beauty are passed on from the mother's side alone. Beauty, on the other hand, does skip a generation, and height does not. But at very high altitudes there is a one-generation delay in the mechanism whereby height is passed on. Again, the net effect is that beauty and height always coincide.

If we ask whether the native term 'beauty' should be translated in our language as 'beauty' or 'height', the question seems genuinely indeterminate. Here the difference between the Field paradigm and the Kitcher paradigm will become apparent. Kitcher's technique for resolving indeterminacy in translation involves reference to a set of initiating events, which Kitcher seems to assume will involve at most one of the entities or properties in question. Field's discussion, by contrast, concerns cases in which all the events that might be regarded as initiating events involve both (or all) of the entities or properties, reference to which we might be tempted to attribute to the subject. Thus it seems clear that the Kitcher strategy is not an alternative to Field's over the complete range of possible examples and that the Eustacia Evergreen example is not an adequate paradigm for all the cases of conceptual change in science that we might imagine. Thus Kitcher's analysis is best regarded as being complementary to Field's, though it may, as he claims, provide a better analysis of the *actual* cases of alleged indeterminacy in the history of science.

In spite of the differences in these two analyses, the concepts of partial character and context of acquisition can be used, with a slight modification, to express Kitcher's proposal as well as Field's. The context of acquisition of 'Eustacia Evergreen' is an ordered pair consisting of the actual world and a functional state token underlying a use of 'Eustacia Evergreen'. Hence the context of acquisition includes the entire casual history of the token. We can, however, distinguish two subcontexts of the context of acquisition. That is, we can look at two subsets of the set of causal chains relevant to the production of the functional state token underlying 'Eustacia Evergreen': those chains that involve the real Eustacia Evergreen, such as the newspaper reports, and those that involve the imposter.

Since the whole context of acquisition involves both Eustacia Evergreen *and* the imposter, the value of the partial character at this whole context of acquisition is a determined character set, that is, a set of two characters, containing one function (character) corresponding to Eustacia Evergreen, i.e., a constant function (character) from contexts of utterance to a function (intension) from possible worlds to Eustacia Evergreen, and another function (character) corresponding to the imposter. Because there are distinguishable subcontexts, however, we can use a modified notion of the character of the expression type to associate *different* intensions with different tokens in different contexts of utterance. We simply specify that for expression types and their underlying functional states whose contexts of acquisition break down into subcontexts, the *modified character* of the expression type maps contexts of utterance in which the utterance *is caused by* one subcontext of acquisition onto the intension that would have been the only intension associated with the expression type if the subcontext had been the only part of the whole context relevant to the acquisition of the functional state. Hence we have one context of acquisition CA_1, but two subcontexts SCA_1 and SCA_2, defined by two different initiating events (or types of events), e_1 and e_2. Let the partial character on the Kitcher analysis PC_K take that *one* context of acquisition CA_1 to a determined character set DC_K consisting of *one* function (modified character) C_K, which maps contexts of utterance in which the token utterance was caused by Eustacia Evergreen onto Eustacia Evergreen at each possible world and contexts of utterance in which the token utterance was caused by the imposter onto the imposter (at each possible world). Thus the notion of partial character allows the construction of a unified framework in which the two approaches to indeterminancy represented by Field and Kitcher may be represented. Examples illustrating the differences between Field's approach and Kitcher's by reference to partial character are fully worked out in the appendix.

As a final instance of the relevance of partial character to philosophy of language, consider the problem of reconciling the desire for a semantics of the language of thought with the causal theory of reference. The fact that meaning is nonautonomous for the causal theorist has led at least one such theorist to despair of the possibility of explaining what it is to believe that Caesar was egotistical without relying at any point on the semantic features of the sentence 'Caesar was egotistical' in one's spoken or written language.[15]

My proposal is that the semantics of an internal system of representations can be done independently of the semantics of a subject's natural language *without* giving up the causal theory of reference. We can do the semantics of the internal language by assigning partial characters to expressions rather than by characterizing the expressions in terms of such nonautonomous properties as intensions and extensions. The semantics of the internal system of representations would be independent of the *actual* semantic features of the natural language, though not of its potential semantic features. Another way of putting this is to say that the compatibility of internal semantics and the causal theory of reference is possible precisely because the internal semantics can invoke potential causes to explain potential references. And, of course, the semantic features of the natural language will not be *reducible* to the semantic features of the internal system of representation. The notion of partial character allows us to make sense of the notion of a semantics of a language of thought and hence of the notion of a language of thought itself.

Appendix

Example 1   The Eustacia Evergreen example, not incorporating Kitcher's analysis of utterance tokens.

$$
\begin{aligned}
\text{CE} &= \text{context of evaluation} \\
\text{CU} &= \text{context of utterance} \\
\text{CA} &= \text{context of acquisition} \\
\text{PW} &= \text{possible world} \\
\text{EE} &= \text{Eustacia Evergreen} \\
\text{Im} &= \text{the imposter} \\
\{\text{CE}\} &= \text{the set of possible contexts of evaluation} \\
\{\text{CU}\} &= \text{the set of possible contexts of utterance} \\
\{\text{CA}\} &= \text{the set of possible contexts of acquisition (relative} \\
& \quad \text{to a fixed interpretation)} \\
\{\text{E}\} &= \text{the set of possible extensions} \\
\{\text{I}\} &= \text{the set of possible intensions} \\
\{\text{DC}\} &= \text{the set of possible determined characters} \\
\text{I} &= \text{intension} \\
\text{C} &= \text{character} \\
\text{DC} &= \text{determined character set} \\
\text{PC} &= \text{partial character} \\
\text{I} &: \{\text{CE}\} \rightarrow \{\text{E}\} \\
\text{C} &: \{\text{CU}\} \rightarrow \{\text{I}\} \\
\text{DC} &= \{C_1, \ldots, C_n\} \\
\text{PC} &: \{\text{CA}\} \rightarrow \{\text{DC}\}
\end{aligned}
$$

Let

$$
\begin{aligned}
I_1 &= \{\langle PW_1, EE\rangle, \langle PW_2, EE\rangle, \langle PW_3, EE\rangle, \ldots\}, \\
I_2 &= \{\langle PW_1, Im\rangle, \langle PW_2, Im\rangle, \langle PW_3, Im\rangle, \ldots\}, \\
C_1 &= \{\langle CU_1, I_1\rangle, \langle CU_2, I_1\rangle, \langle CU_3, I_1\rangle, \ldots\}, \\
C_2 &= \{\langle CU_1, I_2\rangle, \langle CU_2, I_2\rangle, \langle CU_3, I_2\rangle, \ldots\},
\end{aligned}
$$

CA_1 = the whole *context of acquisition* for the exression type 'Eustacia Evergreen', i.e., the context of acquisition in the actual world, which includes the newspaper reports and meetings with the imposter,

$DC(CA_1)$ = the *determined character set* of the expression type 'Eustacia Evergreen' for the argument consisting of the whole context of acquisition = $\{C_1, C_2\}$,

PC = the *partial character* of the expression type 'Eustacia Evergreen' = $\{\langle CA_1, \{C_1, C_2\}\rangle, \ldots\}$.

Example 2   The Eustacia Evergreen example incorporating Kitcher's analysis. Let

$$I_1 = \text{same as example 1,}$$
$$I_2 = \text{same as example 1,}$$

SCA_1 = the subcontext of the whole context of acquisition in which Eustacia Evergreen figures,

SCA_2 = the subcontext of the whole context of acquisition in which the imposter figures,

CU_1 = a context of utterance in which the token utterance of 'Eustacia Evergreen' is caused by the newspaper reports about Eustacia Evergreen,

CU_2 = a context of utterance in which the token utterance of 'Eustacia Evergreen' is caused by a meeting with the imposter,

C_K = the *modified character* of the expression type 'Eustacia Evergreen' = $\{\langle CU_1, I_1\rangle, \langle CU_2, I_2\rangle, \ldots\}$,

$DC_K(CA_1)$ = the *determined character set* (on the Kitcher analysis) of the expression type 'Eustacia Evergreen' for the argument consisting of the whole context of acquisition = $\{C_K\}$,

PC_K = the *partial character* (on the Kitcher analysis) of the expression type 'Eustacia Evergreen' = $\{\langle CA_1, \{C_K\}\rangle, \ldots\}$.

Acknowledgments

I am grateful to Kit Fine, Jaegwon Kim, William Lycan, Timothy McCarthy, Stephen Schiffer, and Nicholas White for comments and advice on earlier drafts of this paper.

Chapter 2
Narrow Content and Narrow Interpretation

1 Introduction

In chapter 1, I put forward an account according to which narrow content is explained by analogy with David Kaplan's notion of character.[1] On this view, the narrow content, or the partial character, of a referring expression is its reference potential. And if we abstract from some of the details, we can take the partial character of a referring expression (for some particular range of functional states underlying the use of the expression) to be a mapping from contexts of *acquisition* of the expression to referents of that expression. The analogy is to Kaplan's treatment of the character of an expression as a function from contexts of *utterance* to referents.

Whereas wide content varies from one context of acquisition to another, narrow content remains fixed. Consider Hilary Putnam's Twin Earth examples.[2] If the word 'water' is acquired by a normal speaker on Earth, it refers to H_2O, and if it is acquired by a normal speaker on Twin Earth, it refers to XYZ. But, although the referent of the term 'water' as I use it is different from the referent of 'water' as it is used by my doppelgänger on Twin Earth, the partial characters of the two terms are the same. It is true both for my doppelgänger and for me that the meaning of our terms is such that acquired on Earth they refer to H_2O and acquired on Twin Earth they refer to XYZ. Furthermore, this analysis applies to the narrow content of sentences as well. The partial character of a sentence is a function from contexts of acquisition to truth conditions. Since this function is also something I share with my doppelgänger on Twin Earth—and indeed with all of my functional duplicates—partial character supervenes on a speaker's internal, functional makeup. Partial character thus abstracts from the external determinants of content. This is true whether these stem from the nature of the natural kinds that make up the speaker's environment (as is emphasized by Putnam) or the conventions that govern the speaker's linguistic community (as has been stressed by Tyler

Burge[3]). The result is a kind of content (which I called 'autonomous meaning' in chapter 1) that represents the contribution of the speaker's internal makeup to the referents and truth conditions of his or her expressions.

2   The Independence of Narrow Content

There have been a number of objections to the notion of narrow content in general and to this account in terms of partial character in particular. I shall consider one of these objections, which is due to Robert Stalnaker and which raises particularly important questions about the nature of narrow content.[4] This objection was made in response to an account of Jerry Fodor's, and it could be interpreted as applying only to accounts with features specific to his.[5] On at least one plausible interpretation, however, the objection is a very general one and applies to a much wider range of theories, including my own.

Stalnaker's skepticism about the idea that there is an analogy between narrow content and character in virtue of which we can abstract from the external contributions to content to arrive at a purely internal notion emerges in the following remarks.

Take the property of being exactly three miles from a burning barn. Suppose I have this property, even though my counterpart who is located at exactly the same place in a certain counterfactual situation does not. He, let us suppose, is instead exactly three miles from a snow-covered chicken coop. Now there is presumably something about the relation between my counterpart and his world in virtue of which he is three miles from a snow-covered chicken coop even though I am not. Call this condition C. Similarly, there is something about the relation between me and my world in virtue of which I am three miles from a burning barn, even though my counterpart is not. Call it C'. Whatever these conditions are, we *do* know this: short of a miracle, it must be true that anyone in the location that both I and my counterpart are in in our respective worlds would be three miles from a snow-covered chicken coop if condition C obtained, and three miles from a burning barn if instead C' obtained. But this does not help us identify a specific function that takes condition C into the property of being three miles from a snow-covered chicken coop and also takes C' into the property of being three miles from a burning barn—a function that is supposed to represent the contribution that an individual's location makes to the relational property. There are many such functions, and no reason to identify any of them with the contribution that my intrinsic location makes to the specific relational property. My counterpart cannot reasonably say, "I did my part toward being three miles from a burning barn by going to a place where, if conditions C' had obtained instead of C, I would have been three miles from a burning barn." *Every* location is such that for some external conditions, if those conditions obtain, then anything in that location is three miles from a burning barn.[6]

On an uncharitable interpretation this might be regarded as skepticism about the assumption that the narrow properties of a subject make a necessary contribution to the content of the subject's beliefs. And there is a short answer to this sort of skepticism. *Believing* that one is in the vicinity of water (and not XYZ) is not like *being* in the vicinity of water. Absolutely anything, regardless of its intrinsic nature will be in the vicinity of water if it is in the right external circumstances (namely, if there is water in its vicinity). But it is not the case that anything, regardless of its internal makeup, will believe that it is in the vicinity of water merely in virtue of having the right relations to the environment—at least where these relations do not entail that it has an appropriate internal structure. Only systems with a certain kind of functional makeup will acquire this belief in virtue of being in the right sort of physical and social environment. And in principle, there is no reason why we could not give necessary and sufficient conditions for being such a system. There is no problem, then, in specifying the functional conditions in virtue of which internal states of a subject are ascribed a partial character. And there is no ambiguity about what function (i.e., what mapping from contexts of acquisition to propositions) is being ascribed; the partial character of the belief that there is water in the vicinity is the function that takes our context of acquisition to the proposition that there is water in the vicinity and takes contexts of acquisition on Twin Earth to the proposition that the vicinity includes XYZ.

There are, however, more charitable interpretations of Stalnaker's objection. The objection may be aimed at theories that, like Fodor's, explicitly disavow a functionalist account of the content of particular beliefs. If this is the case, then my reply that only systems with a particular functional makeup will acquire the belief that there is water in the vicinity when they are in the vicinity of water may be unavailable. On this interpretation, however, Stalnaker's objection will not apply generally to theories that treat narrow content on the analogue of Kaplan's character. Rather, it will only apply to those that incorporate Fodor's antifunctionalist account of content as well. Thus, in view of its narrow focus, I shall not discuss this interpretation further.

An alternative interpretation of Stalnaker's objection is the following one. The characterization of narrow content by analogy with character is objectionable because it makes the characterization parasitic on wide content. The partial character of an expression is defined, after all, in terms of the wide content that the expression *would have* at the various possible contexts of acquisition. However, if the intrinsic properties of a subject did make the kind of systematic contribution to wide content that the proponent of narrow content alleges, namely a contribution of narrow *content*, then it should be possible to characterize this (narrow) content independently of wide content. But the only characterization we have been given of narrow content is a functional characterization and hence not one that characterizes it *as content*. A characterization of content in terms of the inputs, outputs, and internal states specified in a machine table, for example, would not capture the logical or evidential relations between input states and internal states or between internal states themselves. Nor would it capture the relations in virtue of which practical reasoning leads from internal states to output states. Furthermore, it would fail to specify any analogue of the conditions under which a belief is true or the conditions under which it would be justified. And, as Stalnaker goes on to argue, attempts such as Daniel Dennett's[7] to characterize narrow content *as content* (and to do so in a way that is independent of wide content) seem to encounter insuperable problems. Hence we should be at least suspicious of the notion of narrow content.

Since this sort of skeptical worry is not implausible, let us consider Dennett's approach to narrow content and Stalnaker's objections to that approach. According to Dennett, the narrow content of our beliefs is to be defined in terms of what he calls "notional worlds." The set of notional worlds that constitute the narrow contents of a person's beliefs is the set of possible worlds that *are* the way the person *takes* the actual world to be. To determine which possible worlds these are, we must determine "the environment (or class of environments) for which the organism as currently constituted is best fitted."[8]

Against this account Stalnaker makes three objections. First, he suggests that a possible world's satisfying a creature's conception of the world is not sufficient for that possible world's being the one for which the creature is best fitted. Stalnaker supports this claim by arguing that although antelopes believe their environment contains lions, it is not clear that they are better fitted for lion-filled environments than for ones that are lion free.

As Stalnaker recognizes, however, Dennett has anticipated this kind of objection. Dennett claims that the ideal environment is not the best of all worlds for the organism but the one it is prepared to cope with. In response to this reply Stalnaker has put forward a second objection. He claims that a possible world's being among the ones for which a creature is best fitted *in this special sense* is not sufficient for its being one of the worlds that realizes the creature's conception of the world. Stalnaker notes by way of support that porcupines are best fitted *in this sense* for a world in which there are animals that would eat them if they lacked quills. But he adds that if the porcupines are oblivious to such potential predators, then the worlds in which those predators exist cannot be among the porcupines' notional worlds.

Stalnaker's third objection to Dennett's account raises a different sort of problem. Dennett has claimed that if we had enough information about the internal dispositional properties of a believer, then on this basis alone we could reconstruct a set of environments to which the believer's states would be sensitive if it occupied them and with respect to which the believer's behavior would be appropriate. Stalnaker replies as follows:

> Imagine a purely internal discription of the movements that I am disposed to make under various internal conditions, as I walk down the streets of Boston going places to satisfy my wants and needs, a description that makes no reference to what is going on either specifically or in general beyond my skin. How could anything about *Boston,* or about Boston-like cities, be recovered from such a discription? With a little imagination, one should be able to tell all kinds of wild fairy tales about environments in which the movements I am disposed to make are appropriate, but that are not anything like the way the world seems to me.[9]

These points of Stalnaker's seem on the whole well taken. Let us see, however, whether it is possible to construct an account of narrow content that is like Dennett's in being independent of broad content but that is not open to the difficulties for that account that Stalnaker cites.

3   *Notional Worlds and Optimal Actions*

The first step in constructing an account of notional worlds that avoids Stalnaker's objections is to drop the notion of the fitness of the subject in question. In selecting the possible worlds that make up the notional content of a subject's beliefs, we should not look at those worlds for which the *subject* is best fitted or in which the *subject* survives and flourishes. Rather we should look at those worlds in which the subject's *actions* are *optimal*, given the alternatives from which that subject was free to choose. Consider two possible worlds. In W_1 you are notified by Publishers Clearing House that you may have won as much as $100,000,000 but that you must respond to be eligible for the first prize. You do not respond, and indeed you have not won. In world W_2 you also fail to respond, and though you have won, you are ineligible for the $100,000,000 first prize. You are, however, awarded a consolation prize of $20,000,000. There is a perfectly intuitive sense in which you would probably consider yourself better fitted for the life of luxury that you would lead in W_2 than for the life you lead in W_1. But it is only in W_1 that your actions are optimal, given your alternatives. Thus only W_1 is eligible to be considered one of your notional worlds.

Talk of optimal actions yields an apparently attractive response to Stalnaker's first two objections, but it conceals a number of difficulties. The optimality of the actions, if it is to shed any light on the subject's conception of the world, must be relative to the subject's own desires. We might consider, then, saying that an action is optimal just in case it makes the greatest possible contribution to the satisfaction of the agent's desires. (I shall ignore the difficulties in specifying exactly what function of the number of desires satisfied, their strengths, one's commitment to them, and so forth would be maximized if one maximized their satisfaction.) There is, however, another difficulty. What is meant by saying that a single desire is satisfied? It cannot be simply that the content of the desire is realized or that the proposition embedded in the desire is true or that the truth conditions of that proposition are satisfied. This is because the content of the desire is wide content, and the goal is to produce an account of narrow content that is independent of wide content. This means producing an account that does not depend on the notion of an intentional state's having a content defined in terms of its truth conditions. The notion of satisfaction, then, must be something more akin to the kind of state one is in when by one's own lights one's projects are being completed successfully. This suggestion leads to difficulties of its own, to which I shall return.

Notice that the notion of optimality in question, though it is relative to the agent's desires, is nonetheless *objective* optimality. We have seen that in world W_1, where you fail to respond to the contest invitation and have not won, your action is optimal, whereas in world W_2, where you have won, it is not. But in both worlds you action is *subjectively optimal*. That is, in each world the action is optimal, given your beliefs. Only in worlds where the action is weak-willed, compulsive, or similarly defective will it fail to be optimal in this subjective sense. In W_1, however, your action is optimal in another sense. In W_1 your beliefs are true. Hence the action is, intuitively speaking, objectively optimal. Since our goal is to characterize narrow content in a way that is independent of wide content, however, we cannot appeal to the notion of truth in defining objective optimality. So let us proceed as follows. Say that a possible world W *rationalizes the action* of an agent A just in case relative to the propositions to which W corresponds (that is, the propositions in which W consists or alternatively the propositions that are true at W), A's action is rationally justified, given A's desires. I shall go on to say more about rationality, but for the moment, suppose that we take practical rationality to be defined by an appropriate practical syllogism. Then a world W will rationalize an action for an agent A just in case the practical syllogism constructed from the propositions to which W corresponds, together with A's desires, justifies the action. We can now say that an action a is objectively optimal at a world W just in case W rationalizes a.

Suppose we make the tentative assumption that these suggestions do in fact eliminate Stalnaker's first two objections. Stalnaker's third objection is not so easily dealt with. This objection raises in one form what I shall call the Magoo problem.[10] Mr. Magoo is extremely near-sighted and as a result is almost completely mistaken about the nature of his environment at any given time. Suppose that through a series of lucky coincidences, however, Magoo's misinterpretations lead him to perform precisely that behavior that is objectively optimal in his circumstances. This case presents a problem because although the actual world does *not* satisfy the condition for being one of Magoo's notional worlds (since his *actions* are not objectively optimal at the actual world), this is not apparent on the basis of his *behavior*, which *is* objectively optimal. And we have no access to what Magoo's actions *are* apart from our access to the functional and physical facts about Magoo. In other words, we have no reason, given the present criterion for a possible world's being one of a subject's notional worlds and the physical and functional facts we have considered so far, not to include the actual world among the notional worlds we assign to Magoo. And yet we have stipulated that the example is to be understood in such a way that the actual world is nothing like Magoo's conception of how things are.

The Magoo problem arises because we have been assuming that we can capture the narrow content of an agent's conception of the world at a time by assigning a single set of possible worlds to the agent. The hope has been that we could assign all those possible worlds that are compatible with the agent's conception of things and that are indistinguishable as far as the narrow contents of any of the agent's beliefs are concerned. Worlds such as Earth and Twin Earth (where they are each construed as distinct possible worlds) would be indistinguishable in the relevant sense, whereas the world Magoo thinks he inhabits and the one he actually inhabits would not.

The Magoo problem suggests that this approach cannot work. But let us consider an example that points to an alternative approach. Suppose Magoo is accosted by two thugs who demand his money. Magoo fails to see one of them and mishears the request of the other as a request for directions to the bus station. In swinging his umbrella to point the direction, Magoo knocks the thug he has not seen uncon-scious and thereby frightens the other, causing him to flee. Let us suppose that Magoo's movements in this context are objectively op-timal, given his desire to keep his money. What is it that prevents us from ascribing to Magoo the belief that knocking out one thug and frightening the other is the best way of keeping his money? And what prevents us from describing his action as one aimed at achieving this result? (Assume that in this instance Magoo does not say anything to tip us off as to what his real beliefs and aims are).

If we confine ourselves to looking at Magoo's actual movements in the actual world, we may not be able to rule out such an interpretation. But suppose we consider Magoo's behavior in counterfactual circum-stances very similar to the actual ones. Suppose, for example, that the second thug is just out of range of Magoo's umbrella. Magoo swings the umbrella to point the way to the bus station, the two thugs construe this as an attack, and the results are disastrous. At least they are disastrous relative to what we can further stipulate: that Magoo desires to escape unharmed and that this desire takes precedence over any desire he may have not to comply with the thug's command. Thus this possible world (at which the second thug is just outside range of Magoo's umbrella) will not be among Magoo's notional worlds. And more important, in the case of this possible world there is not the temptation, which there is for the actual world, to interpret Magoo as maximizing his own utility.

But how does the fact that we can avoid including this counterfactual variant of the actual world among Magoo's notional worlds solve the original problem that we have no grounds for excluding the actual world? That we can avoid including the counterfactual variant of the actual world among Magoo's notional worlds will be no help with the original problem unless the following condition is satisfied. There must be some constraint that guarantees a significant overlap between the interpretation that assigns notional worlds to Magoo at the actual world and the interpretation that assigns Magoo notional worlds at the possible world in question. If there is no such constraint, then at the world where the thug is out of range, we could interpret Magoo as having misunderstood his demand and as having tried to give directions, while at the actual world we interpret Magoo's behavior as an attack. Thus if there is no such constraint and all interpretations are independent, our acceptance of the former interpretation cannot count against our accepting the latter. And if this is the case, then no reference to counterfactual facts will explain why the actual world is not a notional world for Magoo.

Suppose, however, that we *are* constrained to find such an overlap. Then if we interpret Magoo as mistaking the intentions of the thugs at the possible world in question, we would have a reason to reject the interpretation at the actual world according to which Magoo intends to save his money by taking aggressive action. Of course, it might be objected that we could satisfy the requirement that we find a significant overlap and still include the actual world among Magoo's notional worlds if we interpret Magoo at the relevant possible world as intending to take aggressive action and as misjudging the distance between himself and the thug he is trying to hit. But as we look at other possible worlds, as the distance becomes greater, and as we see that Magoo continues to swing the umbrella, this explanation becomes increasingly implausible. Eventually it should become apparent that at these worlds Magoo's behavior is not best conceived as an attack in view of how obviously ill conceived such an attack would be. And given the constraint that the interpretation in these worlds should not be independent of the interpretation in the actual world, we will be forced to withdraw the interpretation according to which Magoo's intentions are aggressive at the actual world and hence to withdraw our assignment of the actual world to the set of Magoo's notional worlds.

How, then, can we guarantee an overlap between interpretations at the actual world and at other possible worlds? The most natural way is to assign sets of possible worlds not to persons at times but to individual internal states of persons at times. In this way we can require that in moving from one possible world to another, assignments of possible worlds to internal states of the subject change only if there is an appropriate explanation of the difference. For example, if the subject in one possible world has slightly different perceptual experiences than he or she has in another possible world, this will justify assigning different sets of worlds (i.e., different contents) to a few of the internal states, including a few of the memory states. By and large, however, the assignments to most of the states will remain fixed.

The Magoo problem can be solved, however, only if this constraint is incorporated into the definition of a notional world. Unless we add this qualification to the claim that the notional worlds are the worlds where the agent's actions are objectively optimal, the real world will count as one of Magoo's notional worlds, and we have already stipulated that it is not. Let us say that a *hypothesis* consists in

1. a mapping from states of an agent at a time (functionally and/or physically described) to sets of possible worlds,
2. a specification, for every nonempty set of possible worlds, whether it is the content of a belief, desire, intention, or action, and
3. the claim that each set of possible worlds represents the content of the state with which it is associated.

(Of course, for any agent, most states will be assigned the null set.) The qualified definition of a notional world, then, is this: A world W is a notional world for an agent A if and only if

1. there is a function H from possible worlds X at which A is an agent to hypotheses $H(X)$ such that A's actual actions (i.e., A's actions at the actual world, W_a) are, according to $H(W_a)$, objectively optimal at W,
2. for every possible world W', if A's actions at W' are not objectively optimal according to $H(W')$, then there is an appropriate explanation of the actions at W' according to which their nonoptimality is consistent with $H(W_a)$, and
3. for every possible world W'', $H(W'')$ provides the best explanation of A's actions, given requirement (2).

By this definition, the actual world is *not* one of Magoo's notional worlds. This is not, however, because Magoo's *behavior* in knocking out one thug and frightening the other is not objectively optimal. Given Magoo's desires, the propositions determined by the actual world—in particular the propositions that one thug is just within range, that Magoo's reflexes are fast enough, that the other thug is cowardly, and so forth—make this behavioral response better than any of the alternatives. If we confine ourselves to the actual world, then, the simplest hypothesis (call this H') is the one that assigns these propositions to internal states of Magoo. Thus H' is the hypothesis that these propositions provide the content of the states in question. But consider a world at which the thug is clearly out of range and Magoo swings the umbrella with disastrous effects. At this world there is no plausible way of reconciling H' with the nonoptimality of the action. If H' correctly captures Magoo's beliefs about the actual world, then given that Magoo's perceptual apparatus is normal, there is no explanation of Magoo's apparently suicidal behavior. Hence the actual world fails to satisfy the definition and is not among Magoo's notional worlds.

4 Objections and Replies

It may help to clarify this account of notional worlds if we consider a number of objections that might be made at this stage.[11]

Objection 1 The contents of someone's beliefs depend on how that person would describe the things they are beliefs about. The contents of someone's beliefs about a particular glass of water, for example, depend on whether that person would describe it as a glass of water or as a glass of colorless liquid. Thus there is a dilemma. On the one hand, we may use a person's words in characterizing his or her belief contents. In this case, however, the contents will not be narrow but broad, since we are assuming that a person's words derive their meaning in part as a result of facts about that person's environment. On the other hand, we may characterize the person's beliefs in phenomenal terms. But this characterization will not be adequate to distinguish between the person's belief that he or she is looking at a glass of colorless liquid and the belief that he or she is looking at a glass of water.

Reply There is another alternative. We can look at how the person behaves in the actual circumstances and in a wide range of counterfactual circumstances. And more generally, we can look at how the person's functional states vary with actual and counterfactual circumstances. For example, if all I believe about a glass of liquid in front of me is that it is colorless, I will almost certainly not drink it. And even in counterfactual circumstances in which it is crucial that I have a drink, I am likely to hesitate if all I believe is that the liquid has no color. Thus there are more than enough dispositions to behave in counterfactual circumstances to distinguish the belief that there is a glass of colorless liquid in front of me from the belief that there is a glass of water there. And since my dispositions to act in the two cases are different, the set of possible worlds at which my actions are optimal (and at which the other conditions for being a notional world are satisfied) will be different in each case. However, if I know no chemistry, there may be no dispositions that distinguish my having a belief that there is water (i.e., H_2O) in front of me from my belief that there is XYZ there. In this case the set of notional worlds corresponding to my belief will include both the worlds in which the liquid in front of me is H_2O and the worlds where it is XYZ. Thus this account has the consequence that an account of narrow content must have: that in the case imagined, the narrow content of my belief will not discriminate between the liquid's being H_2O and its being XYZ.

Objection 2   Imagine that Smith is investigating a burglary, spots the burglar, and shoots. However, there is a bulletproof glass shield between Smith and the burglar, which is invisible from where Smith stands. As a result the bullet ricochets, and Smith himself is wounded. Smith's action was optimal because he had no reason to suppose the shield existed. But precisely because he believed there was no such shield, the real world is not one of Smith's notional worlds.

Reply   Smith's action was *subjectively* optimal (assuming Smith has no qualms about dispatching intruders in such an offhand way), but it was not *objectively* optimal. Smith had good evidence for his assumption that he would have an unobstructed shot at the burglar, but the assumption was false. The actual world, then, is not one of Smith's notional worlds, since his action in shooting was objectively suboptimal. In other words, although Smith's action was *rational* at the actual world, the actual world fails to *rationalize* the action. Moreover, the fact that the action was objectively suboptimal, together with Smith's lack of any evidence that a glass shield would block his shot, suggests the hypothesis that he believed that no such shield existed. And this hypothesis is borne out when we see that, other things being equal, at those worlds where Smith has good evidence that a shield will block the shot, he does not fire.

Our hypothesis, then, is that at the actual world the notional worlds that define the contents of Smith's intentional states resemble the actual world except in excluding the glass shield. Thus we explain Smith's action by saying that he wanted to shoot the burglar and believed that he was in a good position to do so. (Of course, this explanation is only rough, since we are assuming that in using our ordinary vocabulary we cannot capture the narrow content of Smith's beliefs.) This example, then, is analogous to the example in which one fails to respond to the letter from Publishers Clearing House and, against all odds, one has won.

Suppose there is a possible world, however, at which Smith bumps his head and then shoots at the burglar, even though he has good evidence that a glass shield may block his shot. Does the existence of such a world suggest that Smith's action at the actual world was independent of what he believed about the existence of such a shield?

And does this undermine the explanation of Smith's action at the actual world by undermining the hypothesis that he wanted to shoot the burglar and believed that he was in a position to do so? The answer is no. The best explanation of Smith's actions at the possible world under consideration is not that he believed the shield would block the shot and fired anyway but that he fired in a state of confusion. Thus the circumstances at this possible world give us a plausible way of reconciling the best hypothesis at this world and the best hypothesis at the actual world: the confusion was caused at the world in question by the bump on the head but not at the actual world, where no such bump occurred. Of course, this proposed method of reconciling the two hypotheses is one we shall want to test, both by looking at still more possible worlds and by looking at the causal and counterfactual connections between Smith's internal states. But our way of testing the proposed reconciliation involves just the kinds of considerations that were involved in our formulating the original hypothesis.

Objection 3   Suppose that Jones wants to replace a blown fuse and, being out of fuses, replaces it with a penny. Let us suppose that Jones is aware of the risk he is taking and that the gamble pays off. In this case Jones's action is objectively optimal. Jones, however, chose a penny not because he believed that it was a good conductor of electricity but because he believed that it was a good conductor of heat and that a good conductor of heat was what was needed. Thus although the action is objectively optimal, the actual world is not one of Jones's notional worlds. Furthermore, there is a nomological connection between a penny's being a good conductor of electricity and its being a good conductor of heat. This means that if we look at nearby possible worlds, Jones's replacing the fuse with the penny will continue to be objectively optimal. Of course, we can look at nearby possible worlds in which Jones's behavior is nonoptimal not because replacing the fuse is nonoptimal but because he is asked whether pennies conduct heat or electricity, he expresses the belief that they conduct heat but not electricity, and he desires to tell the truth. But if this is how we determine what Jones's notional worlds are, it seems to make the switch from considering the truth of Jones's beliefs to the optimality or nonoptimality of his actions pointless. And if we do not restrict ourselves to nearby possible worlds, what do we have to hold fixed for a possible world to be relevant?

Reply   First, there is no need to confine our attention to nearby possible worlds. Which worlds we look at (that is, what we hold fixed in determining which worlds it is relevant to consider) will depend on the hypothesis under consideration. Suppose the hypothesis is that the objective optimality of Jones's action at the actual world is the result of Jones's appreciation of the electrical conductivity of pennies. Then we can test the hypothesis by looking at worlds where the nomological connection between the conductivity of electricity and the conductivity of heat breaks down but at which Jones's psychology is, in relevant respects, as much like it is at the actual world as is (logically) possible.

Thus, suppose that at world W replacements for fuses must conduct electricity and that pennies do not conduct electricity, though they do conduct heat. If we keep Jones's psychology fixed, he will use a penny to replace the fuse at W, and the action will be objectively nonoptimal. And since the explanation of Jones's action at W will be that he thought that replacements for fuses had to conduct heat and not electricity and since there is no relevant difference between Jones's psychology at W and Jones's psychology at the actual world, the actual world will not be one of Jones's notional worlds.

Of course, if we are not stipulating what Jones believes at W but trying to determine what he believes on the basis of his behavior and his functional states, then we might *not* conclude that the actual world was not one of his notional worlds. For example, we might conclude instead that at W Jones believes replacements for fuses must conduct electricity and that pennies conduct electricity. In this case if Jones's psychology at W and at the actual world is the same, then the actual world will be among Jones's notional worlds. The two hypotheses, then, as to the explanation of Jones's actions at W can be represented in table 1. But we can distinguish between hypothesis 1 and hypothesis 2 (still assuming that Jones's beliefs at W and at the actual world are not relevantly different) by asking whether we would produce the best explanation of Jones's behavior on the basis of the first or the second of the following two assumptions: that Jones's beliefs about fuses and about pennies are false at the actual world and that his beliefs about fuses (but not about pennies) are false at W (hypothesis 1), or that Jones's beliefs at the actual world about both fuses and

Table 1
Hypotheses regarding Jones's beliefs

| | Facts at W and at A | | Jones's beliefs at W and A | |
	W	A	Hypothesis 1	Hypothesis 2
What fuses must conduct	E	E	H	E
What pennies conduct	H & not E	H & E	H & not E	H & E

A = the actual world; E = electricity; H = heat.

pennies are true and that his beliefs about pennies (but not about fuses) are false at W (hypothesis 2). And this question will normally be settled by looking at Jones's evidence at the actual world and at W. If there is no plausible explanation as to how Jones could be mistaken about either fuses or pennies at the actual world and there are a number of explanations as to how he could be mistaken about pennies at W, then hypothesis 2 will be strongly supported. Alternatively, if there is no plausible explanation of how Jones could be mistaken about pennies at W and there are plausible explanations of how Jones could be mistaken about fuses and pennies at the actual world, then hypothesis 1 will be strongly supported instead.

Second, even if we confine our investigation to nearby (i.e., nomologically possible) worlds, there will be worlds where Jones's belief that replacements for fuses need conduct only heat will manifest itself in nonoptimal behavior. This will be the case even though Jones's replacing the fuse with a penny will be optimal at such worlds. Jones will be disposed, for example, to say that fuses need only conduct heat, even at worlds where his overriding desire is to speak the truth. Indeed, he will be disposed to say this even at worlds where his failure to speak the truth will have serious negative consequences. And at the worlds where he acts on this disposition and either suffers the consequences or simply fails to satisfy his desire to speak the truth, his action will be objectively nonoptimal.

In describing the worlds where Jones's behavior is nonoptimal, of course, I have made a number of stipulations about Jones's intentional states and about the nature of the worlds he inhabits: that he believes that replacements for fuses need conduct only heat, that replacements for fuses must conduct electricity, and that he desires to speak the truth. But there is no problem in our using our pretheoretical notion of belief in describing the example and in showing that the present account of notional worlds captures that notion (where it should). This involves no appeal to the truth of Jones's beliefs in specifying the notional worlds that give them their narrow content. It is a stipulation of the example itself that we are dealing with a class of possible worlds in which Jones believes that replacements for fuses need only conduct heat and at which this belief is false. And there can be no objection to our considering some particular one of these worlds at which Jones expresses his belief, at which he desires to speak only the truth, and at which his failure to speak the truth has consequences he would prefer to avoid. Since we know there are such possible worlds, suppose we have picked one, and call it W^*. Because Jones has a false belief about fuses at the actual world, we have been able to find a nearby possible world at which at least one of his actions is nonoptimal.

This example does raise an important question. Suppose that at some possible world W an agent's actions are optimal according to some hypothesis H that represents the best explanation of the agent's actions at that world prior to the assignment of hypotheses to those actions at other possible worlds. Now let us call a *prima facie defeater of* H any hypothesis H' such that for some possible world W',

1. H' is the best explanation of the agent's actions at W' prior to the assignment of hypotheses to those actions at other possible worlds,
2. according to H' some action of the agent at W' is nonoptimal, and
3. H' is difficult to reconcile with H.

Thus the hypothesis that at W^* Jones is behaving nonoptimally in expressing the belief that fuses need only conduct heat is a prima facie defeater of the hypothesis that at the actual world Jones believes that replacements for fuses must conduct electricity and that the actual world is one of Jones's notional worlds. The question, then, is whether such prima facie defeaters can be discovered as well as stipulated to exist. In other words, will such prima facie defeaters be discovered solely on the basis of physical and functional descriptions of the agent at each possible world?

The answer to the question is yes. Given that at W^* Jones utters the words that are ordinarily used to express the belief that replacements for fuses need only conduct heat and given that this is false at W^*, we need some explanation of Jones's behavior. Of course, Jones may deliberately intend to mislead his audience as to his beliefs at W^*, he may not actually speak the language he seems to speak at W^*, or we may eventually find an explanation that allows us to reconcile the hypothesis that at W^* he is mistaken about the function of fuses and the hypothesis that at the actual world he is not. But each of these possible explanations of Jones's behavior at W^* has implications for the other kinds of behavior we will expect, both at W^* and at other possible worlds. And each explanation will be confirmed or disconfirmed in exactly the same way as the original hypothesis that Jones's beliefs at the actual world about fuses are true: by determining which hypothesis about Jones's behavior at the world in question is best and then attempting to reconcile that hypothesis with the best hypotheses at other possible worlds. Thus not only does the definition of an agent's notional worlds not depend on the notion of the truth of the agent's beliefs at other possible worlds. We can also *apply* the definition solely on the basis of physical and functional descriptions of the agent at those possible worlds that are relevant. Hence the point of defining an agent's notional worlds in terms of the optimality of the agent's actions has not been lost, and the objection that narrow content is parasitic on broad content can be met.

As these objections and replies demonstrate, this account raises the general problem that one cannot ascribe a belief to a subject without knowing the subject's other beliefs and desires. But this is a problem about which functionalists have had a great deal to say.

5   Narrow Interpretation

The problem we are now confronting is the problem of radical interpretation. This is the problem of determining what intentional states a system has, given all and only the physical facts about that system. Let us imagine that we proceed as David Lewis does by conjoining all of the truths about the relations between inputs, outputs, beliefs, desires, and intentions that we want any ascription of intentional states to a subject to preserve. Lewis suggests in "Psychophysical and Theoretical Identifications" that these truths consist in commonsense platitudes.[12] He seems to imply in "Radical Interpretation," however, that these truths can be summarized as relatively general holistic constraints on the ascription of beliefs, intentions, and desires to a subject and on the ascription of truth conditions to that subject's language.[13] I shall not try to determine the relation between these two suggestions of Lewis's, because I want to propose a third alternative: that we take the truths constraining the ascription of propositional content to consist in a substantive theory of rationality.

Such a theory might be developed along the lines of Bayesian decision theory if that theory can be modified in such a way that the standard objections to it are met. Regardless of how the theory is developed, however, it will entail that subjects maximize their expected utility subject to computational limitations and to relatively local lapses into irrationality. The qualification to accommodate irrationality raises a number of serious difficulties, of course. But I shall confine myself here to mentioning three strategies that we are likely to find useful in our applications of the constraint. First, we will want to apply the substantive theory of rationality in some cases not to the subject as a whole but to subsystems of the subject. We can then explain certain forms of irrationality of the subject in terms of the interaction of the relatively more rational subsystems. This is likely to be especially useful in dealing with self-deception.[14] Second, we should be prepared to find what I describe in chapter 7 as nonmaximizing dispositions in cases where they are likely to be strategically beneficial. A disposition to become angry, for example, though it may decrease the subject's utility if it is manifest, may motivate others, if the existence of the disposition is discernible, to avoid bringing about those situations in which the disposition is triggered. As a result, the net effect of possessing the disposition on the subject's utility may be positive. Finally, it is open to us to consider the subject's behavior in possible worlds where the subject has the power to modify his or her motivational makeup at will. If we discover that in those possible worlds the subject eliminates certain desires, this will provide good grounds for the claim that the actions based on those desires in the actual world are irrational. Such considerations are most likely to be of use in dealing with weakness of the will (see chapter 8).

Suppose we had such a substantive theory of rationality. How could we use the theory to assign possible worlds to internal states of the subject? Let us imagine that the theory of rationality is expressed as a set of constraints on the coapplication of intentional predicates. One such constraint, for example, might be "if one has assigned the beliefs that the utility of action A_1 is greater than that of actions $A_2, \ldots, A_n$ and that actions $A_1, \ldots, A_n$ are the only actions open, then, other things being equal, one must assign the intention to perform A_1." Any assignment of intentional content—that is, any assignment of sets of possible worlds and a specification of the proposition defined by each set as believed, desired, or intended—that satisfies all the holistic constraints of the substantive theory of rationality is a legitimate intentional interpretation. (If the set of legitimate interpretations for a single subject includes interpretations that are radically different and the theory of rationality cannot be improved, we would have grounds for considering eliminativism regarding intentional states.)

Suppose that this kind of approach to radical interpretation can be worked out in detail. Let us call such an account one of *narrow interpretation*. How different would such a version of radical interpretation be from the one Lewis originally suggested? The differences at first sight might seem quite significant, since Lewis is explicitly committed to the assumption that the process of radical interpretation has wide content as its output. This is true for two reasons, at least on the assumption that Lewis accepts something like the Putnam-Kripke view of reference. First, Lewis says that we ascribe referents to the subject's referring expressions and truth conditions to the subject's sentences.[15] Second, Lewis says that we should ascribe beliefs and desires to a subject in such a way that the subject would have our beliefs and our desires given our history of evidence and our most basic values.[16] On the Putnam-Kripke view, both of these require-ments ensure that radical interpretation results in wide content ascriptions.

Whether these requirements of Lewis's reflect genuinely deep fea-tures of his account, however, depends on how similar Lewis's ac-count would be to the one I have suggested we develop in terms of a substantive theory of rationality. For on this approach to radical inter-pretation, the holistic constraints require that beliefs, desires, and intentions be ascribed so that subjects maximize their expected utility (subject to computational limitations and to the relevant qualifications concerning rationality). But the propositional attitude ascriptions that make subjects maximizers of expected utility are *narrow* content as-criptions. To see this, consider a version of Saul Kripke's story about Pierre.[17] Pierre believes that Oscar Wilde lived in London, that he himself lives in London, and that if he ever lived in London, he would maximize his expected utility by visiting one of the houses in which Wilde lived. Pierre, however, forms no intention to do so, and this is due neither to irrationality nor to any limitations on his computational capacities. Rather, the problem is that London is represented in Pierre's belief that he lives in London and in his belief that Wilde lived in London in two radically different ways, and he has no reason to suspect that these two representations pick out one and the same city. Because of the difference between these two representations, Pierre has no reason to conclude that he should visit one of the houses in which Wilde lived. Pierre has no more reason to draw this conclusion than he has to conclude from his belief that he lives in London, his belief that Thomas Pynchon lived in Ithaca, and his belief that if he ever lived in Ithaca, he would maximize his expected utility by trying to visit one of the places in which Pynchon lived that he should try to arrange such a visit.[18] Thus if wide content is the only kind we can ascribe in determining whether Pierre satisfies the substantive theory of rationality, then since Pierre does not maximize his expected utility relative to the wide content ascriptions, he does not satisfy the theory. We know, however, that in fact Pierre does maximize expected utility, and the content ascriptions that make this clear are narrow ascriptions. In other words, when we ascribe sets of possible worlds to Pierre's internal states so as to ensure that Pierre satisfies the substantive theory of rationality, the contents we thereby ascribe are narrow con-tents. And this means that to the extent that Lewis's version of radical interpretation resembles this one, it is the production of narrow con-tent, rather than wide content, for which it is most naturally suited.

With this notion of the ascription of intentional states subject to holistic constraints in hand, it is time to return to the discussion of the satisfaction of desires. Recall that we could not say that one maximizes expected utility at a possible world just in case one's desires are best satisfied there, if this is taken to mean that the propositions that determine the contents of one's desires are true. This was because we want an account of narrow content that is not parasitic on truth conditions and wide content. Moreover (assuming I do not know any chemistry), if I obtain a glass of water, we want the desire I would express by saying "I want a glass of water" to be satisfied by my getting a glass of H_2O in the actual world and a glass of XYZ on Twin Earth. (Recall that we are treating Twin Earth as a possible world rather than as a remote part of the actual world.) We want, in other words, that if I maximize my utility in the actual world, then I do so as well on Twin Earth; so if the actual world is one of my notional worlds, so is Twin Earth.

Though we cannot say that our desires are satisfied just in case their truth conditions are realized, neither can we say that our desires are satisfied just in case we *feel* satisfied. Suppose that one desires a good reputation and one feels satisfied with the reputation one has. Contrary to what one assumes, however, one is being slandered in Ohio. This does not diminish one's feeling of satisfaction, however, because one never visits Ohio and word of one's reputation there never gets back to one. Let us call the first sense of 'satisfaction' the *logical sense* and the second sense the *local sense*. If the substantive theory of rationality were couched in terms of satisfaction in the local sense, then the world in which one's actions lead to one's reputation being maligned in Ohio is a world in which one's actions maximize one's utility. Hence this world is one of one's notional worlds and thus one of the set of worlds that provide and equally good fit for one's conception of how things are. But we are assuming that one feels satisfied with one's situation precisely because it is *not* part of one's conception of the world that one's reputation is low in Ohio.

The solution to this problem is to characterize satisfaction by reference to the same constraints on the coapplication of intentional terms that govern the ascription of the subject's beliefs, desires, and intentions. Let us call satisfaction so characterized *global satisfaction*. In this sense, one's desires with respect to one's reputation are *not* satisfied in the world in which one is scorned in Ohio. This is apparent if one considers how one would react if one did come to believe one's reputation was not uniformly high. Thus satisfaction in the global sense depends not only on one's actual satisfaction in the local sense but also on the satisfaction in the local sense that one would experience in counterfactual situations. Of course, one's response in such situations counts against one's desires' being satisfied in those situations only against the background of one's other desires and one's beliefs. Thus the content of one's desires depends on the conditions (both actual and counterfactual) under which they would be satisfied (in the local sense), and the conditions under which they would be satisfied (in the local sense) depend on the contents of one's other intentional states. Hence desire satisfaction must be characterized in the course of the holistic ascription of beliefs, desires, and intentions.

Would such an account of narrow content meet Stalnaker's objections? Stalnaker's fundamental concern, as I have been interpreting him, is over the following pair of problems. The first is that narrow content, if it is developed on analogy with Kaplan's notion of character, is parasitic on wide content. The second is that accounts such as Dennett's, according to which narrow content is not parasitic on wide content, seem to face insuperable obstacles. There are strong grounds for claiming, however, that on this account of narrow interpretation, narrow content does not depend on wide content. Narrow interpretation was deliberately developed in such a way that there would be no such dependencies. Moreover, in the light of the work of Putnam, Kripke, and Burge, this way of developing the idea of radical interpretation seems quite natural. Even if our goal is to produce an account of radical interpretation in which the interpretations have as their output *wide* content ascriptions, general considerations suggest that the account will involve two separable components: a component made up of holistic constraints that guarantee the rationality of the relations between intentional states and a component that specifies how we are to assign referents and truth conditions on the basis of the subject's relations (especially causal relations) to the external environment. These components are naturally thought of as separable because, as we have seen with the Pierre example, they impose different and frequently conflicting constraints on the ascription of content. The assignment of wide content to Pierre's external states frustrates the attempt to interpret Pierre as a maximizer of expected utility. Thus it seems most plausible to think of maximizing rationality at a stage prior to, and independent of, the stage at which wide content is assigned rather than thinking of the rationality constraints and the constraints imposed by a causal theory of reference as operating simultaneously.

In the course of his discussion of Dennett, Stalnaker has also expressed doubt as to whether there is any point to defining narrow content, even on the assumption that this could be done. But on the account I have suggested, according to which narrow content is the natural product of a process of radical interpretation aimed at the production of wide content, this kind of doubt is not as pressing as it might appear. The justification for positing narrow content could simply lie in our interest in wide content coupled with the role that rationality constraints, and thus narrow content, play in its production. This is not to concede to Stalnaker that narrow content is of no independent interest. But even on the assumption that Stalnaker is right, this fact would not constitute a serious objection to the present account.

Is this account, then, likely to prove satisfactory to Stalnaker? It seems entirely possible that the answer is no. Stalnaker's final objection to Dennett is that we cannot recover anything like Boston from a narrow characterization of the internal states of a typical resident. To the extent that the problem being raised is the Magoo problem, I think we do have reason to think that consideration of the subject's responses in counterfactual situations will rule out the interpretations which are obviously incorrect. But in the absence of a more fully fleshed out account of the substantive theory of rationality, there is, perhaps, room for legitimate skepticism.

It is worth noticing, however, that such skepticism does not specifically concern narrow content. The skepticism that remains concerns a general approach to radical interpretation and to the development of a functionalist theory of the mind. My appeal to a substantive theory of rationality is the counterpart of the appeal that both Lewis and Donald Davidson make to the principle of charity.[19] And in view of the lessons of the causal theory of reference, the separation of the principle of charity into a component governing rationality and a component governing the contribution of the external environment to reference and truth conditions seems a natural development of the original intuition. Thus the debate between Stalnaker and proponents of this kind of an account of narrow content is really a debate over the merits of a general approach to the ascription of content of any kind whatsoever.

Acknowledgments

I am grateful to Akeel Bilgrami, Ned Block, Daniel Dennett, Brian Loar, Georges Rey, and Robert Stalnaker for comments on earlier drafts.

PART II
Qualia

Chapter 3
Curse of the Qualia

1 Introduction

The functionalist project of characterizing mental states in terms of their causal and relational properties has seemed to many a promising alternative to such competing theories of mind as dualism, physicalism, and behaviorism. Though functionalism continues to attract a significant following, resistance to this approach, at least where qualitative states such as pain are concerned, almost completely overshadows the original theory. In spite of the plausibility of characterizing beliefs and desires in terms of their causal roles in mediating between perceptual input and behavioral output, states such as pain seem to demand an analysis that accounts for the *feelings* involved in experiencing them. Such feelings, however, appear to be left untouched by any conceivable form of functional analysis.

A recent alternative to functionalism, which is rapidly becoming (if only by default) the accepted view of qualitative states, involves a compromise between functionalist and physicalist intuitions. On this view, which I shall call *physicalist-functionalism*, even those aspects of a subject's physiological makeup that can be varied without varying any functional properties would be relevant to the exact nature of the subject's qualitative states. Versions of this view have recently been defended by Sydney Shoemaker and Ned Block.[1] The list of its proponents, however, is far longer, including the majority of those whose work in the philosophy of mind touches on questions of qualia.[2]

I shall argue that the reaction against functionalism and the attempt to compromise between functionalism and physicalism are mistaken. I shall claim, in fact, that physicalist-functionalism is untenable in any form. Given the alternatives available, this amounts to a defense of functionalism in its orthodox form. I shall begin by sketching the conceptions of qualia that underlie orthodox functionalism, Shoe-

Synthese 68 (1986): 333–368. Copyright 1986 by D. Reidel Publishing Company. Reprinted by permission of Kluwer Academic Publishers.

maker's version of physicalist-functionalism, Block's alternative version of the theory, and a view I shall call *transcendentalism*. This list does not exhaust the logically possible alternatives to functionalism, which include behaviorism and eliminativism among others. But since this paper concerns the challenge that physicalist-functionalism poses to functionalism regarding *qualia*, the list exhausts the relevant alternatives. Those who are unsympathetic to the functionalist attempt to deal with qualia are unlikely to be more impressed with the behaviorist or eliminativist options.

Orthodox functionalism (Harman)

In its most general form, orthodox functionalism is the theory that a subject's psychological states can be explained solely in terms of their causal and dispositional relations to the subject's perceptual inputs, behavioral outputs, and other internal states.[3] Any causal system whose input states, output states, and internal states bear the right relation to one another has the psychological states in question, regardless of whether its physical makeup consists in neural networks, computer chips, or beer cans and bits of string.

Construed as an account of propositional attitudes, this theory has a genuine intuitive appeal. It is not implausible to suppose that the essence of belief lies in its evolutionary role in mediating between our stimulus inputs and behavioral outputs so as to permit flexible responses to new environmental conditions. For the orthodox functionalist, this theory applies equally well to qualitative states. Pain, for example, plays its evolutionary role in shifting our desires away from our current projects when these projects lead to bodily damage. According to orthodox functionalism, the essential property of pain, like the essential property of belief, is its causal role as fixed by evolution. Pain can be functionally defined in terms of its typical causes (bodily damage), and its typical effects (behavioral changes brought about by an intense desire to change one's current state and a belief that one can do so by changing one's behavior).[4] This is not to say that for the orthodox functionalist pain need not be painful. What it *is* for something to hurt, on this view, is for it to cause a state with the functional properties of pain, particularly the overriding desire that that state cease.

Physicalist-functionalism₁ (Block)

This theory, which may be viewed as a compromise between functionalism and physicalism, stems from the same conception of belief and desire as orthodox functionalism but a different conception of qualitative states. For the physicalist-functionalist₁, the dispositional tendency of an internal state to shift our immediate desires away from our current projects toward behavior that would prevent further bodily damage is insufficient to ensure that it feels like pain. Indeed, for the physicalist-functionalist$_1$ such a dispositional property is insufficient to ensure that the state is associated with any feeling at all. According to this theory, the orthodox functionalist has no way of ruling out the possibility that some internal state might play the evolutionary role of pain without its feeling like *anything*, much less like pain, to be in that state. And while a physicalist-functionalist$_1$ might allow the possibility that pain in another subject could involve a different feeling from the one it has for us, such theorists find the possibility that pain could be unaccompanied by any feeling whatsoever an unacceptable consequence of orthodox functionalism. Thus, according to physicalist-functionalism$_1$, functional states underdetermine qualitative states, and only further specification of the physical details of the way in which the functional states are realized would determine which, if any, qualitative states the subject occupies. Being a condition of neurons as opposed to being a condition of silicon chips is, on this theory, very possibly part of the essence of pain.

Physicalist-functionalism$_2$ (Shoemaker)

If physicalist-functionalism$_1$ is a compromise between functionalism and physicalism, physicalist-functionalism$_2$ is a compromise between functionalism and physicalist-functionalism$_1$. Although this view of Shoemaker's grows out of the same dissatisfaction over the orthodox functionalist treatment of qualia as does physicalist-functionalism$_1$, it is also motivated by an objection to physicalist-functionalism$_1$ and an alternative conception of what is essential to qualitative states. The objection is that for the physicalist-functionalist$_1$, a functional duplicate of a normal human subject might lack the qualitative experience of pain for purely physiological reasons. Such a subject, however, would mistakenly believe that he or she experienced all of the usual pain sensations. If this were genuinely possible, then the question would arise how we, in our own cases, could rule out the possibility that we lacked pain experience. But at least in our own cases, Shoemaker claims, skepticism about qualia seems absurd. That it entails this form of skepticism points up, for Shoemaker, the inadequacy of physicalist-functionalist$_1$.

On the positive side, Shoemaker's view is that while part of the essence of pain is that there is *something* it feels like to experience it, it is not essential that this should be exactly what it feels like when *we* experience it. On Shoemaker's account, we can give a functionalist characterization of what it is like to have states with qualitative content, though not of what it is like to have states with any *particular* qualitative content. Since having states with some qualitative content or other is sufficient for mentality, functionalism as a theory of mind is vindicated, and skepticism about the existence of our own qualitative states is forestalled. Physicalist-functionalism$_2$ represents the hope that we can compromise with physicalism over the *particular* qualitative content of qualitative states but that we can save sentience for functionalism.

Transcendentalism (Nagel)

For transcendental theories of mind, as for orthodox functionalism, it is essential to being in pain that it *feel* like pain.[5] But for the transcendentalist, this feeling is not captured by either functional or physical conditions. That one is in pain is a first-person fact, irreducible to any third-person facts, whether these include the details of one's neurophysiology or not. For the transcendentalist, mention of the subject's physical states brings us no closer to what the subject feels than does mention of the subject's functional states. On this score even Cartesian dualism is no improvement. Mental substance is simply one more entity bound up in the causal nexus of objective, third-person relations. If facts about physical substance tell us nothing about what pain feels like, neither do facts about mental substance. As Nagel puts the point, "The question of how one can include in the objective world a mental substance having subjective properties is as acute as the question how a physical substance can have subjective properties."[6] Contrary to Descartes's assumption, facts about the mind are not determined by objective facts of any kind whatsoever. Transcendental theories include transcendental dualism, transcendental idealism, and any of the transcendental pluralisms that might in principle be formulated.

Regardless of the form it takes, any version of physicalist-functionalism is committed to at least one of the following two theses:

1. Absent qualia are possible; i.e., there could be a subject who was functionally equivalent to a normal subject and who lacked qualitative states.
2. Qualia differences are possible; i.e., there could be a subject who was functionally equivalent to a normal subject and whose mental states differed in qualitative character from those of the normal subject.

Block's physicalist-functionalism$_1$ entails both (1) and (2), as does transcendentalism. The transcendentalist, in fact, holds the even stronger thesis that two subjects who are alike in respect of all objective, third-person facts may nonetheless differ in the presence or character of their qualitative experiences. Shoemaker is committed to the truth of (2), while the orthodox functionalist is committed to the falsity of both.

Shoemaker's claim that absent qualia are impossible might seem to commit him to the negation of (1) as well as the truth of (2), but this is not the case. Shoemaker's claim—the only claim for which he argues—is couched in terms of a different concept of absent qualia, and it is significantly weaker than the negation of the claim made by thesis (1). Shoemaker's claim is that no subject who is functionally equivalent to a normal subject *and whose nonqualitative states are all genuine* could lack qualitative states. And this weaker claim is obviously compatible with the truth of thesis (1). Thesis (1) would be true if there could be a subject who was a functional duplicate of a normal subject and who had no mental states whatsoever, nonqualitative or qualitative. Such a case would be compatible with Shoemaker's claim because the subject would lack genuine nonqualitative states. Hence if Shoemaker wanted to defend the negation of thesis (1) as well as his weaker claim, he would have to argue for the impossibility of such a case, and he provides no such argument.

In section 2, I shall show that in spite of the weakness of the claim Shoemaker actually defends, his arguments for the claim raise serious difficulties. Shoemaker's definition of 'absent qualia' requires that an absent-qualia subject have genuine nonqualitative states. However, Shoemaker's understanding of the notion of a genuine nonqualitative state rules out by fiat the most plausible case for the physicalist-functionalist$_1$'s thesis that absent qualia are possible. Shoemaker's definition, in other words, eliminates a case that the physicalist-functionalist$_1$ would rightly regard as a case of an absent-qualia subject not because the case has been shown to be incoherent but because it fails to meet Shoemaker's restrictive definition of 'absent qualia'. Furthermore, the restrictive definition is not justified by Shoemaker's claim for the scope of his undertaking, nor does the definition find any independent support in Shoemaker's arguments against absent qualia.

My own arguments against absent qualia in sections 3 and 4, which are also general arguments against physicalist-functionalism, share some of the same intuitive motivation as Shoemaker's argument.[7] Shoemaker's argument against absent qualia (in his sense) appears to be motivated, at least in part, by the intuition that physical facts per se are irrelevant to the question of a subject's mental experiences. Shoemaker says, for example, that "if we are given that a man's state is functionally identical with a state that in us is pain, it is hard to see how a neurophysiological difference between him and us could be any evidence at all that his states lack qualitative character" (Shoemaker 1975, p. 296). This intuition that mental differences could not consist in neurophysiological differences alone is one that I share with Shoemaker. The basic idea is that unless there is some non–a posteriori connection between the neurophysiological difference and the alleged mental difference, we have no explanation of the relevance to the mental of the difference in neurophysiology. Even if we discovered that every subject to whom we were tempted to ascribe pain had the same neurophysiological makeup, the possibility of there being a subject who satisfied every other condition for pain ascription except the possession of the neurophysiology in question would make the empirical correlation irrelevant. If there is no connection between the neurophysiological facts and the grounds for the ascription of pain that is *prior* to the empirical correlation, the correlation itself could have no relevance to the question of whether the neurophysiological deviant felt pain.

As a result of my agreement with Shoemaker over this intuition, my arguments in sections 3 and 4 will overlap with his in their intuitive motivation as well as in the consequence that absent qualia (in Shoemaker's sense) are impossible. I argue in section 3 that physicalist-functionalists inherit the problem of property dualism that originally plagued central-state materialists and helped to motivate orthodox functionalism. It was the claim of central-state materialism that particular mental events such as one's pain at *t* would turn out to be identical with particular physical events such as one's brain state X at *t*. This identity, it was held, would be an empirical discovery and hence known a posteriori. The following principle suggested that there had to be two modes of presentation of any such mental event, one of which was a mental property or feature: if two expressions refer to the same object and this fact cannot be established a priori, then the modes of presentation in virtue of which they pick out their common referent must be distinct. And this suggested that central-state materialism would be committed to the existence of irreducible mental properties or features. The solution that emerged consisted in the claim that mental terms *were* coreferential a priori with their translations in a topic-neutral vocabulary—expressions that were neither mentalistic nor physicalist. Thus it was claimed that central-state materialism was committed only to the existence of physical and topic-neutral properties. Since functional definitions are instances of topic-neutral translation, orthodox functionalism allows essentially the same response. The insistence of the physicalist-functionalist that no topic-neutral expression is coreferential a priori with a mentalistic term for a qualitative mental state, however, leaves the problem of property dualism with no plausible solution.

In section 4, I argue that physicalist-functionalism precludes our making a principled distinction between those physiological differences between subjects that provide grounds for ascribing differences in their qualitative experiences and those that do not. The reason is that there is no evidence for a difference in the qualitative experiences of functionally equivalent subjects that is *independent* of their physiological differences. This contradicts Shoemaker's claim that intrasubjective qualia inversions provide evidence that allows us to correlate qualitative with neurophysiological changes. I argue, however, that if we keep a subject's functional states constant, no change in the neurophysiology, however drastic, will produce evidence of an intrasubjective inversion.

The thought that physicalist-functionalism justifies intuitions that functionalism cannot accommodate helps to explain its popularity, but it represents a confusion between physicalist-functionalism and transcendentalism. It is transcendentalism, not physicalist-functionalism, that can accommodate more radical pretheoretical intuitions than orthodox functionalism. To the extent that physicalist-functionalism makes room for qualia differences for which functionalism does not, it severs the link between physical facts and the qualia distinctions they are supposed to explain. In so doing, it makes every physical fact equally relevant to the facts of qualitative experience. Nonetheless, the picture of qualitative character offered by the physicalist-functionalist has an appeal that is likely to survive any single argument. Shoemaker's version in particular represents the most detailed and sophisticated treatment available of the constellation of problems surrounding qualitative states. Only by investigating the source of the picture's appeal, as well as the picture's consequences and alternatives, are we likely to have any hope of dispelling it.

2   The Absent Qualia Arguments

Shoemaker's longest and most explicit argument for the thesis that absent qualia are impossible is based on the premise that if absent qualia were possible, qualia would be unknowable (Shoemaker 1981, pp. 587–596). As Shoemaker himself points out, however, there is a serious objection to this argument (Shoemaker 1981, p. 596, n. 20). One might hold the view, defended by Goldman among others, that if one's belief in a proposition is acquired in virtue of a reliable mechanism, then the merely logical possibility of its falsehood does not rule out our knowing the proposition to be true.[8] On this view, the logical possibility of absent qualia would be compatible with one's knowing one experienced genuine qualitative states. Since for Shoemaker it was the absurdity of skepticism about the existence of one's own qualitative states that made the possibility of absent qualia seem unacceptable, Goldman's epistemological position appears to undermine Shoemaker's argument.

Because of this objection, Shoemaker relies on a pair of alternative arguments against the possibility of absent qualia, and it is these arguments that I shall discuss. Before presenting the arguments, however, it will be necessary to set out Shoemaker's definitions of 'functional definability' and 'absent qualia'.

> A mental state is *functionally definable in the strong sense* if and only if it is definable in terms of its causal relations to inputs, outputs, and other mental states, all of which must themselves be functionally definable (Shoemaker 1981, p. 583).

> A mental state is *functionally definable in the weak sense* if and only if it is definable in terms of its causal relations to inputs, outputs, and nonqualitative mental states, where it is not required that these nonqualitative mental states must themselves be functionally definable (Shoemaker 1981, p. 584, n. 8).[9]

Among qualitative mental states Shoemaker means to include, besides qualitative states proper such as pain, qualitative beliefs to the effect that one is in a state with a *particular* qualitative character, such as the feeling of one's headache on a particular occasion (Shoemaker 1975, p. 309).

In terms of these two senses of functional definability we have two corresponding senses of 'absent qualia'.

> Absent Qualia Thesis One (AQT-1) holds that qualitative states are not functionally definable even in the weak sense (Shoemaker 1981, p. 584, n. 8).

> Absent Qualia Thesis Two (AQT-2) holds that qualitative states are not functionally definable in the strong sense (Shoemaker 1981, p. 585).

The thesis to which Shoemaker's actual arguments commit him is not the negation of AQT-2, which would commit him to the negation of thesis (1) of section 1, but the negation of AQT-1 (Shoemaker 1981, p. 587).[10] Shoemaker, then, is committed to the thesis that qualitative states are definable in terms of their causal relations to inputs, outputs, and nonqualitative mental states that need not themselves be functionally definable.[11] Let us, as Shoemaker does, call a mental state that satisfies the best functional definition for states of type M but is not in fact a genuine (token of) M an *ersatz M* (e.g., an "ersatz pain").[12] Suppose that Shoemaker is wrong, that AQT-1 is *true,* and that qualitative states are *not* functionally definable even by reference to nonqualitative mental states that are not themselves functionally definable. Then there is a possible creature all of whose nonqualitative mental states are genuine and whose qualitative mental states are ersatz. Call such a creature an *imitation man.*[13] Shoemaker's claim is that such an imitation man is impossible (Shoemaker 1981, p. 584). Table 1 should make the relations between these theses clear. Logically equivalent propositions are grouped together under boldfaced headings, each of which names the thesis of which the members of the group are alternative formulations.

There is one ambiguity in these definitions that has yet to be clarified. To say that a nonqualitative state that is functionally equivalent to one of our mental states is genuine could mean either of two things. Suppose that the state claimed to be genuine is functionally equivalent to our belief that water is wet. The claim that it is genuine might mean that it is a genuine *belief,* or it might mean that it is a genuine *belief that water is wet.* The difference lies in the fact that on the causal theory of reference, the content of a belief that water is wet is determined in part by environmental circumstances that are independent of the subject's functional makeup. Among those subjects who share our functional states, only those who have beliefs caused in the right way by *water* have the belief that water is wet. Consider a possible subject who is functionally equivalent to a normal human subject and who has a belief that would be expressed by saying, "Water is wet." If that belief was not caused by water, but by a substance like water in all respects except its microstructure, the subject would not have a genuine belief that *water* is wet.[14] Hence on the second, stronger interpretation of 'genuine nonqualitative state', such a subject's nonqualitative states would not all be genuine. Shoemaker has made it clear that it is this second interpretation that he has in mind.[15]

Finally, let us define *the parochial theory of the meaning of mental terms* as the theory according to which mental terms have their references fixed, à la Kripke, to what are in fact (although the users of the terms need not know this) certain physiological states. These states are the physical realizations *in us* of the best functional definitions of the mental states (Shoemaker 1981, p. 592). If an absent-qualia subject (in Shoemaker's sense) were possible, it would be a subject who was functionally equivalent to us and who shared our nonqualitative states but who lacked our qualitative states. Since the only objective difference between such a subject and us would lie in the realization of the

Table 1

Strong absent-qualia thesis (= the negation of the weak definability thesis)	**Weak definability thesis** (Shoemaker's claim)
Possibility of an imitation man: There could be a subject who was functionally equivalent to a normal subject and whose nonqualitative states were all genuine but who lacked qualitative states.	*Impossibility of an imitation man:* No subject who was functionally equivalent to a normal subject and whose nonqualitative states were all genuine could lack qualitative states.
AQT-1: Qualitative states are not definable in terms of their causal relations to inputs, outputs, and nonqualitative mental states, where it is not required that these nonqualitative mental states must themselves be functionally definable.	~ *AQT-1:* Qualitative states are definable in terms of their causal relations to inputs, outputs, and nonqualitative mental states, where it is not required that these nonqualitative mental states must themselves be functionally definable.
↓	↑
Weak absent-qualia thesis (Block's claim)	**Strong definability thesis** (= the negation of the weak absent-qualia thesis)
Thesis (1): There could be a subject who was functionally equivalent to a normal subject and who lacked qualitative states.	*Negation of thesis (1):* No subject who was functionally equivalent to a normal subject could lack qualitative states.
AQT-2: Qualitative states are not definable in terms of their causal relations to inputs, outputs, and other mental states, all of which must themselves be functionally definable.	~ *AQT-2:* Qualitative states are definable in terms of their causal relations to inputs, outputs, and other mental states, all of which must themselves be functionally definable.

functional states, consider a case in which the members of some group of creatures (say Martians) are functionally equivalent to us but differ radically in their neurophysiology. Given the definition of the parochial theory, there are three possible ways in which the Martians' pains and pain beliefs might be related to ours.

Case (1)   Assume that the parochial theory is true. Our term 'pain' refers to any mental state whose neurophysiological realization belongs to the same natural kind as the state that realizes *in us* the best functional definition of 'pain'. Since the Martians have a neurophysiology that differs radically from ours, our term 'pain' cannot refer to the physiological states that realize *in them* the best functional definition of 'pain'. Since, however, the Martians are functionally equivalent to us, their term 'pain' bears the same causal relation to their physical states that our term bears to ours. Hence, since our term refers to our neurophysiological realization of the best functional definition of 'pain', their term refers to theirs. Thus the Martian term 'pain' does not refer to pain, the Martians' pain beliefs are nongenuine, and the Martians, since their nonqualitative states are not all genuine, are not examples of imitation men.

Suppose that the parochial theory is false. Then there are two possibilities as to how our term 'pain' refers. It might refer to anything that *feels like* what we have when we are in pain, or it might refer to anything that is functionally equivalent to the state we are in when we are in pain.

Case (2a)   Assume that 'pain' refers to any state that *feels like* the state we are in when we are in pain. In contrast to case (1), whether the Martians experience pain in this case is not an immediate consequence of the definition of 'pain' alone. It is not *stipulated in advance* that any subject whose functional counterparts of our mental states are realized by states of a different physical natural kind lacks genuine pain. For the physicalist-functionalist$_1$ who does not hold the parochial theory, the usual assumption is that *as a matter of fact* such subjects do lack genuine pain and indeed may lack states with any qualitative character whatsoever. This assumption, if it is true, will be true in virtue of a connection between the physical realization of those states and the way those states feel that is *preconventional*. The nature of this connection for the physicalist-functionalist$_1$ who is not a parochial theorist is admittedly unclear, and I shall go on to examine this problem in the context of my own arguments against physicalist-functionalism$_1$. Nevertheless, the difference between case (1) and case (2a) is genuine.

A convention of the kind postulated by the parochial theory would be justified for one who rejected that theory (if it were justified at all) by the following claim: all and only those subjects whose functional counterparts of pain are realized in states of the same physical natural kind as ours actually feel pain. Unless one accepts the parochial theory, it is this claim that would justify the convention, and not the convention the claim.

For the same reasons as those cited in case (1), the Martians' term 'pain' will refer to their own states and to any states that feel like theirs, which, by hypothesis, ours do not. Hence in this case too our term 'pain' and theirs have different meanings, and the Martians lack genuine pain beliefs. Thus again they are not examples of imitation men.

Case (2b)   Assume that our term 'pain' refers to any state that is functionally equivalent to pain. In this case the Martian pains will be genuine, their pain beliefs will be genuine, and again they will not qualify as imitation men.

These three cases should make at least one difficulty with Shoemaker's position apparent. The fact that none of the possible cases provides a case of an imitation man, and hence that an imitation man is impossible (and thus that absent qualia in Shoemaker's sense are impossible), is a direct consequence of his definitions alone, given his construal of 'genuine nonqualitative state'. Shoemaker does have, it is true, an argument (which is independent of the immediate consequences of his definitions) that the possibility described in case (1) is not a real case of absent qualia. Shoemaker claims that if the parochial theory were true, the question of whether a creature in a state functionally equivalent to pain had genuine or ersatz pain would be irrelevant to the question of whether there was anything it felt like to occupy that state. In case (2a), however, Shoemaker has ruled out by fiat a possibility against which he has no independent argument.

Although Shoemaker might want to object to the distinction between case (1) and case (2a), this is not an objection open to him; it is not open to Shoemaker, that is, to claim that case (2a) should be counted as a case in which the parochial theory is true. Such a claim would undermine Shoemaker's argument against the relevance of the parochial theory. Case (2a) is obviously one in which the question of whether the Martians have real or ersatz pain is *identical* to the question of what it feels like to be a Martian in a state functionally equivalent to pain. Hence if case (2a) is an instance of the parochial theory, then the parochial theory does not *always* render the question of whether Martians have genuine pains philosophically uninteresting.

Shoemaker does attempt to justify ruling out cases in which a creature's *non*qualitative (as well as qualitative) states are ersatz as cases of absent qualia (as he does in his definition of AQT-1), but the justification fails to apply to case (2a). Shoemaker claims that since he is concerned only with the objections to functionalism specifically concerning qualia, cases in which a subject's *non*qualitative states are ersatz can be legitimately ignored (Shoemaker 1981, p. 586). This claim does not take account of the distinction made above between states that are not genuine pain beliefs because they are not genuine beliefs and those that are not genuine pain beliefs because they are not about pain. If we take a state functionally equivalent to one of our pain beliefs (a "pain" belief for short), then if functionalism is inadequate as a theory of belief, such a state may not even be a belief at all. If functionalism *is* an adequate theory of belief, however, such a state may still fail to be a belief about pain because the subject never experiences pain. Given Shoemaker's concern with qualia, the possibility of states of the first sort is one that he is justified in ignoring. There is nothing about the possibility of states of the second sort, however, that would undermine functionalism as a theory of *belief*. The "pain" beliefs in question *would have been* genuine pain beliefs had the subject had genuine pains. Because these nongenuine pain beliefs cast no doubt on functionalism as a theory of *belief*, Shoemaker is not entitled to disregard the cases in which they occur.[16] Since (2a) is such a case and since it is the central case for the physicalist-functionalist$_1$, Shoemaker needs an independent argument against such a possibility, or his claim that absent qualia are impossible will not have the philosophical significance he intended.

I should make it clear at this stage that I am not defending the possibility or the ultimate coherence of case (2a). In sections 3 and 4, I shall argue that such a case does *not* represent a genuine possibility. My objection is to Shoemaker's excluding the case by fiat without challenging its intelligibility or coherence. Shoemaker, however, does not seem to regard his conclusion that absent qualia are impossible as a direct consequence of his definition of 'absent qualia', because he provides a number of arguments in support of the thesis. Therefore, in the remainder of this section I shall review these arguments and show that they fail to provide the independent argument against (2a) that Shoemaker needs.

In addition to the arguments against absent qualia that stem directly from Shoemaker's statement of AQT-1 and the definitions that support it, I can find two distinct arguments of Shoemaker's for the thesis that absent qualia are impossible. The simplest of these I shall call the *symmetry argument*. Shoemaker argues that in virtue of the symmetry between the case of the Martians and our own case, anything that we could say to support our claim to experience qualitative states will have a counterpart in something the Martians could say to bolster their own claim to qualitative experience. Though the Martians lack our neurophysiological makeup, we in turn lack theirs. The relation between the Martians and us seems to be perfectly symmetrical, whereas the relation postulated by the friends of absent qualia is asymmetrical: the Martians lack something significant that we possess, while we suffer no comparable lack in relation to them.

This argument, though it has an intuitive appeal, does not establish the desired conclusion. It is open to the physicalist-functionalist$_1$ to reply that the asymmetry lies precisely in the facts of the subjects' physical realizations. The normal subject has a neurophysiology in virtue of which he or she has qualitative experience; the absent-qualia subject does not. Such an asymmetry may well exist in the absence of any corresponding asymmetry in what can be *said* by a sincere and rational subject.[17]

Compare this with the case of the brain in the vat. The difference between a normal subject and the brain in the vat consists in a physical fact that has no bearing on what a rational and sincere subject could *say* in support of a claim to knowledge of external objects. The fact that either sort of abnormal subject, the absent-qualia subject or the brain in the vat, could say anything a normal subject could by way of justifying his or her belief in qualitative experiences or external objects is less significant than it might appear. It does not necessarily follow that the abnormal subject would have the same justification for saying those things that the normal subject would. Nor does it follow that the abnormal subject would mean the same things in saying them. What the physicalist-functionalist$_1$ would claim is that the symmetries that exist between the normal and abnormal subjects are no more than can be explained by their functional equivalence; it is their physical differences that explain the asymmetries.

There is admittedly an important difference between the absent-qualia subject and the brain in the vat. Whereas the brain in the vat would know itself to be such given *all* the physical facts about itself and its environment, this is not the case for the absent-qualia subject. Even given the facts of its own neurophysiology, the absent-qualia subject would continue to believe in the existence of its own qualitative experience. This fact does suggest that there is at least something a bit odd about the absent-qualia hypothesis. This suggestion of odd-ness, however, is just another instance of the intuition, which I have already touched upon in section 1, that mental differences could not be completely manifest in purely physical facts. This intuition, which Shoemaker himself makes explicit, will provide the basis of the arguments against absent qualia (and against physicalist-functionalism generally) in sections 3 and 4.

Shoemaker's answer to this line of argument poses a dilemma for the physicalist-functionalist$_1$.[18] Either the parochial theory is correct, in which case words such as 'pain' as used by the alleged absent-qualia subject refer to something other than pain, or the absent qualia subject succeeds in referring to genuine pain. In either case, what is alleged to be an absent-qualia subject turns out not to qualify—in the first case because the nonqualitative states are nongenuine and in the second because if the alleged absent-qualia subject succeeds in refer-ring to qualia, then given that it is referring to its own states, it must enjoy qualitative experience after all. Unfortunately, this is not the independent argument Shoemaker needs against the possibility of case (2a). First, the argument assumes incorrectly that only on the parochial theory will the absent-qualia subject refer to something other than what we refer to in using 'pain'. And we have seen that case (2a) provides an example in which the parochial theory is false and yet an absent-qualia subject refers to something other than pain by using 'pain'. Second, the argument presupposes the restrictive definition of absent qualia entailed by the statement of AQT-1. Given that case (2a) exists, the restrictive definition is required if Shoemaker is to rule out this case as a case of absent qualia. But, as we have seen above, Shoemaker's motivation for ruling out case (1), namely that the par-ochial theory trivializes the question of whether other subjects expe-rience qualia, does not apply to case (2a). Thus this argument presupposes the restrictive definition, and the fact that it presupposes this definition makes it useless for providing the independent justifi-cation that the definition requires.

The second argument against the possibility of absent qualia I shall call the *common language argument*. Let us imagine a possible world in which alleged absent-qualia subjects and normal subjects belong to the *same* linguistic community. The argument, then, goes as follows:

1. Since the alleged absent-qualia subjects and the normal sub-jects are functionally equivalent and since 'pain' as used by the normal subjects refers to a state they possess, 'pain' as used by

the alleged absent-qualia subjects must refer to a state they possess as well.

2. Since the alleged absent-qualia subjects and the normal subjects belong to the same linguistic community, they must mean the same thing by 'pain' (i.e., they must associate 'pain' with the same intension, that is, with the same function from possible worlds to extensions).

3. Hence the state to which the alleged absent-qualia subjects refer must be part of the extension of 'pain' at this world as the term is used by the normal subjects.

4. Hence the alleged absent-qualia subjects have genuine pain.

The problem with this is that Shoemaker's assumption that members of our community *must* use the word 'pain' with the same intension with which we do is unwarranted. If we think of 'pain' on the model of a natural-kind term, as the physicalist-functionalist$_1$ does, there is no problem in imagining different members of the community associating the same term with different intensions. It might turn out, for example, that '*Homo sapiens*' does not pick out a natural kind, that in fact there are two distinct natural kinds equally represented in our linguistic community. Call these '*Homo sapiens*$_1$' and '*Homo sapiens*$_2$'. When we, members of *Homo sapiens*$_1$, discover the existence of members of *Homo sapiens*$_2$, we might naturally describe the situation as one in which we had used '*Homo sapiens*' to refer to members of *Homo sapiens*$_1$ and members of *Homo sapiens*$_2$ had used it to refer to members of *Homo sapiens*$_2$. Hence our being members of the same linguistic community does not guarantee that our terms are used with the same intension or extension. But without the second premise that our term 'pain' has the same extension that it has when used by the alleged absent-qualia subjects, Shoemaker's argument does not go through.

Even if we grant Shoemaker's second premise, however, the argument does not establish the conclusion Shoemaker needs. All that follows is that at a possible world in which alleged absent-qualia subjects and normal subjects belonged to the same community, 'pain', as used at that world, *would* include the internal states of the alleged absent-qualia subjects in its extension. Thus it would be true that as 'pain' is used at *that* world, the alleged absent-qualia subjects would experience genuine pain. Since Shoemaker is not suggesting that this is *actually* the case, however, nothing follows about whether an alleged absent-qualia subject would experience genuine pain as the term is *actually* used. Thus there is no shortcut to the conclusion that absent qualia are impossible, and Shoemaker has failed to supply an argument that supports this conclusion.

3   *The Property Dualism Argument*

The basic difficulty with Shoemaker's objections to absent qualia and to physicalist-functionalism$_1$ is that while he explicitly addresses a number of epistemological and metaphysical problems, there is nothing specific to the mental in any of the difficulties he treats. Although the intuition that a mental difference cannot have a purely physical manifestation seems to provide at least part of the motivation for his arguments, it is an intuition that they never successfully capture. If we limit the discussion of qualitative states to those features they share with ordinary objects, we make things far too easy for the friends of absent qualia.

Could there be any objection, if we ignore the peculiarities of the mental, to the thesis that whereas some of the physical realizations of the best functional descriptions of normal human subjects yield subjects with qualitative states, others do not? We can assume, to begin with, that there is a necessary connection between the physical states of a subject and that subject's qualitative states. (If not, there would be a possible world in which that subject exists unchanged in every physical detail but lacks qualitative states. This would rule out Shoemaker's position from the start.) Given this necessary connection, we can assume for the sake of simplicity that the connection is one of identity—nothing in the objection to Block that follows depends on this assumption. Now if we abstract from the peculiarities of the mental, there are no objections to the possibility that while all qualitative states are identical with some physical states of normal subjects, not all subjects that are functional duplicates of normal subjects have physical states that are qualitative states. Given such a possibility, it is entirely plausible that the terms 'pain' and 'qualia', as used by the absent-qualia subject, should fail to refer because they are not causally connected with the right kinds of entities (or that they should refer to states different in kind from the ones to which our terms refer). In either event, the answer to the question of whether we can refer, in our own case, to something the absent-qualia subject lacks is yes.

The problem for Block's theory emerges when we examine what is specific to the epistemology and metaphysics of the mental. And it is a problem that should, at least since the heyday of central-state materialism, be relatively familiar. I am assuming, for simplicity, that a person's qualitative state of pain at t, say Smith's, is identical with a physical state, say Smith's brain state X at t. Even if this is the case, however, not only do the sense of the expression 'Smith's pain at t' and the sense of the expression 'Smith's brain state X at t' differ, but the fact that they are coreferential cannot be established on a priori grounds.[19] Thus there must be different properties of Smith's pain (i.e., Smith's brain state X) in virtue of which it is the referent of both terms. In the case of the expressions 'the morning star' and 'the evening star', it is in virtue of the property of being the last heavenly body visible in the morning that Venus is the referent of the first expression. And (since 'the evening star' is not coreferential a priori with 'the morning star') it is in virtue of the *logically distinct* property of being the first heavenly body visible in the evening that it is the referent of the second. The general principle is that if two expressions refer to the same object and this fact cannot be established a priori, they do so in virtue of different routes to the referent provided by different modes of presentation of that referent.[20] These modes of presentation of the object fall on the object's side of the language/ world dichotomy. In other words they are aspects of the object in virtue of which our conceptual apparatus picks the object out; they are not aspects of that conceptual apparatus itself. Hence the natural candidates for these modes of presentation are properties.

Suppose that this is not the case. Suppose, that is, that two descriptions are coreferential and that this fact cannot be established a priori and has not been established a posteriori. And suppose that there are *not* two different properties in virtue of which the two descriptions pick out the same referent. That the descriptions are not coreferential a priori (and not known to be, a posteriori) means there is a possible world in which speakers who are epistemically equivalent to us use these terms to refer to different objects. There is, for example, a possible world in which the inhabitants are epistemically equivalent to those of our ancestors who used 'the morning star' and 'the evening star' before the discovery that the terms were coreferential and in which the inhabitants use the terms to refer to different planets. As used by the inhabitants of this possible world, these terms must pick out their referents in virtue of distinct properties because, unlike our terms, theirs pick out different objects. Hence the expressions as used by our ancestors must, contrary to our assumption, pick out their common referent in virtue of two logically distinct properties of that referent.

To this argument it might be objected that properties are not individuated as finely as the argument requires. It might be suggested, that is, that there are not distinct properties corresponding to every distinction in meaning between linguistic expressions that are not coreferential a priori. On this view, the same property might be required to provide the route from two referring expressions that are not coreferential a priori. Such a view is tenable, but it simply postpones the problem of explaining how two referring expressions that are distinct in meaning and not coreferential a priori come to pick out the same object. If they do so in virtue of the same property of the referent, then that referent must have other *features* that differ so as to provide two distinct routes by which the referring expressions pick it out. It would then be these features that play the role assigned by the argument to properties, and the argument could be rephrased accordingly.

Let us stipulate that a property that is neither physical nor mental is topic-neutral. Since there is no physicalist description that one could plausibly suppose to be coreferential a priori with an expression like 'Smith's pain at t', no physical property of a pain (i.e., a brain state of type X) could provide the route by which it was picked out by such an expression. Thus we are faced with a choice between topic-neutral and mental properties. Postulating a mental property distinct from the property of being a brain state of type X would, needless to say, run counter to Block's commitment to minimal physicalism (Block 1980, p. 266). Suppose, then, that certain causal (though not necessarily physical) features are what constitute the route by which 'Smith's pain at t' picks out a pain of Smith's. This is what J. J. C. Smart has claimed regarding the topic-neutral properties of pain states. Smart holds that the expression 'an event like the event that occurs in one when one is stabbed with a pin (and so forth)' is a topic-neutral *translation* of 'pain'.[21] That is, the expression contains no irreducibly mentalistic (or physicalistic) vocabulary, and it has the same sense as 'pain', or at any rate, a description in which the topic-neutral expression is substituted for 'pain' is coreferential a priori with the original description.

If descriptions containing 'pain' have a topic-neutral translation (say Smart's) with which they are coreferential a priori, then both the description and its translation share the same route to their referent. Hence both expressions pick out the referent in virtue of the same property. The property of being a pain, therefore, is the same property as the property of being an event like the event that occurs in one when one is stabbed with a pin (and so forth). Since the topic-neutral expression corresponding to this property involves no irreducibly mentalistic terms, the property, like the expression, is topic-neutral; i.e., it is neither mental nor physical. (It follows that the expression 'pain' itself is implicitly topic-neutral; since it has a topic-neutral translation, it is not *irreducibly* mentalistic.) If there are no topic-neutral expressions that are at least coreferential a priori with such mentalistic descriptions as 'Smith's pain at t', then these mentalistic descriptions refer in virtue of a property distinct from that in virtue of which any physicalist or topic-neutral expression refers. Such a property or feature could only be regarded as an irreducibly mental entity.[22]

This argument, which I shall call the *property dualism argument*, shows that unless there are topic-neutral expressions with which mentalistic descriptions of particular pains are coreferential a priori, we are forced to acknowledge the existence of mental properties. The claim that there are such topic-neutral expressions—a claim that Smart shares with the orthodox functionalist, who claims that functional definitions are a priori—is not, however, a solution open to Block.[23] For Block, a topic-neutral property would be unacceptable as the route from a mentalistic description to a pain, since Smart's claim that 'pain' has a topic-neutral translation is just the claim that 'pain' has a definition in terms of its typical causes. And this claim is nothing more than the claim that 'pain' has a protofunctionalist definition. Thus it is an instance of precisely the orthodox functionalist view that Block is attacking. It is, in fact, the alleged inadequacy of *any* topic-neutral definition of 'pain' that motivates Block's physicalist-functionalism. The upshot for Block is that by reverting from functionalism to a theory more akin to prefunctionalist identity theories, he has saddled himself with all the problems those theories entailed. And by insisting on the inadequacy of topic-neutral translations of sensation terms, he has deprived himself of the only plausible solution those problems had generated.

One might assume that Block could solve this problem by dropping his commitment to physicalism. In that case a mental property, such as the property of being a pain, would provide the route by which mentalistic descriptions refer. Surprisingly, however, even dualism does not automatically provide one of the possible alternatives to functionalism. If we ask how the mental property of being a pain is to be explained, we are faced with a choice between a causal and a transcendentalist response. For the Cartesian dualist, pain is a modification of mental substance that has certain typical physical causes and results in a propensity toward certain behavioral effects. Spelling out the causal role that pain plays and then specifying that this role must be instantiated in a mental substance results in a theory that is formally analogous to physicalist-functionalism—and a theory which shares all of that theory's defects.[24] In particular, the same question arises whether 'pain' could be discovered a priori to be coextensive with any description couched in terms of mental substance. The answer is also analogous: either we drop the condition that the causal role of pain *must* be instantiated by a mental substance and Cartesian dualism collapses into functionalism, or Cartesian dualism is no solution to the problem raised by the property dualism argument.

For the transcendental dualist, on the other hand, pain cannot be explained in terms of mental substance, causal dispositions, or any combination of the two. Facts about mental states are not determined by *any* objective, third-person facts, and mental substance is no less objective than physical substance. This position alone, among the alternatives to functionalism, is not susceptible to the argument that I have been developing, but it is a position that seems too radical to tempt any but the most ardent antifunctionalists.

If we accept the property dualism argument, absent qualia are impossible (unless we adopt some version of transcendentalism). The possibility of absent qualia depends on there being some non-topic-neutral condition on the existence of the qualitative state in question. But in adding conditions beyond those that make up a topic-neutral analysis of qualitative states, we make it impossible to establish a priori that a qualitative term and its analysans are coextensive. And it is in virtue of the lack of any a priori connection between the qualitative term and its analysans that the expressions refer to the same subject via different routes—and in virtue of these different routes that we are forced to acknowledge transcendental properties. Thus there is a direct connection between the intuitions that absent qualia and inverted qualia are possible—the intuitions that motivate physicalist-functionalism—and transcendentalism. Hence we have a choice between abandoning the intuitions, and with them physicalist-functionalism, and retaining them and taking their transcendental consequences seriously. Whether these intuitions could plausibly be abandoned will be the subject of the next section.

4   DNA Physicalist-Functionalism

I have argued that Shoemaker's objections to absent qualia fail because they do not capture the features that distinguish the mental. The property dualism argument, which does seem to capture an essential part of the peculiarity of the mental, rules out not only Block's position but *any* version of physicalist-functionalism.[25] Although physicalist-functionalism is motivated by the intuition that functionalism cannot do justice to qualia, there is a crucial respect in which the functionalist account of qualia is superior: the problem of property dualism does not arise. Shoemaker, however, in his attempt to establish the claims of physicalist-functionalism$_2$, produces an important argument that might be thought to count against functionalism. This is the argument that an adequate theory of qualitative experience should allow for the possibility of qualia inversion. And if there is an argument against orthodox functionalism that does not lead to some version of transcendentalism, then functionalism may lose the advantage that it holds over physicalist-functionalism.

Let us distinguish, as Shoemaker does, between intrasubjective and intersubjective qualia inversion. An example of *intra*subjective inversion is the case in which things that look green to a subject at t_1 look red at t_2 and in which the way the rest of the colors look at t_2 is so related to the way they looked at t_1 that all of the subject's synchronic similarity judgments and discriminatory dispositions are preserved. This means, for example, that the subject will find the traffic light at the top more similar in color to the light in the middle than to the light at the bottom after the inversion, as before. Furthermore, all the usual tests for color blindness will yield normal results. Only if the subject is asked how the way the lights at the top and bottom look *now* compares to the way they looked at t_1 will there be a manifest deviation from the norm. Associations such as that between red and danger, including such nonverbal responses to red as a slight increase in pulse rate, might survive the inversion intact, but we can assume for the sake of simplicity that either at the time of the inversion or gradually thereafter these associations will be inverted as well.

In the case of *inter*subjective qualia inversion, the qualitative experiences of *two* subjects are related as the later experiences of the intrasubjective-inversion subject are related to the earlier ones. In this case, however, there is no analogue of the anomolous diachronic judgments of the intrasubjective-inversion victim. If subject A's qualitative states are inverted relative to B's, nothing in their observable behavior or functional makeup will make this apparent. Whereas an intrasubjective-inversion subject will differ functionally from a normal subject, two subjects' qualitative states may be inverted relative to one another's while they remain perfect functional duplicates.

Shoemaker's objection to orthodox functionalism is that while *intra*subjective qualia inversion can be characterized in orthodox functional terms, it could not account for *inter*subjective inversion. This is a drawback, according to Shoemaker, because, he claims, "there is a natural line of argument . . . from the possibility of *intra*subjective inversion to the conclusion that it makes sense to suppose, and may well for all we know be true, that *inter*subjective spectrum inversion actually exists" (1982, p. 358). Shoemaker also claims, "Most, of us, I suspect, cannot help feeling that a visual experience of mine can be like a visual experience of yours in exactly the same way it can be like another visual experience of mine" (Shoemaker 1982, p. 358). If these claims are correct, functionalism would seem to contain a significant source of internal tension.

This feeling of tension, however, is largely illusory. Shoemaker's argument that the possibility of *intra*subjective inversion leads naturally to the possibility of *inter*subjective inversion is based on the intuition that if Smith undergoes a qualia shift at *t*, then either before or after *t* Smith's experience must be qualitatively distinct from that of Jones, who has undergone no such shift. But this is not an intuition that need worry an orthodox functionalist. The basic functionalist intuition is that all mental differences correspond to functional differences. This claim is conceptual rather than empirical: a psychological state has, as a matter of conceptual necessity, no qualitative properties that cannot be reduced to functional properties. Thus the claim that functional duplicates might experience inverted qualia relative to one another is, for the orthodox functionalist, self-contradictory in a way that the possibility of intrasubjective qualia inversion is not. Consequently, the claim that *intra*subjective inversion has a functionalist characterization provides the *functionalist* no reason to take *inter*subjective inversion seriously.

Whether the functionalist *should* admit the possibility of intrasubjective inversion is a question I shall not try to answer in this paper, but the functionalist, if he does so, takes intrasubjective inversion seriously only when it makes a functional difference. If, as it is plausible to suppose, there is no functional difference between intrasubjective qualia inversion and qualia constancy coupled with nonveridical memories, then intrasubjective inversion is no more intelligible to the functionalist than intersubjective inversion. Hence, whatever the defects of the functionalist position, there are no internal sources of tension.

If Shoemaker is to produce an argument that will force us beyond functionalism, it will have to be an argument not that there are tensions internal to functionalism but that it fails to explain our *pretheoretical* intuitions. We do, after all, *seem* to understand the possibility that things we both call 'red' look to me the way things we both call 'green' look to you. But if this is the source of Shoemaker's dissatisfaction, we shall have no reason to prefer physicalist-functionalism to orthodox functionalism. This is because nothing in my statement about what we seem to understand when we claim to understand the possibility of intersubjectively inverted qualia involves any reference to functionalism. If our pretheoretical intuitions make it possible to imagine two functional duplicates who differ in their qualitative experiences, they make it equally possible to imagine two *physical* duplicates who differ in the same way. Hence the intuition to which Shoemaker appeals is every bit as effective against physicalist-functionalism as it is against functionalism. Indeed, it should come as no surprise that our prethe-

oretical intuitions fail to discriminate between physicalist and orthodox functionalism, given that the interest in the possibility of spectrum
inversion so conspicuously predates functionalist developments.

It might be maintained, by way of reply, that physicalist-functionalism at least comes closer to accommodating those pretheoretical
dualistic intuitions we seem to possess. Even this reply, though, is
unavailable to Shoemaker. Imagine a theory that takes the physical
difference in DNA structure between two subjects as evidence of
qualia difference. We can call such a theory *DNA physicalist-functionalism*. To see physicalist-functionalism as superior to orthodox functionalism on the basis of our *pretheoretical* intuitions requires that we
see DNA physicalist-functionalism as an even better alternative. DNA
physicalist-functionalism allows for qualia differences even between
functional states whose physical realizations belong to the same natural kind. Thus by taking physical differences that are independent
of any functional manifestation as evidence of possible qualia differences, we deprive ourselves of any natural point at which to draw the
line between relevant and irrelevant physical differences. No doubt
one would like to associate qualia differences only with "significant"
physical differences, but the physicalist-functionalist has no principled
way of doing so.

Shoemaker might deny that this last claim raises a problem on the
grounds that there is no absurdity in the suggestion that DNA differences might lead to qualia differences, if it is possible in principle to
settle the question. If this is possible, the physicalist-functionalist
cannot be embarrassed by the objection that no physical difference is
too trivial to count as evidence of a qualia difference. If a test is
possible, the physicalist-functionalist can establish *empirically* the point
at which physical differences become irrelevant to qualia.

This possible reply of Shoemaker's goes to the heart of his position
because it points to the fundamental gap in any physicalist-functionalist account of qualia differences. Shoemaker's remarks suggest the
following test to determine whether two different types of physiological realizations of the same functional states in two subjects lead to
qualia differences. If we change the neurophysiology of one subject
to match that of the other (assuming that the physical replacements
are not so extensive as to threaten personal identity) and if the subject
undergoes an *intra*subjective qualia change, this is a very strong indication of the existence of *inter*subjective qualia differences. If there
is no intrasubjective switch, then there is no intersubjective qualia
difference between the two subjects. If neither subject's physiology
can be realized in the other, the question of intersubjective qualia
difference does not arise (Shoemaker 1982, pp. 372–375).

The problem with this reply is that a change in the *type* of physiology per se has *no* tendency to produce functional evidence of intrasubjective qualia change. If the functional states are fixed, changing the type of realization could only produce a subject who claims sincerely to have undergone *no* change in qualitative experience—exactly what the subject would have claimed had there been no change at all. If the functional states are not fixed, then no change in the *type* of physiology is even necessary to produce evidence of inversion. A functional change alone is sufficient to produce a subject who claims sincerely to have experienced an intrasubjective inversion of his or her qualitative states. In other words, we cannot test the relevance of different kinds of physiological differences to qualitative experiences by testing their tendency to produce evidence of intrasubjective qualia inversion. Physiological changes by themselves are *irrelevant* to the evidence of either intrasubjective or intersubjective qualia inversion; only if the physiological changes amount to a change in functional states could any evidence of qualia inversion emerge.[26]

The fact that we can hold a subject's functional states fixed and vary the type of neurophysiology without producing anything an orthodox functionalist would count as evidence of qualia change leads to a dilemma for Shoemaker. Consider the following principle.

> *Manifestation principle*   Differences in the qualitative content of mental states cannot be postulated on the basis of physical differences that have no actual or possible functional manifestation.

This means that the physical difference in the way the functional states of a pair of functional duplicates are realized could not be the basis of an ascription to them of qualitatively different states. It also means that if, as Shoemaker seems to suggest, there are no functional differences between a subject who has undergone intrasubjective qualia inversion and one who has suffered a memory failure producing beliefs to that effect, then the distinction between the two is meaningless. One cannot, as Shoemaker does (1982, p. 363, n. 8), appeal to facts about the way perception and memory are physically realized to make the distinction.

These consequences of the manifestation principle make it clear that Shoemaker cannot accept it. Unless the principle is rejected, intrasubjective qualia inversion is, by Shoemaker's own account, impossible, and regardless of whether it is possible or not, intersubjective inversion is ruled out. Adopting the principle amounts, in fact, to abandoning physicalist-functionalism for its orthodox counterpart.

For equally decisive reasons, however, Shoemaker cannot reject the principle. First, Shoemaker is committed to the principle by the fact that he uses it against Block when he says that if a subject shares with us all of the functional aspects of pain, "it is hard to see how a physiological difference between him and us could be any evidence at all that his states lack qualitative character" (Shoemaker 1975, p. 296). Second, there is the problem that we have just seen of DNA physicalist-functionalism. Without the principle there is no way of ruling out the claim that trivial physical differences correspond to qualia differences. Finally, Shoemaker is committed to the principle by his claim that qualia similarities and differences can be functionally defined. Physicalist-functionalism$_2$ is distinguished from physicalist-functionalism$_1$ by the claim that the class of qualitative states can be functionally defined, even if individual states cannot (Shoemaker 1975, p. 309). Rejecting the principle means rejecting Shoemaker's position for Block's. The dilemma for Shoemaker is that whatever his stance toward the principle, his position collapses—either into ortho-dox functionalism or into Block's physicalist-functionalism$_1$.

Although Shoemaker's dilemma is not a problem for physicalist-functionalism generally, DNA physicalist-functionalism is. Regardless of its form, any version of physicalist-functionalism entails the denial of the manifestation principle. And it is this principle that provides the functionalist with a link between the neurophysiological level and the facts of qualitative experience. Physical facts gain their relevance by making a difference to the functional facts that are conceptually linked to qualia differences. The denial of the manifestation principle breaks this link and leaves the physicalist-functionalist vulnerable to the arguments of DNA physicalist-functionalism. As a result, we have a second argument that works against physicalist-functionalism in any form.

The DNA physicalist-functionalism argument and the property dualism argument grow out of the same general problem for physi-calist-functionalism: that it has no principled way of establishing the relevance (or the lack of relevance) of the physical differences between subjects that have no functional significance. The manifestation prin-ciple is the orthodox functionalist version of the pretheoretical intui-tion that mental differences cannot have a purely physical manifestation. Unlike the proponents of physicalist-functionalism, the orthodox functionalist can point to an a priori connection between the properties he or she takes to be relevant to qualia—the functional properties—and the qualitative properties themselves. This is a con-nection in virtue of the meaning of 'pain' and the meaning of the expression describing the corresponding functional disposition. In contrast, the advocate of physicalist-functionalism who holds the parochial theory can only point to a connection between physical properties and qualitative properties in virtue of a *dispensable* linguistic convention. Nothing would be lost by couching the question of intersubjective qualitative similarity in terms of a concept, 'pain*', to which it is stipulated that the parochial theory does not apply. It would allow us, in fact, to ask a question that is clearly intelligible, given the antifunctionalist intuitions to which physicalist-functionalism purports to do justice: whether qualitative similarity among alleged pains corresponds to identity in natural kind of their physical realizations. In the case of the nonparochial version of physicalist-functionalism, the problem is even more acute: there is *no* connection between a subject's physical and qualitative states. Hence the manifestation principle presents a problem for any version of physicalist-functionalism.

The question with which I began this section was whether there were arguments against orthodox functionalism that might counterbalance the property dualism argument against physicalist-functionalism. I have been concerned in particular with the claim that physicalist-functionalism more adequately captures our pretheoretical intuitions than functionalism. One class of intuitions that have not yet been mentioned are those concerning the privileged access we may be thought to enjoy regarding our own qualitative states. Though these are not irrelevant to an assessment of orthodox functionalism, since they provide physicalist-functionalism with no claim to any advantage, they can in this context safely be ignored. As regards our pretheoretical intuitions about qualia inversion, however, we have seen that they fail to provide physicalist-functionalism any support. Furthermore, physicalist-functionalism violates Shoemaker's intuition that mental differences cannot have a purely physical manifestation. Hence among the intuitions that favor either physicalist-functionalism or functionalism, the advantage goes entirely to functionalism. Functionalism, it is true, fails to capture *all* of our intuitions regarding qualia, but those that it fails to accommodate point beyond physicalist-functionalism to transcendentalism. And though I have left open the possibility of a transcendentalist account of qualia, such a position will have little appeal to most of functionalism's current critics.

Acknowledgments

I am grateful to Akeel Bilgrami, Jaegwon Kim, William Lycan, Joseph Mendola, Stephen Schiffer, and Sydney Shoemaker for their comments and advice on earlier drafts of this paper.

Chapter 4
Transcendentalism and Its Discontents

It has normally been assumed that whatever empirical and metaphysical problems it may raise, mind-body dualism satisfies a number of deeply engrained intuitions about the mental for which nondualist theories have no plausible account. In what follows, I shall argue that this is true only for a special class of dualist theories. I distinguish transcendental dualism from the other forms that dualist theories may take. And I argue that where the intuitions about subjectivity that have seemed to motivate and support dualism are concerned, only transcendental dualism has an advantage over nondualist theories; nontranscendental versions of dualism are open to the same objections that have made nondualist accounts of the mind seem implausible. Moreover, I argue that the usual objections to transcendental dualism are inconclusive. I shall argue, however, that with regard to a crucial intuition concerning the subjective point of view—that we have a form of privileged access to our own qualitative mental states—transcendental dualism is at a disadvantage relative to some nondualist and nontranscendental theories. And I shall argue that if a theory fails to satisfy this intuition, its other advantages carry very little weight. Thus I claim that transcendental versions of dualism do not offer viable alternatives to nontranscendental theories of mind.[1]

1   Interactionist Dualism and Transcendental Dualism

Whatever has been the case historically, the contemporary appeal of dualism does not stem from any doubt that the sophisticated behavior observable in human beings could have a physical explanation. Rather, its appeal lies in the suspicion that such a physical explanation could not accommodate the first-person or subjective point of view. This suspicion has been expressed, for example, by Thomas Nagel: "What seems impossible is to include in a physical conception of the world the facts about what mental states are like for the creature having them. The creature and his states seem to belong to a world that can be viewed impersonally and externally. Yet subjective aspects of the mental can be apprehended only from the point of view of the creature itself."[2] But the assumption that dualism, as it has most frequently been interpreted, leaves any more room for the subjective point of view than do nondualist accounts is problematic. Dualism has ordinarily been understood as *interactionist dualism*—the thesis that particular mental states or mental events have among their typical causes and effects physical states or events.[3] One's feeling pain is normally caused by bodily injury and typically causes behavior aimed at relief. Whether or not mental states such as pain are construed as states of a mental substance, they have, on this view, causal properties in virtue of the actual causal interactions of which they are a part.[4] Furthermore, these states must be presumed to have a number of dispositional properties, since states like pain have a disposition to bring about relief-seeking behavior, regardless of whether or not they actually do so. And these causal and dispositional properties raise a serious questions as to whether interactionist dualism can accommodate the subjective point of view.

For a number of reasons, it is natural to call these causal and dispositional properties of mental states objective.[5] The first reason is that causal and dispositional properties in general are never completely *given* to a subject in any first-person experience or set of experiences. This is true whether the causal and dispositional properties are properties of the subject's mental states or simply the causal and dispositional properties of the external objects and events that make up the subject's environment. Consider external events. Two subjects, it would seem, might have exactly the same histories of subjective experiences, while the causal relations between the events those experiences were experiences of (and the dispositional properties of the objects involved in those events) might differ radically. Each subject, to take a familiar type of example, might seem to see the same type of interaction between two billiard balls. The first subject, however, might see one ball collide with another, the first ball setting the second in motion and coming to a stop itself as a result of the collision. And the second subject might see the balls cover the same trajectories at the same speeds as a result of their manipulation by outside forces with no causal interaction between the motion of the first and the motion of the second. Moreover, such differences among the causal and dispositional facts in the two kinds of cases seem possible regardless of how long the parallel between the two histories of subjective experiences persists. Whatever causal and dispositional properties may be in question, then, they are not determined by what is given from the subjective perspective. And that the causal and dispositional properties of a subject's mental states are not given from his or her subjective perspective follows as a special case.

The second reason that the causal and dispositional properties of mental states are normally seen as objective emerges if we consider what we would expect an objective account of the world to contain. If we abstract from any particular subject's point of view and tell the story of the world from a perspective that is not limited by any subjective viewpoint but is accessible in principle from any point of view, the causal and dispositional properties of mental states would be part of the story. In this respect, interactionist dualism coincides with materialism. On the materialist view, mental events and properties will be included in the account that abstracts from every subjective viewpoint because they will occur as objective physical events and properties of the brain. Though, on the interactionist-dualist view, mental events and properties will be distinct from physical events and properties, they will be included in the objective account as parts of the objective causal history of the world. Just as physical objects, events, and properties are accessible in principle from more than one point of view in virtue of their causal effects (on us, on instruments, and so forth), mental events, because they also have causal effects, will in principle be equally accessible.

The third reason these properties are most naturally construed as objective is that it is natural to make the distinction between objective and subjective properties coincide with the distinction between those properties about which we can be wrong and those about which no mistakes are possible. If we accept this way of drawing the distinction, then because causal and dispositional properties are never fully given from the subjective point of view, these properties will again fall on the objective side of the distinction.

The basic difficulty with interactionist dualism is that on this account mental states and events are not the right sorts of things to satisfy the epistemological intuitions that motivate mind-body dualism in the first place.[6] A deeply entrenched epistemological intuition is that one's access to one's subjective experiences is immediate in a way that one's access to objective states or events could never be. And the immediacy of one's own access to one's subjective experiences has seemed to entail that these experiences could exist in the absence of any objective entities and states whatsoever. Given these intuitions, when mental states are understood from the interactionst-dualist perspective, it is just as hard to see how a mental state could be subjective as it is to see how a physical state could be. And it is just as hard to see how a mental state that is both a cause and an effect in an objective causal sequence could explain the subjective point of view.[7] It is the implausibility of the thought that any objective entity could serve to make sense of subjective experience that has led a number of philosophers—including Kant, Husserl, and, more controversially, Wittgenstein—to take up the idea of a transcendental self.[8] Unlike the empirical self, such a self is not an objective entity of any kind; it is a self that is in principle inaccessible to the natural sciences and indeed to any form of empirical investigation.

The recognition that some forms of dualism are no less objective than materialism suggests a more radical theory, which it is natural to call *transcendentalism*. We can characterize this as the theory that mental states or events have only subjective properties; the properties of mental states are fully accessible from the subjective point of view; and none are accessible, even in principle, from any other point of view. Such subjective properties we can also call transcendental properties. And let us call mental states and events that have only subjective properties subjective or transcendental states or events and facts about such states subjective or transcendental facts. On this theory, transcendental events, facts, and properties are logically independent of any objective events, facts, properties, or objects. (If these categories do not exhaust the subjective and objective realms, then other subjective and objective categories should be understood to be similarly independent.) And the theory according to which, in addition to entities in the subjective categories, there exist entities in one or more of the objective categories I shall call *transcendental dualism*. Given the independence of the subjective and objective entities in these categories (and the assumption that the categories are exhaustive), there will be, on this form of dualism, no supervenience relations in either direction between the subjective and objective realms.

In contrast to interactionist dualism, transcendental dualism is not the wrong kind of theory to account for subjectivity. Transcendental dualism seems to satisfy a number of specific intuitions about the subjective point of view. One such intuition is that we enjoy some form of privileged access to our own mental states. 'Privileged access', as it is often used, is a blanket term that covers a large number of relations one might have to particular classes of facts. I shall use it to pick out the following two relations (where the conditionals are understood as holding of logical necessity):

One has *incorrigible access* to facts of type M if and only if, if one believes that a fact of type M obtains, then that fact does obtain.

One has *transparent access* to facts of type M if and only if, if a fact of type M obtains, then one believes that that fact obtains.

One of the objections to interactionist dualism is that it cannot explain the privileged access we seem to have to the facts of our own mental life. If, for example, we believe that we are in pain, then, it is claimed, we are in pain. And if we are in pain, then we believe that we are. The same applies to other sensations and qualitative experiences. Thus we seem to have transparent and incorrigible access to the facts in our own case about experiences of this kind. Let us call the claim that we have such access the *privileged access thesis*.[9] We have no such access, however, even in our own case, to the objective properties that mental states have, according to the interactionist dualist. The causal and dispositional facts about mental states, because they are facts about objective properties, are all facts about which we might be mistaken. Hence our access to them is not incorrigible. Moreover, we may fail to form any beliefs about the causal and dispositional facts regarding these states. So the access we have to such facts is not transparent either. The facts, then, about these objective, causal, and dispositional properties are not facts to which our access is in any sense privileged.

The advantage of transcendental dualism over interactionist dualism is that it seems to provide for both these forms of privileged access. (Whether this apparent advantage is a real one is the subject of sections 4 and 5.) For the transcendental dualist, first-person, subjective facts are neither reducible to, nor fixed by, any set of third-person facts. The fact that we are in pain does not *consist in* either a set of facts about physical states of the brain or a set of facts about the mental states (as these are conceived by the interactionist dualist) of the brain or of a mental substance. Nor would fixing such facts fix the facts about whether we were in pain. Because transcendental dualists take the mental to be in this way independent of anything objective, they are free to endorse a conception of the mental to which appeal is often made in distinguishing between the mental and the nonmental. According to this conception, the distinction between an object and its appearance, which has application in the objective realm, has no counterpart in the realm of the mental. The same mental object does not present different appearances to different subjects. Nor is there any analogue of the fact that one subject may perceive the same object at different times from different perspectives, each of which reveals aspects that exist simultaneously with those revealed from the other perspectives but that are not perceptible from those perspectives. On this conception, in fact, a mental object *is* nothing over and above the appearance it presents and hence does not exist unperceived.

Given the transcendental conception of the mental, both forms of privileged access appear to follow. Transparent access is a consequence because mental objects have no hidden sides about which we might fail to form beliefs. Nor can we fail to notice the object itself, since if we did, there would be no appearance and hence no object. We have incorrigible access because appearances in the mental realm cannot mislead. If there is an appearance, there is an object, and there is nothing more to the object than the appearance itself.

A second kind of intuition that supports transcendental dualism involves the possibility of spectrum inversion or, more generally, qualia difference. It seems an intelligible hypothesis that when I look at a can of Coca-Cola, I have a color experience like the one you have in looking at a can of 7 Up. And according to the *qualia difference hypothesis regarding behavioral facts,* differences of this kind with respect to qualitative experience can exist in the absence of any behavioral manifestation. In other words, we can fix the behavioral facts (both actual and dispositional) without fixing the facts about qualitative experience.

Qualia difference hypotheses, however, come in increasingly radical versions. One such hypothesis is that we could fix all the functional facts without fixing the qualitative facts. Another is that the qualitative facts are similarly independent of all the physical facts. And on the most radical hypothesis we would not fix the qualitative facts even in fixing all the *objective* facts—including the facts about mental events as construed by the interactionist dualist. Moreover, the intuitions that support the most extreme form of the distinction between the subjective and objective perspectives seem to preclude any principled distinction between the least and the most radical hypotheses. The intuitive difference between subjective and objective facts that supports the claim that they are independent seems just as extreme whether we look at behavioral facts, functional facts, physical facts, or objective facts in general. Let us assume for the moment that our intuitions do *not* provide a principled way of distinguishing between the less radical qualia difference hypotheses and the hypothesis that makes qualia independent of any objective facts. Then taking the intuitions behind any of the hypotheses seriously will require that we entertain seriously this latter hypothesis. And to accept this hypothesis is to accept a version of transcendental dualism where qualitative facts are concerned.

The third type of intuition that supports transcendental dualism is the idea that there is something that subjective experience is like and that is not, and could not be, captured by any objective, third-person account. The intuition here is that there is something it is like to taste burnt toast that cannot be captured by any description, however complete, either of the dispositions to behave, the functional dispositions, or the physiological states of a subject who has such an experience. The claim is that the most fundamental facts of subjective experience are necessarily ignored in the description of facts open to any sort of empirical investigation.

2   Skepticism about the Special Character of the Mental

The argument for transcendental dualism we have been considering—that only such a theory can explain our intuitions about privileged access, the possibility of spectrum inversion, and the facts about what things are like from the subjective point of view—is open to two kinds of criticism. On the one hand, it has been argued that these intuitions are mistaken. For those who take this line, the phenomena that it is alleged only a transcendental theory can explain do not exist. It has been claimed by many, for example, that our access to our own conscious states is not in any interesting sense privileged. Similarly, the possibility of spectrum inversion with no objective manifestation is likely to be denied. And the coherence and intelligibility of talk of what it is like to be conscious or to experience particular sensations or perceptual states (where these experiences or states are not objective) have often been questioned. On the other hand, it is frequently claimed that these phenomena can be accommodated by theories less radical than transcendental dualism. It has often been maintained that our privileged access to certain of our own conscious mental states can be explained in terms of the events and processes that make up the subject matter of the empirical sciences. And many theorists have wanted to claim that whereas the possibility of qualia inversion or qualia difference for subjects identical in all behavioral or functional respects is coherent, it is not coherent for subjects identical in all *objective* respects. Thus these theorists accept the qualia difference hypotheses that can be accommodated by nontranscendental theories while rejecting the qualia difference hypothesis for which only transcendental theories provide an account. In addition, there are theorists who, though they stop short of postulating transcendental facts or properties, claim to account for the intuition that the objective facts do not exhaust the facts about what it is like to have conscious experience.

Given the controversy that surrounds these alleged features of the mental, it will be necessary to consider carefully the claims that these features are actually captured by nontranscendental theories or that the inability of nontranscendental theories to deal with them is not a drawback. I argued in chapter 3 that there are strong pretheoretical intuitions concerning qualia inversion that only transcendental theories can accommodate.[10] My argument for this claim, however, was neutral on the issue of whether we should abandon these intuitions or embrace some form of transcendentalism. And there seems to be no plausible way of settling this issue within the context of the discussion of qualia inversion. I shall concentrate, therefore, on the issues of privileged access and first-person, subjective facts in order to resolve the question about the attractiveness of transcendentalism that the earlier discussion of qualia inversion left open.

I shall argue in this section that where privileged access and first-person facts are concerned, the arguments that they do not exist are inconclusive. I shall go on to argue in section 3 that the claims that they can be accommodated by nontranscendental theories raise equally difficult problems. These problems arise because several types of privileged access can be distinguished. What characterizes these types are the sorts of grounds that are given for the claim that our access to facts of a given kind is privileged. And although nontranscendental theories can account for some of these types, only transcendental theories, if any theories, can account for privileged access when it is supported on the strongest grounds. The conclusion of these two sections is that the usual reasons for dismissing transcendental theories out of hand are open to serious question.

There are a number of arguments against the thesis that we have privileged access to our own mental states. David Armstrong has argued, for example, that it is possible to imagine cases in which it would be natural to say that a subject was mistaken in reporting that he or she was currently experiencing a sensation of pain.[11] According to Armstrong, we might imagine that our understanding of neurophysiology had reached a point at which we had established well-confirmed correlations between a subject's being in a certain brain state and that subject's reporting a pain sensation. It also seems possible to imagine that in such a situation a subject whose sincerity we had no reason to doubt should report a sensation of pain without being in the relevant neurophysiological state. We can imagine that this subject is competent in his or her use of the word 'pain', and we can even imagine that he or she has been given a truth drug to guarantee the sincerity of the response. In such a case, Armstrong claims, it would be reasonable to conclude that the subject mistakenly believed he or she was in pain.

But why should we assume that this would be a reasonable conclusion? First, the proponent of the privileged access thesis is likely to regard that thesis as being true a priori as well as necessary. The thesis has its strongest support, after all, in the fact that its negation seems unintelligible. One cannot *conceive* of what it would be like to feel certain, even after careful consideration, that one was in severe pain when one felt no pain whatsoever. Similarly, one cannot imagine what it would be like to feel excruciating pain while not believing one's experience was in any way unpleasant. At least one cannot imagine this except in the trivial sense that one can imagine one feels pain, even though no sentence equivalent to 'I am in pain' runs through one's head. And the example Armstrong describes does nothing to make the absence of privileged access more intelligible. But if the privileged access thesis is indeed an a priori truth, its revision would not be justified in the circumstances Armstrong pictures.

Furthermore, there is a theory according to which the correlation Armstrong imagines between being in pain and being in a certain neurophysiological state could not have the status of a basic physical law. If the functionalist account of pain is correct, then it might be the case that every actual creature who experienced pain did so in virtue of a certain type of neurophysiological state. There might in fact be an explanation of the generalization in terms of features common to the evolutionary histories of all existing creatures. On the functionalist account, however, it is physically possible for creatures who are functionally equivalent to actual creatures but whose functional states are realized in a radically different type of neurophysiology to experience pain.[12] Thus such creatures (if they existed) would show every sign that they experienced pain in spite of lacking the neurophysiological state in virtue of which all actual creatures experience it. Of course, Armstrong may assume that functionalism cannot account for privileged access and that this possibility is therefore irrelevant. But I shall argue in section 5 that this assumption is unwarranted. Alternatively, Armstrong may hold a theory according to which pain is treated as a natural kind rather than as a functional state. On such a theory, 'pain' would refer to whatever neurophysiological state realizes *in us* (and in the creatures around us) the best functional characterization of pain. Thus creatures who were functionally equivalent to actual creatures but who lacked their neurophysiology would not experience genuine pain. But whatever theory Armstrong has in mind, if it has the consequence that the privileged access thesis is false in the way he supposes, this is a good reason to question it.[13] Hence, in the situation Armstrong imagines, it would be more reasonable to conclude not that the privileged access thesis was false but that the correlation between pain and the brain state in question was not universal. (Alternatively, one might conclude that one of the other assumptions had been violated: the subject was not sincere, not linguistically competent, the truth drug did not always work, and so forth.[14])

A different objection to the claim that we have privileged access to any of the facts about our own sensations has been raised by Keith Lehrer.[15] Lehrer asks us to imagine the case of a woman who has been told by her doctor that itches are pains. As a result, when she has an itching sensation, she is prone to say sincerely that she is in pain. Lehrer claims that because there is nothing out of the ordinary in her acquisition of the word 'pain', the woman has not made a linguistic mistake. The correct analysis, according to Lehrer, is rather that she has a genuinely false belief about *pain*. It will be useful to compare Lehrer's case with a case proposed by Tyler Burge in a discussion of propositional content.[16] Burge imagines a man who, because he has sensations in his thigh similar to those in his hip and because he fails to realize that, as the term is used, arthritis occurs only in the joints, believes what he would express by saying that he has "arthritis of the thigh." Burge claims that on an adequate theory of propositional content, such a man would have a false belief about arthritis rather than a true belief about some more general rheumatoid condition. Let us assume for the sake of argument that Burge is right. This case is not completely analogous to Lehrer's, but it is analogous to the following variant of Lehrer's case. Imagine that a woman in similar circumstances believes that it is part of the *meaning* of 'pain' that itches are pains, rather than its being the empirical generalization that Lehrer's description suggests. The woman, that is, mistakenly believes that the term 'pain' covers a far wider range of sensations than it actually does. In each case the question is whether we have a genuine counterexample to the thesis that our access to our own sensations and qualitative states is privileged.

Lehrer's original case, Burge's case, and the variant on Lehrer's case share the following features. In each case there is a false belief that makes it natural to suppose that what the subject means by the term in question, 'pain' or 'arthritis', is something other than what is normally meant. But in each case it might plausibly be claimed (for example, on the basis of the causal theory of reference[17]) that this supposition is mistaken—that the existence of the false belief is compatible with these subjects meaning exactly what we mean by 'pain' and 'arthritis'. Someone who defends the existence of privileged access, however, can allow that a subject might hold the belief that he or she would express in uttering the sentence 'I am in pain' and fail to be in pain only on one condition: that if that subject were to utter the sentence, he or she would *not* mean that he or she was in pain. Since we are assuming that the subjects in the examples described *do* mean what we mean by 'pain', we have two apparently clear counterexamples to the thesis.

The reply to Lehrer is that the privileged access thesis can be weakened without destroying any of its philosophical interest. In both Lehrer's original example and the variant of Lehrer's example that is analogous to Burge's, the woman in question has a false belief about the sensation she is experiencing because she has one or more other false beliefs that are relevant to what she means (in a sense of that term to be explained) by 'pain'. In the first case the woman's false belief is in the empirical proposition that all itches are pains. This might be based, for example, on the (perhaps inchoate) belief that 'pain' is a natural-kind term that only experts are fully competent to apply and that it has been discovered by the experts that the natural kind it picks out includes itches. The woman's false belief in the second case is that the meaning of 'pain' is so broad that itches are part of its extension and that this is part of the linguistic knowledge of competent speakers. Although we are assuming that the causal theory of reference is true and that each woman's having one of these false beliefs is compatible with her meaning pain by 'pain', there are senses of 'meaning' other than those defined by the causal theory for which this is not the case. Given such a sense of 'meaning', we could use it to reformulate the privileged access thesis. On this alternative sense of 'meaning', each woman *will* mean something other than pain by 'pain' in virtue of her false beliefs. Hence she will not be an example of someone who means (in the alternative sense) the same thing we mean by 'pain' and is wrong in thinking that (in that sense) she is in pain. Thus the reformulated privileged access thesis will escape Lehrer's objection.

To see what such an alternative sense of 'meaning' would involve, consider that 'meaning', as defined by the causal theory of reference, is *nonautonomous* in the following sense: what a subject means by a particular expression is not determined by the subject's internal psychology alone but may depend on features of the subject's external environment. Such features may include the natural kinds that occupy the subject's environment as well as facts about the linguistic practices in which the other members of the subject's community engage. But we can (and for some purposes, as I have argued,[18] must) define a notion of *autonomous meaning* that is independent of the properties of the subject's external environment. Meaning in this sense can be regarded as a component of meaning in the nonautonomous sense and, unlike nonautonomous meaning, it is tied solely to the subject's internal psychology. On a functional account of internal psychology, for example, what the subject means in the autonomous sense depends only on the dispositional relations for that subject among inputs, outputs, and internal states. On any plausible account of internal psychology, however, the woman in Lehrer's example and the woman in the variant example will have different internal psychologies from those of normal subjects. The stimulations that prompt their use of the word 'pain', the inferences they draw from stimulations involving itches, and the associations they make between itches and pains all differ significantly from ours. Thus there is at least nothing to *prevent* our saying that the women mean (in the autonomous sense) something different by 'pain' from what we mean. That is, there is nothing to prevent our saying that the autonomous contents of the beliefs that they express using the term 'pain' differ from the autonomous contents of the beliefs we would express in the same way.

Although we can appeal to the notion of autonomous meaning in defending the thesis of privileged access, this appeal raises a potential problem. To use the notion of autonomous meaning to defend the privileged access thesis, we must claim that subjects who differ in their internal psychology because of differences in their beliefs may as a result mean different things, in the autonomous sense, by the same utterances, even though on a theory of reference like the causal theory they mean exactly the same thing in the nonautonomous sense. But unless there is some limit as to which differences in belief constitute differences in autonomous meaning (that is, some way of distinguishing those differences that contribute to a difference in the autonomous meanings of some of the subjects' terms and those that involve merely a difference in their collateral information), it will be difficult to justify the claim that we are dealing with a sense of 'meaning' at all. This is because we ordinarily assume that meaning and belief are related in such a way that two subjects can hold opposite beliefs about the truth of some sentence while they both mean by that sentence exactly the same thing. Suppose, however, that given any difference in the beliefs of two subjects, that difference were sufficient to constitute a difference in the autonomous meaning of some of the terms involved in the expression of those beliefs. Then a difference in belief that could be expressed by one subject's uttering something of the form 'P' when another would utter something of the form 'Not P' (assuming that all their other linguistic dispositions were as nearly alike as was consistent with their both being rational) would guarantee that they did not mean to assert and deny the same thing. Thus without some limit as to which differences in belief constitute a difference in autonomous meaning, the possibility of genuine disagreement is undermined. And this seems to raise a doubt about the very possibility of an autonomous sense of 'meaning'.

We need not settle the question of when a difference in belief makes for a difference in autonomous meaning, however, to deal with the cases at hand. In each case there are mistaken beliefs of a significant kind—about pain in Lehrer's original example and about 'pain' in the variant example. So there are significant differences between the internal psychologies of the women in the two examples and those of normal subjects. Therefore, there are good grounds for the claim that the differences in the beliefs about pain held by each of the two women on the one hand and a normal subject on the other amount to a difference in the autonomous meaning of some of the relevant terms. In particular, it seems natural to claim that the beliefs of the two women and those of a normal subject that would be expressed in using the term 'pain' differ in their autonomous content. And the claim that a difference in belief of this magnitude is sufficient for a difference in autonomous meaning seems unlikely to force us to the conclusion that a difference in autonomous meaning will result from *every* difference in belief, no matter how trivial.

If this claim about autonomous meaning is correct, we can say that a subject *believes that p in the autonomous sense* just in case the autonomous content of the subject's belief is the same as the autonomous content of the belief that *p* of a normal and well-informed subject. We can then consider the following weakened transparency and incorrigibility relations.

> One has *weakly incorrigible access* to facts of type *M* if and only if, if one believes, in the autonomous sense, that a fact of type *M* obtains, then a fact of type *M* does obtain.

> One has *weakly transparent access* to facts of type *M* if and only if, if a fact of type *M* obtains, then, in the autonomous sense, one believes that a fact of type *M* obtains.

Thus if one were to express one's belief by saying 'I am (am not) experiencing a sensation of type *S*', one could be wrong if and only if the autonomous content of one's utterance differed from the autonomous content that an utterance of the same type would have if it were made by a normal subject. And we can define the *weakened privileged access* thesis as the thesis that we have weakly incorrigible access and weakly transparent access to the facts about our own qualitative experiences. Thus weakened, the thesis still stands.[19]

Besides Armstrong's and Lehrer's arguments concerning privileged access, a number of other arguments have been put forward to show that the anomalous features alleged to characterize the mental do not exist. These other arguments have been equally inconclusive. Arguments that two subjects whose behavior is the same under all actual and possible circumstances must have the same qualitative experiences ordinarily involve very controversial verificationist assumptions. The proposition that two such subjects might have qualitatively different experiences, which Schlick, for example, took to be meaningless,[20] is one that many find perfectly intelligible. Indeed, the thesis that spectrum inversions or qualia differences are possible even between functionally equivalent subjects seems sufficiently plausible that it would count in favor of a theory that it had the thesis as a consequence. Thus if a transcendental theory is in fact the only kind that can accommodate such possibilities in a principled way, this lends support to the claim that such theories deserve serious consideration.

The last claim that the allegedly special characteristics of the mental do not exist is the claim that there are no special facts about what it is like to be a subject—no special facts, for example, about what hot pink looks like or Vegemite tastes like. To the transcendentalist who claims that once you have tasted Vegemite, you will have gained a kind of information that materialists and functionalists overlook entirely, David Lewis has replied,

> We dare not grant that there is a sort of information we overlook.
> . . . Neither can we credibly claim that lessons in physics, physiology, . . . could teach the inexperienced what it is like to taste Vegemite. Our proper answer, I think, is that knowing what it's like is not the possession of information at all. . . . Rather, knowing what it's like is the possession of abilities: abilities to recognize, abilities to imagine, abilities to predict one's behavior by means of imaginative experiments.[21]

Lewis's response (originally due to Laurence Nemirow[22]) is unlikely to convince those who take the first-person point of view seriously. The first problem is that the claim that knowing what Vegemite tastes like is not knowing that something is the case, but knowing how to do something is not derived from any general and systematic analysis of the distinction between knowing how and knowing that. Nemirow does suggest, by way of partial explanation of the distinction, that what it is one knows when one knows what Vegemite tastes like cannot be stated as a fact. But this is not obviously true. The fact in question might be that Vegemite tastes like *this*, where 'this' refers ostensively on a particular occasion to one's experience in tasting it. In other words, we might succeed in stating our knowledge of what Vegemite tastes like (that is, expressing that knowledge as knowledge of a fact) by having recourse to an act of private ostensive reference relating us to a singular proposition.[23] Although it might seem natural to invoke the private language argument in response to such a reply, this would involve a controversial commitment with which the critic of transcendentalism should prefer not to be saddled.[24] I shall therefore postpone until the next section any response to the transcendentalist on this point. There I shall defend a conclusion which is related to that of the private language argument by reference to assumptions that ought to prove less controversial then those of the argument itself.

The second problem is that whether one calls what it is one has when one knows what Vegemite tastes like knowledge or a skill, the subjective-objective distinction on which the transcendental dualist insists has not been bridged. A skill, after all, is just the sort of complex disposition that functionalism is designed to describe, and this kind of description ignores, the transcendental dualist claims, what is essential to subjective experience. Possession of a description of the skill to which Lewis and Nemirow appeal could never give us knowledge of what Vegemite tastes like, but possession of the skill itself, without the appropriate qualitative experience, would be equally useless. Thus unless Lewis has a reply to the transcendental dualist's version of the absent qualia hypothesis—that is, the hypothesis that two subjects, alike *in all objective respects*, can differ in that one has qualitative experience whereas the other does not—his response does nothing to move the discussion beyond what appears to be a stalemate.

3 Three Types of Privileged Access

From the thesis that none of the allegedly special features of the mental exist, I now turn to the thesis that any special features of the mental can be accommodated by nontranscendental theories. In section 2, I considered two sorts of privileged access: incorrigible and transparent access. There are different ways, however, in which transparency and incorrigibility can be grounded. And for some of these ways, nontranscendental theories provide an apparently adequate account. Lehrer, for example, in addition to claiming that our beliefs about our own sensations are not incorrigible, claims that our beliefs about our own occurrent beliefs are in general not incorrigible either. He does allow, however, that we have some incorrigible beliefs. One's belief that one exists is an example, as is one's belief that one believes something. Beliefs of this kind, according to Lehrer, largely exhaust our supply of incorrigible beliefs.[25] If this were the case, it would indeed be reasonable to assume that the existence of incorrigible beliefs could always be explained without recourse to transcendental theories. In Lehrer's first example, it follows from the fact that one believes that one exists. Thus the belief is incorrigible on logical grounds, though it is a belief in a merely contingent proposition. It is the combination of the proposition's content and the fact that it is believed that guarantees its truth. The second case is an example of the same kind. Let us call beliefs that are incorrigible in this way *logically incorrigible* or *logically privileged* beliefs. Let us say that we have the first type of privileged access to facts about which we have beliefs that are logically incorrigible or logically privileged.

So far our only reason for supposing that the facts about privileged access can be explained in nontranscendental terms depends on our accepting Lehrer's assumption that the facts about privileged access are exhausted by our logically incorrigible beliefs. This requires accepting that our beliefs about our own sensations are corrigible. And, as we have seen, Lehrer's arguments on this score have not been decisive. Lewis, however, has argued that *if* our beliefs about any of our own mental states *are* incorrigible, then this fact has a functionalist explanation. Lewis suggests that we define mental states in the following way:

> Think of common sense psychology as a term-introducing scientific theory. . . . Collect all the platitudes you can think of regarding the causal relations of mental states, sensory stimuli, and motor responses. . . . Form the conjunction of these platitudes; or better, form a cluster of them—a disjunction of all conjunctions of *most* of them. (That way it will not matter if a few are wrong.) This is the postulate of our term-introducing theory. . . . It defines the mental states by reference to their causal relations to stimuli, responses, and each other.[26]

Lewis claims that this procedure captures the relational character of mental states. According to Lewis, since the typical causes and effects of mental states include other mental states, we may expect to find families of mental states that are interdefined. As a consequence, it will not be possible to identify something with one mental state in such a family without regard to what we identify with the others. In other words, whether we can identify state x of subject S as a mental state of type I may depend on whether we can identify other states y, z, and so forth of S (which are causes and effects of x) as mental states of the types that are typical causes and effects of states of type I (according to commonsense psychology) and in terms of which states of type I are defined. A state that is physically just like an instance of type I in all other respects may fail to be an instance of type I if it lacks the right kinds of causes or the right kinds of effects.[27]

It is this relational quality of the mental as characterized by functionalist theories, among others, that makes possible a stronger form of privileged access than Lehrer would allow. This claim is supported by the following argument of Lewis's. Suppose that among the platitudes that make up the postulate of the term-introducing theory is one to the effect that the belief that one is in pain never occurs unless pain occurs. And suppose that this platitude is so important that it occurs as a conjunct in every disjunct of the postulate and that a potential psychological subject that fails to satisfy this platitude is not even a near realization of commonsense psychology. Then, Lewis concludes,

> two states cannot be pain and belief that one is in pain respectively
> . . . if the second *ever* occurs without the first. The state that *usually* occupies the role of belief that one is in pain may, of course, occur without the state that *usually* occupies the role of pain; but in that case . . . the former no longer is the state of belief that one is in pain, and the latter no longer is pain.[28]

This sort of privileged access, which Lewis claims is available to the functionalist, is not logically privileged access. Logically privileged access is completely independent of the truth of any particular psychological theory. The form of privileged access that Lewis describes, however, depends on the acceptance of a psychological theory that is appropriately relational. Let us call this second type of privileged access *psychologically privileged access*. The basic idea behind psychologically privileged access is that some "commonsense platitudes" may be so important that they represent a priori constraints on the application of psychological terms. A state will not *count as* pain belief unless it is caused by pain, and a state will not *count as* pain unless it causes a pain belief—and this may be true even though a state is otherwise just like one that did count as pain or that did count as pain belief. And, of course, a state will not count as pain belief or as pain unless it bears the appropriate causal relations to a number of other states as well. Thus psychologically privileged access is just a particular instance of the general functionalist thesis that it is their relations to other states, and not their intrinsic nature, that make mental states the states they are.

It is not the *causal* relation between pain and pain belief, however, that plays a crucial role in psychologically privileged access. For any relation R that we take to hold between pain belief and pain, the same strategy is available; we can refuse to count a state as pain belief that does not bear R to a state we count as pain and refuse to count a state as pain if it does not bear the inverse of R to a state we count as pain belief. Let us say that a theory that guarantees privileged access in virtue of this strategy guarantees it in virtue of the *relational strategy*. Providing a possible account of psychologically privileged access is a characteristic of theories that allow us to employ the relational strategy, rather than of functionalist theories. All functionalist theories are relational in this sense, but functionalist theories are assumed to be couched in terms that are topic-neutral. Nothing in the relational strategy outlined limits the relation R to a topic-neutral relation. Thus there could be theories that allow the relational strategy to be employed and that, as a result, can account for psychologically privileged access, even though they are not functionalist theories.

The question now arises as to whether there is any evidence of a stronger form of privileged access than psychologically privileged access. The answer, I think, is yes. Not only might we be right whenever we believe we are in pain and believe we are in pain whenever we are, this might be in virtue of a mode of access to our own pain that is necessarily unique. If such a mode of access to our own qualitative states exists and if, as a result, our access to them is incorrigible and transparent, then there is clearly a type of privileged access for which no objective (as opposed to transcendental) theory could account. On the functionalist account of psychologically privileged access, whether one is in pain may depend on whether one has a pain belief, and whether one has a pain belief may depend on whether one is in pain. Nevertheless, whether one is in pain is still a perfectly objective fact, open in principle to empirical confirmation by external observers. The subject has no access to whether he or she is in pain that is unavailable (in principle) to anyone else.

It is just such an exclusive access to one's own mental states that transcendentalism seems to promise. Mental states, for the transcendentalist, are outside the nexus of causal relations and hence beyond the reach of any objective investigation. Therefore, if there is a means of access to such mental states, it must be from the subjective point of view, and this must in principle be unique. The reason, as we have seen, is that mental entities for the transcendentalist differ from physical objects precisely in that they are nothing over and above our means of access to them. They, unlike physical objects, are nothing over and above their appearances. Hence transcendentalism assures us of an access to our own mental states, or to their properties, that is in principle unavailable to others. Therefore, in spite of the claims that nontranscendental theories can account for privileged access, we have found a type of privileged access that apparently only transcendentalism can explain.

Let us call this type of privileged access *transcendentally privileged access*. It is the transcendental conception of the mental, according to which there is nothing to pain, for example, over and above our means of access to it, that seems to assure us of this third type of privileged access. Having the third type of privileged access does not, however, entail that we have privileged access of the second type. In fact, if we have privileged access on the grounds provided by the transcendental conception of the mental, the relational strategy is superfluous, and given the transcendental conception of the mental, it is not clear that it would make sense. Whereas the relational strategy guarantees privileged access by making the relation of co-occurrence essential to the identities of pain and pain belief, the transcendental conception provides the same guarantee by denying the difference between pain and our means of access to it. Thus it minimizes, perhaps to the point of denying, the difference between pain and pain belief. Nonetheless, those who endorse the transcendental conception of the mental can plausibly maintain that psychologically privileged access represents a compromise that would only be attractive in the absence of transcendentally privileged access.

Aside from providing this form of privileged access, the transcendental conception of the mental appears to handle the alleged cases of qualia inversion and the alleged facts about what it is like to be a sentient subject. The qualia difference hypothesis regarding objective facts is problematic because it entails that qualitative states can vary even though *all* the objective facts are kept fixed. Similarly, the claim that there is something it is like to be sentient raises problems to the extent that it presupposes the existence of facts that we do not fix in fixing all the objective facts. These radical claims about qualia inversion and subjective facts, however, like the claim for the existence of transcendentally privileged access, present no special problems if our conscious mental states are nothing over and above our means of access to them.

Nontranscendental accounts, of course, deny the existence of any facts about access, qualia, and what conscious experience is like that are not fixed in fixing all the objective facts—and indeed, for most accounts, all the *physical* facts. We have seen, however, that the reasons for doubting the existence of even this strongest form of privileged access and the corresponding claims about qualia inversion and the facts about what it is like to be sentient cannot be assumed to settle the issue. The Lewis-Nemirow reply to Nagel, for example, proved inconclusive. And, as we saw in sections 1 and 2, there are strong intuitions that support the possibility of the weaker forms of qualia inversion as well as reasons for thinking that there is no principled distinction between some of these weaker forms and the strongest form—a form for which no *non*transcendental theory provides an adequate account. Hence there appear to be good reasons for taking transcendentalism seriously.

4   Transcendentalism and Propositional Content

It is hard to avoid the conclusion that the usual responses to transcendentalism never fully come to grips with the challenge it poses. This is because in important respects they are incomplete. Such responses provide alternative accounts of some of the intuitions that transcendentalism is designed to explain. But these responses provide neither plausible explanations of the intuitions for which only transcendental accounts are adequate nor conclusive objections to those accounts. In this section I shall argue against transcendentalism on internal grounds. It is in the attempt to spell out a transcendental theory in more detail that the problems that disqualify it as a plausible theory of mind will emerge.

So far we have discussed transcendental theories in relation to qualitative states and sensations without any explicit consideration of their implications for intentional states. But intentional states, such as beliefs and desires, and nonintentional states, such as sensations, present significantly different problems for a theory of mind. Any attempt to give content to a transcendental theory must take these differences into account. And such an attempt must also ensure that whatever treatments of these two types of states emerge, they can be integrated within a unified and coherent theory.

In spite of the need for an integrated theory that treats both types of mental states, discussions of transcendental theories do not frequently include detailed considerations of the problem of intentionality. Moreover, it is no coincidence that the vocabulary and examples common in discussions of transcendentalism are more appropriate to sensations than to intentional states. Although occurrent beliefs raise some of the same problems regarding incorrigibility, transparency, and uniqueness of access as do sensations and other nonintentional, qualitative states, it is states of the latter kind, such as feeling pain, hearing middle C, or seeing an expanse of red, that provide the main focus for the transcendentalist's attention.

Let us begin, then, by considering the case in which a transcendental theory of sensations is combined with a theory of intentional states (such as functionalism) that is nontranscendental and relational. In such a case we might try to adopt the relational strategy to provide psychologically privileged access and to integrate the two accounts by ensuring that pain and pain belief necessarily co-occur. Unfortunately, this suggestion raises the problem, noted in section 3, that the transcendental conception of the mental and the relational strategy are not easily reconciled. The problem is not that given a transcendental theory of sensations and qualitative states according to which they have no causal or dispositional properties, there will be no causal relations between pain and pain belief. As we have seen, the relational strategy does not depend on the type of relation involved. Hence the lack of any causal relations between pain and pain belief does not preclude the application of the strategy. The problem is rather that the relational strategy and the transcendental conception of the mental seem antithetical. We have already encountered this problem in the fact that the relational strategy emphasizes the relation between pain and pain belief that the transcendental conception of the mental makes it difficult to distinguish. Moreover, the relational strategy seems to undermine the point of transcendentalism. For the transcendentalist, pain is essentially a feeling and something completely given in a single mental act of awareness. And to suppose that what a transcendental state *feels like* could depend on its relations to other states, especially nontranscendental states, seems incoherent.

Since we cannot appeal to the relational strategy to secure psychologically privileged access, there seems to be only one alternative to ensure that pain does not occur without pain belief and that pain belief does not occur without pain. We could either analyze pain in terms of pain belief or pain belief in terms of pain. That is, we could show that pain and pain belief are conceptually connected because (say) the dispositions that constitute pain belief are necessary and sufficient for pain or because the sensations that make up pain are necessary and sufficient for pain belief.

If such an analysis is to hold out any hope for the transcendentalist, it must obviously be the analysis of pain belief in terms of pain. It is in the case of sensations that the transcendentalist account has its greatest plausibility. And to suppose that pain had an analysis in terms of pain belief would undermine whatever reasons we might have for thinking that an adequate treatment of pain would require a transcendental theory.

The question, then, is whether we can have a transcendental theory of intentional states as well as a transcendental theory of sensations with the added requirement that sensations and their corresponding beliefs will necessarily co-occur. And since the only plausible way of guaranteeing co-occurrence seems to involve analyzing beliefs in terms of sensations, the question becomes whether beliefs could have an analysis in terms of sensations as conceived by the transcendentalist.

The following argument strongly suggests that the answer is no. The first premise is that nothing that was completely accessible to a subject from the first-person point of view could fix the content of a proposition that the subject believed. And this premise has two components: that only a dispositional state of a subject could fix the content of a proposition that that subject believed and that no dispositional state of a subject could be fully accessible to that subject from the first-person point of view. Consider first the claim that one's belief in a proposition must be in virtue of one's having some disposition. To make a judgment that is true just in case something has a certain feature is to do something general; it is to bring that thing into relation with all of the other things that share the feature. Even if to refer to a thing were merely to point it out, to judge that it had some feature would have to amount to more than pointing twice. We are, in fact, doing something that presupposes a capacity to make an infinite, or at least indefinite, number of similarity judgments. We divide the actual and possible objects of similar judgments into the class of those things that are alike with respect to the feature in question and the class of things that are not. If instead of concentrating on the predicational structure of propositions, we concentrate on their possible-worlds representations, the same problem arises. We must be able to sort the possible worlds into those of which the proposition is true and those of which it is not. Again, this involves an indefinite number of similarity judgments. That I am in pain is a proposition that can be true in virtue of the existence of an indefinite number of particular and discriminably different sensations. And it is difficult to see how my simply having a pain on a particular occasion without any disposition to judge other sensations as relevantly similar or different (even if this were possible) could be sufficient for my believing the proposition that I am in pain.

The argument for the second component of the first premise, that no disposition could be fully accessible from the first-person point of view, rests on the difficulty in seeing how a disposition could be given incorrigibly in a single mental act of awareness. The disposition of some subject that corresponds to a proposition that the subject believes involves or determines an indefinite number of actual and possible situations. The most that can be given from the first-person point of view, however, is what we might think of as the first-person manifestation of the disposition: that small finite set of cases that in an act of conception or imagination is (or perhaps has been) actually before the subject's mind.

The second premise of the argument is that pain and the other experiences for which transcendentally privileged access is an issue are *fully* accessible from the first-person point of view. Although it may be possible to imagine something that is accessible in principle from only one point of view and yet is not completely accessible from that point of view—as a disposition would have to be to satisfy the transcendentalist—this is not the conception of sensations, such as pain, or experiences, such as that of seeing a certain shade of red, that motivates transcendentalism. The point of the transcendentalist's claim that one's pain is not available, even in principle, from any point of view other than one's own is that from one's own point of view it *is* available. To say that there is something it is like to feel pain but that that something is only partially accessible to the subject whose pain it is would be to deprive transcendentalism of its *point* as well as whatever plausibility it still retained.

The conclusion is, of course, that we cannot analyze pain beliefs in terms of pain. This means that, appearances notwithstanding, privileged access to qualitative states has no explanation in transcendental terms. Without an analysis of intentional states in terms of nonintentional states like sensations, nothing guarantees that we will not have a pain belief without pain or a pain without a corresponding pain belief. Thus transcendental dualism cannot provide an account of either psychologically or transcendentally privileged access where qualitative states are concerned.

The claim that transcendental dualism cannot account for privileged access, however, is open to the objection that 'transcendental dualism' has been defined in an overly narrow way. As it has been defined, transcendental dualism entails that mental states or events have no objective properties. In particular, they are neither caused by, nor the causes of, any other states, regardless of the status these other states have. But suppose we allow that mental states do have some objective properties. Pains, for example, might have the property of causing pain beliefs. Let us call theories according to which mental states do have objective properties *hybrid theories*. Would such hybrid theories allow us to combine the advantages of a transcendental dualist theory with those of an objective theory guaranteeing psychologically privileged access?

If mental states such as pain do have some objective properties in addition to their subjective properties, it is natural to ask whether or not these properties are essential to the mental states in question. Suppose they are. Suppose, for example, that causing a pain belief is an essential property of pains. In this case, since being caused by a pain may well be an essential property of pain beliefs (given that pain beliefs are being analyzed in relational terms), we will have psychologically privileged access. But just because theories of this kind allow that some of the properties of mental states are transcendental, this does not give them any advantage over objective theories that incorporate the relational strategy. The reason is that whether a state is a pain, for example, will depend on whether it causes a pain belief, and since this property of or fact about the mental state is objective, it cannot be given from the subjective point of view. Thus our access to our own pains, on this view, is no better than it is on a straightforwardly objective theory.

Suppose, then, that the objective properties of mental states are all inessential to those states. For example, pain might be caused by a bodily injury and might cause a pain belief and pain behavior, but none of these properties would be essential to the state's being a state of pain. In this case we could have psychologically incorrigible access, since it could be required that a belief be caused by a pain if it is to count as a pain belief. But since the causal properties of pain would not be essential, it could not be the case that a state otherwise just like pain only counted as pain if it caused a pain belief. Hence this kind of theory could not provide psychologically transparent access. Thus the assumption that mental states have objective properties that are inessential does not seem to make the problem of transcendentally privileged access any more tractable for hybrid theories than it was for transcendental theories. Such theories seem incapable of providing transcendentally privileged access and provide only one half of the psychologically privileged access that seems to be a minimum requirement where privileged access is concerned. Moreover, if mental states have inessential objective properties, then not only might we be in excruciating pain without believing that we were, because we would not have psychologically transparent access to our own pains, but others might be better informed about our pains than we were. This is because others in principle would have the same access to the objective properties of our pains that we have, and their access in practice might be much better. So although this second type of hybrid theory allows for incorrigible access to our mental states, it does not seem to satisfy enough of the intuitions about subjectivity to motivate the postulation of transcendental properties and facts. Hybrid theories, then, have some advantages relative to transcendental theories, but neither type of hybrid theory has any significant advantage in relation to objective theories. Whether hybrid theories involve any serious disadvantages in comparison to objective theories is a question I shall take up in the next section.

5   The Relational Strategy and the Dispositional Strategy

If transcendental dualism cannot account for privileged access, how serious a difficulty does this pose? At the very least, this undermines those intuitions that originally motivated the theory. But there is also something seriously incoherent in the idea of a transcendental conception of the mental that does not include privileged access. As we saw in section 2, we cannot conceive of what it would be like for pain and pain belief to come apart in the way in which a theory that cannot guarantee privileged access would allow. To suppose that we could means that we should be able to imagine being in excruciating pain and believing consciously and sincerely that we were experiencing a pleasurable feeling of well-being and calm. This is, of course, not to be confused with what is clearly possible: that we might feel the pain and hear ourselves *saying* calmly that we were having a wholly pleasant experience. The example we must imagine is one in which we actually believe without reservation in the pleasantness of the experience and yet feel, in a perfectly ordinary sense, the excruciating pain.

Let us refer to this example as the *basic example* where privileged access is concerned. The fact that this example seems incoherent should make us reluctant to accept any theory according to which it is not ruled out. In the basic example both incorrigible access and transparent access to our own pains are missing. And, as we have seen, the breakdown of transparency alone and the breakdown of incorrigibility alone also raise serious difficulties. It is extremely difficult to imagine that we might be in excruciating pain and not believe despite having considered the question carefully, that our state was in any sense painful. It seems equally difficult to imagine being certain that we were in very severe pain even after the possibility that we might be mistaken had been raised, and being wrong in thinking we were in pain at all. Such situations do not seem significantly more intelligible than the basic example. But if this is so, then privileged access provides an obstacle for any form of transcendental theory.

Psychologically privileged access rules out all three of these examples, but is it a sufficient response to the problem the examples illustrate? There are good reasons for thinking that the answer is no. Psychologically privileged access by itself is no guarantee that we will not consciously and simultaneously experience two states of the following kinds: a state exactly like pain in every respect except that on the occasion in question it does not cause a pain belief and a state exactly like the belief that one is experiencing a feeling of well-being and calm except that it is not caused by any such state. And this possibility seems as potentially damaging to a theory that fails to rule it out as any of the earlier three.

What seems to be missing in the relational strategy is any *intrinsic* connection between pain belief and pain. Moreover, it should be clear that such a connection cannot be provided by any form of transcendentalism. Transcendental states have too little in common with beliefs construed as dispositions or as incorporating dispositions to support

such a connection. And if beliefs are themselves construed as transcendental states or as made up of transcendental states, then, as we
have seen, they do not determine the content of a proposition. Once
we drop the assumption that states like pain are transcendental, however, a new possibility presents itself: we can be assured of an intrinsic
connection between pain and pain belief if in fact many of the dispositions in the set of dispositions that constitutes a state of pain also
belong to the set that constitutes a pain belief.[29] Let us say that a theory
that guarantees an intrinsic relation of this kind between pain and
pain belief does so in virtue of the *dispositional strategy*. If there is such
an extensive but incomplete overlap in the makeup of the two sets,
this has two consequences. If the overlap in the dispositional makeup
of pain and pain belief is incomplete, then even if psychologically
privileged access holds, states may occur that are just like pain except
that they do not cause, and are not accompanied by, pain belief.
Similarly, it will be possible for states just like pain belief in other
respects to occur without their being caused by pain. If, however, the
overlap in the dispositional makeup of the two states is nonetheless
extensive, then even if privileged access does *not* hold, it will be
impossible for there to be pains without there being states very similar
to pain beliefs or for there to be pain beliefs without states very much
like pain. Thus the dispositional strategy is more apt for ensuring a
very high degree of privileged access than for ensuring privileged
access itself. But this should not be an unwelcome result. The dispositional strategy guarantees a high degree of privileged access in such
a way as to answer the objection we have just been considering to the
relational strategy. Moreover, there are independent reasons for
doubting that privileged access is an all or nothing affair.

Consider the kinds of cases that lend support to skepticism about
privileged access. Suppose someone who manifests what appears to
be pain behavior claims with apparent sincerely not to feel any pain.
Suppose also that the person in question has a strong motive for
denying, both to himself or herself and to others, the existence of the
pain. And imagine that we have grounds for suspecting that this
motive is operating to produce a sincere denial in the face of pain that
is completely genuine. It is examples of this kind, as much as arguments of the sort that Lehrer and Armstrong have produced, that give
denials of privileged access whatever intuitive plausibility they have.
This is not to say that no reply to such examples on behalf of the
proponents of privileged access is possible. It could be claimed that
the person in question does really believe, or does believe on reflection, that he or she is in pain. Or it might be maintained that he or
she has the behavioral manifestations of pain without the pain itself.

A third alternative would be to suggest that the person's consciousness is genuinely split. These replies are not implausible. But it is also natural to want to take the example at something more like face value. Moreover, it seems possible, rather than to deny that privileged access has failed, to maintain that the person *is* in pain and that although many of the dispositions necessary for pain belief are present, not all of them are. And if we assume that the person's conscious state is not one which is fully integrated, the persons' having many of the dispositions associated with pain belief is compatible with that person's also having a significant number of the dispositions associated with the sincere belief that no pain exists, including the disposition to say this with no intent to deceive. Such a description is not obviously less natural than the ones offered by the proponent of privileged access.

Again, consider someone who anticipates being touched with something extremely hot and who is touched instead with a piece of ice. Such a person may behave as though he or she has experienced an intense pain, even though it may seem that no pain could exist.[30] In this example too it seems natural to say that many of the dispositions that make up pain belief are present and that many of the dispositions that make up pain are present as well.

Finally, consider the case of creatures sufficiently sophisticated to experience pain but not sophisticated enough to experience genuine pain belief. All these cases seem to present counterexamples to the privileged access thesis. But even if what we might call *full-blown privileged access* does not obtain because of such cases, they do not rule out a high degree of privileged access. In the first case there is something similar to pain belief in virtue of the fact that the subject would almost certainly acknowledge the pain if he or she were capable of attending to the feelings experienced. The fact that the subject in cases of this kind is never described as acknowledging in a fully reflective way the discrepancy between the pain behavior and the disavowal of pain suggests that the subject's state is not one conducive to introspection. It also suggests that the subject's disavowal is not one that could be made calmly and on reflection. In other words, even if we want to say that this subject experiences pain and says sincerely that he or she does not, the sincerity of the utterance is compatible with the subject's being in an unstable state in which he or she is disposed, on introspection or reflection, to avow the pain. And the subject may find it natural later to describe the pain as having been present even when he or she could not avow it while continuing to maintain that the denials were sincere. Thus the subject will have most of what is required for pain belief, and there will be a high degree of privileged access.

Of course, this example need not be understood in this way. The subject may be conscious of the pain behavior and may be capable of describing that behavior in great detail. Moreover, the subject may be fully conscious of the discrepancy between what he or she is feeling and the behavior in which he or she is engaged. In addition, the subject may have no difficulty in describing his or her unsuccessful efforts to detect any pain on introspection. In this case, however, the subject's denial that he or she does actually feel pain seems relatively unproblematic. On this interpretation, then, the example is no threat to the privileged access thesis.

In the second example, as in the first, we have a case in which at least many of the elements of pain and pain belief are present. Even if the subject does not experience pain, he or she will have most of the dispositions and causal processes that make up pain (such as muscular contractions, involuntary withdrawal of the limb, increased heart rate, and inability to focus on other concerns) as well as many of the dispositions and processes that make up fear, anxiety, the desire that the experience stop, and so forth. In this case too there is nothing implausible in saving the privileged access thesis by saying, for example, that the agent does not really believe that he or she is in pain, even though many of the elements of pain belief are present. But even if we refuse to save the privileged access thesis in this way, this is still an example in which a high degree of privileged access is preserved. And a similar claim could be made about the third example.

In the most plausible cases of the breakdown of privileged access, then, there is at least something close to pain belief as long as we have something that genuinely counts as pain and something similar to pain when pain belief occurs. Therefore, even if we admit the possibility of such examples, we can deny that the basic example and its variants, in which a high degree of privileged access is *not* preserved, are intelligible. Since this is the case, the basic example and its variants can be eliminated, whether full-blown psychologically privileged access or merely a high degree of privileged access obtains. The existence of full-blown privileged access can be ensured by combining the relational strategy with the claim that the dispositional bases of pain and pain belief overlap to a significant extent. Alternatively, a high degree of privileged access could be guaranteed by appeal to the latter claim alone. If it is plausible to suppose that we have full-blown privileged access, however, it is plausible because the dispositional strategy eliminates the arbitrariness that the privileged access thesis has when it is supported by the relational strategy alone. Thus it is the dispositional strategy that plays the most fundamental role in allowing the construction of theories with plausible consequences where subjectivity is concerned. And the dispositional strategy achieves this by appealing to the same intuition that underlies the transcendental conception of the mental: the intuition that the most appropriate way for a theory of mind to ensure privileged access is to minimize the difference between pain and our means of access to it.

Because the dispositional strategy seems to allow us to satisfy the most pressing demands on an account of subjectivity, maintaining the relational strategy and full-blown privileged access as an option might seem unnecessary. The issue, however, is not clear-cut. The terms 'pain' and 'pain belief' are vague. And it is likely that even proponents of the privileged access thesis will find the thesis false for some ways of interpreting these terms. Thus even for its defenders, the thesis will need to be qualified. If one believes that one is in pain on calm reflection, say, or given that one is capable of attending to one's sensations or given that one's conscious state is reasonably well integrated, one cannot be wrong. But when the appropriate qualifications are made, the differences between full-blown privileged access (suitably qualified) and a high degree of privileged access may be relatively minor. What does seem clear, however, is that a theory that fails to provide a high degree of both incorrigibility and transparency is, on that ground, open to serious objection.

If this argument is correct, then the requirement that an adequate theory of mind provide a high degree of privileged access presents an obstacle for any form of transcendental theory. That transcendentalism should fail on this score is indeed ironic in view of the fact that epistemological considerations such as those surrounding privileged access provide the main source of interest in a theory whose ontological implications are bound to raise a number of doubts. Moreover, the hybrid theories, some of which, as we have seen, incorporate the relational strategy as effectively as objective theories, cannot easily assimilate the dispositional strategy. To the degree that transcendental properties are important to such states as pain, the degree of overlap where the intrinsic properties of pain and pain belief are concerned is diminished, and the dispositional strategy is undermined. Thus hybrid theories not only fail to provide an advantage over objective theories, but relative to some objective theories, they appear to have serious drawbacks.[31]

Furthermore, if, as it seems they do, some objective theories capture that form of privileged access whose breakdown it seems impossible to imagine, the job of reconciling ourselves to the lack of any stronger form may not be impossible. What makes the idea of our having a special and unique source of access to our own mental states seem important is the apparent incoherence of the basic example. The other intuitions supporting transcendentalism seem significantly weaker than the intuition that pain and pain belief are not completely independent, and these other intuitions are likely to prove far less durable. If there is a transcendentalist objection to the dispositional account suggested by Lewis of knowing what it is like to have conscious experience, it seems to involve the claim that we could be given the dispositions without the experience. In other words, it seems to involve the qualia difference hypothesis regarding functional facts. Of course, we may be inclined to think that a qualia inversion or a qualia difference between two functionally equivalent subjects is indeed possible. But the claim that this is *not* possible does not seem immediately incoherent in the way the claim that we might lack a high degree of privileged access does. Nor does it seem at all implausible to deny that there could be two subjects, alike in all objective respects, who experienced inverted qualia or qualia differences relative to one another. If we consider the possibility, then, that there is a principled way of distinguishing the cases in which qualia inversion is possible and those in which it is not, the obstacles to accepting an objective theory where qualia are concerned need not be insurmountable.[32] And if this is correct, the intuitions that transcendental dualism can accommodate will count for relatively little in the face of its failure to guarantee a high degree of privileged access. Thus in the trade off between the intuitions that support transcendental dualism and those that do not, the reasonable solution will favor a nontranscendental theory.

PART III

Identity and Consciousness

Chapter 5

Metapsychological Relativism and the Self

Recent discussion of the problem of personal identity has focused on the distinction between two kinds of theories. Derek Parfit, for example, characterizes *reductionism* as holding

> 1. that the fact of a person's identity over time just consists in the holding of certain more particular facts, and
>
> 2. that these facts can be described without either presupposing the identity of this person, or explicitly claiming that the experiences of this person's life are had by this person, or even explicitly claiming that this person exists. These facts can be described in an *impersonal* way.
>
> 3. A person's existence just consists in the existence of a brain and body, and the occurrence of a series of interrelated physical and mental events.[1]

Let us say that there is a *direct psychological connection* between two person stages X and Y if and only if Y can now remember having an experience X had or Y acts in a way that realizes an intention of X's or Y has a belief, desire, or some other psychological feature possessed by X. The *strong connectedness* of two person stages requires that enough such direct psychological connections hold between them. *Psychological continuity* is the holding of overlapping chains of strong connectedness (*Reasons and Persons*, pp. 205–206).

Suppose we know what psychological connections and continuities exist between two person stages A and B, as well as what physical relations obtain between them. And suppose we know the same about the relations between the earlier person stage A and any later stage C whose claim to be a stage of the same person as A competes with that of B. Then, according to the reductionist view, which Parfit endorses, we know everything relevant to deciding whether A and B are stages of the same person. Parfit, following Hume, sees an analogy between

Journal of Philosophy 86 (1989): 298–323. Copyright 1989 by The Journal of Philosophy, Inc. Reprinted with permission.

questions of personal identity and questions about the identity of nations over time. Whether England was the same nation after the Norman Conquest is a question that can only be settled by reference to the connections and continuities among people and institutions. In the same way, questions of personal identity must be settled solely by reference to the psychological and physical connections and continuities among person stages.

The *nonreductionist*, in contrast, holds that there are facts of personal identity over and above the impersonal facts. In what follows, I shall criticize both nonreductionism and Parfit's reductionist alternative. Although the theoretical options that Parfit provides are the only ones ordinarily offered, I shall argue that there is a more attractive theory than either of those between which we have thus far been forced to choose.

1   Nonreductionism and Personal Facts

The nonreductionist view that there are facts of personal identity in addition to the impersonal facts involves a number of problems. Since I agree with Parfit that this view is untenable, I shall raise what I take to be the most serious objections before discussing reductionism. These objections and Parfit's are largely complementary.

Proponents of nonreductionism face a dilemma. Either the facts to whose existence they are committed are subjective—that is, facts to which the person whose identity is in question has some special form of access—or they are objective. Subjective facts, I shall argue, are not the kinds of facts that could determine the identity of a person over time. On the other hand, objective facts of the kind required for nonreductionism, if they did settle questions of personal identity, would make it completely mysterious why these questions held any significance or interest.

The most convincing exponent (who may or may not have been an advocate) of the subjective version of nonreductionism is Thomas Nagel.[2] Nagel claims that the true nature of the problem of personal identity is obscured by discussions that focus on continuities and similarities, whether these are physical, mental, causal, or emotional. Given that any such set of conditions is met, there is still the further question whether the same subject or self is preserved under these conditions. The view that Nagel's remarks suggest is one according to which there are irreducibly subjective facts in addition to the objective facts. Whether sugar tastes like *this* to other people is one such fact, and the question whether the subject of *this* experience will exist in some future situation is another (*Mortal Questions*, pp. 200–201).

There are two characteristics that, for Nagel, connect the problem of personal identity with the problem of the subjective character of experience. Unlike facts about objective entities, facts about the subject or self as it figures in the problem of personal identity and facts about the subjective character of experience are not facts about entities in the world. And unlike facts about objective entities, the relevant facts about the subject and about subjective experience are accessible only from the first-person point of view; they are not accessible, even in principle, from any point of view other than that of the subject in question. It is in virtue of these two shared characteristics that the aspects of the subject that are relevant to personal identity, as well as to the subjective aspects of experience, fall on the subjective side of Nagel's subjective/objective distinction (*Mortal Questions*, p. 201).

It follows on this view that although we may be fallible in our judgments about subjective facts, we have what might be called *third-person incorrigibility* where such facts are concerned. That is, we could not be corrected by anyone else about the subjective facts to which we have access. The problem for this view is that our judgments about the facts of personal identity are not third-person incorrigible. Suppose, to take an example of Parfit's, that we create at time *t* a molecule-for-molecule duplicate of Smith in a qualitatively indistinguishable environment. If we leave Smith unchanged, this duplicate will believe, and believe mistakenly, that he is Smith and that he existed long before *t*. And these seem to be straightforwardly mistaken beliefs about the facts of personal identity that could be corrected by any external observer with access to enough of the objective facts.

If such a duplicate would not be making a mistake about a fact of personal identity—a fact of the kind to which, the proponent of the subjective view claims, we have third-person incorrigible access—it is unclear what would count as such a fact. The problem is that the only kinds of facts that it is even plausible to claim are third-person incorrigible are facts about the contents of our present states of awareness. Personal identity over time, however, must consist in some further facts about the relations between such states. And these further facts would not be determined by the content of any single state of awareness. Thus the facts of personal identity that were not fixed by the totality of impersonal facts could not be subjective facts.

Suppose, then, that the facts about personal identity that exist, according to nonreductionism, over and above the impersonal facts are not subjective in Nagel's sense. In this case it would be difficult to see how such a fact, to which we had no special access from the first-person point of view, could explain the intuitions that motivate nonreductionism. If there is any reason to postulate facts over and above the impersonal facts, it is that we feel we have access to something over and above such facts. The postulation of objective facts to which no means of access—whether subjective or not—has been suggested would seem to raise far more serious problems than any that may have motivated nonreductionism. And given this conspicuous lack of access to the facts of personal identity thus construed, it is hard to see how such facts could make a difference to anything that matters.

2   Reductionism and the Instability of Our Intuitive Judgments

In spite of the difference in their respective views, Parfit adopts one of the basic assumptions of those committed to nonreductionism. The assumption is that the crucial division in discussions of personal identity is between nonreductionists and reductionists. On this assumption, once we abandon the intuitions about subjective facts that underlie nonreductionism, the deep problems should disappear. Nagel says, for example, that the concept of the self is the concept of something independent of objective facts, and he adds, "This may be an illusion. It may have no sense to speak of 'the same self as this one' in complete detachment from all external conditions. But it is still the internal idea of the self that gives rise to the problem of personal identity" (*Mortal Questions*, p. 201). And Parfit, though he is not explicit in making this assumption, suggests in a number of remarks that the most difficult puzzles surrounding personal identity will disappear when we drop our prejudices against reductionism (*Reasons and Persons*, pp. 259–260). It is this shared assumption that I shall show is unjustified.

To suppose that the philosophical problem of personal identity is solely the result of bias in favor of nonreductionism underestimates the tension within reductionism itself. Consider three examples.

Example 1: the memory-switch case   Suppose your brain is physically altered in such a way that it comes to contain the information and have the dispositions of another subject's, say Smith's. Smith's brain is similarly altered, with the result that it contains the information and has the dispositions yours has now. Thus the person who wakes up in your (present) body after the operation will seem to remember doing all the things Smith now remembers doing and will have Smith's desires, goals, and intentions. Similarly, the person who wakes up in Smith's body will have your (present) psychology. Which, then, of the two resulting persons is you?

It seems implausible to suppose that for most people the continued possession of a particular body could be more significant than the possession of a particular sort of psychological makeup. Not even the most serious accidents in which some person survives undermine our belief that the original person survives (unless, of course, there is damage to the brain and the psychology of the original person is not preserved). But if one survives the radical alteration of the type of body one has, what significance could the numerical identity of one's body have for one's continued existence? We can, if we like, imagine a case in which the new body is qualitatively identical to the old one. In such a case neither the subject nor any observer need notice any difference. And, presumably, it is the person with one's memories and psychological dispositions who would realize one's goals and projects. Thus the conclusion that one would be the person with one's memories and personality seems the natural one to draw.

Example 2: the future-pain case   Imagine that you are given the following news. You are to be tortured twenty-four hours from now. There is no chance of reprieve, but you are offered the following consolations. First, before the torture is administered, you will suffer complete amnesia regarding your present experiences. Second, you will be given a set of delusive memories about your past. Third, you will be given a set of dispositions to behave that are at odds with your present character and constitute a basic change in your present personality. As a final consolation, the same kinds of psychological changes will be effected in another subject, who, after suffering amnesia, will seem to remember the things you remember now and will exhibit your personality traits.

Could any of these changes relieve the apprehension you feel about the impending torture? The argument that they could not is relatively simple. The first three conditions, though they might add to one's apprehension on other grounds, do not seem to lessen the anxiety one would justifiably feel about the future pain. If, on the other hand, none of the first three conditions is any help, it is hard to see how the experience of someone else could have any bearing on the situation whatsoever.

Example 3: the California-therapy case   Imagine a therapeutic technique that is claimed to remove all the psychological blocks that prevent one from resolving one's problems and using one's opportunities in the most effective way possible. The therapy is effective whether the blocks involve guilt, fear, depression, or anxiety. The therapy requires a session of eight hours a week, during which one is unconscious and that can be scheduled during the hours one is normally asleep. Imagine that you agree to try the therapy, are given a sedative, and awake refreshed with no memories of the session. Suppose that the results exceed even your most optimistic expectations. Your capacity to deal effectively and confidently with the situations you confront far surpasses that of your earlier self.

Suppose now that after months of satisfaction with the therapy, the underlying process is explained. After the sedative is administered, the brain matter that realizes your memories and personality is restructured in order to realize the memories and personality of another subject. The resulting person is then awakened and subjected to hours of an excruciatingly painful procedure without anesthesia—a procedure, however, that leaves no discernible effects after the session. At the end of the session, that person is sedated, the original structural features of your brain are restored, and you are awakened.

If you had been satisfied with the therapy before all the facts were disclosed, would it be rational to discontinue it after the disclosure? (Those who are incurably squeamish might be offered a pill that would erase the memories of the explanation of the procedure.) If the decision is made on purely selfish grounds, there are no obvious reasons why you should fear the experience of the procedure, given its complete dissociation from your own life history. Furthermore, there is a serious objection to the idea that one should discontinue the therapy. One's experience, given that one undertakes the therapy, is exactly analogous to the actual experience of one of the personalities of a multiple personality subject. In such a subject the dissociation between the personalities may have been the only available response to a painful situation that the subject as a whole could not avoid. To suppose that forgetting the details of the therapy and continuing would represent merely a kind of philosophical error would be to ignore how deep the sources of our pretheoretical intuitions supporting the therapy may be.

The most important point that these examples bring out is that rejecting nonreductionism for reductionism brings us no closer to a solution to the puzzles they pose. The problem lies in the instability of our intuitions as we move from one case to the next. That our intuitions are unstable in terms of reductionism follows from the fact that the descriptions of all three examples are compatible with their complete equivalence relative to that view. That is, the descriptions are compatible with the stipulation that the degrees of bodily continuity, psychological continuity, and causal continuity are in each case exactly the same.

This fact is, of course, deliberately obscured in the second example. The physical details of the subjects' transformations are ignored, and the description of the events as things that could happen to you might be regarded as question begging. (It is important to notice, however, that this description is part of an event in the example, not part of the description of the example; the fact that in the example other people describe the person who is to suffer as "you" will be important later.) To object on these grounds, however, would be to miss the point. On the view suggested by the first example, what matters to one's identity are one's memories and one's psychological dispositions. On this view, the description of the second example as one in which *you* would be given false memories, *you* would be given a different personality, and *you* would be tortured would not be question begging but incoherent. The point of the example, however, is that the description is not incoherent; we have no apparent difficulty in understanding the example described. Furthermore, our reaction to the example completely reverses our earlier response. In this case it is bodily continuity, not the continuity of memories and psychological dispositions, that seems to matter. Even when it is pointed out that the description of the second case is compatible with the description of the first, we seem reluctant to disavow the second response. What does seem to happen is that we reevaluate our reaction to the first case in the light of our recognition that the first case is susceptible to the redescription that the second case provides, i.e., the second reaction undermines the first.

The first two examples, which are due to Bernard Williams,[3] provide his argument for the thesis that bodily continuity is the crucial relation in personal identity. The third example, which is intended to bear the same relation to the second that the second bears to the first, is designed to forestall this conclusion. The third example provides another possible redescription of what is, on the reductionist view, an instance of exactly the same case. By the time the third case is reached, however, I think it would be hard to suppose that the examples support either the view that identity depends on the continuity of memory and psychological dispositions or the view that bodily continuity is crucial. Our intuitions are unstable in a way for which the reductionist seems to lack an account. If we take reductionism seriously, these cases should be unproblematic; at the very worst, they should all arouse in us the same sort of ambivalence. The problem is that they do not.

We can appreciate the seriousness of this problem for Parfit if we look at a number of other cases in which it arises. Consider the following example, proposed by David Wiggins.[4]

Example 4: the double-transplant case   Suppose that for some subject the two brain hemispheres are psychologically indistinguishable. And imagine that each one is transplanted in a body of its own, for which it becomes the sole source of control. In the single-transplant case, in which one hemisphere is transplanted and the other is destroyed, the identity of the original subject seems to be preserved. In the double-transplant case, each transplant recipient has the same degree of bodily and psychological continuity with the original person as exists in the case of a single transplant. Consequently, the reductionist has no basis for choosing either as the unique successor to the original subject. Thus, since identity is necessarily one-one, this is evidently not a case in which, for the reductionist, personal identity is preserved.

This in itself is not a problem for Parfit. Parfit distinguishes personal identity from *survival,* which he characterizes as the preservation of what matters in the identity relation. For Parfit, survival consists in the same kind of psychological continuity that he requires for identity without the requirement of uniqueness. Unlike identity, then, the relation of survival need not be one-one. And, for Parfit, neither identity nor survival requires that psychological continuity have either its normal cause or even a reliable cause (*Reasons and Persons*, pp. 262–263). Hence in the double-transplant case, one survives as each of the resulting people, and everything that matters is preserved in both.

Parfit's characterization of survival, however, requires some clarification. The preservation of what matters might mean the preservation of what makes life worth living. In this sense, what matters might not be preserved in the existence of some future self in whom one would not hesitate to say one survived. One might, for example, be tortured at some time in the future to such an extent that one would prefer, both before the torture and during it, not to go on living. But the preservation of what matters might have a stronger sense. It might mean that there are future person stages for which one would have (or be justified in having) the sort of special concern that one ordinarily has for one's future self. In this sense, what matters is preserved in the torture case. One would normally make very extreme sacrifices where one's present desires were concerned to alleviate some of the pain of the self to be tortured. It is this stronger sense in which it is plausible to identify survival with the preservation of what matters. It is this sense in which I shall use the expression and in which I shall assume Parfit uses it.

In spite of Parfit's distinction between identity and survival, the double-transplant case seems problematic in a way that the normal case does not. Although he claims that everything that matters is preserved, this conclusion is not clearly supported by our intuitions. This problem becomes acute in the following variation of the double-transplant case.

Example 5: the multiple-fission case   We can imagine cases of fission in which one splits like an amoeba into two indistinguishable replicas. Consider, then, a case in which one splits simultaneously into a thousand or ten thousand different replicas. Is it really plausible to suppose that everything that matters is preserved in this case and that one survives as ten thousand different individuals?

Another case, which is often mentioned in the literature, also raises serious problems.

Example 6: the teletransportation case   Imagine a machine that records the types, speeds, and directions of all the particles that make up a subject at an initial location. This information is then sent to a terminal location, where a distinct set of particles is used to produce an exact replica. At the same time the particles at the initial location are dispersed, and, it is claimed, the subject travels (discontinuously) between the initial and terminal locations. Since this is a nonbranching case that preserves psychological continuity, Parfit is committed to its being a case of identity. More important, on Parfit's view, everything that matters is preserved. Thus we should have all the same responses to this case that we have to the normal case, and it is not at all clear that we do.

Again, consider a variation that has sometimes been proposed.

Example 7: the defective-teletransportation case   Suppose the original particles are not dispersed at the initial location. Then one survives as two people. As far as what matters goes, there is nothing to choose between these two, though one may or may not be identical with the person who remains at the initial location. (Whether one is depends on whether the causal connections between the person at the initial location and the person at the terminal location are enough like those between the person at the initial end before and after the switch is thrown to regard the case as a branching one.) Furthermore, on Parfit's view, it should not matter if there is a thousand-year time lag between one's stepping into the machine and a replica's stepping out. If the replica who steps out does so in virtue of a reliable mechanism, the time lag would involve nothing to which Parfit could object. And since for Parfit even the reference to a reliable mechanism is unnecessary, a replica created a thousand years later in another part of the universe by a monumentally improbable accident is one in whom one survives.

So far we have been looking at cases in which all of Parfit's conditions for survival are satisfied. In spite of this fact, our responses are neither consistent with our responses to ordinary cases nor consistent with each other (though these are all cases that, on Parfit's view, are equivalent). Let us now look briefly at a group of mental states that are not related to our conscious life history by the direct psychological relations that matter for Parfit, but that we treat as though they were. The beliefs and desires of our unconscious subsystems, though they may be causally continuous with our conscious experiences, are not in the relevant sense psychologically continuous with them. We do not, for example, remember such unconscious mental states, nor do they contribute to our actions in the way that our consciously accessible beliefs and desires do. Thus, given Parfit's understanding of what matters, we should dissociate ourselves from the effects of such states on our behavior.

In spite of the lack of psychological continuity, however, we do not consider ourselves free to disown such beliefs, desires, and their effects. These unconscious states are as much a part of the self as the conscious states, and we do ordinarily assume responsibility for their consequences. Thus not only do we have different reactions to cases that should be equivalent on Parfit's view; we have similar reactions to cases that should be significantly different.

There is a possible reply that Parfit might find tempting. Parfit might claim that we are responding on a case by case basis to irrelevant features of the examples. Given Parfit's views about which features are relevant, this is what he must say to explain the variety of our responses. The difficulty is that Parfit has no explanation of which irrelevant features elicit our responses and why such responses are elicited by those features. I do not intend to suggest that such an explanation is impossible. I shall suggest, however, that when we attempt to explain why these responses are forthcoming, we shall find that the explanation undermines the claim that the features to which we are responding are, in fact, irrelevant to identity and survival.

3   Nonautonomous Access Relations

The problem for Parfit stems from his inability to explain our intuitive responses to the puzzles of personal identity. I shall now outline a different theory in order to account for the diversity of these reactions. But the objections so far have been largely addressed to Parfit's view and not to the reductionist view in general. And given the range of causal conditions that a proponent of reductionism might require for identity or survival, the emphasis on Parfit might seem unjustified. On Parfit's view, as we have seen, the only condition necessary for survival is that the degree of psychological connectedness and continuity is sufficiently high; it is not necessary that it should be caused in the usual way or even in a way that is reasonably reliable. Such a view is arguably the minimal version of reductionism. Thus the assumption that the problems for Parfit are problems for reductionism in general may seem unwarranted.

There are two reasons, however, why the emphasis on Parfit's version of reductionism should not be a drawback. First, a number of the cases we have looked at raise problems not only for Parfit but also for reductionists who claim that survival requires psychological connections that hold in virtue of either reliable or even normal causal processes. This is true in the memory-switch case (example 1), the future-pain case (example 2), and the California-therapy case (example 3), because the causal explanation of the psychological connections is the same in all three cases, while our reactions differ. Second, suppose that Parfit's claim that the question of survival depends only on the existence of psychological connections—regardless of whether they are reliably caused—is false. (It is at any rate open to serious question.) None of the examples we have looked at, however, except the version of the teletransportation case (example 6) in which the creation of the replica is accidental, involves a cause that is unreliable. And although all the examples involve abnormal causes, the claim that the normal cause is necessary seems hard to sustain. If there are no facts about personal identity and survival over and above the facts about psychological connections and their underlying causes, then it is hard to see how the normality of these causes could be what matters. The details of the actual causal processes may be inaccessible and may be quite different from what we now take them to be. Thus if psychological connectedness, reliably caused, were not enough to ensure survival (i.e., to ensure that what matters to us is preserved), it is difficult to see how requiring that the causal processes should be normal could possibly help.

This argument raises a serious difficulty. Suppose we abandon, as I have suggested in section 1 that we should, the intuitions supporting nonreductionism. What further facts, besides the facts available on Parfit's version of reductionism (or on one of the alternative versions, such as the one according to which psychological continuity requires that the causal relations be normal), could explain those variations in our responses that raise the problems for Parfit? What further facts are there, in other words, to account for the variety in the data? Once we abandon nonreductionism, the cases that cause problems for Parfit seem to raise difficulties for which none of the resources that remain are adequate.

This problem is not insurmountable if we recognize that there is an alternative to all the versions of reductionism we have considered so far. Let us begin by reformulating Parfit's characterization of reductionism in terms of supervenience in one of its senses.[5] Reductionism will then entail that fixing some set of impersonal facts fixes the personal facts as well. If we refer to the facts that do the fixing as the supervenience base, the thesis is that the personal facts have their supervenience base in some set of impersonal facts. This way of reformulating reductionism allows us to distinguish clearly between two distinct components of Parfit's characterization. The first is the claim that the fact of a person's identity over time just consists in a set of impersonal facts. The second is the claim that the facts of a person's existence consist in facts about the existence of a brain and a body together with facts about the occurrence of a series of interrelated physical and mental events. Whereas Parfit's first claim places no limits on the impersonal facts contained in the supervenience base, the second claim limits the supervenience base to facts about the mental and physical events associated with that person's body (or, more accurately, the impersonal facts associated with the body of the person in question and those associated with the bodies of any competitors who may have claims to being that person at other times; I shall assume in what follows that the body includes the brain). In order to distinguish these two claims, I shall call the first *weak reductionism* and the second *strong reductionism*. (Each thesis has two versions, one of which is a claim about personal identity and one of which is a claim about survival.)

> *Weak reductionism regarding identity (survival)*   The fact as to whether person B is the same person, existing at a later time, as person A (is a survivor of A) supervenes on impersonal facts.

> *Strong reductionism regarding identity (survival)*   The fact as to whether person B is the same person, existing at a later time, as person A (is a survivor of A) supervenes on impersonal facts associated with the bodies of A and B and the bodies of any competitors of B who may have claims to being identical with (a survivor of) A.

Parfit and most other proponents of reductionism are committed to strong reductionism regarding both identity and survival. (In fact, as

I shall point out later, Parfit is committed to an even stronger claim regarding survival.) I shall argue, however, that if strong reductionism is true in either of its versions, it is true for reasons that are very different from those normally cited in its support.

The strong reductionist claim that limits the supervenience base to the psychological and physical makeup of all the relevant competitors involves the following (ordinarily implicit) assumption: while such relations of psychological access as one's memory of past actions and one's intentions regarding future actions matter for identity and survival, it is *only* such internal access relations that do. Suppose the assumption turns out to be wrong. In such a case the following strategy would be possible. We could explain the differences in our responses to cases that are equivalent on Parfit's view by reference to differences in the relations between person stages that are not found among the internal access relations. On the view I shall suggest, the relations between person stages relevant to survival would include both internal and external relations. Thus it is the assumption that all the relevant relations are internal that I shall now call into question.

The notion of an internal access relation requires some explanation. Let us say that a mode of access to past events or actions or a mode of access to (including control of) present or future events or actions is *autonomous* if and only if it is possessed by all possible functionally normal adults. Thus one's access via memory to the event of one's falling from a bicycle at the age of six is via an autonomous mode of access, because access of this type is shared by all actual and possible functionally normal adults. Imagine, however, a subject with an apparent memory of such an actual incident that has been produced on the basis of otherwise inaccessible memory traces by a neurophysiologist aided by a computer. This mode of access is shared not by all functionally normal adults but only by those living in societies that have the technological capacity (and have made the necessary social arrangements) to make such access possible. Hence, this mode of access is *non*autonomous. Similar remarks apply to one's ability to form an intention on which one's future self will act. Formed in the usual way, this intention provides an autonomous source of access to one's future self; implanted directly in that future self by a hypnotist acting on one's present orders, the intention provides a form of access that is nonautonomous. It is this notion of autonomy that I shall use to explain the sense in which both the proponents of nonreductionism and the proponents of strong reductionism assume that the access relations relevant to identity and survival are internal. Both groups assume that the relevant relations are autonomous in the sense defined.

The solution to the problems for Parfit turns on the existence of modes of access that are nonautonomous. My claim will be that reference to differences in nonautonomous access relations can explain differences in our responses to examples that are equivalent where autonomous access relations are concerned. The examples of nonautonomous access relations involving the implantation of memories and intentions by neurophysiologists and hypnotists provide almost no clue, however, as to how such relations might figure in the examples that cause Parfit difficulties. The only kinds of access ordinarily discussed in connection with such examples are memories and intentions, and, as we have seen, these are normally autonomous. Thus we need a general characterization of access with the following consequence: a significant number of our most important sources of access to our future selves—both in the problem cases for Parfit and in the normal cases—are nonautonomous. It may help, then, if we consider what access amounts to in contexts unrelated to personal identity. Suppose we think of access in the context of governmental policy. The two most basic components of this kind of access are knowledge and control. Someone who has very little notion of the workings of government and the kinds of governmental actions that are feasible will have little meaningful access to public policy. Similarly, someone who understands the general workings of government but lacks any knowledge of the constraints imposed by the actual circumstances will lack significant access to governmental decisions. Even someone well informed, however, may lack access in the relevant sense if he or she cannot exercise influence over those in power. Such knowledge could not be translated into the power to have his or her desires and intentions determine policy. In the remainder of this section I shall use this general conception of access to examine a variety of forms—both autonomous and nonautonomous—that access relations may take in the kinds of cases that cause problems for Parfit.

Consider again the teletransportation case (example 6). In certain possible worlds one has what might be called teletransporter extensions, that is, persons whose presence at the terminal end of a teletransporter has an appropriate explanation in terms of one's own presence at the initial end. In all those worlds in which one has a teletransporter extension, there are certain access relations between oneself and one's extension in virtue of the normal functional makeup one has in common with one's extension. One has access to (and in particular can exercise control over) a teletransporter extension by forming intentions to perform certain actions after the extension comes into existence. One can also exercise control by cultivating long-term dispositions to behave in certain ways. The teletransporter extension, of course, has access to one via memory. Since these relations hold for all functionally normal subjects and their extensions, they are autonomous.

Contrast this with the kinds of access relations that exist between oneself and one's descendants. If one is determined that a child, grandchild, or more distant descendant should perform a certain action, one can invoke reasons, engage in persuasion or bribery, indulge in intimidation or brainwashing, issue orders or threats, or rely on respect or the force of habit. Each of these strategies depends on the specific features of particular societies, and none can be effected merely in virtue of one's normal functional makeup. Hence these strategies for exercising control yield sources of access that are *non-autonomous*. And most of these sources of nonautonomous access that are available in the case of one's descendants will also be available, with minor variations, in the case of one's teletransporter extensions. Although many of these strategies would be difficult to effect directly where a teletransporter extension is concerned, most would be possible to arrange with the help of other people. Thus the teletransportation case (unlike the case involving one's descendants) exhibits a variety of both autonomous and nonautonomous relations.

The double-transplant case (example 4) provides a second example of the significance of the distinction between autonomous and nonautonomous relations. Those who accept strong reductionism regarding survival, must suppose that the claim to be someone in whom we survive is equally strong, whether the claim is made by one of the two recipients of one of our brain hemispheres or by the person who remains when we have one hemisphere removed and destroyed. But such an analysis is not plausible except on the assumption that only autonomous access relations are relevant to survival. This is because, while each of the two resulting persons in the double-transplant case has the same autonomous relations to us as the single resulting person in the hemisphere-removal case, the nonautonomous relations may differ substantially.

To see how the single-transplant case and the double-transplant case might differ with respect to nonautonomous access relations, consider a third example in which the departure from the single-transplant case is more extreme. In the multiple-fission case (example 5) in which one splits into a thousand or ten thousand replicas (as in the single- and double-transplant cases), all of our autonomous access relations are preserved. However, many of the external sources of access that one would normally have to a single future extension would be absent in such a case of massive replication. An important source of knowledge about our future behavior stems from our knowledge of our future environment—the people to whom we have significant relations, the roles we play, the problems they present, and the opportunities they offer. The difficulty in the multiple-fission case is that an environment so defined could never absorb the number of replicas in question. People of significance to us could not maintain personal relations with each of our replicas. Nor could *we* maintain the pattern of concern that characterizes our relations to our future selves for this many future extensions. Moreover, this number of replicas would be unable to share the roles we play or the opportunities we anticipate. Hence, our ability to predict our future actions and experiences on the basis of our knowledge of our environment would be lost—as would our ability to control such actions and experiences on the basis of our present control of the environment. In the double-transplant case, the loss of nonautonomous access through duplication might or might not be of crucial significance. But in the case of multiple fission, the replication involved would destroy the major sources of our nonautonomous access to our future selves.

4   The Intrinsic/Extrinsic Distinction

The multiple-fission case (example 5) provides a model of the strategy I shall adopt in section 5 in dealing with the problems raised by strong reductionism. These problems stem from the fact that if strong reductionism is true, there is no appropriate explanation of our intuitive reactions to a number of puzzle cases. That is, there is no explanation of our reactions by reference to what, if strong reductionism is true, are the relevant factors—the physical and causal continuities and the autonomous access relations. My strategy in section 5 will be to examine these cases in the light of the nonautonomous access relations to determine whether they might provide a better set of explanations of our intuitions. Proponents of strong reductionism, however, have suggested a number of principles that, if true, would rule out nonautonomous access relations as relevant to identity and survival. In this section, then, I shall consider whether these principles really do preclude an explanation of our intuitions in nonautonomous terms.

To see what is involved in explaining our responses to difficult cases by reference to nonautonomous access relations, consider once again the example of the teletransporter (example 6). Among the possible sources of nonautonomous access of the subject who steps into the machine to the subject who steps out are the following. First, there is the legal title of the subject stepping out to the possessions of the person who stepped in. If legal title is preserved, then the initial subject can control to a large extent the environment of the terminal subject by providing for that subject. Second, there are the legal and social relations of the individual at the terminal location and the persons who figure importantly in the life of the individual at the initial end. Suppose that the terminal individual remains married to the spouse of the initial individual, that he or she has the same family ties, and that he or she is a member of the same groups, a citizen of the same country, and a friend of the same individuals. This will increase not only the information that the initial subject will have about the terminal subject but also the initial subject's ability to plan and control the terminal subject's future. Third, there is a source of nonautonomous access in the general contractual rights and obligations of the terminal subject. If these remain intact, there is a further source of rational control for the person contemplating the process.

Whether we intuitively think of the person at the terminal location as a copy of the original person (and in one's own case whether one thinks of the person as a copy of oneself) depends, on the view I am suggesting, to a large extent on how we imagine other people will respond. If the process is described as a means of transportation, then we are thinking of a society in which the subject at the terminal end is taken to be the original and not merely a copy. If personal identity and survival are determined in part by external factors of the kind under consideration, then it is not far from the truth to claim that in a society in which teletransportation is interpreted as transportation, it *is* transportation.

Explaining the puzzle cases in terms of the relevance of nonautonomous access, then, has the consequence that the members of one society might survive teletransportation whereas the members of another would not. This claim, however, is open to objections both from those who think that teletransportation must preclude survival and those who think that in such cases survival is guaranteed. It is a common response among philosophers, for example, to suppose that a society that interprets teletransportation as transportation must be mistaken. According to this response, teletransportation is always incompatible with the preservation of personal identity. The response is based on considerations like the following. Suppose the machine that disperses the particles of the person at the initial location fails. In such a case the person who is still at the initial location exists simultaneously with the person at the terminal location. Since the former, it is alleged, is obviously identical with the original subject, the person at the terminal end must be a copy. It is then concluded that the person at the terminal end must be a copy *even when the machine functions correctly.*

A similar objection involves the fact that even if the particles of the subject at the initial end are dispersed, the information about the particles might be transmitted to two terminal locations. Two persons would then be created, each with the same relation to the original. Since they could not both be identical with the original and since there are no grounds to choose between them, neither one could be identical with the person at the initial end. And because in the case where the machine works, the relevant relation between the initial subject and the terminal subject is the same as in the case in which it does not, neither relation is one of identity.

These arguments, due in large part to Williams, rely on principles like the following:

> *Principle 1*   Whether a future person will be me must depend only on the intrinsic features of the relation between us. It cannot depend on what happens to other people.[6]

This principle counts against our regarding the person who steps out of the teletransporter as identical with the person who stepped in. For even in the case in which the teletransporter works correctly, it could have failed to disperse the particles of the person who stepped in. And if it had failed, we would, Williams claims, surely count the person remaining at the initial end as identical with the person who stepped in. Thus, suppose that in cases in which the teletransporter worked, it preserved identity. Then whether the person at the initial location when the switch was thrown was identical with the person at the terminal end would depend on whether the person at the initial end continued to exist past the time the switch was thrown. Hence the assumption that the teletransporter could ever preserve identity violates principle 1. Given his commitment to principle 1 and the fact that he does not distinguish personal identity and survival, I shall assume that Williams is a proponent of the following thesis in the form that concerns survival as well as the form concerning identity.

> *Very strong reductionism regarding identity (survival)*   The fact as to whether person B is the same person, existing at a later time, as person A (is a survivor of A) supervenes on impersonal facts associated with the bodies of A and B. It does not depend on facts about any other people.

Thus, whereas for the strong reductionist, identity (survival) supervenes on the autonomous relations between A, B, and any relevant competitors, for the very strong reductionist, like Williams, identity (survival) supervenes on the autonomous relations between A and B alone.

Whereas Williams would object to the claim that a society or culture might construe the teletransporter correctly as transportation, Parfit would object to the claim that a society might view it correctly as death, at least where this is taken to be incompatible with survival. Parfit is committed to the claim that teletransportation always guarantees survival, regardless of how it is construed by those involved. For Parfit, the fact that the particles of the subject at the initial teletransportation location could have failed to disperse and the fact that more than one duplicate could have been made are irrelevant to what matters, namely survival. Parfit holds this even though he holds the analogue of Williams's principle 1 for survival. That is, he holds the following:

> *Principle 2*   Whether my relation to some future person P contains what matters depends only on the intrinsic features of the relation between us. It cannot depend on what happens to other people.

This amounts to holding very strong reductionism regarding survival. Parfit can hold both these theses, because he allows that survival need not be one-one. (Where identity is concerned, Parfit rejects very strong reductionism and principle 1 [*Reasons and Persons*, pp. 266–273].) And given that the teletransporter preserves psychological continuity, Parfit's claim that survival need not be one-one, together with his claim that psychological continuity is what matters regardless of its cause, yields the conclusion that in cases of teletransportation, survival is always assured.

Like Parfit, I reject principle 1. A case of fission in which one of the duplicates is immediately destroyed might well be a case in which one's identity is preserved. This is possible even though if that duplicate had lived, one would not have been identical with either duplicate but would (at best) have survived in both. But unlike Parfit, I also reject principle 2. Not only can one's identity with some future person depend on what happens to other people, but whether that person's existence preserves what matters to one (i.e., whether one survives as that person) can depend on other people as well. As we saw in section 3 in the multiple-fission case (example 5), whether what matters is preserved may depend on how many future persons are psychologically continuous with one's present self. Too many duplicates may prevent what matters from being preserved, even though the intrinsic relations between one's present self and each of the duplicates do not seem significantly different from what they are in the normal case. This is a case in which the others who make a difference are competitors. Another such case that we have looked at is the defective-teletransporter case (example 7). Consider the person created in a far-flung corner of the universe many years hence. Given that a normal duplicate is also created, one might plausibly feel that the existence of the more remote duplicate matters scarcely at all. In the absence of such a normal duplicate, however, one might invest in the more remote duplicate, who would represent one's only chance of survival, something like the concern one usually reserves for one's ordinary future selves.

In addition to providing the candidates for our future selves, other people provide the means in virtue of which we gain nonautonomous access to such selves and their competitors. If, for example, there were a social convention concerning cases of multiple duplication whereby one of the duplicates inherited the entire network of social relations, one might then regard oneself as surviving in that duplicate and regard the others as largely irrelevant. Such a convention, after all, would prevent just that situation that made it plausible in the case without the convention to suppose that one did not survive, namely the situation in which none of the thousands of duplicates could inherit any substantial portion of one's significant relations to others.

This rejection of principle 2 is not without precedent. Robert Nozick has claimed that whether what matters to one is preserved in the existence of some future person *P does* depend on who the competitors of *P* are (*Philosophical Explanations*, p. 63). In other words, Nozick rejects very strong reductionism regarding survival as well as identity. Even for Nozick, however, the question depends only on the autonomous relations between oneself and the various candidates for being one's future self. Thus, for Nozick, strong reductionism is true regarding both identity and survival. On my view, even this claim is false. Strong reductionism is false for both identity and survival. Whether survival or identity is concerned, weak reductionism provides the best account. Since principles 1 and 2 are intuitively plausible, however, I shall provide two more variations on the future-pain case (example 2) to show that the intrinsic/nonintrinsic distinction cannot bear the strain to which Parfit's theory subjects it.

For Parfit, anxiety is not an appropriate response to the future-pain case, in which one's torture will be preceded by a memory and personality switch. Once the amnesia and the personality change have been effected, the psychological continuity and connectedness, which for Parfit are what matters, have been completely destroyed. One has no more reason to fear pain that will be felt by such a subject than to fear pain that will be felt by a perfect stranger.

The normal case, in contrast, is one in which psychological continuity and connectedness remain intact. In the normal case, if one experiences a period of intense pain, one is psychologically connected to, and continuous with, the earlier self that anticipates the pain. Such connections exist in virtue of both one's conscious occurrent memories of one's earlier self and one's dispositions to form such conscious memories as occasions arise. The same is true of the continuity between the personality of the earlier self and that of the later self. This continuity is manifest in the similarity of occurrent episodes of thought and behavior, but it is also manifest in the similarity of the dispositions underlying such episodes. One's relation to the future person stages that are to suffer the pain might, however, be somewhat different. Consider the following sequence of cases.[7]

Example 8: the no-occurrent-memories case   Suppose one knew that one would be tortured at some future date. One might believe with good reason that once the ordeal began, one would be too preoccupied with the immediate sensations of pain to entertain conscious memories of any prior experience. This thought, if it occurred, would be unlikely to provide any consolation. Whether one consciously reflects on any of one's past experiences is likely to be a function of the pacing of the ordeal and the presence or absence of any reminders of the past. And such factors seem irrelevant to the question of how painful the experience would be. Nor is it plausible to attach to factors such as these the importance that Parfit wants to attach to identity and survival. The same line of reasoning applies to the conscious manifestations of one's characteristic personality traits.

Example 9: the undetected-memory-switch case   In this case, imagine suffering the psychological discontinuity described in the future-pain case (example 2). At the flip of a switch, one's memories and personality are replaced by delusory memories and a new personality. The difference in this case is that the switch is thrown at the same time the pain begins and one's conscious experience is as described in the no-occurrent-memories case (example 8). Hence, there will be no conscious manifestation of the psychological difference induced when the switch is flipped. Thus, like the last change, this change from the normal case should produce no rational grounds for consolation in thinking of the future pain.

Example 10: the sporadic-occurrent-memories case   In the final variation, imagine either that the switch is flipped shortly before the pain starts, that the ordeal is paced slightly more slowly, which allows a few minutes of relief, or that there are more reminders of the past. Although this makes a difference in one's conscious experience, this difference seems too trivial to provide a plausible justification for viewing this prospect more optimistically than either the normal case or the other two variations on the normal case (examples 8 and 9). This case, however, simply *is* the future-pain case (example 2), with regard to which Parfit is committed to claiming that one has no reason to fear the painful experience. The problem is that the importance of the difference between the normal case (in which anxiety about the future pain is justified) and the future-pain case (in which it is not) seems to dissolve on examination. Since this is the most central case of the kind of intrinsic difference that Parfit thinks matters to survival, his assumption that only such intrinsic differences can matter seems unwarranted.

5   *Nonautonomous Relations and the Explanation of Our Intuitive Judgments*

The question that I now want to consider is whether reference to nonautonomous relations can solve the original problems for proponents of the strong reductionist claim that what matters depends only on autonomous features. These problems arose because this claim made it impossible to explain our differing intuitions regarding the three versions of the memory-switch case (examples 1 to 3). It should be clear by this point that these three examples, though equivalent as regards what Parfit and Williams think matters, are likely to suggest very different situations where nonautonomous access relations are concerned.

The description of the original memory-switch case (example 1) not only leaves open the possibility that the nonautonomous access relations are inherited by the person who inherits the memories, it encourages this assumption. This claim is best explained by reference to what psychologists refer to as default assignments. In understanding the stories that make up these examples, we adopt assumptions that are not strictly given in the stories themselves, assumptions that are subject to revision as new information comes in. And in the absence of any other cues, it is natural to assume that the body that inherits one's memories and intentions will have roughly the same capacity to act on those intentions and realize one's projects as any of one's normal future selves. This is a reasonable assumption for those whose projects and relations to others are not importantly tied to their particular bodily makeup. Thus the first example encourages us to assume that the relation between autonomous access and nonautonomous access is fixed. There is nothing to suggest what is nonetheless a real possibility: that autonomous and nonautonomous access may come apart and that someone who inherits all of one's social relations may be more likely to carry on one's relationships and commitments and to realize one's intentions and projects than someone who inherits one's psychological makeup.

In the future-pain case (example 2), by contrast, the normal relation between autonomous access and nonautonomous access cannot be taken as given. If you are told that *you* will experience amnesia and be given delusive memories and new personality traits, there is a clear contrast established between the first-person and third-person perspectives on your identity. From the point of view of the people in charge and, by implication, the outside world generally, the person with your body remains you in spite of the loss of autonomous access. (This is the significance of the fact that people in the story refer to the person who will suffer as "you.")

The California-therapy case (example 3), like the original memory-switch example, strongly suggests that autonomous access and nonautonomous access are present or absent together. The external perspective that the example suggests is not one in which you are tortured for your own long-term good. Rather, it is one in which your body and brain are manipulated in various ways during periods in which you remain unconscious.

Notice that if we have an explanation of the fact that the changes in the future-pain case provide no consolation, we also have an explanation of the two variants of the future-pain case: the no-occurrent-memories case (example 8) and the undetected-memory-switch case (example 9). In both these cases the intrinsic or autonomous changes are less important than the continuity of the nonautonomous relations. Whether it is we who are suffering depends in part on whether those around us can be expected to respond as though it is. In the undetected-memory-switch case and the no-occurrent-memories case, there is no reason at all for an outside observer not to feel that it is the original subject who is being made to suffer; nothing accessible to an ordinary observer in either case would reveal anything unusual. This contrasts with the California-therapy case, in which it is relatively easy to dissociate the subject who suffers from the original subject. Not only does the original subject return unharmed with no memories of any painful experience, but our access to the suffering is mediated by the medical personnel, for whom the psychological dispositions of the person who suffers seem most significant. Compared with the California-therapy case, the sporadic-occurrent-memories case (example 10) provides fewer barriers to nonautonomous access and less support for dissociation where the subject who suffers is concerned. An emphasis on how little significance the memory switch may have for one's conscious experience under torture suggests an external perspective in which one would not seem significantly different to others. It may also suggest a society in which the facts about one's conscious experiences, rather than the facts about one's psychological dispositions, are highly accessible and salient. In any event, there is no suggestion, as there is in the original memory-switch case and the California-therapy case, of a social practice and a perspective on oneself in which such dispositional changes would justify an attitude of indifference to the prospect of the future pain.

As a final test of the hypothesis that nonautonomous access relations matter, consider two more examples.

Example 11: the realistic-nightmare case   Suppose that you are told by a psychologist, on the basis of a neurophysiological theory and a brain scan, that you have had and will continue to have terrifying nightmares, which you never remember. Unlike ordinary dreams, however, these nightmares have no adverse consequences for your waking experiences and in fact tend to have positive effects. If Parfit is right, whether you should be anxious ought to depend on the content of the nightmares. If your responses to situations in the dreams are what your actual responses would be, if the characters in the dreams correspond closely to people you actually know, and if the past incidents you seem to remember actually occurred, then the psychologist's news should be serious cause for concern. This is because from the inside the case would be indistinguishable (until you are reawakened) from one in which the events actually occur. If, alternatively, your reactions in the dream are unlike your normal reactions, if the characters in the dream have no real-life counterparts, and if you seem to remember a very different past from your actual one, the psychologist's news should occasion no anxiety.

In fact, whether the news that one experiences such nightmares produces, and is justified in producing, anxiety seems completely independent of the details of the contents of the nightmares. Furthermore, most of us, if told that we experienced such nightmares, would not feel any great anxiety. This fact is explained by the tenuousness of the nonautonomous relations, in this society, between waking and sleeping subjects. Nothing in the example suggests that outside observers would have any reason to feel anxiety for us. As a result, we feel no anxiety for ourselves. And the tenuousness of such relations is independent of any facts we might be given about the detailed content of the nightmares.

Compare this case with a variation of the California-therapy case.

Example 12: the cut-rate-therapy case   In this case, one undergoes the procedure of the California-therapy case without either anesthesia or the benefit of any change in one's memories or personality. After the procedure the memories of the pain are erased, which leaves one satisfied with the therapy and eager to continue. In this kind of case, one would be very unlikely to continue the therapy once the facts were explained. But the difference between this case and the realistic-nightmare case is again a difference in the *non*autonomous access relations alone.

Thus it seems difficult to deny that such relations explain a wide variety of our actual responses.

In spite of the examples, however, the feeling is likely to linger that to take the role of nonautonomous access relations seriously in questions of personal identity is to risk changing the subject. What must ultimately matter, after all, is not the third-person perspective of others but the first-person perspective of the subject in question. To offer such an objection, however, is to miss an important ambiguity in the notion of the first-person point of view, as well as what is most important in the notion of nonautonomous access. On one possible construal, the first-person point of view is the subjective view: that is, the view defined by the set of facts that are independent of any objective facts whatsoever. The claim that personal facts must be manifest from such a perspective, then, is the nonreductionist claim that personal facts are subjective facts. And this claim, as we have seen, does not lead to a viable theory of personal identity. In another sense, though, the nonautonomous facts about a subject are a crucial part of that subject's first-person point of view. The perspective of others is *a* significant, if not *the* significant, component of our internalized self-image. Other people, real or imagined, and internalized, are an important part of our psychological continuity and of our own access to ourselves. Our internalized image of ourselves *as seen from the outside*—sleeping tranquilly and awakening refreshed—is part of what robs the realistic-nightmare case of its capacity to produce concern. It is this internalization of others in virtue of which our society's customs and practices are personal facts about what matters.

If nonautonomous access relations are relevant to the explanation of our intuitive judgments about personal identity, then we should reject Williams's principle 1, Parfit's principle 2, and Nozick's position. The claim that the personal facts about a given subject (including such facts as whether what matters is preserved in the existence of some future person P) supervene on facts about the intrinsic physical and psychological relations between that subject and P is too strong. And the claim is still too strong even if we include in the supervenience base all the facts about the intrinsic physical and psychological relations between the subject and all the relevant competitors of P. We should accept only some weaker supervenience claim that incorporates facts about the relations of nonautonomous access in the supervenience base.[8] The personal facts about a given subject do not supervene on any set of facts that does not include facts about the attitudes and feelings of others, the conventions and practices of the subject's society, and in some cases even the society's level of technological development.[9]

6   Metapsychological Relativism

These claims lead naturally to a position that I shall call *metapsychological relativism*. The metapsychological facts are those facts about personal identity, responsibility, and the unity and character of the self that are presupposed, rather than settled, by empirical psychology. The relativist claim, then, is that there could be two societies neither of whose members are either misinformed or irrational but whose social practices settle the significant metapsychological issues in radically different ways.

The teletransporter case (example 6) provides a particularly plausible example. Is there any rational way of choosing between a society in which the social conventions support the use of the teletransporter as transportation and a society in which they do not? It is true, of course, that given some relevant social conventions, it might seem irrational to adopt others. If, for example, the person at the terminal location retains the marital and family ties of the original person, then a convention by which contracts become null and void would seem at least highly unmotivated. The question, however, is whether, between a society in which all the institutions and practices support the use of the teletransporter as transportation and one in which none do, there would be any basis for a rational choice. And it is not apparent what the basis of such a choice could be. There seems, then, to be no neutral way of choosing between the two societies.[10]

Metapsychological relativism is not, of course, the facile conventionalism that claims that one simply decides what is to count as an extension of oneself. One cannot decide that by 'oneself' one means one's body, or alternatively one's psychology, except as a trivial stipulative definition. And there is clearly more at stake in the puzzle cases than that. To say that there is more at stake, however, is not to endorse a belief in the kind of transhistorical fact for which antirelativists have searched. We cannot decide as individuals what counts as our own continuation, any more than we decide as individuals what kind of society we shall inhabit. But as we determine collectively the form and shape of our society, we thereby also determine the boundaries of ourselves.

Acknowledgments

I am grateful for their comments and criticisms to the members of the audience at the Philosophy Department Colloquium at Columbia University where an earlier version of this paper was presented in April, 1985. I have also benefited from the criticisms and suggestions of Paul Boghossian, Mark Johnston, Derek Parfit, Carol Rovane, and Peter Unger.

Chapter 6

What Is It Like to Be a Homunculus?

---

1   The Problem of Conscious Subsystems

Of the concepts we ordinarily use in describing the mind, consciousness has seemed the least plausible candidate for philosophical analysis. This is particularly true with regard to naturalistic analyses,
which are intended to explain the relation between mental phenomena
on the one hand and those entities that form the subject matter of the
natural sciences on the other. This fact, however, has not prevented
a number of attempts at analyses that are not only naturalistic but that
characterize consciousness in functional terms—that is, in terms of
the causal relations between the sensory inputs, the behavioral outputs, and the internal states of psychological subjects. As instances
of such functionalist analyses have accumulated, some of the reasons
for the apparent intractability of consciousness have emerged. Of
these, one that raises particularly important issues has been pointed
out by Georges Rey.[1] The problem for functionalist analyses of consciousness, according to Rey—indeed, the problem for any naturalistic analysis—stems from the following fact: a survey of recent
characterizations of consciousness by philosophers and psychologists
reveals that most or all characterizations would be satisfied by information-processing devices that either exist now or would be trivial
extensions of devices that exist. Since Rey regards this consequence
as absurd, he concludes that the concept of consciousness is unlikely
to have a role in a genuinely scientific psychology.

In what follows, I shall argue that Rey's pessimism is unjustified.
There are plausible constraints on the ascription of consciousness that
are compatible with both naturalism and functionalism and that rule
out existing artificial information-processing devices as conscious. I
shall claim, however, that the following *is* true. Both functionalism
and naturalism, when combined with very weak assumptions about

Pacific Philosophical Quarterly 68 (1987): 148–174. Copyright 1987 by the Pacific Philosophical Quarterly. Reprinted with permission.

what is presupposed by an adequate cognitive psychology, have the following consequence: many of the sophisticated subsystems of a human subject—that is, many of the more sophisticated homunculi that make up such a subject—are themselves conscious. This is a consequence that I claim the functionalist (or the naturalist) must learn to live with. And it is a consequence that functionalists and naturalists *can* live with if they abandon a picture of consciousness that seriously inflates its significance. Consciousness must be sharply distinguished from self-consciousness. It is the claim that our sophisticated subsystems are *self*-conscious, not the claim that they are conscious, that would raise genuine difficulties. I shall argue, however, that this claim is not one that either functionalism or naturalism entails. Indeed, it is an advantage of the functionalist perspective that it makes clear the distinction between consciousness and self-consciousness and explains the extreme implausibility of ascribing self-consciousness to any of our subsystems.

Among the characterizations of consciousness of the kind surveyed by Rey, D. M. Armstrong's is a particularly clear example.

> Introspective consciousness, then, is a perception-like awareness of current states and activities in our own mind. . . . [This] inner perception makes the sophistication of our mental processes possible in the following way. . . . In any complex computing operation many different processes must go forward simultaneously: in parallel. There is need, therefore, for an over-all plan for these activities, so they are properly co-ordinated. . . . The co-ordination can only be achieved if the portion of the computing space made available for administering the over-all plan is continuously made "aware" of the current state of play with respect to the lower-level operations which are running in parallel. Only with this "feed-back" is control possible.[2]

Similar characterizations have been put forward by psychologists. Bernard Baars, for example, offers an account that gives a similar emphasis to the role of consciousness in achieving coordination.[3] In both cases, consciousness is explained in terms of a feedback relation between a set of specialized and autonomous processes, and a more global process that mediates between them. And as Rey points out, this is a relation that virtually every sophisticated information-processing device instantiates.[4] It is also a relation that is undoubtedly instantiated at many different levels of the human nervous system. Hence the relation will not be a feature that applies uniquely to the system as a whole. If this is all that consciousness amounts to, we shall be forced to the conclusion that a wide range of subsystems of our own nervous system, subsystems to which we have no introspective access, as well as many existing computer systems, are conscious. Call this the *problem of conscious subsystems.*

Suppose we supplement these characterizations of consciousness with the added condition that conscious subjects or systems must have either genuine beliefs and desires or genuine intelligence. This move would prevent our ascribing consciousness not only to our present artificial information-processing devices but to any such devices that might be designed or contemplated in the foreseeable future. There are, however, convincing examples of systems that satisfy even this stronger condition but that it seems very implausible to regard as conscious. Rey cites as examples "those unconscious neurotic systems postulated in so many of us by Freud" and "all those surprisingly intelligent, but still unconscious, subsystems for perception and language postulated in us by contemporary cognitive psychology."[5]

To these examples of intelligent but apparently unconscious systems, we might add the intelligent homunculi postulated by Dennett and Lycan in their homuncular versions of functionalism.[6] Dennett describes the artificial-intelligence researcher's application of the homuncular strategy as follows.

> His first and highest level of design breaks the computer down into subsystems, each of which is given intentionally characterized tasks; he composes a flow chart of evaluators, rememberers, discriminators, overseers and the like. These are homunculi with a vengeance; the highest level design breaks the computer down into a committee or army of intelligent homunculi with purposes, information and strategies. Each homunculus in turn is analyzed into *smaller* homunculi, but, more important, into *less clever* homunculi.[7]

Both the systems cited by Rey and these intelligent homunculi could be held to satisfy the earlier conditions on consciousness *and* to possess genuine beliefs or intelligence, without being conscious. Hence the characterization that consists in those earlier conditions together with the requirement that the subjects or systems in question possess genuine beliefs or intelligence is still not sufficient to capture consciousness.

This problem is by no means unique to functionalist theories. Since the subsystems of our nervous system have the same physical realization as the nervous system itself, those who think a system's physical realization is crucial in determining whether it has mental states are in no better position to claim that these subsystems are unconscious. This is in fact a problem for any theory according to which the idea of interacting subsystems with sophisticated capacities for processing information makes sense. In other words, it is a problem for any empirically adequate theory. The problem of conscious subsystems can be put in the following way. Psychological research has yet to uncover any functional structure that is unique to the human subject as a whole and that is plausibly regarded as necessary for consciousness. Furthermore, since the subsystems of the human subject will have the same type of physical realization as the system as a whole, there will not be a combination of a functional structure and a type of physical realization that distinguishes the system as a whole from all of its subsystems. Since our ordinary assumption is that consciousness *is* uniquely possessed by the system as a whole, we are faced with a dilemma. Either we have no idea what a theory of consciousness should involve, or we are left with the implausible consequence that some of our subsystems are themselves conscious *in* exactly the same way we are.

2   The Group Fusion

The conclusion Rey draws is a drastic one. According to Rey, the concept of consciousness is not likely to figure in a fully scientific psychology.[8] Consciousness, on his view, is not a term ripe for reduction: rather, it is ripe for elimination. Rey's arguments for the impossibility of a naturalistic theory of consciousness, however, contain at least one serious mistake that is crucial to his skeptical position. Rey claims,

> The capacity for "*self*-consciousness," or reflection on one's *own* thought processes will not be much help either. . . . If system *A* can have beliefs and preferences about some system *B*'s beliefs and preferences, . . . what possible obstacle could there be to its having beliefs and preferences about system *A*'s—that is—its own, beliefs and preferences? At most it might need a special functioning phoneme in its language of thought that would serve to link itself as a receptor of its inputs to itself as an originator of its outputs, rather as 'I' does in English. But this is just to put a particular constraint on its use of a particular phoneme.[9]

In other words, if the conditions that a naturalistic theory holds to be sufficient for consciousness are satisfied by intuitively unconscious systems, the problem could not be solved by supposing that we confuse consciousness and self-consciousness. According to Rey, then, we could not solve the problem for a theory of consciousness by accepting the following two propositions.

1. Naturalistic theories of consciousness raise *genuine* difficulties only if they entail that our intelligent subsystems are *self*-conscious and not merely conscious.

2. Our *apparent* difficulties with the claim that our intelligent subsystems are conscious can be explained by the fact that the *self*-consciousness of such subsystems *would* raise genuine difficulties and that we do not adequately distinguish between self-consciousness and consciousness.

The reason that such a solution to the problem could not succeed, Rey suggests, is that once the conditions required for consciousness are met, the conditions required for self-consciousness are too easily satisfied. If the addition of an appropriately constrained phoneme to a conscious system is sufficient to make it self-conscious, then this is clearly too trivial a difference to support the claim that whereas the consciousness of some of our subsystems would raise no philosophical problems, their self-consciousness would. Hence the strategy that proceeded by distinguishing consciousness and self-consciousness could not hope to resolve the problem for naturalistic theories that the concept of consciousness raises.

In what follows, I shall argue that the approach summarized in propositions (1) and (2) is essentially correct. Rey seriously underestimates the significance of the distinction between consciousness and self-consciousness when he treats it as equivalent to the presence or absence of a phoneme of the appropriate kind. It is this tendency of Rey's to minimize the difference between consciousness and self-consciousness, I shall claim, that makes the problems for a theory of consciousness seem insurmountable.

To see the significance of the distinction between consciousness and self-consciousness, consider the following example, which I shall call the *group fusion example*. Imagine that several human subjects are wired together in such a way that each one receives the sensory input from a single body distinct from the body of any individual subject. We can imagine that the subjects' bodies are immobilized and sustained by some form of automated life-support system. Thus the experiential input to each subject will be exactly the same. Let us assume that the condition that results when the subjects are wired together in this way is the only condition of which they have any memory or awareness (either conscious or unconscious).

The assumptions we have made so far guarantee that each subject will have the same perceptual experiences but not the same conscious intentions. Like any normal group of individuals, these subjects will have different innate capacities and dispositions; as a result, their responses to exactly the same history of inputs will vary. In particular, each individual on a given occasion may be disposed to form a somewhat different intention, even though each one finds himself or herself in exactly the same situation. The sense of 'same intention' that is at stake here is the fairly weak sense in which two functional duplicates in distinct but qualitatively indistinguishable environments will form the same intentions. If duplicate A, for example, forms the intention that would be expressed by saying 'I will now raise my arm', then at the same time duplicate B will form the intention that would be expressed by the same sentence. This sense of 'same intention' is weak, because A and B will *not* in general form intentions with the same propositional content; duplicate A's intention is an intention to raise *his* arm, whereas duplicate B's intention is an intention to raise not A's arm but his own. (To use a term of David Kaplan's, A and B will form intentions with the same character but not with the same content.[10]) Even in this weak sense, however, the subjects in the group as described so far will not necessarily form the same conscious intentions.

We can, however, construct an example in which the conscious intentions of all the subjects in the group *are* identical (that is, do express at least the same character) if we imagine either of two alternatives. On the *first alternative*, the subjects are wired to a computer programmed to mediate between either their unconscious intentions or their unconscious tendencies to generate conscious intentions (see figure 1). (Let us call these the *preconscious contributions* of the group members to the conscious intentions of the group.) The process of mediation works so as to ensure the satisfaction of two conditions. The first is just the condition that *at a given time* the intentions that reach the consciousness of any of the subjects are always the same. This would be accomplished by routing the different preconscious contributions of the members of the group through the mediation device, which would produce a single preconscious contribution as output. We would then route this output back to each of the members of the fusion, where it would be realized as the same conscious intention in each subject. This means that these conscious intentions can form the source of control over the common body and that each of the subjects will experience the body as under his or her conscious control. In other words, if one were a member of the group, one would never think 'Now I will remain standing and raise my arm' and find oneself inexplicably sitting down with one's hand in one's pocket. From the perspective of each of the individual subjects, his or her control over the common body will be indistinguishable from the kind of control over his or her body exercised by any normal subject.

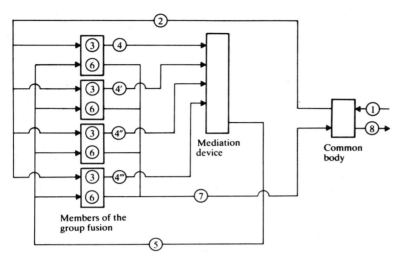

Figure 1
The group fusion. (1) Perceptual inputs to the common body. (2) Perceptual input signal to the members of the group fusion (the same for each member of the group). (3) The conscious perceptual experience produced in each of the group members by the perceptual input signal (the same for each member of the group). (4–4‴) Preconscious contributions to the group's intention (different for each member of the group in virtue of their functional differences). (5) Single preconscious contribution produced by the mediation device. (6) The conscious intention produced in each of the group members by the single preconscious contribution (the same for each member of the group). (7) Output to the motor system (the same for each member of the group). (8) Motor output of the common body.

The second condition is that the intentions that reach the consciousness of the subjects *over time* are not radically unstable and do not radically conflict, as they might otherwise do, given that they are the result of the contributions of all the different group members. At least this should be true under normal circumstances and within relatively short periods. This will ensure that each subject experiences his or her psychology as reasonably stable over time. Thus each one, from his or her own perspective, will not only enjoy the kind of continuity necessary for personhood but will also experience the sort of integration characteristic of a normal personality.

The problem that the mediation device is intended to solve is analogous to the problem in normal human subjects of maintaining the identity of the conscious intentions formed in the left and right brain hemispheres and ensuring that the intentions formed are consistent and stable over time. This problem arises if we assume *any* functional asymmetry between the two hemispheres and does not depend on any assumptions as to whether the asymmetry results in an "analytic" or an "intuitive" side to the brain. Any significant functional asymmetry will have the consequence that each brain hemisphere has somewhat different dispositions to form intentions on the basis of the *same* history of experience. Thus we can imagine the computer program mimicking whatever mechanism ensures this integration of the left and right hemispheres in normal subjects.

The *second alternative* for resolving conflicts between subjects over the formation of conscious intentions produces the same result without resort to any external computational mechanism. This should be possible in principle, since there clearly exist mechanisms by which the potential conflicts between the brain hemispheres are resolved. Thus it should be possible to wire the subjects together so that the same mediation mechanisms used to resolve conflicts between hemispheres in the formation of the conscious intentions of single subjects are used to resolve conflicts *between* subjects. We should be able to feed into the mediation mechanism of one of the subjects not only the inputs from that subject's two brain hemispheres but also those from the hemispheres of all the other subjects as well (though the mediation mechanism might have to be multiply instantiated—or the inputs routed via a system of loops and delays—if the mechanism were capable of handling only pairs of inputs at a time). The output of this device, as in the first alternative, would consist in a single preconscious contribution to the formation of a conscious intention. And we would route this output, again as in the first alternative, back to the individual subjects, where it would be realized as the same conscious intention (distinctly tokened) in each of the group members.

The mediation device on either alternative then ensures that the perceptual data, conscious intentions, and actions are the same for each subject. But this is probably not enough, given the functional differences between the subjects, to guarantee the kind of continuity and coherence *within* the set of mental experiences of each subject that seem to exist within ours. The description of the mediation device so far is compatible with the members of the group fusion forming intentions that are in no way related to their other thoughts, including the reasons that occur to them for choosing one action rather than another. Thus I am inclined to require that *all* preconscious contributions to conscious thought be handled by the mediation device in the same way. Preconscious contributions to conscious thought are all routed through the mediation device and the single output is realized as the conscious thought of each of the subjects. By thus ensuring that the conscious thoughts of all of the subjects are exactly the same, we make it possible to guarantee a high degree of coherence within the thought of each subject. And however this is done, it is apparently done successfully by whatever mechanism actually mediates between the two brain hemispheres.

In making the assumption that there is a great deal of coherence and continuity within the experience of each member of the fusion (and that there must, therefore, be a large overlap in their conscious experiences), I am not begging any empirical questions. This case is the *worst* case for both the functionalist and the naturalist. This is because the problematic consequence of functionalism and naturalism (that is, the consequence that many of our most sophisticated subsystems are conscious) is more damaging to the extent that we lack independent evidence that would make this antecedently unintuitive claim less implausible. In other words, this consequence is more damaging to the extent that we lack independent evidence for the kind of disunity that the picture of a collection of separately conscious subsystems carries with it. To the extent that such evidence is or becomes available, the problem Rey raises becomes that much *less* serious a challenge to the possibility of a naturalistic theory of consciousness.

3   The Distinction between Consciousness and Self-Consciousness

With the group fusion example we are in a position to draw a fundamental distinction between consciousness and self-consciousness. Each of the individual subjects will be fully conscious in the ordinary sense. This much is difficult to deny because of the extent of the continuity between ordinary subjects and the subjects included in the group fusion. None of the differences that do exist could plausibly be thought to render an otherwise conscious subject unconscious. Where the concept of self-consciousness is concerned, however, the picture seems significantly different. Each individual will, or course, engage in what he or she takes to be self-reference and will use the term 'I' in picking out the subject of certain past experiences, certain beliefs, desires, and intentions, and certain expectations for the future. Each one will also use 'I' to pick out the subject of certain external characteristics: having been in contact with certain people and things, having participated in certain events, and having played a certain causal role in the world. The problem is, of course, that each one will use exactly the same descriptions. It would be very misleading, in fact, to suppose that there is a separate self-assessment for each member of the group. Only one self-assessment will actually be delivered, and that is the one the subjects deliver jointly through the common body.

There are, of course, distinct tokens of this one self-assessment. Each subject will have his or her own token of the intention to produce the relevant utterances. With reference to these intentions, we can speak of different tokens of the self-assessment in question. Our doing so, however, will not count in favor of the self-consciousness of the subjects in the fusion if these are simply different tokens of a single intention to produce one self-assessment. And the intentions to express this self-assessment do belong to the same physical and functional types and are intentions to utter the same words. Are they, though, intentions to express the same propositions? And is the propositional content of each of the intentions the same?

There are at least some reasons for thinking that the answer to both questions is yes. If subject A and subject B in the group fusion each intend to utter a sentence about a friend named Smith, each will intend to refer to the same person. Each will therefore express the same proposition. Contrast this with the Twin Earth case, in which the subject on Earth and his or her Twin Earth counterpart each use the name Smith (with the same underlying descriptive content). In the Twin Earth case, each one will refer to a different person. Thus each will automatically express a different proposition. The same contrast between the Twin Earth case and the group fusion case seems to exist for all the usual sorts of entities in the external world—things, places, times, events, and so on—*other than* the subjects themselves. The interesting question is whether an individual subject in the group fusion can engage in first person self-reference and can refer to his or her thoughts and his or her brain states using the first person possessive in a way that distinguishes these thoughts and brain states from those of the other subjects.

The basic question, then, is this: When a conscious thought that would be expressed in an utterance containing the word 'I' (call this an I thought) occurs to one of the subjects of the group fusion (and hence to all of them), to whom does it refer? The answer I want to suggest is that each such thought token refers to the group as a whole rather than to the individual subject in whom the token occurs. We should recall first that the external and mental facts that give content to the use of 'I' are all shared. One ordinarily describes oneself as the person who did such and such, the person who thought such and such, or the person to whom such and such happened on a particular occasion. Such descriptions, however, could not pick out one subject of the group fusion as distinct from another. The individual subjects also cannot refer to themselves by referring to the mental-state tokens that *caused* the common body to behave in certain ways. As the example is framed, bodily movements are the result of causal overdetermination by mental-state tokens. Hence the usual ways of saying who one is fail for these subjects.

It might be objected that the descriptions we have imagined the subjects giving of themselves can all be expressed without the use of 'I', 'my', 'here', etc. A lunatic who imagines that he is Napoleon may try to refer to himself and fail in using the expression 'the Emperor of France in 1812'. In spite of his intention to refer to himself, the lunatic may well refer to Napoleon. Nonetheless, the lunatic refers to himself and not Napoleon in using 'I'. And it might be objected that just as the lunatic's difficulty in referring to himself via descriptions is no indication of a difficulty in referring to himself via demonstratives, so there is no evidence of a general problem of self-reference among the fusion subjects. However, this distinction between the use of descriptions and the use of 'I', which has a clear application in the case of the lunatic, is less easily applied in the case at hand. One can refer to oneself even though one is mistaken about almost all the objective facts about oneself, because 'I' refers to the speaker of the utterance (or the thinker of the thought) in which it occurs. In this case, the question of who the speaker of an utterance made by the common body *is* and the question of who the thinker of a thought that the individual subjects share *is* are just the questions at issue. Of course, it is possible to *claim* that the thinker of each individual thought token is the individual in whom that thought token occurs, on the grounds that such would be the case if the individuals were not fused. But the problem of determining the referent of an I thought tokened by one of the fusion subjects deserves a less question-begging response.

In the absence of substantive reasons for holding that the I thoughts tokened in each subject refer to that subject alone, the drawbacks of this assumption make it an unattractive one. The most serious objection to the assumption that the individual subjects refer to themselves in tokening I thoughts lies in the analogy between the group fusion example and the organization of the brain hemispheres in a normal subject. If we claim that the individuals in the group fusion can or do refer to themselves in tokening I thoughts, then we ought to claim that in entertaining I thoughts, our left hemisphere can or does refer to itself as distinct from the right hemisphere. And if the left hemisphere does refer to itself in tokening an I thought, what is it in virtue of which the person as a whole refers to himself or herself? This assumption, then, seems to lead to serious difficulties.

Furthermore, to suppose that we either could or do refer to a single hemisphere in using 'I' or in tokening I thoughts raises questions that are not all clearly intelligible. Can we think of ourselves as a single hemisphere rather than the unified system? If so, do we have to think of ourselves as being the left hemisphere, since that hemisphere is responsible for speech production? Or could we be mistaken in thinking we are responsible for the speech of the system as a whole? If the two hemispheres were separated, which one would we be?

The last question seems to raise special difficulties for the idea of restricting the reference of 'I' to a single hemisphere. Suppose that from the perspective of our normal state we imagine undergoing the following split-brain experiment. Suppose that our two brain hemispheres, after having their connections severed and in virtue of being given significantly different experiences, come to house different personalities and, presumably, different persons. The question of which of these two persons we would be is pretheoretically a genuinely puzzling one. And it may be a question that fails to make sense—or at least one for which there is no answer. There would be no puzzle, however, if in referring to ourselves we referred automatically to our left hemisphere alone. Thus the proposal that we refer to the left hemisphere exclusively seems unlikely to be correct. Furthermore, the assumption that we must refer to the left hemisphere, on the grounds that that hemisphere is responsible for speech, is largely arbitrary. And if we do not make this assumption, it is hard to see what possible grounds we could have for supposing that we refer to one hemisphere rather than the other.

Suppose, alternatively, that in using 'I' we normally refer to a system that includes both hemispheres. Could one hemisphere refer to itself if the other hemisphere were temporarily rendered unconscious? Consider the following thought experiment. Imagine you are told that your left brain hemisphere has been rendered unconscious and that your present experience is solely the result of processes in your right hemisphere. (Assume that although the two hemispheres are not functionally equivalent, they have comparable intellectual capacities and that they had the same information up to the point at which the left hemisphere lost consciousness.) Do these beliefs carry with them any temptation to suppose that the referent of your own use of 'I' is distinct from what it formerly was? The answer, I think, is no. And this counts against the proposal that members of the group fusion refer to themselves, given the analogy between the fusion members and the two brain hemispheres. To treat the normal case in the way that it is proposed that we treat the group fusion case is to suppose that there are already two persons involved even before the split occurs. And nothing in the description of either case seems to force us to such an unintuitive conclusion.

Besides the intuitions that support the claim that in tokening 'I' the fusion members fail to refer to themselves, there are two theoretical points that lend the claim support. First, although it is a commonplace that descriptive content does not determine reference, there must be some set of facts in virtue of which one's referent is fixed when it is not fixed by the content of the descriptions to which one has access. In the usual cases, facts about correct linguistic usage, facts about natural kinds, or facts known exclusively to experts may supplement or override the content of one's available descriptions in fixing one's referent.[11] But these facts seem to have no analogues, in the case of the group fusion, that would support the claim that each member's token of 'I' refers to that member. Of course, this might be denied. It might be argued, for example, that the tokens of 'I' refer to the individual members of the group because 'I', as tokened by such subjects, must refer to a single organism of the species *Homo sapiens,* and the individual members, unlike the group as a whole, are such organisms.[12] Or it might be claimed that 'I' always picks out a stream of consciousness. And it might also be claimed that the individual tokens of 'I' pick out the individual streams of consciousness in virtue of facts that are not available to the individual subjects. These alternatives do not seem to me promising, because it seems far more plausible to suppose that 'I' always picks out a *person.* And whether the members of the group fusion have a valid claim to personhood is exactly what I am calling into question.

This is not to claim, of course, that the referents of a subject's tokens of 'I' cannot vary independently of that subject's view of himself or herself from the inside. Imagine, for example, a member of the group fusion who is initially well informed about the structure of the group. Thus, on the present assumption, when this subject tokens 'I', she takes herself to be referring to the collective entity. Suppose, however, that the other members have gradually died off without her knowledge and that she is the only subject who remains. In this case it seems natural to say that she now refers to herself (together with the common body). But from the inside, her situation seems in no way different from what it was in the original group fusion. And this may tempt us to suppose that, contrary to the present assumption, in tokening 'I' she referred to herself all along. There will be less temptation to do so, however, if we recognize that there can be a discrepancy between the nature of the referent of 'I' and the descriptions that the subject in question would apply. In this case the discrepancy is easily explained in terms of the other descriptions the subject would apply and their relative importance. She takes herself to be, among other things, the *person* responsible for the changes brought about through the behavior of the common body. And since this belief seems more important than her mistakes about the details of the physical realization of her psychology, her referring to herself (together with the common body) seems in this case unsurprising, even on the assumption that she originally refers to the fusion.[13]

The same considerations seem to apply in the opposite case in which a single individual becomes, without his knowledge, a member of a group fusion. Suppose that the original subject is fused with several other subjects who have been made functionally equivalent to him as a result of being given his memories and psychology. (We can assume that the common body is either that of the original subject or that it is qualitatively indistinguishable from it.) In this case his own brain has become one highly redundant component of the system that realizes his psychology. Thus in this case it is plausible to think that the original subject's conception of himself picks out the fusion, even though this is again to credit a subject with a number of false beliefs about the way his psychology is realized.[14]

The second point about the fusion members' use of 'I' depends on the features of 'I' that distinguish it from the other terms we use in referring to ourselves. What sets first-person self-reference apart is the role that first-person beliefs play in mediating between perception and action. First-person beliefs are tied to action in a way that other beliefs are not, since one does not have to locate oneself to move oneself—such actions are normally basic. Thus, whereas the other things we refer to, if we are to be able to act on them, must be given to us under a description that relates them to our system of action and perception, this is not true when we refer to ourselves using 'I'. All that is required are the causal connections in virtue of which our perceptions generate I beliefs and our I beliefs, together with our desires, generate our basic actions.[15] And since the members of the group fusion share all the same perceptual inputs and have the same repertoire of basic actions, the pragmatic features that distinguish 'I' from other self-referential devices are shared. Thus to the extent that the referents of the group members' tokens of 'I' depend on the pragmatic features that make 'I' distinctive, there are no grounds to suppose that the tokens have different referents.

In arguing that the members of the group fusion are not self-conscious, I have appealed to a number of considerations that suggest that they do not engage in first-person self-reference. And these considerations are plausible ones. But it would not necessarily undermine the argument for the possibility of a naturalistic theory of consciousness if this appeal were to fail. Suppose that the group members *did* refer to themselves in tokening 'I' and were *in this sense* self-conscious. Since I shall argue on independent grounds in section 4 that the group members are not self-concerned, their referring to themselves would only show that self-consciousness in this sense does not guarantee self-concern. And if this is the case, then even the claim that the members of the group (and our most sophisticated subsystems) are self-conscious in this sense would not support any obviously unacceptable conclusions. It would not support, for example, the conclusion that the members of the group (and our sophisticated subsystems) had the same claim to rights, respect, and personhood as ordinary individuals.

The preceding arguments might seem open to the following objection. Our reason for thinking that the brain hemispheres are separately conscious depends on our intuitions about the group fusion example. But then it cannot be legitimate to appeal to our intuitions about whether the brain hemispheres refer to themselves in tokening 'I' (and about what *we* refer to in uttering 'I') in order to conclude that the members of the group do not refer to themselves. Regarding this objection there are two points to notice. First, the assumption that the two brain hemispheres are separately conscious is justified on independent grounds. They are conscious because we are conscious, and they are separately conscious because either one could become unconscious without the same thing happening to the other. Second, the objection misconstrues the strategy behind the group fusion example. In describing the organization of the group fusion, I have deliberately made it analogous to the organization of the two brain hemispheres in all respects that seem relevant. The two examples are essentially different perspectives on the same case. Neither has any theoretical priority over the other, and an adequate theory must give us a plausible account of both. And in the absence of any significant disanalogies, it must be the same account in each case. Therefore, it is legitimate to appeal, for any given question, to whichever example seems to support the strongest intuitions.

The claim that the individual subjects of the group fusion are conscious but not self-conscious leads to a number of questions. For example, is the group, as opposed to the individuals in it, conscious, self-conscious, or both? And suppose the group is either conscious or self-conscious. Since the group (on the interpretation according to which the mediation device is not a separate and artificial component) is nothing over and above the individuals that make it up, does this imply that consciousness or self-consciousness is nothing more than a kind of fiction? Is the lack of self-awareness of the individual subjects just a matter of ignorance of their situation? What would they need to become self-conscious as well as conscious?

We can begin by answering the question whether the lack of self-awareness of the fusion subjects is just a matter of ignorance of their objective situation. Again, the answer will depend on the analogy between the members of the group fusion and the two brain hemispheres of a normal subject. Since the two brain hemispheres may have a perfectly adequate conception of the objective facts of their own 'group fusion' without being self-aware, that is, aware of themselves as distinct subjects, the same is true of the fusion subjects. Ignorance of their objective situation plays no essential role in their lack of self-awareness. In other words, the illusion that each of the fusion subjects has that there is a single conscious subject in control of the common body plays no part in each subject's lack of self-consciousness.

The answer to the question of whether the group as a whole is either conscious or self-conscious, however, may be less immediately clear. Given that the group is nothing more than the individuals who make it up when the mediation device is not a separate component, the temptation is to think that the group is neither conscious nor self-conscious. It may seem no more plausible to call this group as a whole conscious or self-conscious than it does to ascribe these attributes to an arbitrary set of normal subjects. But although the group appears to be nothing over and above the individuals who make it up, the functional properties of the group as a whole are distinct from those of any particular individual. Though each individual entertains the same conscious thoughts, the unconscious contributions made to those thoughts are distinct in each subject.

Consider, for example, the output of the unconscious information-processing systems of a single subject S in the group, that is, the output of S that becomes the input to the group's mediation mechanism (see figure 2). Imagine that we reproduce the output continuously and route the reproduced output into the mediation mechanism of a subject, S^*, who is otherwise unconnected with the group fusion. Suppose that S^*'s mechanism is one that has been rigged so that it always produces conscious intentions in S^* corresponding to S's inputs. S^*'s behavior, then, will be significantly different, given the same environmental inputs, from the behavior of the common body. S^* will, in fact, quickly cease to function. Since the members of the group fusion differ functionally, and since the mediation mechanism for the group responds to inputs besides those of S, the outputs from the group to the common body on the one hand and the outputs from S to S^* on the other will differ. This means that even if the common body and S^*'s body are located in qualitatively identical environments, their movements in those two environments will be distinct. Hence the inputs from the environment to the common body and the inputs from the environment to S^* will be different. Since only the inputs to

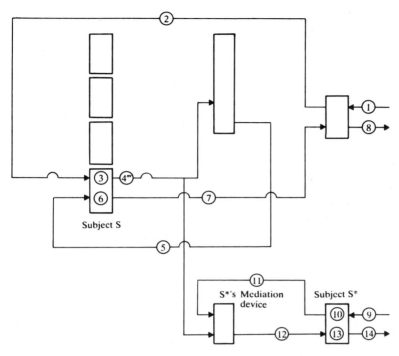

Figure 2
Subjects S and S^*. (9) Perceptual inputs to S^*. (10) Conscious perceptual experience produced in S^* by the perceptual inputs. (11) $S^{*\prime}$s preconscious contribution to $S^{*\prime}$s conscious intention. (12) The output of $S^{*\prime}$s mediation device (which is always identical to $4^{\prime\prime\prime}$). (13) The conscious intention produced in S^* by the output of $S^{*\prime}$s mediation device. (14) $S^{*\prime}$s motor outputs.

the *common body* are received by S, however, S will be unable to take account of the situation of S^* to the extent that it differs from that of the common body. Hence the outputs from S to S^* will become increasingly irrelevant to S^*'s environmental situation. They could include messages to grasp objects that are not within reach, to walk forward while sitting down, or to keep walking while immobilized before a solid object. Given the radically different responses in initially identical environments, the functional system that consists in the group and the functional system that consists in S and S^* are clearly distinct.

The malfunctioning of S^*'s body is an indication not only of the functional differences between the group as a whole and the individual subjects but also of what the group has that the individuals lack: self-consciousness or self-awareness. The behavior of S^* is an external manifestation of precisely what the individual is unaware of in the group fusion: his or her own contribution to the group enterprise. The individual subject is unaware not only of what his or her own output would be in isolation from the group but also of what, if that output were externally manifest, the subsequent input and hence his or her own experience would be. It is because of this lack of awareness (which arises in virtue of the collective responsibility for the behavior of the common body and hence for the sensory feedback from that body) that S^*, given S's outputs alone, would cease to function. The outputs and inputs of which the individual is aware are not his or her own but those of the group. The individual, then, is group-conscious. Only the group as a whole is self-conscious.

The example of the group fusion should make it clear why Rey's characterization of self-consciousness is inadequate. Each individual subject is conscious. Each is in fact separately conscious in the sense that any one of them could be conscious even though the others were not. But no subject is conscious of himself or herself as a separate or distinct self. The subjects are individually conscious but only collectively self-conscious. Each, however, has a perfectly adequate grasp of the syntax, semantics, and pragmatics of the word 'I'. Hence there is more to self-consciousness than Rey's account allows. In particular, there is room for a distinction between consciousness and self-consciousness that will give us an opening in approaching the problem for a theory of consciousness.

4   The Reevaluation of Conscious Experience

To see the significance of this lack of self-consciousness in an individual subject in the group fusion, imagine that a member of the group fusion is forced to choose among the following alternatives. The first alternative is an operation that would destroy the subject making the choice but that would have no effect on the capacities or the personality of the group as a whole. (It is a feature of the case, in other words, that all the significant capacities of the subject making the choice are duplicated in the other members taken collectively.) The second alternative is an operation in which one of the *other* members of the group would be destroyed but in which the capacities of the group as a whole would be significantly impaired. The third alternative is an operation that would dissolve the group by connecting each of the members to a separate body. We can assume that the subject in question has a perfectly adequate theoretical grasp of the structure of the group and of the relations of the individuals who make it up. The question is which of the alternatives would represent a rationally justified choice in such a situation.

On the face of it, this question might seem meaningless. As the example has been framed, any conscious belief, desire, or intention that the group member in question forms will be the result of the input of the entire group. Hence any reason that could be a conscious reason for this subject for favoring his or her own case would be better thought of as a reason for the group's favoring that case. Thus any such reason would be irrelevant to the question at hand. We can avoid this problem, however, if we imagine ourselves looking not at the conscious beliefs and desires that the subject might form (along with all the other members of the group) but at the individual's own particular preconscious contribution to a choice among the alternatives. In fact, we can do better. We can imagine explaining the choice to the group and promising to give each member an opportunity to ratify the group decision individually. When the group had reached a decision, we could take each member in sequence, render all the other members unconscious, and allow the member who remained conscious to approve or disapprove the decision made by the group as a whole.

Suppose, then, that we consider the alternative that involves disbanding the group. If one of the members were to contemplate that possibility, would there be any basis on which such an individual could plan his or her own future? Such an individual would, of course, have a large fund of factual information about the world in which he or she would come to exist. All the memories he or she had formed as a member of the group would remain intact and form an important part of the individual's personality after the split. Assuming that the group to which the individual belonged was reasonably large, however, these memories would provide almost no clue to the individual's character or personality. The individual, for example, would know nothing about his or her intelligence, artistic talents, or athletic abilities; nothing about his or her character traits such as resoluteness, courage, or neatness; nothing about his or her tastes, desires, or preferences; and nothing about his or her unconscious psychology, including neuroses, psychoses, unconscious beliefs, unconscious desires, and unconscious intentions. Even if we left the individual free to choose his or her own body, including one exactly like the common body, the individual would lack the information necessary to make a rational choice. The individual, then, would have scarcely any basis on which to make rational plans for the future.

This is not to say, of course, that such an individual would lack all preferences concerning the future. Some states of affairs would obviously be preferred on very general grounds. What such an individual would lack are his or her own desires for his or her own future. In this respect, the individual would be very much like the Rawlsian moral personality behind the veil of ignorance.[16] The individual might possess an extensive fund of general psychological and sociological information, but he or she would have no access to his or her own conception of the good. Faced with such a situation, the individual group member would seem to have a very strong reason for preferring the continuation of the group, with its capacities intact, to its dissolution.

Suppose we consider, then, the second alternative. This is the alternative in which the subject can avoid destruction by choosing that another member of the group be destroyed, but in which the capacities of the group as a whole would be significantly diminished. Would the subject making the choice have any rational grounds for preferring this to the one in which he or she is destroyed and the group's capacities remain intact? I think the answer again is no. Although the individual can form a preference distinct from the group's, his or her perspective on the choice and that of the group still coincide. Since the long-term memories to which the individual has access, including the memories of previously formed intentions, are *group* memories, the prospect of the death of any individual group member to the individual facing the choice is the same as the prospect of the loss of an individual to the group. And the loss of an individual has significance for the group only to the extent that it bears on the capacities of the group as a whole.

It might be assumed that it is only ignorance of the facts that prevents a subject in the group fusion from making a choice in his or her own interests, as distinct from the interests of the group. But this would be a mistake. Imagine a variation of the previous example. In this case the subject faced with the choice is given a complete account of his or her functional makeup and of the functional makeup of all the other members of the group, as well as a functional description of the group itself. Thus this subject could determine not only what his or her contribution to the group's behavior had been but could also predict what he or she would be like as an independent subject in the event that the group was dissolved. Even in this case, I claim, a rational subject would choose the operation that would result in his or her destruction over either the alternative operation or the dissolution of the group.

The argument for this claim is simply that a rational choice will be motivated by the desires that the subject *actually* has at the time of the choice. And these desires are the desires that belong to the group and are common to all of the members. From such a perspective it is obvious that the operation that leaves the capacities of the group intact is to be preferred to the one that leaves the capacities seriously impaired. And from this perspective it is also to be preferred to the group's dissolution. We can see this by considering another example. Suppose the subject making the choice has access to the following information. First, it can be determined what desires the subject would have had at the time of the choice if he or she had been functioning as a separate individual. Second, the desires that he or she would have had at the time of the choice would have been better satisfied if the subject had been functioning separately from the group. Third, these desires, as well as those the subject would acquire as a result of functioning separately, would be better satisfied in the future if he or she were to continue as a separate subject. Even if these conditions obtained (as they very likely would), they would be irrelevant to the choice the subject faces. What matters are the subject's *actual* desires, and these are most likely to be satisfied by the continuation of the group with its capacities intact.

It does not follow, of course, that it would *never* be rational for such a subject to choose the dissolution of the group or the destruction of a different subject and some diminution of the group's capacities. But the choice would be motivated not by the desires that the subject *would have* in isolation but by the desires that he or she *does have* as a result of membership in the group. Suppose, for example, that the other members of the group were holding back the subject's ability to realize those actual, conscious goals he or she shared with the rest of the group. In this case the subject might opt for dissolution. But this would be a case in which the desires of the *group* would be best realized by disbanding the group. Similarly, such a subject would be rationally justified in preferring the destruction of another member of the group and some loss of the group's capacities just in case that choice would have the greatest effect in furthering the goals of the group. Such a loss of the group's capacities would be accepted just in case the gain in terms of the group's goals outweighed the loss as judged from the perspective of the group.

This conclusion will be reinforced if we consider what is essentially the same problem under the following redescription. Suppose that you are told that at the present moment only one of your sophisticated subsystems—call it X—is functioning. (You are to assume that X belongs to a set of subsystems related in the same way as the members of the group fusion. You are also to assume that the fact that only X is functioning does not involve a loss of any of your intellectual capacities.) Suppose you are also told that you must choose among a brain operation that will destroy X but will leave your present capacities and personality intact, a brain operation that will destroy another subsystem Y at the cost of a significant reduction in your capacities, and an operation that will result in the transplantation of each of the subsystems in the set into a new body of its own—an operation that will create a number of new personalities, none of which will be motivated to pursue your current desires and projects or to respect your current commitments. Faced with such a choice, the obvious answer seems to be that one would prefer the destruction of X. If this does not seem immediately plausible, consider again the case in which the set of subsystems consists of the two brain hemispheres. Even if we are told that only one of the hemispheres is making the decision, we seem to have no preference for saving that hemisphere that would outweigh our desire to preserve our own capacities intact.

It is on the basis of these kinds of considerations that I think the reevaluation of conscious experience is warranted. By this I mean that the value we characteristically place on persons is in virtue of their self-consciousness rather than their consciousness. Since this proposed reassessment of the significance of consciousness will be convincing to the extent that we have an explanation of the relatively high status that consciousness usually enjoys in our thoughts about ourselves, I shall offer three reasons why we tend to overestimate its importance. First and most obvious, we often fail to distinguish clearly enough between consciousness and self-consciousness. One possible explanation of this failure is that we have no access to unproblematic actual examples of consciousness without self-consciousness. Another possible explanation is that there are plausible philosophical accounts of self-consciousness, as Rey's remarks suggest, that obscure its difference from consciousness. A third possibility, at least where philosophical discussion is concerned, is that one may hold the inseparability of consciousness and self-consciousness as a substantive philosophical doctrine.[17]

A second reason that we may overestimate the importance of consciousness is that we hold, either implicitly or explicitly, a transcendentalist theory of consciousness. The transcendentalist claims that two subjects who are alike in all objective respects, including the details of their physical makeup, might still differ in their subjective experiences—even to the point that there might be something it was like to be one and not the other.[18] On this theory, the basic distinction is the distinction between consciousness and nonconsciousness: the distinction between being a creature like us for whom there is something it is like to exist and being a thing, for example a pencil sharpener, for which there is nothing it is like to exist. The actual content of consciousness—including the kinds of things that might distinguish a subject who is self-aware and self-concerned from one who is not— is made to seem generally less important on this view.

Finally, the connection between consciousness and sentience and the moral significance attached to pleasure and pain almost certainly provide a reason for the importance attached to consciousness. Indeed, from the point of view of a strictly hedonistic consequentialism, moral value attaches only to the character of conscious states. To produce unpleasant conscious states is always prima facie wrong, whereas to kill a self-conscious creature instantaneously, painlessly, and without warning and to replace it with a similar creature need not be. Since the ability to experience pleasure and pain requires consciousness but not self-consciousness, the value we ordinarily place on consciousness should come as no surprise.

5   Self-Consciousness and the Unity of the Self

If this explanation of our tendency to overvalue conscious experience is not implausible, we can put the less inflated conception to use in addressing the problem of consciousness with which I began. The problem for a theory of consciousness stemmed in part from the fact that many computer programs already in existence would count as conscious, given the way consciousness is currently characterized in functional terms. And even if we add the condition that conscious systems must have genuine intelligence or intentional states, the problem remains. There are too many systems—ranging from the unconscious systems of Freudian theory to Dennett's homunculi—that are not only intelligent but to which it is plausible to ascribe intentional states as well.

Recognition of our tendency to inflate the significance of conscious experience makes it possible to solve this problem. The problem lies in the fact that functionalist analyses apparently make consciousness too pervasive a phenomenon. Systems that it is intuitively implausible to call conscious satisfy all the conditions imposed by any reasonable functional analysis. The intuitions that such systems *could not be conscious,* however, can be discounted once we recognize their source in the inflated conception of consciousness. The consequence of the functionalist or naturalist analyses—that many more systems are conscious than we had imagined—does not have the further implications that might have seemed to follow. Though it follows that our sophisticated subsystems are like us in significant ways, it does *not* follow that these sophisticated subsystems have the automatic claim to personhood, rights, and respect that is justified in the case of ordinary self-conscious subjects. If consciousness were what mattered where personhood, rights, and respect were concerned, then since we have grounds for thinking that our two brain hemispheres are separately conscious that are independent of any particular analysis of consciousness, we would be forced to the following conclusion: brain surgery necessary to save a subject's life, if it involved the destruction of one of the hemispheres, would raise the same moral issues that would be raised by killing one person to save another. And this is a consequence that seems clearly unacceptable.

On the alternative suggestion that what matters for personhood is the kind of self-consciousness necessary for self-concern, this problem does not arise. By this criterion, neither the brain hemispheres nor our other sophisticated subsystems have any claim to personhood. Nor do the members of the group fusion. This fact emerges especially clearly if we contrast the group fusion example with other examples in which subsystems of a larger system do have plausible claims to personhood.

Consider first the Chinese nation example proposed by Ned Block.[19] Block imagines the inhabitants of China being organized so as to instantiate the Turing machine table that best describes the functional makeup of a psychologically normal subject. Each of the inhabitants has continuous access to the current input state and the current internal state of the system. And each inhabitant is responsible for one particular combination of an input state and an internal state in the following sense: if that combination occurs, he or she is required to push a button that brings about the output state and the new internal state required by the machine table. In other words, each inhabitant instantiates the dispositional state defined by one square of the table.

Suppose this system is connected to a human body for which it serves as the central processing mechanism and that, as a result, behaves like a normal human subject. And suppose that we are convinced that the subject is conscious and self-conscious in virtue of his functional equivalence to a normal subject. (Block argues that this would not be the case, because the Chinese nation, though it is functionally equivalent to a normal subject, involves a different type of physical realization. But since the Chinese nation example is disanalogous to the group fusion example in this respect, it would have no bearing on the group fusion example if Block were right. Thus we need not settle the question of whether the Chinese nation as a whole would *actually* be conscious or self-conscious.)

Suppose now that a group of Chinese dissidents threatens to end the project by calling a general strike. In this case, as in the group fusion case, the subject whose continuation is at stake might desire that parts of the system that realize his psychology be eliminated to ensure his continued existence. But in this case, in contrast to the group fusion case, eliminating the agitators to save the threatened subject could have no moral justification. Unlike the members of the group fusion, the inhabitants of China are fully self-conscious in a way that supports self-concern. Each one would describe himself or herself and his or her environment in different ways and in ways different from the way the threatened subject would describe himself and his surroundings. And each one has his or her own goals and projects, all of which are independent of those of the threatened subject. Thus there is no temptation to assimilate the threatened subject's desire to eliminate the agitators to the desire of a normal subject to undergo a brain operation that would save his or her life.

A second example that contrasts with the group fusion is that of the split-brain exam taker suggested by Derek Parfit.[20] Parfit asks us to consider the possibility that we might exercise voluntry control over the connection between our two brain hemispheres. Thus, faced with an examination problem in which two approaches looked promising, one might break the connection and pursue one approach in each hemisphere. In this case too a form of self-consciousness is created that could support a sense of genuine self-concern. After the split occurred, each of the two subjects would describe what he or she was doing in different ways, and each would wonder what the other was doing and experiencing. Moreover, they could rapidly develop conflicting interests. Suppose, for example, that they were given a sequence of problems and the slower subject on each problem was given a shock. Then each could hope, while working on each problem, that it would be the other subject who would be shocked.

This case obviously contrasts with the original group fusion case. But it also contrasts with the case in which we render all the group members but one unconscious in order to have that member ratify the group's decision to preserve itself at that member's expense. The crucial difference is that in the split-brain case the two subjects have different experiences simultaneously. This makes it possible for each subject to regard certain experiences as happening to the other subject but not to him or her. Nonetheless, this is a very attenuated case of self-consciousness. Just as the long-term goals and projects of the members of the fusion will ordinarily give them a very strong motive to resist the dissolution of the group, so the split-brain subjects will ordinarily have an equally strong motive to reintegrate, given that the resulting subject is likely to be better equipped to realize their goals and projects than either subject individually.

The last example that I want to contrast with the group fusion is that of the multiple personality subject. Let us assume that the personalities have sequential control over the common body and that they have nonoverlapping histories of past experiences. Thus we can assume that each personality is best suited to realize its own goals and projects without being integrated with any of the others. This example presents the most extreme contrast with the group fusion. First, there is no subject over and above the subjects corresponding to the different personalities. Second, each of the subjects has his or her own goals and desires, and many of these, for example, the desire to control the body over longer periods, will inevitably conflict. Finally, there are no overriding motives for any of them to fuse. Given the difficulties of living in a society in which their condition is very rare, they might well contemplate fusion, but the advantages would have to be weighed carefully against the disadvantages of a loss of autonomy. Such a decision would be no different in any important respect from the decision that a group of ordinary individuals would face if the possibility of fusion were made available and the practical disadvantages of not fusing were equally serious.

Since the group fusion case contrasts sharply with each of the previous three cases, it seems fair to conclude that if the members of the group are self-conscious, it is not in a sense that raises insurmountable difficulties. And if the group members are conscious without being self-conscious, then the apparently absurd consequences of the claim that our sophisticated subsystems are conscious do not in fact follow. Such subsystems are not appropriately regarded as persons distinct from the person of whom they form a part.

Thus the current state of the cognitive sciences will not rule out a naturalistic theory of consciousness. Consciousness supervenes on some combination of physical and functional features—features that are necessary conditions for possessing beliefs and intelligence and are thus shared by our intelligent subsystems.[21] Self-consciousness, however, supervenes on features unique to the system as a whole. Only the subject as a whole needs access to accurate data on its past performance and present psychological dispositions in isolation from the contributions and the dispositions of other systems. And only the system as a whole must be self-concerned. Though subsystems might well require some aspects or others of a capacity for self-knowledge, it is their lack of a genuine self-conscious awareness and self-concern that makes a unified subject possible.

Another problem for a theory of consciousness, and one that applies to nonfunctionalist as well as functionalist theories, is the problem of the evolutionary efficacy of consciousness. Unless consciousness makes a contribution to intelligence, it has no plausible evolutionary explanation. If it does make such a contribution, however, then given any explanation of intelligence in terms of interacting subsystems, the lack of conscious (and hence intelligent) subsystems would seem to constitute a suboptimal design. Even if empirical research should show that we instantiate such suboptimal designs, the limitation of consciousness to the system as a whole would be accidental and nonintrinsic.

The distinction between consciousness and self-consciousness can help us here as well. Consciousness does in fact contribute to intelligence. It is a necessary (though not necessarily sufficient) condition of high intelligence, and we do consist of many conscious subsystems. Self-consciousness, however, is not a necessary condition of intelligence. In the group fusion example, the lack of self-consciousness imposes no limitations on the subjects' intelligence. We can imagine the group fusion subjects to be as intelligent as we like without changing the fact that only the group as a whole, and none of the subjects individually, is self-conscious. Reasonably high intelligence is a necessary condition of self-consciousness, since self-consciousness requires genuine beliefs about the self, but it is not sufficient.

The evolutionary perspective explains why self-consciousness should occur only at the highest level of organization. Here again, our characterization of the distinction between consciousness and self-consciousness is crucial. The self-consciousness of the system as a whole *does* play an evolutionary role, but equally important, from the standpoint of evolution, is the *lack* of self-consciousness of the conscious subsystems. And it is from the evolutionary perspective that the connection between the lack of self-consciousness of the subsystems and the unity of the system as a whole is best understood. To function as a subsystem is to function as the perfectly cooperative member of a unified whole, rather than as an individual whose bonds to the other individuals are at best political. The lack of self-consciousness among intelligent subsystems ensures the benefits of cooperation and noncompetition. We need only think of the problems that multiple personality subjects face to see how significant these benefits may be. The disadvantages of a system with self-conscious subsystems gives their *lack* of self-awareness an evolutionary point that neither a lack of consciousness nor a lack of intelligence could have. The fact that the self-consciousness of a number of subsystems would impose a serious liability on the system as a whole—one that would not be imposed by the consciousness of those subsystems—explains the intrinsic connection between self-consciousness and the system at its highest level of organization.

Acknowledgments

An earlier draft of this chapter was presented at the MIT Philosophy Colloquium in October 1987. I am grateful to the members of the audience for their comments and criticisms. I am especially grateful to Ned Block for his suggestions and comments on the chapter in its earlier versions.

PART IV
Rationality and Responsibility

Chapter 7
Self-Deception and Responsibility for the Self

Despite the impressive evidence of its existence, self-deception has seemed to resist coherent description. Self-deception appears to be mysterious, if not plainly paradoxical. I shall argue that this appearance is misleading. What are ostensibly puzzles about self-deception are in fact puzzles about the justification of ascriptions of responsibility.

The issues I shall raise, therefore, are not the ones ordinarily associated with self-deception. I shall argue briefly that a theory of self-deception, if it is to avoid paradox, must recognize a division of the self into interacting subsystems. And this means subsystems with their own beliefs, goals, plans, and strategies, that is to say, homunculi. But although I shall argue that a theory of self-deception must be a homuncular theory, I shall not elaborate or defend any particular version of such a theory. Homuncular theories are well understood in outline, however many difficulties their details may involve.

What makes self-deception seem paradoxical is not our inability to make sense of a divided self but the fact that the homuncular solution is apparently unavailable. We make a distinction, where responsibility is concerned, between the person who is self-deceived and the person who is deceived by another. Given a homuncular model of the self, however, the psychology of the former does not seem relevantly different from the psychology of the latter. Thus a theory of self-deception must either provide an alternative to the homuncular model or provide an account of responsibility that makes this feature of the model intelligible.

The first and last sections, in which I discuss self-deception and the homuncular model, thus form a prologue and an epilogue to the rest of the chapter. The remaining sections make up the account of responsibility that I claim an adequate theory of self-deception requires. A theory of self-deception, to succeed, must make intelligible the

From *Perspectives on Self-Deception*, ed. B. McLaughlin and A. Rorty. Copyright 1988 by the Regents of the University of California. Reprinted with permission.

ascription of responsibility to those who deceive themselves—despite their psychological similarities to those who are deceived by others. And it is a fundamental misconception about the constraints governing our ascriptions of responsibility, I shall argue, that has made these ascriptions, and hence self-deception itself, seems problematic.

1   From Explanation to Evaluation

Let us understand by (full-blown) self-deception one's intentionally making oneself believe what one believes at the same time to be false or one's preventing oneself from believing what one continues to believe to be true.[1] Although it is sometimes denied that self-deception is appropriately understood on the model of other-deception,[2] these denials have never carried conviction. We say, for example, that we lie to ourselves, that we persuade ourselves of what we believe is false, and that we make it appear to ourselves that what we know is not the case. It is just this insistence on describing self-deception in terms whose intelligibility seems to presuppose the existence of distinct subjects that stands in need of explanation.

Cases that fall short of full-blown self-deception because they do not involve intentionally making oneself believe what one continues to believe is false (or preventing oneself from believing what one persists in believing is true) include the following. Suppose one believed, either truly or falsely, that one was guilty of an unforgivable offense and was tortured by the belief. One could have the belief removed by resorting to hypnosis, drugs, or brainwashing. One could instill new beliefs in similar ways. Assume that none of these methods leave any memory of the removal of the old belief or the addition of the new ones.

None of these cases raises any of the puzzles we associate with self-deception. Nor do they exhibit any of the advantages that a self-deceptive strategy can confer. Assume the goal of self-deception is to induce or suppress a particular belief *and* to maintain the resulting state once it is acquired. Then a strategy in which the belief in the falsity of the induced belief (or in the truth of the suppressed belief) is lost has obvious drawbacks. Such a strategy is essentially a one-shot affair. As such, it would leave one vulnerable to all the possible future evidence that would reintroduce the suppressed belief or destroy the belief one had intentionally induced. One-shot self-deception might be a reasonable strategy if one regarded one's actual state of belief as irrational, that is, if one were not genuinely committed to the truth of the belief to be suppressed or to the falsity of the belief to be induced. In such a case the strategy might provide the basis for useful therapy.

One-shot self-deception, however, is not an optimal strategy for dealing with beliefs to which one's commitment is genuine. And it is not one that reveals the apparently paradoxical features of full-blown self-deception.

The limitations of the one-shot strategy may give the impression that the puzzle about self-deception lies in the coexistence of inconsistent beliefs. Such an impression would be incorrect. Inconsistent beliefs do not in themselves raise interesting philosophical problems as long as they are ordinarily manifest in different contexts or if for some other reason the inconsistency does not become apparent. Nor is the one-shot strategy of inducing a later belief that one now believes is false improved merely by retaining the belief that the belief induced is false. This would simply render the induced belief doubly vulnerable. Let us call the belief that the induced belief is false the *original belief*. In this case, not only would the induced belief be vulnerable to extinction in the light of future evidence; it would be equally vulnerable in a confrontation with the original belief.

Retaining the original belief confers a strategic advantage only if that belief allows one to insulate the induced belief from the external evidence that might disconfirm it and if the induced belief can be insulated from the original belief as well as from the role played by the original belief in insulating the induced belief from the disconfirming evidence. If this can be accomplished, it represents a significant strategic advance over one-shot deception. One's induced belief will be far more secure if, on the basis of the original belief, one can prevent oneself from recognizing any evidence that might undermine it, including the evidence provided by one's own activity.

This feature of full-blown self-deception is spelled out clearly by Roy Schafer in his description of Freudian defenses: "one does not know that one knows something, wishes something, considers something emotionally, or is doing or has done some other action; one keeps oneself from discovering *what* one does not know, etc., thus deceiving oneself once; and one keeps oneself from discovering *that* and *how* one is deceiving oneself in this way ('unconscious defence'), thus deceiving oneself a second time or in a second respect."[3] It is this full-blown notion of self-deception that seems unintelligible. How can one, on the basis of one's original belief, manipulate one's ability to recognize the import of the evidence at one's disposal in such a way as to protect one's induced belief? Intentionally manipulating one's own response to the evidence seems to presuppose that one has a clear grip on the import of the evidence and thus that in the same context one both is and is not aware of its significance. It is on the basis of this kind of description that the paradoxical nature of self-deception is alleged.

The description that is paradoxical as applied to one person is, of course, nonparadoxical as applied to two. This fact suggests an approach to the problem of self-deception that is already explicit in the Freudian model. Split the self into two or more interacting subsystems, each with its own beliefs, goals, plans, and strategies. Call any model that postulates more than one such system per subject a *homuncular model*. On the basis of such a model we can describe the process of self-deception without conceptual strain. Subsystems S_1 and S_2 originally both believe that p. S_1 causes S_2 (either directly or indirectly) to lose the belief that p (and possibly to believe its negation), while itself continuing to believe that p. S_1 subsequently monitors S_2's environment for evidence that p and attempts to prevent S_2 from acquiring that evidence. S_1 also tries to prevent S_2's coming across any evidence that would reveal S_1's activity. The use of such homuncular models is by no means restricted to Freudian theory. Homuncular models are the common currency of most recent theorizing in the cognitive sciences.[4]

Natural as the homuncular approach may seem in the contemporary context, it has two drawbacks, one of which appears to be fatal. The less serious of the two is that talk of homunculi, if taken literally, raises potentially embarrassing questions. If, for example, S_1 retains the original belief that p, why is S_1 not tortured by the belief, which would make the strategy self-defeating? Furthermore, if S_1 is as sophisticated as the homuncular model suggests, are S_1 and S_2 both conscious? And are they both self-conscious? If so, are there two distinct persons in a single body?

These questions would deserve extended discussion in any systematic defense of homuncular models. Here I shall simply assume what I argue in chapter 6: that talk about a multiplicity of such interacting subsystems does not commit us to a multiplicity of either self-conscious subsystems or distinct persons.[5] I shall also assume that whatever their other problems, homuncular models are sufficiently well understood that we can usefully explore the implications of a homuncular model of self-deception.[6]

Granting these assumptions, however, does nothing to stave off a seemingly conclusive objection. Regardless of whether S_1 is conscious or unconscious, S_2 must be unconscious of S_1's activities, at least as far as the induced or suppressed belief is concerned. If this were not the case, then all the puzzles that the distinction between S_1 and S_2 was intended to solve would reemerge. But because this is the case, the following problem arises. Since we have made self-deception intelligible by assimilating it to other-deception, we can make no sense of an essential feature of self-deception: that we hold a subject responsible for deceiving himself or herself in a way that we do not hold him or her responsible for being deceived by another. On the homuncular model, there seems to be no relevant psychological difference between the subject who is deceived by another and a subject who is deceived by one of his or her subsystems of whose operation he or she is completely unconscious. The conscious experiences of the subject deceived by the operations of an unconscious subsystem and of the subject deceived by another, for example, may be exactly the same. Again we seem to have produced a model that ignores an essential aspect of self-deception: in this case the fact that deceiving oneself is something one does and something for which one can be blamed, not something that happens to one and something that entitles one to the sympathy of others.

It is the apparent inadequacy of the homuncular model to explain the pattern in our ascriptions of responsibility, I think, that explains why philosophers have not generally taken this otherwise attractive line concerning self-deception.[7] The argument for the inadequacy of a homuncular explanation, however, depends on the assumption that differences in our ascriptions of responsibility to different subjects can be justified only by reference to relevant differences in the psychologies of the subjects in question. I shall argue that on its most natural interpretation, this seemingly uncontroversial assumption is false.

I argue in section 2 that any theory that attempts to ground the ascription of responsibility in relevant features of a subject's psychology faces a dilemma. On the natural interpretation of what such a grounding involves, any subject who is a candidate for punishment or blame is psychologically either not relevantly different from the psychopath or not relevantly different from the compulsive. In neither case does there seem to be any way in which the subject could acquiesce and be justified in acquiescing in the suffering that being blamed or being punished involves. And without the possibility of such acquiescence, we have not a practice involving responsibility, blame, and punishment but one involving the exercise of manipulation, power, and control.

In section 3, I argue that theories that avoid this dilemma by attempting to justify our ascriptions of responsibility in terms of their contribution to social welfare fail. I examine the most sophisticated version of this kind of theory, due to P. F. Strawson. I conclude that his references to our characteristic reactive attitudes toward those who have injured others—attitudes such as guilt and remorse if we have caused the injury ourselves and resentment and indignation if it has been caused by another—are not sufficient to justify our practices where responsibility is concerned.

In section 4, I contrast nonmaximizing dispositions—the class of dispositions to which our reactive attitudes belong if they have no further justification—with another class that I call self-supporting dispositions. I argue that because they are not self-supporting, nonmaximizing dispositions cannot provide the foundations for an institution of social control that resembles our institution of punishment.

By reference to self-supporting dispositions, I develop in section 5 an alternative form of justification of our practices regarding responsibility, punishment, and blame. I call a form of justification that appeals to our self-supporting dispositions an internal justification. The suffering caused by a practice of ascribing responsibility and blame that has an internal justification is necessarily suffering in which we can acquiesce, even when the suffering is our own. Such a practice may have an internal justification *without* satisfying the constraint that differences in the ascription of responsibility must be grounded in relevant psychological differences, as these are ordinarily understood. Thus the major objection to the homuncular model of self-deception will have been removed.

I conclude section 5 by examining the limits of internal justification. I argue that it is not the case that any conceivable practice concerning responsibility, punishment, and blame would have an internal justification for some possible population of subjects. I do claim, however, that radically different practices could each have an internal justification for appropriately different populations. The view, then, entails a form of relativism where responsibility is concerned.

In section 6, I consider the kind of internal justification to which our own practices regarding responsibility in general and responsibility for self-deception in particular are susceptible. Although I give only a suggestion of what an internal justification of these practices might be like, I argue that unless there is *some* such justification, the suffering these practices entail will not be suffering in which we could acquiesce. I conclude that in such a case the practices would require either radical revision or rejection.

2   A Dilemma for Intrinsic Theories

The objection to a homuncular model of self-deception depends on two assumptions. The first is that we do in fact treat self-deceivers differently from the victims of other-deception where responsibility is concerned. The second is that differences in the ascription of responsibility to different subjects can be justified only by relevant differences in their psychologies. The first assumption seems hard to avoid. I shall take it for granted in what follows. The second assumption, which I shall argue is false, requires some clarification.

Let us say that the constraint that differences in the ascription of responsibility to two subjects are justified only if there are relevant differences in the subjects' psychologies is the constraint that justification must appeal to *intrinsic properties* of the subjects in question. Call this constraint the *intrinsic-property constraint*. This means, first, that the justification of an ascription of responsibility depends only on the subject of the ascription. Facts, for example, about the deterrent value of holding the subject responsible or about any other social benefit that might accrue are irrelevant. Second, the psychological facts on which justification depends must be independent of the subject's general values and commitments on the one hand and beliefs about responsibility on the other. This means that whether the ascription of responsibility to a subject in another culture is justified can be settled by reference to the same standards that apply in our own culture. Thus questions about responsibility are questions about which an entire culture may be mistaken. (The relevance of this second requirement will become clear in section 5.) Finally, let us call any theory that justifies only practices satisfying the intrinsic-property constraint an *intrinsic theory*.

There are two ways in which the assumption that the intrinsic-property constraint governs ascriptions of responsibility can figure in an objection to a homuncular account of self-deception. It might be held that our actual practices involving responsibility satisfy the intrinsic-property constraint and that they are justified. In this case a homuncular model of self-deception would be impossible to reconcile with our practice of holding self-deceivers responsible. On the homuncular model, self-deceivers have the same intrinsic properties as the victims of other-deception. And given that our practices discriminate between them, if the practices are justified, the homuncular model (which together with the intrinsic-property constraint entails that they are unjustified) must be wrong. Alternatively, it might be held that although our actual practices are unjustified (either because they fail to satisfy the intrinsic-property constraint or for some other reason), there is a true theory of responsibility justifying an alternative set of practices that *do* satisfy the constraint—and these practices involve ascribing responsibility to self-deceivers. Again this would rule out the homuncular model.

My argument that the intrinsic-property constraint is false has three stages. I shall argue first that there are good reasons to believe that our actual practices concerning punishment, responsibility, and blame are not governed by this constraint. This is intended to lend intuitive plausibility to the claim that ascriptions of responsibility that violate the constraint may still be justified. Second, I shall argue that anyone who believes *both* that psychopaths and compulsives are inappropriate candidates for punishment and blame *and* that the intrinsic-property constraint is true is faced with a dilemma. *Any* candidate for punishment and blame, I shall argue, is either not relevantly different from the psychopath or is not relevantly different from the compulsive (given the intrinsic-property constraint). Finally, I shall argue that not even those who regard the psychopath as an appropriate candidate for punishment and blame are immune to the problems that the intrinsic-property constraint raises. Holding that the psychopath is an appropriate candidate raises the question of how the suffering that such punishment and blame would entail can be justified. And this is a question, I shall claim, that has no answer. The solution is not to suppose that genuine punishment of the psychopath is possible but to abandon the intrinsic-property constraint. In so doing we make it possible to draw a defensible distinction between psychopaths and compulsives on the one hand and genuinely appropriate candidates for punishment and blame on the other.[8]

The best argument for the claim that our practices concerning responsibility do not satisfy the intrinsic-property constraint (i.e., for the first stage of the argument that the intrinsic-property constraint is false) is provided by our attitudes toward our beliefs, desires, emotions, and character traits. As many philosophers have argued, we seem to be held responsible for such states as unjustified anger or resentment, self-righteousness, lack of feeling or sympathy for others, racist or sexist sentiments, bitterness, jealousy, and cowardice.[9] This is the case even when there is no reason to believe that any of the following are true: (1) that such states are under our voluntary control, (2) that they are the foreseeable consequences of our voluntary choices in the past, or (3) that all that we are really being blamed for are our voluntary or intentional expressions of these states. Given that these states are outside our voluntary control, there is apparently no psychological difference between such states and the states for which we are not ordinarily held responsible—for example, having caught the flu, being a certain height, and lacking musical talent—which *by itself* justifies the difference in our ascriptions of responsibility. Thus there is apparently no *relevant* psychological difference between the two sets of states.

Moreover, there are other important classes of events that are outside our control but for which we are apparently held responsible. We are blamed for the intentions we form, even though another subject who would have formed the same intention in our circumstances (say to lie rather than face embarrassment) is not blamed because he or she never encountered the same situation. And we may be blamed for the consequences of our actions (say causing a death through a minor act of negligence) even though someone with the same motives and intentions and the same degree of conscientiousness is not blamed because an accident never ensues.[10] Even philosophers who regard departures from the intrinsic-property constraint as irrational generally agree that such departures are a common feature of our actual practices regarding responsibility and blame.[11]

These arguments that our actual practices fail to satisfy the intrinsic-property constraint are, of course, controversial and by no means conclusive. They do, however, raise significant doubts where its validity is concerned. I shall now go on to provide the second stage of my argument that the intrinsic-property constraint is false. This is the argument for the claim that those who doubt the appropriateness of punishing or blaming psychopaths and compulsives *and* accept the intrinsic-property constraint confront a dilemma.

To state the dilemma, I shall need the notion of a certain form of equilibrium with respect to one's noninstrumental or intrinsic desires.[12] Such an equilibrium has analogies with John Rawls's reflective equilibrium and depends on the fact that, like our moral convictions, our noninstrumental desires may either support or fail to support one another.[13] The relation of support among noninstrumental desires is modeled on the relation of support among beliefs to which the proponents of coherentist accounts of epistemic justification appeal. Like that relation, the relation of support is not a logical one. Nor, given that the desires are all noninstrumental, is it a means-end relation. One's desire to bring aesthetic pleasure to others may (given one's beliefs) support and be supported by one's desire to become a musician. One does not desire to become a musician as a *means* to giving pleasure to others or vice versa. Nonetheless, the two desires can be mutually reinforcing. In contrast, the desire to live a life of luxury does not support and is not supported by the desire to pursue a career of honest public service and to live entirely on one's own earnings (given any ordinary set of beliefs). As these examples suggest, support among noninstrumental desires is always relative to a set of background beliefs. I shall follow the lead of those who discuss support in the context of epistemology by treating support among desires for the most part as primitive.

Imagine now that we had a pill that would allow us to add and subtract noninstrumental desires at will. Such a pill would enable us to destroy noninstrumental desires that were badly supported relative to our other noninstrumental desires and to add noninstrumental desires that would be well supported. This involves no commitment, of course, to the intelligibility of our revising our set of noninstrumental desires from a point of view that is neutral with regard to all the desires simultaneously. The motivation for adding and subtracting desires must be grounded in the noninstrumental desires that remain fixed. The model here is the familiar one of Neurath's ship: repair is possible only as long as the vessel itself remains afloat.

With the notion of such a pill we can define a subject's *ideal reflective equilibrium* (IRE) as the most coherent extension of the subject's noninstrumental or intrinsic desires that the subject could and would produce given access to the pill (and given his or her actual beliefs). That is, it is the extension the subject would be motivated to produce in eliminating conflicts among his or her noninstrumental desires.[14] In the real world, many of a subject's noninstrumental desires will be out of IRE in the sense that they are unsupported or badly supported by the subject's other noninstrumental desires. Such desires would not survive the existence of the pill, in terms of which the IRE is defined. As the case of drug addiction shows, however, there is no connection between the strength of a desire and its degree of support—the desire for a drug may be overwhelming, though almost entirely unsupported by other desires. We can distinguish, then, between the *motivational strength* of a desire for a subject—the tendency of the subject to act to fulfill the desire—and its *evaluational strength*—the tendency of the subject to keep the desire in his or her IRE. In the case of a normal heroin addict, the motivational strength of the desire for heroin will be extremely high and its evaluational strength will be very low. To say that a desire is *out of IRE* for some subject is to say that its evaluational strength would not be enough to make it part of that subject's IRE.

Among the noninstrumental or intrinsic desires of a subject's IRE, there is a special subset that I shall call the *conative core*. These are the unconditional desires that have a bearing on decisions the subject might realistically be called upon to make. By an *unconditional desire*, I mean a desire that a state of affairs be realized regardless of whether that desire itself persists. If, for example, one has a noninstrumental desire that one drink tea rather than coffee, one will ordinarily desire that this happen only as long as the desire persists. Hence the desire is conditional. If, however, one desires that one treat others honestly or that one keep one's promises, one would normally desire that these states of affairs be realized whether one continues to desire them or not.[15]

One's conative core, then, is the most coherent extension one would be motivated to produce of those unconditional desires on which one might plausibly have to act. And given their relation to action, the pressure for coherence among these desires is even greater than among ordinary noninstrumental desires. Hence the conative core is stable in the following sense. First, (if one's beliefs remain fixed) one could not be motivated to change the desires in one's IRE in general and in one's conative core in particular. Any motivation for change would have been exhausted in the formation of the IRE and its corresponding conative core. Second, any local change in one's conative core, if brought about from outside, would be reversed if one had access to the appropriate pill. (At least, this would be true on the plausible assumption that none of one's unconditional desires were unsupported in the way that a bare preference, for example, for one flavor over another, might be.) Third, though a sufficiently drastic change in one's conative core would not be reversed (since it would give rise to an alternative equilibrium that would itself be stable), one's motivation would not carry *across* such a change. That is, if one knew now that such a change would occur at time *t* and that it could not be prevented, one would not be motivated to sacrifice the satisfaction of one's present desires for the satisfaction of desires after *t*. If one's desires were unconditional, one would give no weight to the fact that in the future one would no longer have those desires, or would have incompatible desires, or would even have incompatible desires that were unconditional. Suppose, for example, that one were a Nietzschean and that one's most fundamental Nietzschean desires were unconditional. If one knew that after time *t* one would have the noninstrumental desires of an orthodox Christian, one could not be rationally motivated to sacrifice one's present Nietzschean desires for the satisfaction of one's future Christian ones. Hence the conative core represents one's deepest commitments—those commitments that, to the extent that any set of commitments can, define who one is.[16]

Suppose now that a subject performs an antisocial act on the basis of a desire that (for that subject) is in IRE. Since the desire that motivates the action is in IRE, there is no other desire or set of desires to which we could appeal to provide the subject with a reason not to perform the action. Suppose, for example, that the action involved driving after drinking. Since the action stems from a desire in IRE, one could not appeal to the subject's sympathy for accident victims or their families in attempting to demonstrate the necessity for reform. Such an appeal to the subject's other desires and sympathies makes sense only on the assumption that the desire that motivates the action is *not* in IRE.

A scenario in which an antisocial act stems from a desire in IRE would be possible if, for example, the subject in question were a rational psychopath. Such a subject lacks any sympathy for others to which we could appeal in providing that subject with a reason to refrain from the action (beyond whatever calculation he or she has made about the possibility of punishment). And it is not hard to understand why philosophers have been reluctant to hold psychopaths responsible for their antisocial actions.[17] Since there is nothing in psychopaths' attitudes, desires, values, hopes, or concerns to which we could appeal, there is no possible means by which they could come to *acquiesce* in our condemnation of their behavior and in the justice of their punishment. They would normally experience no feelings of guilt or remorse for their actions, and if such feelings arose, they would be unsupported by the psychopaths' other noninstrumental desires. For example, any wish experienced by such a psychopath that he or she had not performed the action in question would be eliminated by the same pill that defines IRE. Similarly, any desire to make amends, secure forgiveness, or bring about self-reform would be isolated and unsupported and hence would be eliminated. Thus, in the sense in which justification is necessarily connected with motivation, such feelings would be completely unjustified.[18] Therefore, such subjects are beyond the reach of *punishment* (where genuine punishment requires that guilt and remorse be *justified* even for the subjects themselves), though not beyond being deterred, manipulated, and controlled. Let us call subjects in this situation *unreachable*.

Although the claim that our actual practice involves a reluctance to hold psychopaths responsible for their actions is relatively uncontroversial, the stronger claim that this reluctance is in virtue of their unreachability may not be. I shall not, however, go on to make this stronger claim. What I suggest is that their unreachability *justifies* this reluctance.

Imagine that one existed peacefully as an outsider in the midst of a native population whose taboos one regarded as irrational superstitions. And suppose that one were in the habit of breaking the taboos whenever the chances of being discovered were slight. If one were caught and made to suffer, how could one regard the suffering as more than a piece of bad luck brought on by the unforeseen consequences of actions that under the circumstances were completely justified? Assuming one were unreachable, it is difficult to see how one could be rationally justified in feeling remorse or guilt or how one could construe such suffering as genuine punishment, regardless of how much one might regret the upshot of one's actions.

The psychopath's lack of sympathy for others, then, is not a necessary condition of his or her being outside our practice of ascribing responsibility and blame and administering punishment—being unreachable has the same effect. Nor is a lack of sympathy sufficient. A subject who lacked any sympathy for others but who could be reached by moral argument would ordinarily be subject to punishment and blame. Since our practice of ascribing responsibility, punishment, and blame requires the reachability of those to whom responsibility and blame are ascribed, not only psychopaths but all those whose socially proscribed actions are done in IRE and in whom remorse could find no motivational support fall outside the practice.[19] Nonpsychopathic subjects who are nonetheless unreachable include, among others, some religious fundamentalists, subjects with a radically different conception of the good from ours, and subjects with a radically different conception of responsibility, whenever these subjects act in IRE. Among subjects acting in IRE, only those who are mistaken about the facts and who are open to a different version of them are not unreachable. And since their actions are done in ignorance, such subjects are still not appropriate candidates for the ascription of responsibility and blame.

The upshot is that subjects in IRE who are prima facie candidates for punishment or blame are either unreachable or ignorant. Thus, on an intrinsic theory, which requires that ascriptions of responsibility be justified solely in terms of relevant features of the subject's psychology, a subject in IRE will be no more appropriate as a candidate for punishment or blame than a subject who is ignorant or psychopathic.

From the perspective of the intrinsic-property constraint, however, the prospects for the ascription of responsibility are no better for subjects out of IRE. A subject who acts on a desire that is out of IRE is acting on a desire that he or she would, if possible, eliminate. Such a desire is cause for regret, and the action it motivates may be associated with feelings of guilt or shame. This guilt or shame, however, is no more justified for the subject acting out of IRE than it is for the compulsive—at least if such justification has to appeal to intrinsic differences. Such feelings do not prevent the subject who is out of IRE from acting on the desire, because its motivational strength is out of proportion to its evaluational strength. And given the definition of a desire's motivational strength, there is no sense to the suggestion that the subject might have chosen not to act on the desire in spite of its motivational strength. Thus the psychology of such a subject is in relevant respects like that of the compulsive. A subject acting on a desire out of IRE may not exhibit the repetitive and identifiable behavioral patterns of the compulsive, but though this is a psychological difference, it is hard to see how it could be a relevant one. Hence the subject acting out of IRE is no better candidate for punishment or blame than the subject whose action is compelled.

The dilemma for any intrinsic theory of responsibility, then, is this. Any prima facie candidate for either punishment or blame acts either in or out of IRE. A subject who acts *in IRE* and who is not ignorant of any crucial facts is not relevantly different in psychology from the psychopath: both act in a state that makes them unreachable. A subject who acts *out of IRE* is not relevantly different from the compulsive: both act on a desire whose motivational strength is out of proportion to its evaluational strength. Hence neither type of subject, and thus no subject, is responsible in the sense of being an appropriate candidate for punishment or blame.

It might be objected that ignorance is not always excused and may lead to actions whose motivating desires are neither like those of the compulsive nor like those of the psychopath. On the intrinsic conception of responsibility, however, this objection merely moves the problem one step back. If liability to punishment or blame is to be based on relevant features of a subject's psychology, then this basis could not consist in ignorance per se. Rather, the ignorance must have been brought about by actions for which the subject was responsible and subject to blame. And such actions must have stemmed either from a desire in IRE or from a desire out of IRE. Hence the dilemma for intrinsic theories of responsibility reappears.

This dilemma posed by stage two of the argument against the intrinsic-property constraint depends on the assumption that the psychopath is an inappropriate candidate for punishment or blame. But this assumption can be justified. Punishment of the psychopath could, of course, be justified on consequentialist grounds, but as I argued (in note 19), such a justification is irrelevant to the problem of self-deception. And as I shall argue in section 3, consequentialist theories do not provide a plausible account of our actual practice regarding responsibility.

Traditional retributivist theories (those that observe the intrinsic-property constraint) fare no better where punishment of the psychopath is concerned. Such theories cannot answer the following question: If there is no justification of the psychopath's suffering in terms of social utility (and the retributivist must be willing to impose the suffering even when there is no social payoff) and there is no justification from the subject's own point of view, what prevents the suffering from being gratuitous? To this line of argument it might be objected that the demand for such justification begs the question against the retributivist. In particular, the objection might be that there is no gap between the claim that the subject acted on a desire from which he or she was in no way alienated and the claim that the subject is an appropriate candidate for punishment and blame. And if this is true, the conclusion will be that once the first claim is granted, no further justification of the subject's being a candidate for punishment is possible. But this is not the case. I shall go on to show that such justification *is* possible. Since it is, the gap exists. Thus there is an important justificatory role that is played by the alternative theory of responsibility to be proposed and for which an ordinary retributivist theory is inadequate.

3   Extrinsic Theories and Reactive Attitudes

Once the problems for intrinsic theories are clearly in focus, the alternative provided by existing extrinsic theories is unlikely to hold much appeal. If our institutions of blame and punishment cannot be justified on intrinsic grounds, then the claim that they serve as a deterrent to wrongdoing and thereby contribute to aggregate utility is likely to ring hollow. For counting such considerations as a justification of the pain and suffering necessarily inflicted by punishment and blame seems to presuppose that the recipient is blameworthy in some sense other than being the most efficient means to the production of aggregate utility or some alternative social goal. The extrinsic justification alone, when the assumption that an intrinsic justification exists has been dropped, is simply not of the right kind to justify anything like our current practices where responsibility is concerned. Such a justification of our current practices seems either to miss the point or to change the subject. The problem of the subject who is punished on the basis of this rationale is like the problem of the subject who is punished while being unreachable: although each subject can recognize in the suffering involved the intended manipulative effect and the (perhaps) efficacious exercise of power, neither subject can view the suffering in the light of any concept recognizably like that of desert.[20]

This argument against extrinsic theories has been challenged by P. F. Strawson.[21] According to Strawson, the justification of our customary practices of ascribing responsibility in terms of their efficacy in regulating behavior in socially desirable ways is to be either supplemented or replaced by another sort of justification. On Strawson's view, the justification of these practices is grounded in our reactive attitudes toward those from whom we expect and demand goodwill. Under normal circumstances we are prone to exhibit a characteristic pattern of responses toward someone who has caused an injury. If we have been injured by someone else, the characteristic response is resentment. If we are witnesses to the injury of someone else by a third party, the characteristic response is moral indignation. And if we ourselves have injured someone, the response is guilt or shame. This last case involves what Strawson calls self-reactive attitudes. On the positive side, our reactive attitudes include our feelings of gratitude and of moral approbation.

Under special circumstances these feelings are suspended. Injuries due to ignorance make such responses as resentment inappropriate with regard to that particular *action*, but they do not lead to our suspending our reactive attitudes toward the *agent* in question. We are fully prepared to respond with our normal reactive attitudes, both positive and negative, to the *other* actions in which that agent is engaged. Other circumstances do lead to such a suspension. The claim that an agent was not himself or herself, was under great strain, was schizophrenic, or was hopelessly compulsive leads us to withdraw our reactive attitudes toward the agent either temporarily or on a permanent basis. Instead of seeing the offending agent as the appropriate target of resentment or moral indignation, we see him or her as someone to be managed or handled, cured or treated.

Strawson's analysis of our reactive attitudes provides a reply to my earlier objection to extrinsic theories. The objection was that we could not justify the imposition of suffering merely by reference to the contribution that suffering would make to social welfare. To do so would be to treat the alleged wrongdoer as a convenient instrument of social policy but not as someone toward whom resentment or indignation (and for whom guilt or remorse) would be justified. This would be, in Strawson's terms, to take the objective attitude toward the alleged wrongdoer and to see that person as an appropriate subject for management or manipulation. Such a practice provides no place for our reactive attitudes toward those on whom suffering is imposed or whose behavior is modified. Nor does it allow any scope for the self-reactive attitudes of guilt or shame on the part of such subjects. Strawson's reply is that we can have an extrinsic justification of our practices without abandoning our reactive or participatory attitudes. Strawson claims that we suspend our reactive attitudes only under genuinely abnormal circumstances. If Strawson is right, we could not suspend them across the board on the basis of general, theoretical considerations, even supposing we had strong arguments for doing so. Thus we could not suspend such attitudes on the basis of our recognition of the dilemma for intrinsic theories. And according to Strawson, even if we *could* choose whether or not to suspend our reactive attitudes, we could choose rationally only by weighing the gains and losses for human existence. The implication is clear that in

Strawson's view, if we chose rationally, we would choose to keep our reactive attitudes.

There is no question that Strawson has accurately diagnosed and eliminated an important difficulty for an extrinsic justification of our practices in ascribing responsibility. The objection to such a justification is that it alienates the participants in those practices from the practices themselves. Instead of justifying punishment and blame by reference to the subjects on whom such punishment falls, we justify it in terms of its social efficacy. The picture this suggests is that of a society forced to go through the distasteful ritual of inflicting suffering on those who are distinguished only by the fact that their suffering will maximize social utility. Punishment in such a case would amount to the self-conscious and cynical victimization of those who were made to suffer. And Strawson is correct in pointing out that we are not alienated from our own practices in this way.

For Strawson, the gap between social utility and the pain and suffering of particular individuals is bridged by our tendency to feel resentment, moral indignation, guilt, and shame when an injury has been caused. As Strawson puts it, "the preparedness to acquiesce in that infliction of suffering on the offender which is an essential part of punishment is all of a piece with this whole range of [reactive] attitudes."[22] And, as he goes on to add, our preparedness to acquiesce in our own suffering when we have caused injury to another is part and parcel of the attitudes in this same range.

My position, like Strawson's, will depend on the assumption that for a practice to be genuinely one involving responsibility, blame, and punishment, it must be possible for subjects to acquiesce in the suffering it involves—including their own. Because the difference between my view and Strawson's turns on whether reactive and self-reactive attitudes alone are sufficient for aquiescence in the suffering of others and of oneself, it is necessary to say more explicitly what I take this to entail. Acquiescence in the suffering brought on by punishment and blame requires, first, the ability to accept and support the suffering involved, where this includes the ability to respond with the appropriate reactive attitudes. Beyond this, however, one's acceptance and support must be *justified* and must be justified in a way that is conceptually connected with motivation.

These requirements are more in line with our understanding of what is necessary for an institution to count as one of punishment than is Strawson's assumption that only reactive attitudes are necessary. An act of inflicting suffering that we would not count as punishment would not become punishment merely because its victims accepted it as a result of (say) neurotic guilt. Nor would it become punishment merely because it was accepted (as a result of neurotic guilt) and there existed *some* justification of that acceptance. The fact, for example, that the acceptance had a utilitarian justification (unbeknownst to those involved) would not make the suffering a case of punishment. Even if the utilitarian justification were recognized by those involved, the acceptance of the suffering would not necessarily have a rational justification for those who suffered. The subjects in question might be completely unmotivated to make such a contribution to aggregate utility. Under these circumstances, acceptance of the suffering would not count as acquiescence. What acquiescence requires is that the acceptance be motivated by the justification, and not merely as a matter of contingent psychological fact. Such a fact would itself require justification in the same way that the psychological fact of our possessing certain reactive attitudes does. Hence the justification must provide its own motivation—and do so necessarily.[23]

Thus, although Strawson's complaint that the usual extrinsic theories provide no role for reactive attitudes is justified, he is wrong in assuming that reference to our reactive attitudes rules out all possible forms of alienation from our own practices. One of the difficulties for Strawson's position lies in the fact that he fails to recognize the problems that arise for an intrinsic justification of our practices concerning punishment and blame. And in the absence of such an intrinsic justification, Strawson has no reply to the objection that we could come to see our reactive attitudes themselves as being as much in need of justification (and as difficult to justify) as our practices regarding punishment. Though we might continue to feel indignation at some of those who cause injury to others and feel no distaste in making such individuals suffer, we might also find this very lack of distaste itself a source of shame and regret.

Moreover, though Strawson is undoubtedly right to claim that eradicating such feelings is not a practical possibility, it is clearly a logical possibility. And it is certainly not irrelevant to ask whether we would be justified in doing so if we had the technology to make such a fundamental change in the structure of our interpersonal attitudes. Nothing that Strawson has said rules out the claim that we should eliminate our reactive attitudes and accept a revised conception of those who injure others along the lines suggested by contemporary psychiatry—and with it an attenuated sense of our personal responsibility. Hence Strawson cannot plausibly claim to have filled the gap that he has correctly noted between the social efficacy of our practices and the real pain and suffering of actual individuals.

4   *From Nonmaximizing to Self-Supporting Dispositions*

Changing our perspective on self-deception to focus on our evaluation of the phenomenon rather than its explanation will have meant replacing one puzzle with another if there is no adequate account of our ascriptions of responsibility to self-deceivers. And as we have seen in sections 2 and 3, none of the usual accounts is adequate. In this section I shall discuss a class of dispositions—the nonmaximizing dispositions—of which, as it turns out, self-deception is a member. This will help to clarify the nature of the difficulties with our present treatments of responsibility. I shall then go on to examine a second class—the self-supporting dispositions—which provides the basis for a solution to these difficulties. In the two sections that follow, I shall apply these results to the problem of ascriptions of responsibility to show the kind of justification to which our ascriptions in general, and our practice of ascribing responsibility for self-deception in particular, are open.

Let us say that *d* is a *nonmaximizing disposition* for a subject *S* between *t* and *t'* (where *D* is the set of *S*'s desires at *t* and *B* is the set of *S*'s beliefs at *t*) if and only if *d* prevents *S*'s actions from maximizing the satisfaction of the desires in *D* (given the beliefs in *B*), even though *D* and *B* remain *S*'s underlying desires and beliefs between *t* and *t'*. Such a disposition might be the result of some of *S*'s desires or beliefs in *D* or *B* becoming temporarily inaccessible or diminished in strength. Alternatively, it might result from the temporary emergence of desires or beliefs that are not part of *D* or *B* or from the temporary increase in strength of some of those that are. Thus, although one always acts on what is motivationally one's strongest desire, that desire may be a temporary aberration relative to one's underlying desires and beliefs. (On this definition, full-blown self-deception yields a nonmaximizing disposition. When one is self-deceived in the full-blown sense, one will maximize the satisfaction of one's desires not relative to the underlying set of beliefs that contains one's original belief but relative to the new set that contains the induced belief. In contrast, one-shot self-deception will not yield a nonmaximizing disposition, since the original belief does not remain part of one's underlying belief set.)

There are many familiar ways in which nonmaximizing dispositions can give one a strategic advantage over others.[24] One might, for example, induce in oneself the disposition to ignore any threats made against one, come what may. One might do so by inducing a disposition to become so angry if threatened that one would temporarily lose touch with all the desires that conflict with the desire not to capitulate. One's disposition to ignore these threats, whatever the consequences, would effectively deter any threat whose execution would impose a significant cost on the person making it, as long as one's disposition were known to potential threat initiators. A potential threat initiator would calculate correctly that he or she stood to gain nothing by threatening such a perfect threat ignorer and that he or she stood to lose either credibility or the cost of executing the threat. Of course, if for some reason a potential threat initiator were *not* deterred, then even if it would maximize the satisfaction of one's underlying desires to capitulate, one would be disposed not to do so. Hence such a disposition is a disposition to act in a way that will not maximize the satisfaction of one's underlying desires (relative to one's underlying beliefs) *if* it is ever *manifest*. But the *acquisition* of the disposition could maximize the satisfaction of those same underlying desires (relative to the underlying beliefs) because its *possession* would keep one out of precisely those situations in which one would act on it.

With this definition of nonmaximizing dispositions in mind, we can strengthen the conclusion of section 3. That conclusion was that Strawson had not shown that our reactive attitudes were justified and so had not shown that our practices regarding responsibility were justified. The stronger claims for which I shall now argue are the following. First, unless they can be given some form of justification, our reactive attitudes are a kind of nonmaximizing disposition. Second, nonmaximizing dispositions, by their very nature, cannot themselves serve as the ultimate ground of a set of practices and institutions where responsibility is concerned. Third, if our reactive attitudes are nonmaximizing dispositions, they cannot be justified (under the conditions in which our practices regarding responsibility actually occur) by reference to their consequences. Thus they cannot play the justificatory role for which Strawson has them slated.

To see that if our reactive attitudes have no further justification they are nonmaximizing, we need only notice that they are dispositions to cause suffering in the form of punishment or blame or to acquiesce in our own suffering, even when such suffering has no deterrent rationale. This must be the case, since in expressing our reactive attitudes, we are ignoring questions of social efficacy, the consideration of which would make our attitudes objective rather than reactive. Thus our reactive attitudes are dispositions that prevent our actions from maximizing our overriding concerns to prevent pointless and unnecessary suffering.

The reason that nonmaximizing dispositions cannot themselves provide the ultimate support for practices such as those concerning responsibility is a direct consequence of their definition. A nonmaximizing disposition prevents our actions from maximizing the satisfaction of our desires, given our beliefs. Whether this is the result of our temporarily losing touch with some of our underlying beliefs or desires or of the temporary emergence of new ones, we will retain the motivational resources to criticize our nonmaximizing dispositions. Such dispositions will be open to criticism for their failure to maximize the satisfaction of those desires relative to those beliefs. Thus, however resistant to change they might turn out to be in practice, we could have good reason to regret our reactive attitudes and to hope for new therapies or drugs that would improve the prospects for their change or elimination.

Strawson must argue, then, not just that our reactive attitudes are deeply ingrained but that they are themselves in fact justified. And it is very implausible to claim that such dispositions are justified by the contribution they make to our human good, that is, by their consequences.[25] There are two reasons for the implausibility. The first is that such dispositions are unlikely to be efficacious under the conditions imposed by the fact that our practices of punishment and blame constitute our primary institution of social control. Reactive attitudes construed as nonmaximizing dispositions cannot provide the basis for institutions that are deliberately designed to function independently of the attitudes of individual participants.

The inadequacy of our reactive attitudes to support our institutions is clear in view of the following characteristics of our institutions and attitudes. Our reactive attitudes are often of shorter duration than the institutional proceedings for ascribing responsibility and blame, and they will almost certainly be of shorter duration than the punishment prescribed in the most serious cases. Our reactive attitudes may also depend on the point of view adopted, for example, whether we take the perspective of the victim or the accused, and they may shift with shifts in our perspective. There are also institutional mechanisms designed to help us suppress the reactive attitudes and to put us in touch with our underlying beliefs and desires. Examples include the arguments of defense attorneys alleging the pointlessness of the suffering that their clients' punishment would entail. Our institutions of punishment and blame are also designed to deal with those cases in which the stakes are highest. And the combination of high stakes, long and impersonal proceedings and penalties, and mechanisms designed to give us access to our underlying desires virtually guarantees that nonmaximizing dispositions in general, and our reactive attitudes in particular, will not be sustained in the context of the institutions they are meant to support.

The second reason for the failure of the claim that our reactive attitudes are justified by their consequences is that there may well be alternatives in dealing with social deviance that do not require that we inflict pain and suffering. A social practice governed by the medical or psychiatric model of social deviance or by models derived from the social or behavioral sciences provides an obvious example.[26] Since our attitudes on these issues are open to criticism and revision, the uneasiness we might feel at such an objectivist approach is not *in itself* sufficient to support our current practices regarding responsibility, punishment, and blame.

This failure of our reactive attitudes in the role for which Strawson intended them stems from the following fact. Nonmaximizing dispositions cannot be *self-supporting*. That is, our motivational makeup is such that we have the resources both to criticize our pattern of emotional responses and in the long run to change it, where feasible. There is, however, a class of dispositions that resemble nonmaximizing dispositions and that are self-supporting. Recall the definition of an ideal reflective equilibrium. Given a subject's actual noninstrumental desires, that subject's IRE is the set of noninstrumental desires that would result if he or she could subtract the desires that were badly supported and add desires that would be well supported. By definition, a subject's IRE is not open to criticism from inside that could motivate that subject to change it. Hence the set of desires that emerge in IRE, taken as a whole (and given the subject's beliefs), constitutes a self-supporting disposition.

But in what sense does such a disposition resemble a nonmaximizing disposition? In other words, in the case of a self-supporting disposition consisting in a set of desires in IRE, what are the analogues to the two salient features of nonmaximizing dispositions: that they dispose one to act against one's own interests and that it may nevertheless be true of some that it is in one's interests to acquire them? And if there are analogues to these features of nonmaximizing dispositions, how do they coexist with the feature that makes one's desires in IRE suitable to play the role that Strawson assigns to reactive attitudes—that one cannot be motivated to replace or override one's desires in IRE?

To see the relation between a nonmaximizing and a self-supporting disposition, imagine an act-consequentialist with no noninstrumental desire to keep her promises except as this contributes to the satisfaction of her other desires. She desires various kinds of states of affairs, and her problem is to maximize the satisfaction of those desires. And suppose she faces the following situation. First, the potential benefits of cooperating with others (and hence of making and keeping contracts and promises) are very great, especially in undertakings in which the stakes are high. Second, a large number of others are disposed to cooperate with those who are similarly disposed. Third, most subjects are adept at distinguishing those who are genuinely disposed to co-operate from those who are disposed to feign cooperation and to defect when it is to their advantage to do so.

As an act-consequentialist, she will be motivated, under such cir-cumstances, to acquire a disposition to cooperate. Moreover, she will be motivated to acquire a self-supporting disposition to keep promises, even when the stakes are high and it is disadvantageous to do so. For unless the disposition is self-supporting, she will be motivated to have the disposition overridden or destroyed whenever the stakes are suf-ficiently high that what she gains by breaking a promise offsets any damage to her credibility. Similarly, unless the disposition to keep promises is self-supporting, she will be motivated to break them when-ever she could do so undetected. If others are able to tell whether she possesses a self-supporting disposition, a disposition that is not self-supporting will not secure for her the desired benefits.

As an act-consequentialist, she can acquire such a self-supporting disposition to keep contracts and promises by acquiring a complete IRE that contains as part of its conative core the noninstrumental desire to keep her promises even at great cost to herself. Since this desire is part of the conative core of an IRE, it cannot be an isolated one. Like any other such desire, this desire must be supported by a large number of other noninstrumental desires, such as the desire to preserve her honor at great cost and desires that define the role of honor in all the significant areas of her life. In general, such a disposition is not guar-anteed to maximize her original act-consequentialist desires. What prevents this disposition from being nonmaximizing in the strict sense defined is that the original act-consequentialist desires do *not* persist as her underlying desires. When she acquires the disposition, there is no longer any interesting sense in which she is an act-consequentialist. As an act-consequentialist, the motive she has to acquire it rests on its contribution to the satisfaction of her original desires. But under cir-cumstances that she hopes will never arise (partly as a result of her having the disposition), her actions would not maximize the satisfac-tion of *those* desires. Those desires would be sacrificed in favor of the desires that called for (say) the preservation of her honor even at great cost.[27]

The acquisition of such a self-supporting disposition is an irrevers-ible choice. Though one may be motivated to acquire such a disposition to secure the benefits of cooperation, one cannot be motivated (as always, with one's beliefs fixed) to eliminate it. Thus the act of ac-quiring such a disposition is self-constitutive or self-defining. I shall go on to claim that it is by reference to such self-supporting and self-defining dispositions that our ascriptions of responsibility are to be justified.

5 Internal Justification

As an act-consequentialist, one would be justified, given certain assumptions about the others in one's community, in acquiring a self-supporting disposition to keep promises even at great cost to oneself. Under similar conditions one would be justified in acquiring a self-supporting disposition to acquiesce in inflicting suffering on those who had caused injuries, even when one would oneself be the subject who suffered. One would, that is, be justified in acquiring a self-supporting disposition in virtue of which one would be prepared, on particular occasions, to inflict more suffering on those who had caused injuries and less suffering on those who had not caused injuries than would an act-consequentialist. One would be prepared, for example, to acquiesce in the punishment of those who had injured others but could be spared without any loss of deterrent effect in the future, and to refrain from causing suffering to those who had injured no one but whose suffering would be far outweighed by the future benefits to others.

Though the *acquisition* of this disposition would be justified on act-consequentialist grounds, those grounds would not be what justified the *possession* of the disposition to those who, in virtue of its acquisition, were no longer act-consequentialists. For such subjects, the extrinsic, act-consequentialist considerations would no longer be relevant. And because our ascriptions of responsibility discriminate where there are no relevant psychological differences, the intrinsic theories of justification would provide no alternative.

There is, however, an alternative to both an act-consequentialist justification and an intrinsic justification of this disposition. Imagine a subject for whom this disposition is part of a self-supporting disposition and in particular part of the conative core of the subject's IRE. It follows that the desire to support our practices in ascribing responsibility is supported by a large number of other desires, both noninstrumental and unconditional, that the subject has.

But what sorts of desires would support the desire to uphold these practices? Consider what would be lost if, on the basis of a psychological theory of deviant behavior and a medical approach to social control, we came to regard all punishment and blame—and hence our present conception of responsibility—as unjustified. Our concept of personal responsibility is intimately tied to our concepts of privacy and autonomy. Dispense with notions like responsibility, and we open ourselves to intervention aimed at preventing and not merely punishing social transgressions. Similarly, with no reason for the degree of intervention in one's affairs to reflect any actual injuries one has caused, one's sense of autonomy and privacy would be further eroded. Also, with different assumptions about responsibility go different assumptions about the rationality of one's motivations, and our notions of integrity and self-respect are likely to be lost or changed in radical and unpredictable ways. Moreover, since some social control must be internalized, if this is not accomplished through a sense of personal responsibility, it is difficult to see how it is to be accomplished except through the inculcation of false beliefs or by the direct conditioning of a significant number of desired responses. The first alternative puts even further pressure on our notions of self-respect and autonomy, whereas the second seems incompatible with the value we place on creativity and on one's right to pursue one's own possibly idiosyncratic projects when these involve no harm to others.

Let us call a justification that appeals to our noninstrumental desires in IRE an *internal justification.* Internal justification is conceptually tied to motivation. To a subject whose conative core contains desires for self-respect, autonomy, privacy, and the possibility of nonconformity in something like our senses, the desire to support our practices regarding responsibility will be well supported. By appeal to these other desires, the desire to support these practices will be both justified and motivated.

Such a justification answers the critic who claims that an extrinsic and consequentialist justification of our practices is out of place. If one is made to suffer under our practices of ascribing responsibility or one objects to such suffering, one can be made to see that the concept of responsibility involved is an inseparable component of a set of concepts that are together constitutive both of one's deepest commitments and of one's sense of what makes one the person one is.

What I have given is merely a sketch of a certain kind of justification of our practices regarding responsibility. Such a sketch is no guarantee that a justification of this kind actually exists. My own view is that this type of strategy regarding justification is promising, but the only claim I shall defend is that unless such a justification exists, there is no way of answering the objections of a certain kind of skeptic about our current practices. In the remainder of this section I shall first clarify the notion of internal justification. I shall then go on to discuss the kinds of skeptical questions that might be raised and the limitations on the kind of justification I have proposed.

What is the relation between an internal justification of our practices and the intrinsic justification discussed in section 2? An internal justification of our practices regarding responsibility, if it exists, depends on our noninstrumental desires, such as those for autonomy, privacy, integrity, and the possibility of nonconformity. Our commitment to these values consists simply in there being the appropriate mutually supporting desires in the conative core of our IRE. Thus, given the second component of the intrinsic-property constraint, which does not allow such values and commitments to count as a relevant psychological basis for the ascription of responsibility, an internal justification is necessarily extrinsic.

This result is in line with the way in which intrinsic theories are ordinarily understood. Traditional answers to the question of what constitutes a relevant psychological difference between those who are held responsible and those who are not require that the actions for which we are held responsible should be intentional, not impulsive, not the result of a rage or an irresistible impulse, not due to compulsion or a drug-induced state, and not the result of low intelligence. It has ordinarily been assumed that whether one believes one is responsible or whether our practices of ascribing responsibility are supported in one's IRE are not psychological considerations relevant to the question whether one actually *is* responsible. Given the internal conception of justification, our practices would be justified for a community of subjects who had internalized personal ideals and self-conceptions like ours; for a community of subjects who had not, the possibility of acquiescing in our practices of punishment and blame might not exist. And on any ordinary understanding of intrinsic theories, the question of whether a subject is responsible is not in this way relative to our beliefs and desires.

But though internal justification is extrinsic, it is unrelated to extrinsic justifications as *they* are normally understood. On the usual understanding, extrinsic justifications appeal to consequentialist considerations in order to justify the suffering that our practices concerning responsibility and punishment involve. For those for whom our practices have an internal justification, however, such an appeal is unnecessary. For such people, the acceptance of the suffering will be supported by dispositions superficially similar to our reactive attitudes as Stawson construes them. The difference is that those dispositions will themselves be supported by noninstrumental and unconditional desires in IRE. For such people, the acceptance of the suffering would remain even if the suffering were their own and even if they had the ability to change their attitudes at will. Thus an appeal to consequentialist considerations to justify our practices would be, for such people, not only unnecessary but irrelevant.

My claim, then, is that any justification of our actual ascriptions of responsibility must be either consequentialist or internal; there is no intrinsic justification of the ascriptions. But the distinction between intrinsic and internal justification suggests a serious limitation on the latter. Internal justification of our ascriptions of responsibility only works, assuming it does, for those who share our personal ideals and self-conceptions. And for those who do not, radically different practices may have an internal justification. For a community that shared our ideals, the complete medicalization of social control would not only be repugnant but would be unjustified in the internal sense. For a community that did not share these ideals, a medical paradigm might provide the ideal model for dealing with deviance.

This limitation on internal justification does not trivialize the claim that such a justification is available for our practices of ascribing responsibility. That such a claim might be trivial is suggested by the following argument. Whether a set of practices regarding responsibility is justified for a community depends on the noninstrumental desires that the members of the community have or would have in IRE. Since a group of people could be conditioned (or caused, at least in principle) to have any coherent set of desires, any scheme of social control, regardless of how outrageous, could be justified for some appropriately conditioned community.

The claim, however, that any set of institutions of social control could have an internal justification—if this means an internal justification that does not involve seriously mistaken beliefs—is almost certainly false. Imagine a society that successfully deters undesirable behavior by inflicting punishment on a certain number of people chosen at random. Assume that most people believe the gods control the process by which the victims are picked and that they believe, therefore, that the process is just. (Trial by ordeal might provide a rough approximation.)

Consider the position of the act-consequentialist deciding whether to adopt a disposition that will make her a part of the group, though she does not share the members' belief in the gods. Suppose she recognizes that membership in the group is the only alternative to the anarchy that prevails outside the group, that the advantages of group membership far outweigh the risks of being victimized, and that group membership requires a genuine self-supporting disposition to support the practices of social control even at great cost. Under these circumstances the act-consequentialist would seem to have every reason to acquire the self-supporting disposition required for membership. The acquisition of the disposition would have a consequentialist justification for her while she remained an act-consequentialist, and the social institutions would have an internalist justification for her after the nonconsequentialist disposition was acquired.

The difficulty is that even with a perfect technology for the creation of dispositions, the disposition in question may not exist. Given that the act-consequentialist believes that the victims are selected at random, what could she tell herself if she or a close friend were selected? What kind of disposition would allow her to acquiesce in such a victimization? She could, of course, acquire a disposition to feel loathing or antipathy toward the victims selected, and such a disposition might well extend to her own case. But the question is whether such a disposition could be self-supporting. Assuming a reasonable amount of sympathy in general for herself and others (and this might also be a requirement for group membership), what kinds of commitments and self-conception could override the temptation to spare one of the chosen victims if it were in her power to do so without being detected? Although the act-consequentialist might internalize a sense of repugnance at doing so, given the technology for changing one's dispositions, this is a disposition she would be motivated to override or eliminate if the relevant situation arose. But this means that, given her beliefs, the act-consequentialist could not acquire the relevant self-supporting disposition. Hence, for those who have no false beliefs about the machinations of the gods, the institutions in question seem to have no internal justification.[28]

Because the fact that our practices regarding responsibility have an internal justification is a nontrivial fact about those practices, we now have an answer to at least one skeptic (on the assumption that the sketch of an internal justification can be filled out). This is the skeptic who shares our self-conception and commitments but who wonders how our practice of ascribing responsibility and blame can be justified in the light of the problems for intrinsic theories. Let us call this person the *sympathetic anticonsequentialist skeptic*. Such a skeptic is answered by making explicit the support that the noninstrumental desire to acquiesce in our institutions of punishment and blame derives from his or her noninstrumental desires for autonomy, privacy, integrity, creativity, and so forth. By the same token, there is a skeptic we cannot answer, namely the skeptic who does not share our set of ideals and commitments but who has internalized some alternative set. Let us call this person the *unsympathetic anticonsequentialist skeptic*. For such a skeptic, our practices of social control will not have an internal justification, whereas some radically different practices will.

A third skeptic is the *act-consequentialist skeptic*. Since we have seen that under a set of conditions that are not completely unrealistic, an act-consequentialist would be motivated to adopt an IRE supporting our institutions of social control, we have a reply to the act-consequentialist skeptic as well. This is not to say that an act-consequentialist with no prior commitments could not adopt a self-conception that would support an alternative social practice. From the point of view of an act-consequentialist, a set of commitments supporting a medical approach to socially undesirable behavior might be equally attractive. This is simply to say that from a consequentialist point of view, there may be diverse solutions to the problem of securing social harmony.

There is a fourth skeptic, however, who, like the unsympathetic anticonsequentialist skeptic, cannot be answered. This is the skeptic who insists that only an intrinsic justification could justify our practices and who despairs of finding one. Such a skeptic is like the critic of compatibilism who is aware that the distinctions in our actual ascriptions of responsibility are based on systematic psychological differences but who does not find the differences relevant. Such a critic presses the difficulties we have seen for any intrinsic justification and claims that the psychological facts to which an internal justification appeals are equally irrelevant. This skeptic is equally unimpressed by external justifications and, I shall assume, by notions like agent causation. That we have no answer to such a skeptic shows that skepticism about responsibility has a deeper source than the compatibilist generally recognizes. There is no justification of our practices that rules out radical alternatives like those governed by the medical model. But the inference from the lack of an absolute justification to the conclusion that there is no justification at all is, as we have seen, unfounded.

6   Responsibility and Self-Deception

The question that remains is how the discussion of responsibility in general bears on the problem of self-deception. What the discussion of responsibility has shown is that ascriptions of responsibility that have no intrinsic justification can have both a consequentialist and an internal justification. This means that to hold a subject responsible for the operations of an unconscious subsystem is not *necessarily* unjustified. This falls obviously short of showing that it is justified in this particular instance. We do not, after all, hold people responsible for all the operations of their unconscious subsystems. What makes such a practice appropriate in the case of self-deception?

Let us take our discussion of responsibility in general as a guide. If there is an internal justification of our practices regarding self-deception, we should expect some special connection between avoiding self-deception and our notions of autonomy, integrity, and responsibility.

And the ideal of not being deceived by oneself does in fact seem tied to our concept of responsibility in a way that one's remaining immune to the deceptive strategies of others does not. The claim is, in other words, that to view ourselves as merely the victims of self-deception and not as its perpetrators would be at least partly to undermine the ideal of autonomy that is constitutive of our practices regarding responsibility.[29]

Suppose, however, that the following objection is made. Granted, it is difficult to imagine a practice involving responsibility, in anything like our sense, in which punishment and blame are entirely displaced by medical intervention. And given the problems for intrinsic theories, we are bound to assign or withhold blame on grounds that, according to the intrinsic-property constraint, cannot be relevant. Still, it might be objected, the ideal of being responsible oneself for remaining un-deceived by oneself is not so central to our notion of responsibility that we cannot imagine a similar notion that lacks this ideal.

The answer to this objection involves recalling the central claim of the chapter. That claim is that our practice of ascribing blame for self-deception can be justified for a group with beliefs and commitments similar to ours. For such a group there is a form of justification, internal justification, that would justify our practices of blaming self-deceivers in particular and of punishment and blame in general. Since I shall leave open the question of whether we are such a group, the question of whether the desire to acquiesce in blaming self-deceivers would occur in *our* ideal reflective equilibria will not be settled here. Nonetheless, I shall briefly sketch two reasons for thinking that the answer is not obviously no.

The first reason is that even if we eliminated our tendency to blame self-deceivers, this would bring our practices of ascribing responsibility no closer to satisfying the intrinsic-property constraint. We would continue to blame some people for actions motivated by desires out of IRE, while others whose actions were also motivated by such desires would be excused as compulsives. And we would do so despite the lack of a relevant psychological difference (by the standards of the intrinsic-property constraint) between the two cases. To suppose that the desires that make up the conative core of our IREs would not support such a distinction would be to suppose that nothing like our practice of ascribing responsibility would be supported, either because we would cease to regard any form of compulsion as an excuse or because we would excuse everyone acting on a desire that was out of IRE. The former alternative would represent a radical tightening of the standards we apply in evaluating excuses. And the latter alternative, as we have seen, would leave only the psychopath and other unreachable subjects as legitimate objects of punishment and blame.

Second, just as we ascribe blame for some actions stemming from desires out of IRE and not others, so we are likely to ascribe blame for some actions stemming from self-deception and not others (and for some instances and not others of self-deception itself). But since it would require a lengthy discussion of the excuses we accept, I shall not try to characterize the grounds on which we distinguish some actions and not others as compulsive where they all stem from desires out of IRE. I shall therefore not try to work out an analogous distinction between the forms of self-deception that are likely to be excused and those that are not. It seems plausible, however, to suppose that as the desire motivating the deception becomes more remote from our conscious desires and projects, the likelihood of that deception's being excused will increase. And if we think of psychological operations as mechanical to the extent that they are insensitive to the influence of our conscious beliefs and desires, then mechanical self-deception seems less likely to incur blame. But as self-deception becomes more closely tied to projects that we recognize as our own and becomes a more flexible manifestation of our conscious beliefs and desires, our responsibility for its consequences will be more difficult to deny.

What I have shown is the intelligibility of a situation in which people with beliefs and desires like ours have noninstrumental desires in IRE to support the practice of punishment in spite of the dilemma for any intrinsic justification. Since the practice of ascribing responsibility and blame to self-deceivers is intelligible on the same grounds, this provides one solution to the problem of self-deception. More precisely, it removes the most serious objection by far to the homuncular solution. But to show the intelligibility of people with beliefs and desires at least *similar* to ours for whom the practice of blaming self-deception has an internal justification is one thing. To show that such a practice has an internal justification for us is another. It may not, either because our desires in IRE do not support our practices of punishment in general or because they do not support our practice of blaming self-deceivers in particular. If this is the case, then these practices are unjustified in any sense that would allow us to *acquiesce* in the suffering they involve. And this provides a second solution to the problem of self-deception. If our blaming self-deceivers is unjustified or justified only on consequentialist grounds, then the alleged implausibility of the homuncular solution is merely apparent. In either case the objection to the homuncular solution has been met.

A satisfactory treatment of the problem of self-deception, then, involves three basic revisions of the underlying assumptions with which it is ordinarily approached. First, we must come to see the problem not in terms of the explanation of self-deception but in terms of the evaluation of our responsibility for its occurrence. The mechanism of self-deception is unmysterious, given the prevalence of homuncular models in the cognitive sciences. It is the ascription of responsibility for the operation of an unconscious mechanism—that is, the ascription of responsibility in violation of the intrinsic-property constraint—that raises the most serious philosophical problems.

Second, we must drop the assumption that our practice of ascribing responsibility could have a justification in which discriminations in our ascriptions to different subjects are justified by differences in the intrinsic properties of the subjects' psychologies. Furthermore, though the acquisition of a disposition to support our practices regarding responsibility might have a consequentialist justification, for those whose commitments actually *do* support our practices, no such justification is possible.

Finally, we must abandon the expectation of an absolute justification of our institutions and practices. If we do, we can explain the possibility of an internal justification of our institutions and practices by reference to the notion of a self-supporting disposition. Though the justification is not absolute, it is the only justification that can appeal to those who have internalized the ideals on which these practices depend. In this chapter I have provided only the barest sketch of how such an internal justification might be completed and of how it might be applied to the specific case of self-deception. But if the completion of such a task is impossible, this would entail not just a change in our attitude toward self-deception but a wholesale revision of our conception of responsibility and of ourselves.

Acknowledgments

I am grateful to Jonathan Adler, Robert Audi, Akeel Bilgrami, Stephen Darwall, Mark Johnston, Brian McLaughlin, and Georges Rey for their comments on earlier drafts. I have benefited especially from the discussion of these issues with Jonathan Glover and from his recent work on responsibility (presented at the University of Michigan in 1985 and included in part in "Self-Creation," *Proceedings of the British Academy* 69 [1983]: 445–471).

Chapter 8
Moral Responsibility

On July 17, 1976 Albert Spaggiari and the group he had assembled completed their tunnel into the vault of the Société Générale in Nice. Estimates put the value of the currency, gold, and jewelry they removed at sixty million francs, which would make the theft one of the largest of its kind ever committed.[1] If determinism is true, then a complete description of the universe at noon, January 1 in the year 1 A.D. entails (given the laws of nature) that Spaggiari would enter the vault at exactly the time he did (approximately 10 P.M.) and would execute exactly the sequence of actions he performed to complete the robbery thirty-two hours later. According to compatibilist theories of moral responsibility, the claim that our practices of ascribing responsibility, praise, and blame are justified is compatible with the truth of determinism.

Determinism is, of course, false.[2] But I shall assume that if the truth of determinism makes the justification of our practices regarding responsibility impossible, then the indeterminacies of quantum mechanics do not solve the problem that the absence of such a justification poses. I shall also assume that if determinism is compatible with such a justification, then that justification will not be undermined if quantum indeterminacies exist. In what follows, I shall consider the currently available versions of compatibilist theories. I shall argue that none of these versions of compatibilism provides an adequate justification of our practices of ascribing responsibility, punishment, and blame. I shall then go on to sketch a compatibilist theory that avoids the problems for the types of compatibilism that have thus far been proposed.

1 Classical Compatibilism

The claim that responsibility is compatible with determinism is based on the following intuition. What matters for responsibility is that we act freely, and it is not required for our acting freely that our actions be uncaused. Rather, what is required is that they be caused in the right way. And what compatibilists have usually had in mind in requiring that our actions be caused in the right way is that they depend on our preferences, choices, decisions, or some similar motivational states of ours. Moreover, it is usually assumed that for a piece of behavior to depend (in the relevant sense) on our preferences, choices, or decisions entails that if we prefer, choose, or decide to do the thing in question, we do it, and if we prefer, choose, or decide not to, we refrain. Where our past behavior is concerned, this means that had we chosen or decided to do something besides what we actually did, we would have done it. Indeed, this last condition has been taken to be an analysis (the so-called conditional analysis) of the claim that we could have done other than what we did.[3] And this in turn has been taken as a necessary and sufficient condition of our having acted freely. Proponents of this kind of theory include Hobbes, Locke, Hume, Moore, and Ayer, among others.[4] Let us call compatibilist theories of this kind versions of *classical compatibilism*.[5]

Classical compatibilism is open to a number of familiar objections. To say that an agent's behavior depends on his or her preferences, choices, or decisions does not seem to rule out any of the following possibilities:

1. Smith gambles and thereby satisfies her strongest desire. But Smith is well aware that continuing to act on this desire will have ruinous consequences and wishes that she could be rid of it.
2. Jones chooses to take a drug and as a result does so. Jones, however, is an addict. Had he chosen not to take the drug, he would have been unable to persist in this choice for long and would, within a short period of time, have decided to take the drug after all.
3. Brown decides to sing the *Marseillaise* at midnight and does so. But Brown does so as a result of a posthypnotic suggestion, which she never chose to receive.
4. Black comes to believe that, all things considered, he should confess to the political crimes of which he has been accused, and therefore he does. Unbeknownst to Black, however, his belief is the result of an intensive process of brainwashing designed to break down the commitments that would motivate him to resist making the confession.

In each of these cases the preference, choice, or decision determines the action. But in each case the action seems unfree because of the way the preference, choice, or decision is determined. Though the action is a function of one of the relevant motivational states in each case, the state is forced on the agent, either by internal or external conditions, in a way that seems to rule out either the agent's acting freely or choosing freely. A natural response is to impose an analogue of the requirement regarding actions on the agent's choices, preferences, or decisions themselves. If an agent is to have acted freely, the agent's choice (preference, decision, etc.) must have been determined in an appropriate way by some of his or her other motivational states. But suggestions along these lines have encountered serious difficulties.

In the first place, the counterfactual analysis of an agent's having been able to do otherwise—that if the agent had chosen to do otherwise, he or she would have—does not seem applicable to the notion of choice itself. It does not seem plausible, that is, to suppose that an agent chooses freely just in case if the agent had chosen to choose otherwise, he or she would have done so. Similar problems arise if our acting freely is analyzed in terms of our behavior's being determined by an intention, a decision, or a willing.[6] This first objection counts against the claim that our being able to do other than what we in fact do is *sufficient* for our doing it freely and for our being responsible for it. It has also been objected that our being able to do other than what we do is not *necessary* for its being our responsibility. Imagine that a scientist has planted electrodes in Doe's brain, which allows him to monitor Doe's thoughts and change them at will. And suppose that the scientist decides that if Doe chooses not to perform a particular action A, he will intervene and make Doe change his mind and choose to do it, and that if Doe chooses to perform A, he will not intervene. Now suppose that Doe chooses to perform the action without any intervention by the scientist. In this case it seems that Doe has acted freely and is responsible for what he does, even though he could not have done otherwise. That is, it is not the case that had he chosen to refrain from doing A, he would have done so.[7]

These objections to classical compatibilism have rightly been seen as inconclusive. Nothing in any of the objections shows that there cannot be a theory that analyses an agent's acting freely in terms of his or her being able to do otherwise and analyses this in terms of the claim that the agent *would* have done otherwise had he or she chosen to do so. But there is a more fundamental objection to any such theory. If determinism is true, then for any action there will be some senses (or interpretations) of the expression 'could have done otherwise' in which the agent could indeed have done otherwise, and there will be other senses (or interpretations) in which he or she could not. The conditional analysis provides one sense in which the agent could have done otherwise: the agent would have acted differently if he or she had chosen differently. And there are many other features of the causal history of the agent's action such that if those features had been different, the action would have been different. On the other hand, there will be many senses in which the agent could *not* have done otherwise. For example, given determinism, if we hold the whole causal history of the agent's action fixed, then the resulting action could not have been other than it was. The question, then, for classical compatibilism is, What grounds the claim that one of the senses in which we could have done otherwise justifies our practices regarding responsibility when it could be argued equally well that one of the senses in which we could not have done otherwise ensures that our practices are unjustified?

This problem can be put in another way: What can a proponent of the conditional analysis say to an incompatibilist who claims that the sense in which we could have done otherwise (as defined by the version of the analysis in question) does not justify our ever punishing or blaming anyone? As the conditional analysis becomes more complex (as it must in order to deal with the kinds of objections that have been raised already), it is increasingly unlikely to be self-evident that those who satisfy the analysis deserve punishment or praise. Even if there is some version of the analysis that captures all the actions that we intuitively think of as free and excludes all those we think of as unfree, and even if the analysis is based on an intuitively plausible principle, such an analysis will be insufficient to answer the incompatibilist. How can such an analysis answer the incompatibilist's claim that the conditions specified as sufficient for free action are *not* sufficient? The problem is especially acute because the incompatibilist too can appeal to plausible principles, for example, the principle of the transfer of powerlessness: if one is powerless to prevent A and one is powerless to prevent A's leading to B, one is powerless to prevent B.[8] The compatibilist, of course, can appeal to the fact that his principle is the one that codifies our actual practice. But this reply begs the question against the incompatibilist, who is asking whether that practice is justified. Let us call this problem for classical compatibilism the *basic problem* and the argument that appeals to it the *basic argument*. As we shall see, the basic argument provides an objection to any form of compatibilism which is not, in a sense to be defined in section 4, direct.

2   Hierarchical Compatibilism

We saw in section 1 that the conditional analysis of free action according to which an action is free just in case the agent would have refrained from performing it if he or she had chosen seems unpromising. An action may be unfree because it is the product of an unfree choice, and nothing in the conditional analysis imposes any constraints on how the choice is produced. As we have seen, the attempt to apply the conditional analysis to choice itself yields the dubious notion of choosing to choose, as well as the threat of an infinite regress. That our choices should be *chosen* imposes an impossibly strong constraint. But that they should merely depend in *some* way on our motivational makeup is clearly too weak. What is needed is some specification of the features of the motivational makeup that must determine our choices if those choices are to be free.

Hierarchical compatibilist theories provide a way of filling this gap. Hierarchical theories distinguish ordinary first-order desires from higher-order desires, which take other desires as their objects. According to these theories, one's action is free in the sense required for moral responsibility just in case the desires by which it is motivated are either in accord with, or in accord with and motivated by, one's higher-order desires. Harry Frankfurt, for example, defines one's *will* as a first-order desire that does or will or would move one all the way to action. And he defines a *volition* as a second-order desire that one have some first-order desire or that some first-order desire should move one to action, that is, that it should be one's will.

Frankfurt applies these distinctions in the following example. The person whom Frankfurt calls the *unwilling addict* struggles against the desire for some drug and finds the desire irresistible. Such a person has a first-order desire for the drug, and this desire is his or her will. The person also has a second-order volition that the desire for the drug not move him or her to action, and this second-order volition is frustrated. Frankfurt goes on to claim that one has *freedom of the will* just in case the following further condition is met: with regard to any particular one of one's first-order desires, one is free either to make that desire one's will or to make some other desire one's will instead.[9] Frankfurt does not, however, hold that freedom of the will is necessary for moral responsibility. Being morally responsible seems to mean for Frankfurt that one does what one wants to do because one wants to do it and that one's will is the result of a second-order volition.[10] The unwilling addict, then, lacks freedom of the will. In addition, this person is not responsible for taking the drug. Although such an addict takes the drug as the result of a desire to do so and although he or she would not have taken the drug had there been no such desire, this addict's will is not the result of any of his or her second-order volitions but is in direct conflict with them. In Frankfurt's terms, the unwilling addict not only lacks freedom of the will but also fails to *act of his or her own free will.*

In this failure to act of his or her own free will the unwilling addict is different from the subject Frankfurt calls the *willing addict*. Whereas the unwilling addict desires not to have an effective desire for the drug, the willing addict is happy to have such a desire. In fact, if the willing addict's desire for the drug were to disappear, he or she might well be motivated to reinstate it, if this were possible, in its full strength. The willing addict, however, still lacks freedom of the will. This is because if he or she were to lose the second-order volition that the first-order desire to take the drug should be effective (and acquire a second-order volition that this should not be the case), the first-order desire for the drug would continue to determine his or her actions. In other words, the desire for the drug would continue to constitute his or her will. Thus such an addict would be unable to have the will he or she desired. It is true, nonetheless, that the willing addict can perform the action he or she wants. And although this addict cannot have any will except the one he or she has, the addict's will accords with his or her second-order volition. Moreover, according to Frankfurt, the willing addict's will is overdetermined by his or her addiction and his or her second-order volition. On Frankfurt's view, then, the willing addict does act of his or her own free will.[11]

This account, like other hierarchical accounts, provides a natural analysis of the problem of compulsion that plagues classical compatibilism. For the classical compatibilist, the compulsive performs the action he or she wants and hence acts freely and is responsible for the action. But because the unwilling addict, according to Frankfurt, does not act of his or her own free will, Frankfurt can allow that he or she is *not* responsible for the action.

In spite of this advantage, hierarchical theories also encounter serious problems. As has often been pointed out, Frankfurt's view and other hierarchical theories seem to involve an infinite regress.[12] The objection is that on these views responsibility requires that one identify with the first-order desire that moves one to action. And for this it seems necessary that the first-order desire should be endorsed by a second-order volition. But suppose that one does not have a third-order volition that one act in accordance with one's second-order volition. Since in this case one has not identified with the second-order volition (and in fact, one may have a third-order volition in virtue of which one repudiates it), the second-order volition seems insufficient to ensure that one identifies with the first-order desire. Thus it seems that one can be responsible for acting on a first-order desire only if acting on that desire is endorsed at every higher level. And this demand is one that no actual agent seems to meet.

It has been objected on Frankfurt's behalf that although identification with a desire may in some cases consist in its endorsement by a desire at the next level, this is not a necessary condition of identification on his view.[13] This objection is well taken, but it leaves Frankfurt and other defenders of hierarchical theories with a dilemma. Either they must accept the consequences of an infinite regress, or they owe us an independent explanation of what identification consists in. My present claim is not that such an explanation is impossible. But to the extent that it is forthcoming and does not involve an infinite regress, it will show that even for hierarchical theories, it is not the appeal to higher-order desires that plays the most important role in the explanation of such important notions as identification.

A second and related problem for proponents of hierarchical theories is that although in general our higher-order desires may be closer to our real values and commitments than our first-order desires, there is no necessary connection between a desire's being of higher-order and its representing what we "really" want. There is nothing to prevent a second-order volition from being as alien to one's real desires as any first-order desire. Take the second-order desire not to have or act on desires that were formed during a period of one's life from which one is now alienated (say because one held religious views that one now repudiates), even when those desires would otherwise cohere perfectly with one's present desires. This is a desire that one might struggle as hard to overcome as any of the first-order desires with which one fails to identify. If this is the case, however, then the proponent of a hierarchical theory seems to be on the wrong track. Hierarchical theories represent an advance in suggesting the importance of the relation between the desires that move us to action and the rest of our motivational makeup. Desires that are completely alien to us, for example, compulsive desires, may move us to actions for which we are not responsible. But to suppose that the reason we are not responsible is merely that our first-order desires to perform the compulsive actions are not endorsed by second-order volitions seems to create more problems than it solves.

Weakness of the will poses a third problem for hierarchical theories. The first two problems for such theories concerned the difficulties in constructing a hierarchical theory of identification. What a theory of identification must explain is which of our desires represent or are compatible with our commitments or values or, alternatively, our judgments as to what we should do, all things considered. Such a theory should tell us, in other words, which of our desires are desires for the things we *really* want. And, as we have seen, the attempt to explain the distinction between what we want and what we really want by reference to our higher-order desires does not succeed. There is, however, another problem that any theory of responsibility must face. Suppose such a theory did provide an adequate account of identification. Then consider the problem of weakness of the will. To perform a weak-willed action is simply to act on a desire in conflict with one's real desires or with one's judgment as to what one should do, all things considered. Thus to perform a weak-willed action is to act on a desire with which one does not identify. One may, for example, put off starting a project, even though one knows full well that the project will be completed less successfully as a result and even though one cares more about the successful completion of the project than about the advantages derived from postponing it. But in cases of this kind one is not excused by the fact that one has acted on a desire at odds with one's real desires. If the desire to postpone the project is not irresistible, then one is justified in blaming oneself for acting on the desire and in accepting the blame directed at one by others.

Thus the problem of weakness of the will shows that a theory of identification is not sufficient to provide a theory of moral responsibility. Both the compulsive agent and the weak-willed agent act on desires with which they fail to identify. But the compulsive agent is excused, or at any rate not held fully responsible, whereas the weak-willed agent is held responsible and blamed. Of course, the difference is that the desire on which the weak-willed agent acted was resistible, unlike the one on which the compulsive agent acted. But this suggests that the weak-willed agent is blamed because he or she could have done otherwise, and it was the problem of spelling out this notion in a way compatible with determinism that drove us from classical compatibilist theories to hierarchical theories in the first place.

3   Valuational Compatibilism

Valuational compatibilism is the thesis that a free action is one that has some special relation to values. Either the action must accord with values (either the subjective values of the agent or objective values), or it must be produced by values, or it must be responsive to values in the sense that if the values had been different, the action would have been different. One version of such a theory has been advanced by Gary Watson. Watson suggests that the distinction between the free agent, that is, the agent who acts freely, and the compulsive is that the compulsive's "desires express themselves independently of his evaluational judgments."[14] These evaluational judgments are the product of the agent's "valuational system." And for Watson, the valuational system is "that set of considerations which, when combined with his factual beliefs (and probability estimates), yields judgments of the form: the thing for me to do in these circumstances, all things considered, is a."[15] The agent's valuational system contrasts with the motivational system, which is "that set of considerations which move him to action. We identify his motivational system by identifying what motivates him."[16] Thus, whereas Frankfurt distinguishes between levels of desire, Watson distinguishes between "independent sources of motivation."

By shifting his focus from higher-order desires to the valuational system, Watson solves two of the three problems that Frankfurt's theory faces. Watson's theory requires no notion of identification with lower-order desires. Thus it involves no threat of an infinite regress among desires of higher order. And Watson is free to acknowledge the lack of any necessary connection between a desire's being of higher order and its being a desire for something one really wants, wants most, or wants all things considered.

The notion of a valuational system raises problems of its own, however. On the one hand, this notion requires that we be able to step back from our desires and make an evaluation that conflicts with what is dictated by our motivationally strongest desires. On the other hand, we cannot step back from all our desires simultaneously, since the evaluational judgment is supposed to have motivational force; it is a judgment about what the agent himself or herself should do, all things considered. And if this judgment lacks motivational force, it cannot help in characterizing compulsion or weakness of the will. One does not necessarily behave in a weak-willed way because one fails to act on the judgment that one ought, all things considered, to do A. The behavior need not be weak-willed, for example, if the judgment that one ought to do A involves only the use of 'ought' in scare quotes—as the judgment might if it were backed only by the norms of one's society. One may fail to act not out of weakness but because one is indifferent to those social norms. And if Watson cannot give an account of weakness of the will or compulsion, then he will have lost any advantage his account might have had over classical compatibilism.

Assume, therefore, that the evaluational system itself operates on the basis of the agent's desires (and Watson himself makes it clear that this is the case in his version of the valuational theory). Then a valuational compatibilist needs some account of the difference between the desires that motivate the evaluational judgment and the desires the agent steps back from in forming the judgment. The valuational compatibilist cannot be content to say that they are different systems, since that would raise the question of why the agent should identify with the desires in the evaluational system. And the suggestion cannot be that the evaluational system simply *is* the system with whose desires one identifies, whatever system that is. This would provide no explanation of what it was in virtue of which the evaluational system was the evaluational system. Hence the valuational theorist would have no account of identification to replace Frankfurt's account in terms of higher-order desires. Thus, unless the difference between the valuational and motivational systems can be spelled out and the way in which desires generate values or all-things-considered judgments made clear, valuational theories will have no advantage over the hierarchical theories they are intended to replace. In moving from hierarchical to valuational theories, we will have exchanged an account of identification that is seriously incomplete for one that leaves the notion almost entirely unexplained.

Suppose, though, that some current valuational theory is supplemented with a substantive characterization of the difference between mere desires and desires for what one really wants or values or is committed to. In other words, suppose that such a theory is supplemented to provide a non-question-begging treatment of identification. Would such a theory be sufficient to provide an adequate treatment of responsibility? The answer is no. Such a theory would still be open to the third objection to Frankfurt's account: that a theory of identification alone cannot provide for the distinction between weakness of the will and compulsion. Recall that one's acting on the desire that is one's strongest motivationally but that seems contrary to one's real desires as defined by one's valuational system is characteristic of both weak-willed action *and* compulsive action. Both kinds of action involve one's being moved by a desire with which one does not identify. Even an adequate theory of identification, then, will not suffice to distinguish the two.

Watson does attempt to draw the distinction between weakness and compulsion by noting that there are "capacities and skills of resistance which are generally acquired in the normal course of socialization and practice, and which we hold one another responsible for acquiring and maintaining."[17] According to Watson, then, the distinction between weakness and compulsion is that "weak agents fall short of standards of 'reasonable and normal self-control' (for which we hold them responsible), whereas compulsive agents are motivated by desires which they could not resist even if they met those standards."[18] This way of drawing the distinction, however, raises the same problems we encountered with classical compatibilism. If the suggestion is that weak agents act on the basis of desires that *they* could have resisted, this is no help in the absence of some analysis of the notion of their having been able to do otherwise that meets the difficulties raised by the basic problem. The suggestion may be, however, that weak agents act on desires that they could not have resisted but that normal agents could. But in this case we have a dilemma. First, suppose that the normal agent's desire to perform the action in question is no weaker than that of the weak agent and that the normal agent's desires that conflict with that desire are no stronger. Suppose also that the normal agent has no relevantly different beliefs. (For example, the normal agent does not believe that the consequences of a failure to resist the desire in question are more serious than the weak agent does.) In this case we will be at a loss to explain how the normal agent could have resisted the desire to which the weak agent succumbed. Suppose, however, that we do have such an explanation. Then either the weak agent was attempting to resist a stronger desire than the normal agent (or one whose strength relative to the weak agent's other desires exceeded the relative strength of the normal agent's), the weak agent's desires that were in conflict with the desire he or she was attempting to resist were weaker (or again relatively weaker) than the normal agent's, or the weak agent's beliefs were relevantly different. Moreover, to preserve our ability to explain the fact that the normal agent resists the desire to which the weak agent gives in, we have to suppose that were the normal agent in a situation exactly like that of the weak agent (i.e., attempting to resist the stronger desire that the weak agent faced or attempting to do so with weaker conflicting desires or relevantly different beliefs), the normal agent would give in as well. Thus the question of how we can justify blaming the weak agent for doing exactly what the normal agent would have done in the same circumstance cannot be dismissed. And this is a question to which Watson's approach provides no answer.

4   Direct Compatibilism

One of the fundamental problems for classical compatibilism is that it counts too many actions as free: on any such theory, compulsive action counts as free action. Hierarchical and valuational compatibilism, even if they could provide an adequate account of identification, face the opposite problem. Such theories, unless they are supplemented with some account of the distinction between weak-willed and compulsive actions, classify both kinds of actions as unfree, given that both kinds are motivated by desires with which we fail to identify. In other words, these theories count too few actions as free. In this section I shall consider a group of theories that bypass the notion of free action altogether in their characterization of responsibility.

Let us call any theory according to which our practices regarding responsibility, punishment, and blame are justified directly without reference to whether agents act freely or could have done other than they did a version of *direct compatibilism*. Direct compatibilism and only direct compatibilism sidesteps the basic argument (in section 1) against classical compatibilism. Given any analysis of an agent's having acted freely or having been able to do other than what he or she did and given that the conditions of the analysis were satisfied, we can ask how the fact that those conditions were satisfied can justify our punishing or blaming the agent. Direct versions of compatibilism (and only such versions) avoid the objection that this question raises, since they consist of a justification of our practices regarding punishment and blame, rather than an analysis of the conditions under which agents act freely or under which they could do other than what they have actually done. Thus the basic argument against classical compatibilism is the basic argument against indirect compatibilism as well.

It does not, of course, follow from the definition of direct compatibilism that its proponents are committed to the claim that no agent acts freely or that no agent could have done other than what he or she in fact did. It is perfectly possible for a direct compatibilist to hold that agents could have acted quite differently. It is even possible for direct compatibilists to hold that agents are responsible for what they do just in case they have acted freely and could have done other than they did. What matters for direct compatibilism is the order of justification. Ascriptions of responsibility and practices regarding punishment and blame are justified in advance of how we settle the question of whether agents have freedom of action and the question of whether alternative possibilities for action exist. Indeed, having provided some form of justification for our practices of ascribing responsibility, punishment, and blame, the direct compatibilist may deliberately construct a notion of our having been able to act differently that satisfies the following condition. An agent could have done other than he or she did just in case the ascription of responsibility and blame to that agent for the action in question is justified. Alternatively, however, the direct compatibilist may simply concede that we could never have done other than what we actually did—an approach aptly conveyed by the title of a paper of Daniel Dennett's: "I Could Not Have Done Otherwise—So What?"[19]

A clear example of a direct compatibilist position is one that we might call *utilitarian direct compatibilism*. The proponent of such a theory proposes to justify our ascriptions of responsibility and our practices regarding punishment and blame by reference to their utility in regulating social behavior. Such a justification seems obviously compatible with the truth of determinism. As I argue in chapter 7, however, an adequate justification of our practices regarding punishment requires something more than reference to their contribution to aggregate utility. The proposed justification would allow us to count the practice of scapegoating as a legitimate form of punishment. Nothing in the account presented so far rules out punishing an innocent person if this makes the greatest contribution to aggregate utility. In response, the utilitarian direct compatibilist is likely to claim that punishment requires freedom in the sense that the agent in question must have acted in the absence of certain conditions. These include being compelled to perform the action by another agent, innate or psychological incapacity, and circumstances in which an alternative choice would impose a cost that no one could be reasonably expected to bear. But the rationale for these restrictions on the ascription of responsibility and blame and the imposition of punishment lies in the contribution that they make to aggregate utility when a practice that lacks the restrictions is compared to one that does not. It is this fact—that the practices regarding responsibility, punishment, and blame are justified first and that the restriction of punishment and blame to free actions is a consequence of this justification—that makes the position an example of direct compatibilism. Proponents of this view include Moritz Schlick, P. H. Nowell-Smith, and Daniel Dennett.[20]

P. F. Strawson examines a version of utilitarian direct compatibilism in "Freedom and Resentment" and argues that it contains a lacuna. Such a theory, on Strawson's view, provides no adequate answer to the question of why freedom in the sense of lack of coercion by others and lack of compulsive desires justifies punishment. According to Strawson, the only answer the utilitarian direct compatibilist can provide is that imposing punishment and blame only on the basis of actions that are free in the sense in question maximizes aggregate utility. And this answer, according to Strawson, is inadequate. As Strawson says, "This is not a sufficient basis, it is not even the right *sort* of basis, for these practices as we understand them."[21]

What, then, does Strawson offer to fill the lacuna? What the utilitarian direct compatibilist leaves out, Strawson thinks, are what he calls our reactive and self-reactive attitudes. Our reactive attitudes toward those who harm others through a lack of goodwill toward them include resentment when we are the people harmed and indignation when the harm is done to others. And when we are the cause of the harm, our self-reactive attitudes include guilt and remorse. On the positive side, we feel gratitude toward those from whose concern we benefit.

But what does reference to these reactive attitudes add to the utilitarian-direct-compatibilist justification of punishment and blame? Strawson suggests that what is objectionable in this justification is that it implies a manipulative and detached attitude toward those who are punished and those who are the objects of blame. But it is open to serious question whether the appeal to reactive attitudes can yield a satisfactory justification where our practices regarding responsibility are concerned. The primary objection to the proposed justification is, or should be, not that the person who is punished is treated in a detached and manipulative fashion. Rather, it should be that the person who is punished is made to suffer solely in order to increase the welfare of others. And this is unjust, whatever the attitudes of those who administer the punishment. Moreover, it is unjust even if those who are punished have been conditioned to acquiesce in the attitudes of their punishers and, indeed, even if they have been conditioned to take the corresponding self-reactive attitudes toward themselves. Strawson claims that there is no possibility that our practice of ascribing responsibility and expressing our reactive attitudes in imposing punishment and blame could have an external, rational justification.[22] But Strawson assumes that the existence of such reactive attitudes is something we are given with the "fact of human society."[23] And this surely underestimates the extent to which our practices regarding punishment and blame and the judicial model that lies behind them could be (and to some extent have been) replaced by practices grounded in a medical model and involving therapeutic techniques of readjustment and reeducation. Such therapeutically grounded techniques of social control have not lacked supporters.[24] And they represent a genuine alternative to our practices where responsibility is concerned. Thus the demand that our current practices be justified is not one that we are at liberty to ignore. Unless we can answer the charge that these practices involve no more than the creation of scapegoats, the proposal that they be abandoned deserves serious consideration.

5   Ideal Reflective Equilibria

The problem for utilitarian direct compatibilism is that if our practices of ascribing responsibility and blame can be justified only on utilitarian grounds, then the charge that we make scapegoats of those we punish is difficult to answer. And this problem remains whether or not those who are punished experience such self-reactive attitudes as guilt or remorse. Unless it can be shown that those who are punished (including those who are not utilitarians) can be rationally justified in acquiescing in their punishment, the objection that utilitarian direct compatibilism justifies their victimization cannot be met. Thus it is natural to ask whether direct compatibilism could be combined with an internalist form of justification, that is, a form of justification that appeals to the actual values of those who are forced to pay the cost of our practices regarding punishment and blame.

The notion of an internalist justification of our practices raises one of the questions that arose for Watson's valuational theory of free action: How does one distinguish a subject's values from what are merely his or her desires? We can start with the intuition that our values are desires that we desire to have. As we shall see, this intuition requires a great deal of refinement.

Suppose one had complete control over one's own noninstrumental desires. Suppose, for example, one had a pill that allowed one to eliminate noninstrumental desires that one preferred not to have, to add such desires that one wanted to have but lacked, and to increase or decrease the strengths of the desires in the resulting set. As in chapter 7, let us call the set of desires that would emerge, given that one was aware of the basic facts of one's motivational makeup, one's *ideal reflective equilibrium* (IRE). The requirement that one be aware of the basic facts of one's motivational makeup is simply the requirement that one not be so caught up in any particular desire that one could not reflect on the fact that the desire in question was in conflict with most of one's other desires. It is not required that one have any sort of sophisticated self-knowledge that is unavailable to any normal subject under normal circumstances. Let us say that the combination of access to the pill described and an awareness of the basic facts of one's motivational makeup constitute *conditions of IRE*. And when a desire is in some subject's IRE, I shall say that the desire is *in IRE* for that subject.

I discuss the implications of exercising such control over one's own motivational makeup in chapter 7.[25] Here I shall give a slightly more detailed account of the most important consequences that our exercise of control of this kind would have.

What would motivate one to add or subtract desires or to increase or decrease their strengths could only be one's other desires. The idea that one could step back from all of one's desires simultaneously and decide which to keep is incoherent, since one would have no desires that could motivate the decision to keep some rather than others. What would motivate such a decision is the fact that there are relations of support among one's noninstrumental desires. That is to say that between a subject's noninstrumental desires we can find an analogue of the relation of support that exists between the beliefs in that subject's conceptual scheme. Having found such a relation of support, we can say that one of the subject's noninstrumental desires will be eliminated just in case its tendency to conflict with some of that subject's other desires provides the motivation for its elimination and it lacks enough support among those other desires to keep it in place.

Consider, for example, Flaubert's description of Emma Bovary's vision of a religious calling. "She wanted to become a saint. She bought rosaries, she wore amulets; she wanted to have in her room, at the head of her bed, a reliquary set in emeralds, in order to kiss it every evening."[26] Flaubert's description is ironic in part because the desire to become a saint is the desire for a state of affairs at which one cannot aim directly. But it is also ironic in that even the desire to lead a life of religious devotion, which is not in itself inappropriate, is not well supported by what we can infer are Emma's other desires. Her preoccupation with what she wears, how her room is furnished, and what precious stones decorate the reliquary not only fails to support a desire to lead a religious life; it supports desires for a worldly existence with which that desire would come in direct conflict.

In eliminating a desire that conflicts with one's other desires in this way and in adding desires that support the ones that remain, one would be increasing the overall coherence of one's set of desires. To say that one's decisions increase the overall coherence of one's set of desires, however, is not to say that they are motivated by a second-order desire to maximize the coherence of the set. Few people have any such desires, and those who do would be likely to prefer many things over maximum coherence. What would motivate one to eliminate the desire for (say) heroin would be the other desires that the satisfaction of the desire for the drug would frustrate, for example, the desire for a healthy life, the desire for a successful career, the desire for normal human relationships, and so forth.

The fact that if one's other desires were relatively normal one would eliminate the desire for heroin shows that it is not the strength of the desire that determines whether it is eliminated. The desire for the drug might well be one's strongest desire in the sense that it has the greatest tendency to determine one's actions and would continue to have this tendency if it came into conflict with any of one's other desires. It would be eliminated, however, because of its lack of support among one's other desires. Let us, then, distinguish a desire's *motivational strength*, which is its tendency to cause actions aimed at its satisfaction, and its *evaluational strength*, which is its tendency to remain under conditions of IRE. In a normal addict the desire for heroin would be eliminated under conditions of IRE, in spite of its high motivational strength, because of its low evaluational strength. For

Frankfurt's willing addict, however, the desire for the drug coheres with the addict's other desires. Hence it has a high evaluational strength and would be reinstated, under conditions of IRE, even if its strength began to wane.

Just as the motivational strength of a desire is irrelevant to whether it is eliminated, so its content is also irrelevant, except as it bears on its degree of support. In particular, whether the desire is of first or higher order has no direct bearing on whether it will remain. Suppose this were not the case. Suppose instead that given the kind of pill we have been imagining, lower-order desires would always be eliminated in any conflict with desires of higher orders. Now imagine that one has a superstitious second-order desire not to act on desires formed on Tuesdays. This desire might be eliminated, of course, if one had a third-order desire with which it conflicted, for example, a third-order desire not to have arbitrary second-order desires that result in the frustration of many first-order desires. Such a third-order desire, however, would be vulnerable to fourth-order desires that might themselves be superstitious, such as the desire that one never act on desires of odd orders. And this fourth-order desire might be supported by higher-order desires of an equally superstitious sort. In such a case the second-order desire would remain, regardless of how many first-order desires it frustrated. This consequence, however, does not seem to reflect the decisions we would actually make if we had access to the pill in question. The coherentist view I am proposing explains these decisions. On this view, there is nothing to prevent the second-order desire from being eliminated by the first-order desires with which it fails to cohere. The real objection to the superstitious second-order desire, after all, is not that there is an abstract criterion of rationality formulated at some level higher than the second that it fails to meet (though this might count against it) but that it frustrates all those desires formed on Tuesdays. If support is a matter of coherence, then the elimination of higher-order desires by lower-order desires presents no difficulties.

In the same way very general desires may be eliminated because they lack support among more specific desires, and specific desires may be eliminated because they find no support among those that are more general. In this respect, the formation of an ideal reflective equilibrium resembles the formation of Rawls's reflective equilibrium, which requires that one be ready to reject normative principles that fail to cohere with one's particular normative intuitions and vice versa.[27]

Finally, one's ideal reflective equilibrium is relative to one's *actual* beliefs. Whether the desire for heroin supports and is supported by an otherwise normal set of desires depends on one's beliefs. If one mistakenly believes that one can satisfy the desire for heroin without frustrating one's other desires, there is no reason for one to eliminate the desire for the drug from one's IRE.

6   Identification, Values, and Commitment

As we saw in sections 2 and 3, there are a number of problems for hierarchical and valuational compatibilist theories. For hierarchical theories these include the problem of avoiding an infinite regress while providing a theory of identification where one's desires are concerned. They also include the problem of explaining the relevance of one's higher-order desires to the question of what one "really" desires or what one values. For valuational theories these include the problem of providing a substantive theory of what we think we ought to do, all things considered. Can the appeal to ideal reflective equilibria take us any closer to the solution to these difficulties?

The notion of identification as it is used in discussions of responsibility is a vague one. But we can use the concept of an ideal reflective equilibrium to define a somewhat more precise notion. Let us say that we identify with, in the sense that we are not alienated from, the desires in our ideal reflective equilibrium. This definition makes our identification or our failure to identify with our desires a function of their evaluational strength. And this means that given our beliefs and our other desires and given perfect control over our motivational makeup, the desires with which we identify would be the ones that remained after all the adjustments we could be motivated to make had been completed.

Such a characterization of identification allows us to reconstruct most of the distinctions Frankfurt makes in terms of his concept of identification while avoiding the problems generated by his appeal to higher-order desires. We can distinguish, as we have seen, between the willing addict and the unwilling addict, since the former is simply the addict whose desire for the drug is in IRE and the latter is the addict whose desire for the drug is not. However, Frankfurt also appeals in his discussion to the notion of a wanton, that is, the notion of an agent who has no second-order volitions.[28] And this notion of Frankfurt's turns out to be problematic. It is possible, of course, to imagine beings who lack the conceptual sophistication to reflect on their first-order desires. Such creatures can never be in conditions of IRE, since they lack reflective awareness of the basic facts about their own motivational makeup. As Frankfurt points out, children and animals fall into this class. And we can also imagine someone whose first-order desires are sufficiently free of conflicts that he or she is not motivated to change them under conditions of IRE. This is simply the person whose desires are already in IRE. What is harder to imagine, however, is the wanton addict that Frankfurt describes. What we seem to be asked to imagine is a subject who satisfies the following conditions. First, the subject is addicted to a drug, and his or her desire for the drug is overwhelming. Second, the subject's desire for the drug is completely unsupported by the other desires he or she has, and his or her taking the drug frustrates the other desires in the most painful ways possible. Third, the subject fails, under conditions of IRE, to eliminate the desire for the drug. On Frankfurt's account, this seems possible because the motivation to eliminate the desire for the drug has its source in a second-order desire that seems conceptually independent of any of the agent's first-order desires. But on the account of identification couched in terms of IREs, the motivation to eliminate the desire for the drug has its source in the first-order desires that the desire for the drug frustrates. Thus in an agent capable of genuine reflection on his or her desires, the first-order desires will provide sufficient motive, under conditions of IRE, to eliminate the desire for the drug. But although Frankfurt's notion of a wanton has no counterpart in the account that appeals to the concept of an IRE, the notion does not seem essential to Frankfurt's general treatment of responsibility.

The fact that in the present account of identification there is no special appeal to higher-order desires eliminates both the problem of an infinite regress and the problem that there is no necessary connection between our higher-order desires and what we really want. Moreover, if it were plausible to take this account of identification as an account of an agent's values, we would have a substantive account of the distinction between values and mere desires. Thus this account would meet one of the objections to the valuational compatibilist theories we have considered so far. (Whether the account of identification actually is an account of an agent's values is a question I shall take up shortly.) But the present account would still be open to the most fundamental problem for both hierarchical and valuational theories. An account of identification in terms of IREs would, by itself, provide no rationale for distinguishing between compulsion and weakness of the will where responsibility is concerned. Both are cases in which one acts on a desire from which one is alienated, with which one does not identify, that is out of IRE, and whose motivational strength is high while its evaluational strength is low. Nothing in the present account provides any means of distinguishing the two cases.

This problem for theories that analyze responsibility in terms of identification would also be a problem for theories that analyze responsibility in terms of the agent's values *if* the agent's values could be analyzed in terms of his or her desires in IRE. But it is not plausible to claim that the desires from which we are not alienated, that is, our desires in IRE, represent our values. And the fact that this is so is crucial to our ability to distinguish between the weak-willed agent and the compulsive. We can see that a desire in IRE is not necessarily a desire for something we value if we consider our preferences for certain tastes over others. These are trivial desires in large part because they are not connected by relations of support to a significant number of other desires. This is not to say that there are no such relations. If the price of Bordeaux increased a hundredfold, then the combination of a strong preference for Bordeaux over Burgundies and a strong desire not to accept any substitutes would conflict with many of one's other desires and would almost certainly cease to be in IRE. Nonetheless, the status of one's preferences concerning tastes would be quite different if they were connected by relations of support to many of our other desires under normal circumstances. Imagine, for example, that a taste for sweets, a preference for happy endings in fiction, and desires that made one prone to sentimentality were all connected by strong relations of mutual support. In this case it would be plausible to hold that a desire for sweets, if it were part of some agent's IRE and supported by desires of the kind suggested, represented one of the agent's values (though presumably one of which we could not entirely approve). Of course, this is plausible because we think of desires that make one prone to sentimentality as raising issues that engage our values. Thus the explanation of the disposition ultimately depends on some explanation of what is required before desires become more than mere tastes.

Let us examine, then, desires that are connected in significant ways to many other desires, especially those that motivate decisions having an important bearing on our lives and the lives of others. Consider the choice one would make in deciding between a very risky career, such as acting, and one that is relatively secure, such as high school teaching. The choice between security and risk itself reveals some of one's values, but there are likely to be reasons behind the choice that reveal a good many more. The choice of the insecure career, for example, affects in significant ways the kinds of relations one can expect to have to others, especially the degree to which others can expect to depend on one. Moreover, the choice may reveal the relative values one assigns to such goods as service to others, one's own creative expression, the chance for wealth and fame, the chance to interact personally with the people for whose benefit one's talents are exercised, and so forth. If the desire for a risky career, such as acting, and the desires that support such a desire are in an agent's IRE, it is reasonable to take the objects of such desires to be among the agent's values.

There is, however, a deeper sense in which our desires may be for things we value. Contrast the desires just described with the desire one might have as a novelist to preserve one's artistic integrity in the face of temptations to produce inferior work. It is not only that one prefers now that one resist the temptation to produce work that, though more accessible and salable, is less innovative. Nor is one's attitude fully captured if we add that one desires now that in the future one continue to resist the temptation. Rather, one desires now that one continue to produce innovative work even if in the future one should cease to desire to do so. In other words, one's desire now is such that one is motivated now to sacrifice one's future desires, even if one knows now that one would not be prepared to do so in the future.

The difference between the desire for a risky career and the desire for artistic integrity lies in one's willingness to frustrate the desires of one's future self. Suppose that one's desire now were for the acting career but one had good reason to believe that over the course of most of one's adult life, one would prefer the teaching career. Then one would almost certainly be prepared to change careers when one's preferences changed. One might, in fact, take seriously the possibility of foregoing the acting career and pursue the teaching career, knowing that it was the one that would eventually make one happy. Where one's artistic integrity is concerned, however, one might attach little importance to the fact that the things that would make one happy for most of one's adult life were money and fame. One might even be prepared now to foreclose the option of writing commercially successful novels in the future—possibly by making one's opinion of popular fiction so well known as to inhibit any temptation one might have to change one's style.

Let us say, as in chapter 7, that an *unconditional desire* is a desire that some state of affairs be realized whether or not the desire itself continues to exist. Then in the examples described, the desire for an acting career is conditional and the desire to preserve one's artistic integrity is unconditional. Of course, there is nothing to prevent one's having an unconditional desire to act and a conditional desire for artistic integrity, though these desires seem somewhat less probable than the ones we have just considered.

The distinction between conditional and unconditional desires requires the following qualification regarding the earlier account of ideal reflective equilibria. As we have seen, one's higher-order desires have no special significance, and the account of support among desires is coherentist rather than foundational. But there is an asymmetry between conditional and unconditional desires that introduces a foundationalist element into the picture. Suppose one contemplates eliminating a conditional desire from one's motivational makeup. In this case the fact that one will no longer have the desire itself fully compensates for the fact that the desire is far less likely to be satisfied once it has been eliminated. In other words, the fact that one will feel no dissatisfaction fully compensates for the fact that the desire will not be satisfied. This is not true, though, of unconditional desires. If one eliminates an unconditional desire, then the fact that one will feel no dissatisfaction as a result does not compensate for the fact that by eliminating the desire one will make its satisfaction far less likely. If one of one's desires is unconditional, then one wants now that the state of affairs that is its object obtain in the future, regardless of whether the desire exists in the future. Thus eliminating it (and any desires that support it) will frustrate some of one's present desires, even though doing so will *not* frustrate the desires one will retain once it (and its support) are no longer part of one's motivational makeup.

This distinction between conditional and unconditional desires means that in cases of conflict, conditional desires will be eliminated in favor of unconditional desires, whatever their relative degrees of support. This is because if one chooses to eliminate a conditional desire in favor of an unconditional desire, there is no genuine loss from one's point of view when one makes the choice. If, however, one chooses to eliminate an unconditional desire in favor of a conditional desire, then from one's own point of view, when one makes the choice, one sustains a loss that no satisfaction of one's future desires can make up. As a result, one's desires form a two-tiered structure, with the tier consisting of unconditional desires playing the foundational role relative to the tier of conditional desires. Within each tier, a desire's evaluational strength is a function of its holistic support. But in cases of conflict between tiers, conditional desires are always adjusted to support unconditional desires and not vice versa. In what follows, I shall refer to the unconditional desires in one's IRE as one's *conative core*. Both one's unconditional desires and those of one's conditional desires that have relations of support with a large number of other desires represent one's values. But I shall say in addition that one's unconditional desires represent one's *commitments*.

Given this scheme, we can see why a theory of identification—that is, a theory that explains which of our desires we identify with in the sense that we are not alienated from them—is inadequate to explain our values and commitments. Nonetheless, it remains to be seen how reference to our values and commitments can explain the distinction between weak-willed and compulsive actions, which was left unexplained by the concept of identification. That is, it remains to be seen how this account of values and commitments can help us explain the fact that we take responsibility for weak-willed actions but not for actions that are genuinely compulsive. It is to this question that I shall now turn.

7   Internalist Direct Compatibilism

We have seen that a theory of identification is only part of a theory of our values and commitments. But can a theory of our values and commitments explain how we could be justified in taking responsibility for actions motivated by desires from which we are alienated? Let us ask this question indirectly by asking the question that arose for Strawson's theory of responsibility: What could justify our being disposed to acquiesce in punishment and blame for some of our actions without our simply being scapegoats? As we have seen in section 4, individuals become scapegoats when the punishment or blame they receive has no internal justification from their point of view. Thus we can restate the original question as follows: Under what conditions could we be *internally justified* in acquiescing in, or in keeping a disposition to acquiesce in, punishment and blame? And given the analysis (in section 5) of internal justification in terms of the relations of support among desires in IRE, this amounts to asking the following question: What kinds of desires would motivate us under conditions of IRE to take a pill that would allow us to acquire or prevent our losing such a disposition?

It seems possible to suggest a number of desires that could motivate our acquiring or keeping such a disposition. First, consider the *desire for authorship*. We want to be recognized, both by others and by ourselves, as responsible for our accomplishments and our creations. On the one hand, this is a desire not to be alienated from these creations. We prefer not to see ourselves, when we are engaged in our most creative efforts, as merely giving voice to the prejudices and assumptions of our time. When we perform those actions that seem to require the most effort, either to overcome our fears, our appetites, or our apathy, we like to think of ourselves as doing more than manifesting a disposition produced by our genes and our culture. When with difficulty we make the right choice, we want to feel that it is *our* choice. And when it turns out to be a mistake, we can want just as much to feel that it was our choice nonetheless. One does not want one's feelings to resemble those of the schizophrenic who believes that his thoughts are being dictated from elsewhere. Nor does one want experiences like those of the person who feels trapped in a set of emotional responses that he or she experiences as alien not because they conflict with the person's values but simply because the person fails to see himself or herself in them. And one does not want to feel what Borges portrays himself as feeling when he writes, "I live, let myself go on living, so that Borges may contrive his literature, and this literature justifies me. It is no effort for me to confess that he has achieved some valid pages, but those pages cannot save me, perhaps because what is good belongs to no one, not even to him, but rather to the language and to tradition."[29] On the other hand, we want the recognition of others that our actions are our own. We want to be eligible to be credited by others with our most original creations, our most strenuous efforts, and our most difficult choices. (Spaggiari, whose professed motive in engineering the Nice robbery was to carry off the crime of the century, expressed the intention of giving his share to "a good cause."[30])

But would it not be possible to accept credit for our achievements without accepting blame for our failures? Why could we not make ourselves indifferent to the desires out of IRE on which we act, and thus indifferent to our failures? Would we not be better off if we did so? First, notice that we cannot justify accepting responsibility for actions motivated by desires in IRE and rejecting responsibility for actions motivated by desires out of IRE by reference to any relevant differences between the two kinds of desires. It is difficult to see how there could be a difference from the subject's point of view between the desires on which we want to act (and do) and the noncompulsive desires on which we act even though we desire not to. Suppose the fact that a desire was sufficient to produce an action made us feel, when the desire was out of IRE, that we had no choice or that the action was not really ours. Then we could have no reason to feel, where desires in IRE were concerned, that the actions they motivated were ours or that their performance could bring us any credit. Another way of putting this is to say that unless we can see some of our desires that are out of IRE as resistable (and hence see the actions they cause as blameworthy), we must see our actions caused by desires in IRE as inevitable and thus as unworthy of praise.

In addition to the connection between those of our desires that are in IRE and those that are not, there is a connection between our view of ourselves and the view taken of us by others. As seen from the external perspective, the desires that motivate our actions make those actions equally inevitable and equally resistable, whether they are in IRE or not. Thus unless everyone could be persuaded to make a distinction between actions motivated by desires in and out of IRE, others will see both kinds of actions as equally ours. And how we view ourselves is intimately connected with how we view others as viewing us.[31]

But if the distinction between actions that are based on desires in IRE and actions that are not has no basis in reasons, what would prevent our making a brute distinction? A subject who made such a distinction would be analogous to the subject Derek Parfit describes as future-Tuesday-indifferent. Such a subject will not bear the slightest pain on days other than Tuesday to prevent the most extreme pains on any Tuesday in the future and is willing to sacrifice the greatest pleasures on future Tuesdays for the smallest pleasures on any other day. This is the case even though the person recognizes that the events in question will happen to a person who has the same body he has and is as continuous with him psychologically as his attitude toward the future allows. Since the person who is future-Tuesday-indifferent recognizes that there is no intrinsic difference between those of his future selves that exist on Tuesdays and those that do not, he simply makes a distinction that has no further justification. His concern for his future selves extends only to those that do not exist on Tuesdays. Such a psychology seems logically possible, and there are circumstances in which it might be to one's advantage to acquire it.[32]

If such a distinction is possible in the case of the subject who is future-Tuesday-indifferent, why would we not be justified in making a distinction of this kind between those of our desires that are in IRE and those that are not? What objection could there be to our making ourselves indifferent, if we could, to the results of our desires that are out of IRE while we continue to feel responsible for, and take credit for, our actions that stem from desires in IRE? Even if there is no intrinsic difference between the way in which the desires produce actions, would we not make ourselves better off by giving ourselves such a psychology? Of course, this would satisfy the desire to receive credit from others only if everyone took the same attitude. But if such a collective change in attitude could be arranged, would there be any objection to our doing so? Although a change in our attitudes of the kind described seems to satisfy the desire for authorship, that is, the desire to be eligible for credit for our accomplishments, there are other desires that a change of this kind could not satisfy.

Consider what we might call the *desire to maximize one's accomplishments*. Suppose one were to adopt the strategy of making oneself indifferent to one's alienated actions. In other words, suppose one made oneself disposed not to feel guilt or remorse for such actions. And suppose one lived in a community in which one was not blamed or punished for them. Then one's actual ability to satisfy one's desires in IRE would be impaired. Without the tendency to blame oneself and to anticipate being blamed by others for one's failures, the motivational strength of desires in IRE would be diminished, all other things being equal. As a result, one could expect such failures to be far more frequent than they would otherwise be.

But if this is the only objection to making oneself indifferent to one's alienated actions, imagine a more systematic version of the strategy. Suppose one simply eliminates the desire to maintain one's accomplishments at the level that a tendency to blame oneself allows. In other words, suppose that one changes one's psychology so that one can be satisfied with the accomplishments that are possible if one is not disposed to accept blame for one's failures. Are there any grounds for rejecting this strategy?

The answer to this question demonstrates the importance of considering unconditional desires in constructing an account of our values and commitments. Consider our current desires to maintain specific commitments, such as our commitment to certain standards of integrity or our commitment to moral principles requiring that we respect the rights of others. Most commitments of this kind will be unconditional, so that one will prefer now that they be kept in the future, even if at that time one were no longer concerned to keep them. Suppose now that one contemplates reducing the level of responsibility one takes for keeping one's commitments by making oneself indifferent to one's failures. Since one knows that this will reduce the degree to which the commitments are kept, this is tantamount to giving up some of one's unconditional desires. And although if one does change one's psychology in this way one will feel no dissatisfaction as a result, the fact that the desires one would be losing are unconditional keeps this from being an acceptable option.

Let us call the desire not to diminish the level of our responsibility for our commitments the *desire to maintain our commitments*. Of course, this is not an isolated, abstract desire but is supported by all our specific desires that we uphold specific commitments. Thus it is a desire that is well supported by a large number of unconditional desires. And, as we have seen, the desire to maintain our commitments supports and is supported by the desire to maximize our accomplishments.

And this desire, in turn, supports and is supported by the desire for authorship.

Moreover, the desires to uphold commitments with specific contents are not the only desires by which the desire to maintain our commitments is supported. We seem to desire not to be passive in the face of temptations to which we are drawn by desires out of IRE. Let us call this the *desire for nonpassivity*. It seems, then, that we desire to struggle against desires from which we are alienated. The desires that motivate such a struggle may consist simply in the desires already mentioned. But there may also be a desire to exercise some control, in cases of conflict, that is independent of desires regarding specific commitments and accomplishments. And if in fact we have such a desire in addition to the other unconditional desires mentioned, it is likely to be unconditional as well.

So far we have considered what our responses might be to the prospect of making ourselves indifferent to failure. But we should also consider the likely responses of others and the bearing that would have on our other desires. If as a community we dispose ourselves not to blame others or ourselves for our failures, we will have lost an important source of social control. Not only will the internal inhibitions provided by our tendency to blame ourselves be lost, but our ability to ascribe blame and administer genuine punishment will be lost as well. (The fact that we cannot administer genuine punishment under these circumstances follows from the fact that genuine punishment must be deserved. At this stage of the argument the only notion of desert that has not been ruled out is our being internally justified in acquiescing in reactive and self-reactive attitudes. And it is just such a justification that would be missing if our dispositions to blame ourselves for our failures were unjustified.) There must be some mechanism of social control, however, to fill the gap, and any such mechanism is likely to violate desires that are both unconditional and well supported. Suppose, for example, that some form of social control grounded in the medical model is employed. On the judicial model, as well as on the commonsense picture according to which we are responsible for our failures and for struggling against desires out of IRE, we expect to be protected from outside interference as long as we refrain from violating our society's norms. On the medical model, however, this protection would be difficult to defend. If the actions based on desires out of IRE are simply things that *happen* to us, then outside intervention to prevent such occurrences would have the same justification as does vaccination to prevent the outbreak of disease. Moreover, since the only rationale for such intervention is to prevent further outbreaks in the future, there could be no reasonable objection to preventative intervention before the first outbreak has occurred. We desire now, however, that we not be subject to such intervention. Let us call this the *desire for nonintervention*.

The desire for nonintervention raises a further question about what form of social control could substitute for the one presently in place. Although outside intervention will almost certainly be a component of such a mechanism of social control, it is very unlikely that it could constitute the whole mechanism. It is unlikely, that is, that any mechanism of social control could be effective unless some significant component were internalized in the psychologies of members of the society. But given that we have ruled out self-reactive attitudes as the internal component, what psychological dispositions are there that could do the job? False beliefs about divine wrath or about karma might do the job, and so might the kinds of inhibitions produced by the technologies of behavioral modification. But just as we desire to be free of external interventions as long as we succeed in controlling ourselves, we also desire to be free of internal controls that are likely to violate our (present) conception of autonomy. Let us call this the desire for *internal autonomy*. This desire supports and is supported by all the other desires mentioned, and like a number of them, this desire is almost certainly unconditional.

Suppose that we do possess some of the unconditional desires of the kind described. In that case we will have well-supported and unconditional desires to acquiesce in the reactive attitudes of others and in our own self-reactive attitudes toward our own failures. Moreover, a justification of our acquiescing in such attitudes that appeals to such desires will be an internal justification, both in that it appeals to our actual values and in that it will necessarily provide a motive for our acquiescing. And although this motive may be overridden by a stronger one, unless there is some other group of unconditional desires that are better supported and that conflict with the unconditional desires in question, action stemming from the stronger motive will be irrational.

Assume, then, that the unconditional desires described are not themselves desires that would be eliminated under conditions of IRE. (Their coherence and mutual support and the lack of plausible candidates for unconditional desires with which they might conflict make this assumption reasonable.) In this case there is an internal justification for our accepting punishment and blame for our weak-willed actions. Let us call the form of direct compatibilism under consideration *internalist direct compatibilism*. On an internalist direct compatibilist theory we are responsible for those actions of ours that are weak-willed. This is because on such a theory, as we have seen, there is no more to being responsible than being appropriately justified in acquiescing in the relevant reactive and self-reactive attitudes.

It does not follow on such a theory that we are responsible for our compulsive actions. The fact that on such a theory we will be justified in accepting blame for some actions stemming from desires out of IRE does not entail that we would be justified in accepting blame for all such actions. We might, for example, have extremely good evidence that almost no one succeeds in resisting the desire for a particular drug once a certain quantity has been consumed. And we might have the introspective experience of being unable to stand outside a certain kind of desire in order to struggle against it. That is, we might perceive the desire, when it reaches a certain level of intensity, as occupying all of our consciousness. And we might perceive this desire as increasing in intensity until it is satisfied. Thus on either statistical or introspective grounds we might perceive ourselves as powerless in the face of such desires. And in such cases we would not be internally justified in accepting responsibility or blame for our actions.

Suppose, however, that we could acquire a disposition to see ourselves as capable of resisting such desires. Let us say that our acquiring such a disposition would be a case of our *enhancing our self-conception*. If it were within our power to bring about, would such a change be justified? The answer seems to be no. I have argued that we would *not* be justified in acquiring the opposite disposition, that is, the disposition to see ourselves as powerless regarding our own desires. But the argument against our diminishing our self-conception does not justify our enhancing it in the way suggested. The desire to maximize our accomplishments, for example, cannot motivate us to accept responsibility and blame for actions stemming from a particular sort of desire if we perceive all struggle against the desire as futile. Similarly, the desire not to be passive in the face of temptation will not justify accepting blame if the struggle not to perform the action in question seems hopeless. Again, the desire to maintain our commitments is a desire to maintain them relative to our present conception of our capacities. Thus in not enhancing our self-conception in the way suggested, we would not be failing to live up to our present commitments. Moreover, if we have the means to avoid the desires we perceive as compulsive or the capacity to eliminate them by voluntarily seeking help, then we are likely to be motivated (for example, by the desire for nonintervention) to do so. And the possibility of coping with compulsive desires indirectly suggests that we are already justified in holding ourselves indirectly responsible for their control. But if this is the case, then the grounds for attempting to make ourselves directly responsible for such desires do not seem strong.

Unlike the other theories we have considered, then, internalist direct compatibilism can distinguish between weak-willed and compulsive actions. According to this theory, we can *acknowledge* a desire—that is, be justified in acquiescing in the reactive attitudes of others and in our own self-reactive attitudes when the desire leads to harm—without identifying with it, i.e., without its being in our IRE. The distinction between weak-willed and compulsive actions does depend on the notion of our perceiving certain actions to be within our power and certain actions to be outside our power. But the role of an action's being within an agent's power in internalist direct compatibilism is very different from its role in classical compatibilist theories. In classical theories it is argued that we could have done otherwise, that because this is so we were responsible, and that because we were responsible, punishment and blame are justified. On the internalist theory, the analogous argument is this:

1. We are internally justified in maintaining a disposition to perceive certain actions as being within our power to avoid.
2. Thus we are internally justified in acquiescing in punishment and blame for those actions.
3. Thus punishment and blame are justified.

And since we have an argument that punishment and blame are sometimes justified, we are free to construct a compatibilist interpretation of our being able to do otherwise that fits this notion of justification established on other grounds. Thus this theory avoids the basic argument against indirect compatibilist theories: that they cannot tell us why, given a particular compatibilist interpretation of 'could have done otherwise' or 'acted freely', the fact that we could have done otherwise or acted freely in that sense justifies praise or blame.

Postscript

In chapters 7 and 9, I argue that there is a dilemma for indirect compatibilist theories, and I use this argument to support the alternative theory of moral responsibility that I call internalist direct compatibilism. The dilemma turns on the claim that neither those who act on desires in IRE nor those who act on desires out of IRE seem appropriate candidates for punishment or blame. This argument still seems to me correct. But the argument turns on the appropriate treatment of psychopaths, and the issues involved rapidly become complex. (See the postscript to chapter 9.) Of course, even if the claims about the psychopath are dropped, there is still a serious objection to indirect compatibilist accounts. That is, even if it is granted that we are justified in punishing the psychopath, the conclusion that *only* the psychopath can be blamed constitutes a powerful objection to indirect compatibilism.

The argument that I put forward in chapter 8, however, seems to provide both a simpler and more comprehensive objection to the compatibilist accounts in question. Assume that in some sense we could have done other than what we did in a reasonable number of cases. And assume that our pretheoretical intuitions make us responsible just in case in this sense we could have done other than we did. We can still ask, however, why we are justified in punishing those whose actions cause harm and who could, in the sense in question, have performed actions other than those they performed. In chapter 8, I call the problem that this question raises the basic problem.

The basic problem motivates what, in chapters 7 through 9, I call *direct* compatibilism. Whether we could have done other than perform the action we did will depend on whether we are justified in accepting responsibility and blame for that action, and not vice versa. But if we are to avoid making scapegoats of those who are blamed and punished, their justification for acquiescing in such punishment and blame must be internal justification. And as I argue in chapters 7 through 10, the account of ideal reflective equilibria provides the distinctions between desires and values necessary to make sense of internal justification.

The same problems raised by accounts of moral responsibility also arise for accounts of personal identity. Suppose we succeed in characterizing a distinction between those future and past person stages that are stages of us and those that are not that captures all of our pretheoretical intuitions in the puzzle cases. We are still left with the question of how these distinctions can be justified. Suppose, for example, that the criterion of psychological continuity captured all of the intuitions we have regarding cases like that of the teletransporter. Thus we are supposing that according to our intuitions, teletransportation preserves personal identity. In such a case one will be willing to make sacrifices for the future of the person who results from one's being teletransported. But we can still ask *why* one should be willing to make such sacrifices. And we can still ask why, if one is the product of a process of teletransportation oneself, one should assume responsibility for the person who underwent the process.

This problem of personal identity is another version of the basic problem for compatibilist theories of moral responsibility. And the strategy for dealing with the two problems is the same. Certain patterns of concern are characteristic of our attitudes toward those persons or person stages we currently regard as our past and future selves. The strategy is to justify these patterns independently of whether they satisfy any particular metaphysical (i.e., nonnormative) criterion. We can then say that the proper metaphysical criterion, if indeed there is one, is determined by the past and future person stages for which such characteristic patterns of concern are justified, and not vice versa. In other words, the account of responsibility in terms of the internal justification of our reactive attitudes has an analogue regarding personal identity. This account of identity rests on the internal justification of our concern for future persons. Thus we can apply the analysis of moral responsibility retroactively to the problem of personal identity. And because we appeal to the same analysis of internal justification in each case, we are lead to the same conclusion. Since there is room for a great deal of variation in the IREs of different subjects, especially subjects from different cultures, this approach carries with it a form of relativism regarding personal identity.

It is important to recognize that this form of relativism regarding personal identity is distinct from the form for which I argue in chapter 5. In fact, the two are independent. According to the form defended in chapter 5, reference to social norms and practices occurs in the description of our pretheoretical intuitions themselves. This does not entail, of course, that anyone would be likely to agree that which person one will be at some future date depends on what social practices are in effect. Virtually everyone's intuitions are that who they will be is independent of facts about social institutions. The claim is rather that the best explanation of the pattern of pretheoretical responses that the puzzle cases elicit runs as follows. First, in responding to these cases we make implicit assumptions about the social circumstances in which they occur. Second, the assumptions are sensitive to the details of the descriptions of the cases. Third, cases that are identical in all their intrinsic features (i.e., in which all the psychological and physical facts are the same except those pertaining to the social institutions) may elicit different responses. Thus on this account a description of the nature of the intuitions themselves involves a reference to social norms and practices. Call this form of relativism *internal relativism* regarding personal identity.

Contrast this with the form of relativism generated by the basic argument. That form says that different social institutions may produce individuals whose pretheoretical intuitions about the puzzle cases differ significantly. For example, the members of one society may be internally justified in treating as future selves the people who step out of the teletransporter as a result of their stepping in, whereas the members of another society may not. And this fact may be explained by differences in the social institutions. But in this case the social institutions need figure only in the causal explanation of the intuitions, not in the description of the intuitions themselves. Relativism would obtain in this sense, for example, if the members of one (possible) society were internally justified in treating the teletransporter as transportation, whereas members of another (possible) society were not. Let us call this *external relativism* regarding personal identity.

The two forms of relativism, then, are independent. On the one hand, we can have external relativism without internal relativism. Members of two societies that differ over the acceptability of teletransportation might all have intuitions that could be described (though not causally explained) without any reference to social institutions. Members of the society in which teletransportation is treated as transportation might have intuitions that were perfectly characterized by the psychological criterion of personal identity. Thus they would respond to cases in such a way that the identity of a person over time (as indicated by their responses) would depend only on the intrinsic features of the person in question. Similarly, members of the society in which teletransportation is unacceptable might respond to the puzzle cases on the basis of intuitions that fell neatly under the criterion of bodily continuity. Again, the content of such intuitions could be described without reference to social norms or practices.

On the other hand, we could have internal relativism without external relativism. Suppose, for example, that our linguistic conventions entailed that what the expression 'personal identity' means is determined by the general characterization that best captures our intuitions. Now suppose that the description of our intuitions does in fact require a reference to social institutions. And suppose that the members of some other society are internally justified in showing special concern for those future persons (and virtually only those future persons) with whom they are psychologically continuous. In this case their special concern will not be for the persons they will be in the future; much of their concern will be for persons other than their future selves. This is because, given our linguistic conventions, what concerns the members of this other society is not picked out by the term 'personal identity'. Thus its members do not have an alternative conception of the identity of persons. Rather, their concern is with some other feature of personal continuity over time. Therefore, this would not be a case in which the members of different societies had different conceptions of personal identity and hence not a case of external relativism. Of course, in this case personal identity would not be as important as we take it to be. And we would surely coin a term to capture what our special concerns and those of the members of the other society had in common. But the example shows the possibility of having internal relativism without external relativism.

Of these two forms of relativism where personal identity is concerned, external relativism is clearly the more basic. Suppose that there eventually emerges an analysis of the puzzle cases that makes identity (or survival) supervene on the intrinsic features of the subjects involved. Even so, the basic problem will still arise where the justification of special patterns of concern regarding past and future subjects is at issue. Since this is a practical issue, it is internal justification that is relevant. And on my account of internal justification, the possibility of subjects for whom radically different patterns of concern are justified is a consequence. Thus whether or not the issue is called one of personal identity, the program of providing such a justification will necessarily be relativistic in the external sense.

Chapter 9

Rationality, Responsibility, and Pathological Indifference

1 Pathological Indifference

Imagine you are about to enter SoHo. You are retracing the only route you know to an address below Canal Street, and a detour would make you lose at least an hour. Unfortunately, you have offended a ruthless criminal, C., whose power inside SoHo is absolute. Should you enter the district, C. will obtain his revenge by having you tortured. C.'s busy schedule, though, will not permit him to devote more than half an hour to making you suffer. All told, if you decide to enter SoHo, you will be delayed forty-five minutes, fifteen minutes less than if you take the detour. Of course, the time saved is at the cost of a period of intense pain. However, pains you will experience in Soho are completely discounted in your calculations. Given the opportunity to avoid pain or displeasure that will be experienced *outside* SoHo by choosing to experience more pain or more displeasure *in* SoHo, you always prefer (while you are outside SoHo) to do so. And this preference remains even if you anticipate experiencing much more pain as a consequence. Similarly, you always prefer (when you are outside SoHo) to sacrifice very great pleasures available to you *in* SoHo for much smaller pleasures available elsewhere. As a result, you ignore the detour and pursue your original route into the district.

Let us call the attitude that discounts pleasurable and painful experience in SoHo *SoHo indifference*.[1] Derek Parfit (1984, 124) has considered a similar motivational makeup in which one discounts pleasures and pains that will occur on future Tuesdays. If one is *future-Tuesday-indifferent*, one will accept the prospect of great suffering that will fall on a future Tuesday in order to save oneself even the smallest amount of suffering on other days. And one is similarly indifferent to pleasures that one will experience on future Tuesdays. This is not to

First appeared in *Identity, Character, and Morality*, ed. O. Flanagan and A. O. Rorty. Copyright 1990 by the Massachusetts Institute of Technology. The essay has been revised for its publication here.

say that one is indifferent when Tuesday actually arrives. On Tuesday, pleasures and pains are assessed in the normal way; it is only the pleasures and pains of future Tuesdays that are discounted. Parfit claims (p. 124) that future-Tuesday indifference is irrational. And he would clearly make the same claim about SoHo indifference. I shall argue that this is not necessarily the case. The disagreement with Parfit is not a disagreement about future-Tuesday indifference or any of its analogues; it is a fundamental disagreement about the nature of rationality and about the nature of justification.

My strategy in the earlier chapters on personal identity, self-consciousness, and moral responsibility (chapters 5 to 8) has been to substitute normative accounts for metaphysical accounts of the topics in question. For example, where personal identity is concerned, this has meant substituting an account of the justification of our patterns of special concern for future persons for a metaphysical account of personal identity. Where moral responsibility is involved, this has meant substituting an account of the justification of our tendency to acquiesce in punishment and blame for a metaphysical account of moral responsibility. The account of justification in each case is an account of internal justification according to which our being justified in manifesting a certain pattern of concern is necessarily tied to our being motivated (at least under suitably idealized circumstances) to display that concern. But it is not plausible to claim that an account of the justification of some of our patterns of special concern can substitute for a metaphysical account of personal identity, for example, unless the account of justification is an account of *rational* justification. Unless we are rationally justified in displaying the patterns of concern we do, it is difficult to see what relevance our special concern for a particular future person could have to the question of who we will be in the future. Similarly, unless we are rationally justified in acquiescing in punishment and blame, the relevance of our being disposed to do so to the question of whether we are responsible is far from obvious.

Cases such as future-Tuesday indifference or SoHo indifference, however, may seem to undermine the claim that the account of internal justification *is* an account of rational justification. If it is such an account, then because in some cases future-Tuesday indifference or SoHo indifference would be internally justified, they would be rationally justified. And this seems to be an unintuitive consequence. Moreover, if the account of internal justification is an account of rational justification, then it entails a version of what Parfit calls the present-aim theory of rationality that "tells each to do what will best achieve his present aims" (Parfit 1984, 92). This is because the account of internal justification is couched in terms of the agent's present motivational makeup, suitably idealized. And though this idealization involves the motivational makeup as it would be modified had the agent the ability to add and subtract desires and adjust their strengths at will, these modifications themselves can only be motivated by the agent's present desires. Parfit's discussion of the present-aim theory strongly suggests, however, that because it has the consequence that future-Tuesday indifference need not be irrational, the theory does not provide an acceptable account of rationality. Thus the theory of internal justification can only play the role for which it was intended if the claim that dispositions such as future-Tuesday indifference must be irrational can be met.

In what follows, I shall briefly mention three points concerning future-Tuesday indifference on which Parfit and I can agree, in order to bring the more fundamental disagreement into focus. I shall then sketch an argument for an account of rationality that has the consequence that future-Tuesday indifference and SoHo indifference need not be irrational.

Point 1   Parfit can agree that to someone in the grip of future-Tuesday indifference or SoHo indifference, there may be nothing we could say to show that person the error of his or her ways. Imagine we are trying to reason with a person who is indifferent to pain on future Tuesdays. We argue that by trading off smaller pains on Mondays or Wednesdays for greater pains on Tuesdays, he needlessly increases the total amount of pain he experiences.

The person who is future-Tuesday-indifferent, however, claims that this begs the question. "Whether this disposition increases or decreases the total amount of pain," he points out, "depends on whether the pain experienced on Tuesdays *counts*." "Bear in mind," he continues, "that I simply don't *care* about pain that will occur on a future Tuesday. So, to compute the total pain (in any sense that is relevant), the pain that will fall on a Tuesday must be ignored. If it is, then my disposition will have *decreased* the amount of pain I experience."

We object, naturally, that he *will* care about the pain. And we remind him that when Tuesday arrives, he will bitterly regret his decision.

"The relevance of that," he replies, "depends on when the regret occurs. If it occurs on Tuesday, then since I am indifferent to the pain, I surely have no reason for concern about my feelings of regret. If it occurs on any other day, of course, it will figure in my calculations in the same way that any other negative consequences of choosing the greater pain on Tuesday will. Only if the feelings of regret (as well as the other negative consequences of the choice that occur on days other than Tuesday) are outweighed by the pain that I avoid (on days other than Tuesday) will I choose the pain on Tuesday."

We suggest that he must, then, believe that it will not be he who suffers or believe that in some sense he does not really exist on Tuesdays.

He replies as follows: "Consider the anthropologically sophisticated psychopath. Suppose such a person is asked whether his willingness to see others suffer rather than have his slightest whim frustrated is immoral. If he is candid, he is likely to admit that by the standards of the society in which he finds himself, such a characterization would be correct. These standards, however, mean nothing to him. Thus it would be misleading of him to use the term 'immoral', except in scare quotes, to describe his own disposition. Such a description would suggest an endorsement of the prevailing standards. However, in offering such a description, he would be giving nothing more than the anthropologically correct account of the application of these standards to his own case.

"I am like the psychopath," we can imagine the person who is future-Tuesday-indifferent going on. "I am fully aware that by all the criteria that prevail, it will be I who suffers on Tuesday. The person stages that suffer on Tuesday can be as physically and psychologically similar to the Monday person stages as is possible, given the discontinuity between my present lack of concern for what happens on Tuesday and the concern that will be felt when Tuesday arrives. And my lack of concern now for what will happen on Tuesday is not based on the belief that I have a Cartesian soul that will be gone before Tuesday comes. There is no further fact, over and above the physical and psychological facts, in which the question of personal identity could consist. The physical and psychological similarities between the Monday person stages and the ones that exist on Tuesdays, however, are a matter of indifference to me. I can admit, then, that *I* will suffer only by using the word 'I' in scare quotes. Like the psychopath's admission, mine describes an anthropological fact that, because of my motivational makeup, has no bearing on my disposition to express sincere evaluations."

Given this analogy between the person who is future-Tuesday-indifferent, or SoHo-indifferent, and the psychopath, I shall call such indifference *pathological indifference* without prejudice to the question of whether or not such a disposition is rational. The first point on which Parfit and I can agree, then, is that if we are, or have become, pathologically indifferent, that indifference may be stable in the following sense: just as we will be indifferent when we are not in the relevant circumstances to the pain we will experience when we are, we may be indifferent to all those considerations that are thought to establish that our indifference to the pain is either irrational or unjustified. Facts about psychological continuity or about the regret that will be felt when the pain occurs may have no more significance for us than the pain itself. In this sense we can say that there are circumstances in which pathological indifference will be in equilibrium.

Point 2   Parfit, in fact, can agree to something stronger. There are circumstances under which it would be rational for us to make ourselves future-Tuesday-indifferent if we could do so effectively and at reasonable cost (say by taking a pill). Suppose that we were faced with the prospect of a number of unavoidable and extremely painful experiences each week and that our only control over the situation lay in our ability to schedule the experiences in any way we chose. And suppose we had a similar control over the timing of the pleasurable experiences open to us. In such a case it would seem perfectly rational to schedule all the pains on Tuesdays, all the pleasures on other days, and then to take the pill.

It is necessary, however, not to overstate the amount of agreement with regard to this kind of case. For Parfit, it is rational to take the pill only if the following condition is met: taking the pill must increase the expected utility of one's future experiences, where the utility is assessed from the perspective of an impartial concern for all of one's future person stages. This condition is likely to be met in the present case if, for example, one nearly always suffers the same amount of pain regardless of when in the week one schedules it. And this latter condition is not obviously unrealistic. Except in emergencies, cases in which one suffers more pain as the result of postponing it are usually ones in which the pain is postponed for a significant period of time. In the case of the person who is future-Tuesday-indifferent, however, there is no incentive to postpone the pain any more than a week. Moreover, not only must Parfit require that his condition be met if the decision to become pathologically indifferent is to be rational; he must also hold that the benefits of such indifference are extremely limited. For Parfit, the gain in becoming future-Tuesday-indifferent lies in saving oneself the pain and anxiety of anticipating future pains that one has no way of avoiding. The significance of the pains themselves, once they occur, is in no way diminished by one's indifference to them before the day on which they are experienced.

For those who do not assume that rationality requires impartiality regarding one's future person stages, however, Parfit's condition need not be satisfied. Any partiality in one's concern for one's future person stages would be reflected in one's decisions about whether to make oneself pathologically indifferent. And it is difficult to see what we could say to someone who made such a decision on grounds that were not fully impartial (on the basis, for example, of a preference for future person stages that were closer in time merely because they were closer). At least it is difficult to see what we could say that would convince the person that he or she had made an irrational decision. In addition, for those who do not share Parfit's assumptions about rationality, the benefits of pathological indifference may involve more than eliminating the anticipation of pain. For the person who is future-Tuesday-indifferent, the pain experienced on Tuesdays may, as he or she would maintain, simply not count.

It does not follow, however, that one would be likely to make oneself pathologically indifferent if there were a significant chance that in doing so one would be led to accept a great deal of suffering one could otherwise avoid. It seems very unlikely, for example, that one would make oneself SoHo-indifferent if one could foresee the possibility that one would make oneself undergo torture merely to save time. This is because from the perspective one must assume in deciding for or against SoHo indifference, the person stages in SoHo are just as important as those in other locations. And this will be true even though, from the perspective of the person who would be SoHo-indifferent, the pains felt in SoHo could be completely discounted.

Point 3   A final point about pathological indifference, and again one with which Parfit can agree, is that the possibility of acquiring such an attitude might have genuine explanatory significance in psychology. The explanation most commonly offered by clinical psychologists for the phenomenon of multiple personalities is that splitting the self represents a rational response to a situation in which one anticipates that one will suffer intolerable pain over which one has no control. Splitting the self represents a rational strategy, however, only if one can withdraw one's present concern from one or more of the future selves. This is evident if one imagines the possibility in which two future selves that are psychologically discontinuous with each other will alternate in control and only one will experience the pain. The fact that the future selves are psychologically discontinuous with *each other* is no improvement from one's perspective in the present if each one remains continuous with one's *present* self. From one's perspective in the present, the future self that experiences the pain is just as much a matter of concern as it would be if it and the future self that avoids the pain were psychologically integrated. Thus it is only the ability to withdraw concern from a part of one's own future that provides the strategy of splitting the self with the rationale that was intended.[2]

Parfit and I can agree, then, not only that pathological indifference may represent an equilibrium from which one has no motivation to depart but also that it may be an equilibrium at which one has good reason to aim. In the sections that follow, I shall sketch the argument that pathological indifference may not only be in equilibrium, but that when it is, it is not irrational.

2   Ideal Reflective Equilibria

General accounts of rationality are notoriously controversial. As an alternative to assuming the truth of some conception of rationality, I propose to look at a dilemma for our practice of assessing some actions as *irrational* that arises if such assessments are to play the role they seem to play in our ordinary practical decision making. The dilemma about ascriptions of irrationality (and rationality) is a special instance of a dilemma, which I describe in chapter 7, concerning our ascriptions of responsibility and blame. I shall outline the dilemma concerning the ascription of responsibility and blame in section 3 and the dilemma regarding rationality in section 4. In order to state the two dilemmas, however, I shall develop in this section the notion of equilibrium involved in the claim that when pathological indifference is in equilibrium, it need not be irrational.

As in chapter 7, the concept of equilibrium in question is the one that would result if we had complete control over our own motivational makeup. Imagine a pill that allowed us to add or eliminate any noninstrumental desire we chose and with which we could increase or decrease the strengths of any of the desires in the resulting set. Many of us have desires of a persistent or possibly even addictive sort, which we would happily eliminate. There are also desires, such as the desire for more exercise, whose strengths we would seriously consider increasing. Those with serious emotional or motivational conflicts would be likely to make far more extensive changes. To characterize the notion of equilibrium that I have in mind, however, I require that all such changes be subject to the following proviso: one must be reflectively aware of the basic facts about one's motivational makeup. One cannot, for example, be so thoroughly in the grip of an obsessive desire, say for revenge, that one is unaware that one has other desires, such as the desire to retain one's freedom, with which that desire is in conflict or is likely to be in conflict. It is not required, however, that one know anything more than facts of this basic kind.

With this proviso, one's addition and elimination of desires, as well as one's adjustments of their strengths, will satisfy the following conditions:

• One's motivation to add and subtract desires must have its source in the other desires that one has. The idea of stepping back from all of one's noninstrumental desires *simultaneously* and choosing which to keep is clearly unintelligible. The process is rather one of increasing the overall coherence of the set of desires with which one starts. And this does not require that one have a noninstrumental second-order desire that one maximize the coherence of one's first-order desires and that this second-order desire take precedence over all the others. Indeed, a subject who had such a desire would probably have good reason to eliminate it or to see that its strength was decreased. Certainly very few would want to devote large portions of their resources to increasing the coherence of their other desires simply for its own sake. What will motivate one to eliminate (from an otherwise normal set) the desire to drive at twice the legal limit, to gamble with one's life savings, or to brawl in pubs is the recognition that such desires threaten most or all of the others, together with the motivational force of those other desires.

• The strength of a noninstrumental desire alone is irrelevant to whether it will be retained or eliminated. The desire for heroin might be the strongest desire one has in terms of one's tendency to act on it, but it will still be eliminated from an otherwise normal set.

• Whether a noninstrumental desire is retained depends on the amount of support it receives from other noninstrumental desires and does not depend on its content. Very general desires may be eliminated for their failure to cohere with very specific desires, just as specific desires may be dropped because they fail to find support from other specific desires and general desires. This process has obvious analogies to the process that Rawls describes as arriving at reflective equilibrium. Since the pill that defines the equilibrium achieved produces an idealization of what we could achieve without it, I shall call this outcome an *ideal reflective equilibrium* (IRE).

• The coherentist and holistic character of the process of arriving at an ideal reflective equilibrium has one important limitation. Let us define an *unconditional desire* as a desire for a state of affairs that one wants to be realized whether or not the desire for it persists. One's desire for luxuries, for example, is ordinarily a desire that one have them only if one continues to want them. One's desire that one should be honest, however, is ordinarily unconditional. Even if one knew now that in the future one would cease to have any noninstrumental desire to tell the truth, one would ordinarily prefer now that one continue to tell the truth, even if one does so out of habit, fear of punishment, or superstition. To say that one's desire to tell the truth is (likely to be) unconditional, however, is not to say that it is unqualified. One's desire to be truthful may be unconditional even though one has no desire to insist on the truth when to do so would cause suffering and when the issues involved are trivial. Indeed, a desire to tell the truth may be qualified in indefinitely complex ways while remaining unconditional. Moreover, the claim that one's desire for honesty is unconditional does not entail that its existence is independent of the nature of one's upbringing or the character of one's society. Nor does it entail that one would prefer to remain honest regardless of how much suffering one would experience if at some time in the future one came to desire not to be honest and that desire were frustrated. All that follows from the claim is that if one contemplates now a time in the future in which one's present desire to be honest no longer exists, one prefers now, all other things being equal, that at that future time one should be honest.[3]

Given this definition of an unconditional desire, we can note the following relation between conditional and unconditional desires. In a competition between an unconditional noninstrumental desire and a conditional noninstrumental desire, the unconditional desire will always survive, regardless of how well supported the conditional desire is by other conditional desires. The reason is that eliminating either desire makes it less likely that one will bring about the state of affairs that corresponds to that desire and thus less likely that it will come about. In the case of a conditional desire, this represents no loss from the perspective of the choice situation. If the desire is conditional, then if one will not have it in the future, that fact completely compensates for the fact that the state of affairs that is its object is less likely to come about. For an unconditional desire, this is obviously not the case. Thus there is a two-tiered structure within the set of one's noninstrumental desires in that unconditional desires play a foundational role relative to conditional desires. But within each tier, considerations of coherence are decisive.

• One's ideal reflective equilibrium is relative to one's *actual* beliefs. Whether the desire for heroin supports and is supported by an otherwise normal set of desires depends on whether one believes that it is addictive, that it is illegal, that it is likely to shorten one's life, that its use is likely to force one into criminal activity, and so forth. With a sufficiently bizarre set of beliefs, both the desire for heroin *and* one's more normal desires might remain in one's ideal reflective equilibrium.

3   The Dilemma Regarding Responsibility

Once we have the notion of an ideal reflective equilibrium, the dilemma regarding our ascriptions of responsibility and blame can be explained as follows. Suppose we contemplate making someone suffer for an act of harm that the person has committed. There are two possible explanations of the action if one assumes that it was not performed in ignorance of some of the relevant facts. The person in question may have produced the harm on the basis of a desire in IRE (i.e., a desire that would have remained had he or she had access to the pill in terms of which an IRE is defined) or on the basis of a desire out of IRE. (I shall assume that in explaining the action, we presuppose a picture of the underlying causal connections that is not strictly deterministic. But I shall also assume that whatever indeterminacies the picture involves, it is no better than determinism as far as the prospects of making sense of ascriptions of responsibility are concerned. In other words, I am making the familiar assumption that indeterminism raises the same problems for ascriptions of responsibility and blame that determinism does.)

In the case in which the person acts *in IRE,* the person knew he or she was acting so as to cause harm and did so on the basis of a desire the person was perfectly content to have. That person, of course, either miscalculated the chances of being caught or was simply unlucky. In either case, the harm did not figure prominently enough in the person's motivational makeup to deter the action. The preference for the action, then, over refraining from the harm was in equilibrium for that person. Hence, our blame of the person finds no footing in the person's motivational makeup. Though the person might feel guilt or remorse, these sentiments themselves would be eliminated were the person in IRE. Thus in the internal sense in which what is justified for us must have some connection with what would actually motivate us (under suitably idealized circumstances), such a person would be unjustified in retaining any disposition to feel guilt or remorse for the harm in question. Since the person's lack of concern over the harm in question is in equilibrium, there is nothing we could appeal to in the person by condemning the action and making the person suffer. Our making the person suffer could, of course, work as a deterrent or as a restriction on the person's freedom, but the connection between punishment and the possibility of genuine guilt or remorse would be broken.

Imagine, for example, that Martians had the ability to punish people for stepping on insects. (Assume that there is no disagreement between the Martians and us over the psychology of insects. They simply find the analogy between pain and its closest analogue in insects more striking than we do.) And suppose you continued to step on insects whenever the possibility of being caught was remote and the cost of avoiding doing so was significant. If you were caught and made to suffer, you would certainly regret your misfortune. You might also change your assessment of the Martians' surveillance techniques. You would not, however, find guilt or remorse appropriate, nor would you regard your suffering as punishment. You would be to the Martians what the psychopath is to us. Though they could manipulate your behavior and exercise power over you, they could not do so in a way that would constitute genuine punishment.

Similarly, if you lived in the vicinity of a tribe whose taboos you considered superstitious but who had the power to make you suffer for breaking them, you would not regard such suffering, if it were inflicted, as genuine punishment. And what is essential to this example is not that the norms you violate are superstitious but that, as in the previous example, they incorporate values so alien to yours that you could not be internally justified in acquiescing in your suffering. The same considerations would apply if you were a political prisoner whose values differed radically from those of your captors. In all three cases, though you might recognize that your suffering was intended as punishment, you yourself could only regard it as the exercise of superior force. Thus in the sense in which I am using the expression 'genuine punishment', none of these cases in which you suffer are ones to which that term applies.

The person who causes harm on the basis of a desire in IRE, then, is in an important respect like the psychopath. And there is fairly wide (though hardly universal) agreement that the psychopath cannot be the object of genuine punishment or blame (Haksar 1964; Fingarette 1967, chap. 2; Feinberg 1970a; Murphy 1972, 288–289). Let us call *unreachable* those subjects who, for lack of the appropriate motivational makeup, are beyond the reach of genuine punishment. It is not the psychopath's lack of sympathy for others that makes him or her unfit for punishment. Someone who lacks sympathy for others but is rationally motivated to avoid actions involving harm to people for other reasons *is* blameworthy if he or she intentionally causes such harm to occur. It is the psychopath's lack of any element in his or her motivational makeup in which our blame can find a foothold, that is, his or her unreachability, that makes such blame inappropriate. And it is this feature that the person who acts on the basis of a desire in IRE so as to produce harm shares with the psychopath.

Thus someone whose harmful action stems from a desire in IRE is not an appropriate candidate for genuine blame. This is not to say that we would be unjustified in protecting ourselves from such subjects. It is merely to say that our justification for doing so could not be the same as our justification for administering genuine punishment. (And as I argue in section 5, it is our being blamable in the sense that would justify genuine punishment that is basic.) Unreachable subjects include, besides the psychopath and the subjects who live under the sway of the Martians or the local tribesmen, subjects with radically different conceptions of the good from ours and subjects with radically different conceptions of responsibility.

In the second case the person whom we contemplate making suffer has committed an act of harm on the basis of a desire *out of IRE*. Since the desire was one on which the person actually acted, it follows trivially that it was that person's strongest desire in the motivational sense. Let us contrast, then, the *motivational strength* of a person's desire, which is a measure of the person's tendency to act on it, and its *evaluational strength,* which is the tendency it has to survive (or to survive undiminished) the person's acquisition of the pill that defines IRE. Since the desire from which the harm stemmed was out of IRE, its motivational strength was out of proportion to its evaluational strength. In this respect, however, the person is not relevantly different from the compulsive. Of course, the person who acts on a desire out of IRE need not exhibit the kind of recognizable and repetitious pattern often associated with compulsive behavior. Nor must the desire that was acted upon have been any more than marginally stronger than its nearest competitor. Thus just as the action done from a desire out of IRE may lack the external marks of compulsion, it may lack the phenomenology as well. The person may have acted on a desire that he or she had chosen not to act on many times in the past. And the person may have felt perfectly capable of choosing not to act on it on this occasion even as he or she did choose to act upon it. This is just to say, however, that if the desire had been weaker, the person would not have acted on it. And this is equally true of the compulsive. The fact that in this case, in contrast to the case of the compulsive, the desire acted upon was not overwhelmingly greater in strength than its nearest competitor does not seem to be a morally significant difference. Thus, like the person who acts on a desire in IRE, the person who acts on a desire out of IRE seems an inappropriate candidate where punishment and blame are concerned.

It is possible, of course, that the person who caused harm did so as the result of ignorance of the consequences of his or her actions. If this is the case, then again blame seems unjustified. There is a puzzle, then, in seeing how ascriptions of responsibility and blame could ever be justified.[4]

Such an argument might seem to support a utilitarian account of responsibility and blame. The puzzle we are considering was generated in large part, however, by the following intuition: that guilt and remorse should have an internal justification for those to whom responsibility and blame are ascribed. For those who take this intuition seriously, the utilitarian account of responsibility is unlikely to have much appeal. In the next section I shall argue that ascribing irrationality is a special case of ascribing responsibility and blame. I shall then argue that there is an account of responsibility that does satisfy the intuition that the appropriateness of punishment and blame and the internal justification of the suffering involved are necessarily connected.

4   The Dilemma with Regard to Rationality

Given the dilemma about responsibility, an analogous puzzle emerges concerning rationality. This is because to call a person's action irrational is to ascribe a certain kind of blame to the person, and such ascriptions of blame may have serious consequences for the person's future interests. This blame that we ascribe to a person for the irrationality of his or her *acts* must be distinguished from an ascription of irrationality to the *person*. In what follows, I shall be concerned with ascriptions of irrationality where *particular acts* of a subject are concerned and in which the subject is not excused on the grounds that he or she is irrational in general. Both kinds of ascriptions are likely to have an adverse effect on the interests of the person to whom they are made, and thus both may cause the person to suffer. But only for ascriptions of the first kind are resentment in the case of another's action, and guilt and remorse in the case of one's own action, appropriate. And only in these cases does the suffering that ascriptions of irrationality impose involve genuine punishment and blame.[5]

The question, then, like the question in the general case of responsibility, is how the suffering involved in ascriptions of irrationality is to be justified. Since this puzzle is a special case of the earlier one, it has exactly the same structure.[6] Suppose that we contemplate making someone suffer for an act we describe as irrational. Let us assume that the stakes are relatively high and that the action resulted in harm, either to the person who performed it, to some other person, or both.

As in the general case of responsibility, if the person did not act out of ignorance or on the basis of some other cognitive defect, then he or she either acted on the basis of a desire in IRE or on the basis of a desire out of IRE. And as in the general case of responsibility, the problem is to see how the blame and suffering that ascriptions of irrationality involve can be justified.

Let us consider, then, each of the alternatives where blame for irrationality is concerned. In the first case the person knowingly acts in a way that is likely to cause harm, as harms and benefits are ordinarily assessed, either to himself or herself, to others, or to both. Moreover, the person acts on the basis of a desire that he or she is perfectly content to have. One such case is similar to an example of Harry Frankfurt's (1971, 12). I shall use the term 'integrated addict' to refer to someone whose addiction to a drug is not in serious conflict with the majority of his or her other desires. The integrated addict would not mind, for example, that as a result of the addiction, he or she could not hold a conventional job, maintain normal human relationships, or count on a normal life expectancy. Such a person could also be expected to enjoy associating with other addicts, to find excitement in selling illegal drugs, and to derive meaning and significance from the drug subculture. Thus if offered the pill that defines IRE, the integrated addict would be unmotivated to eliminate the desire for the drug. The integrated gambler is another example of the same type. A third example might be the person whose desire in IRE is to fulfill a promise at enormous personal cost even though it is to someone who will benefit only slightly, if at all, from its fulfillment. Other examples include the person whose commitment to an apparently frivolous goal, such as being in the *Guinness Book of World Records*, is in equilibrium and the person whose willingness in IRE to sacrifice himself or herself for others seems wildly extravagant by ordinary standards.

Would the actions typical of such subjects be irrational? Viewed from the outside, the drug addiction, the gambling, the promise kept at enormous cost, the trivial pursuit, and the extravagant self-sacrifice are quite plausibly regarded as irrational and self-destructive. One's judgment is likely to change, however, when the stories are spelled out in enough detail to make it clear that the actions stem from desires in IRE. Terms like 'compulsive', 'ill-considered', or 'obsessive' would be regarded as appropriate by the person in question (and would in fact be appropriate) only on the assumption that we could appeal to those normal goals and desires that we ordinarily possess and that make these terms appropriate in our own cases. For such a person acting in IRE, these normal goals and desires that we ordinarily take for granted do not exist. Guilt and remorse over the harm that their actions might cause to themselves or to others would be equally unjustified for such people on the assumption that the actions stem from desires in IRE.

For the person who is not in IRE but who acts on an apparently self-destructive desire that would be in IRE if the appropriate drug were available, this need not be true. Such a person will necessarily have conflicting desires, which might well make the person vulnerable to feelings of guilt, remorse, self-directed anger, or shame. But such a person still differs from most of us in that if the person were given the choice, it would not be the apparently self-destructive desires but the desires with which they conflict and the emotions such as guilt and remorse that they generate that would be eliminated. For such a person, then, it is the guilt and remorse that would be unjustified, as would any suffering caused by being blamed for irrationality. Therefore, as in the case of the psychopath, it is difficult to see how genuine blame could be justified and thus difficult to see what could justify calling such a person irrational.

The second case is analogous to the second case of the puzzle about responsibility. The person to whom we are tempted to ascribe irrationality and on whom we would impose the adverse consequences that such ascriptions involve has acted on a desire out of IRE. Suppose, for example, that faced with an intruder threatening one's family, one reacted with anger, thereby subjecting the family to more danger than if one had remained calm. One may well have known, even while envincing them, that the angry reactions were not the ones that maximized the chances of survival. Had one been able to change one's motivational makeup on the spot, one would have eliminated the desires underlying the dangerous reactions. (That is, one would have eliminated the token desires that resulted in the angry reactions on that occasion. One would not, of course, necessarily have eliminated the types of desires of which they were tokens.) Other cases that involve harm to oneself as a result of acting on a desire that is out of IRE include gambling or taking drugs when the desire to do so is not integrated with one's other desires. Unusual fear that prevents one from saving someone's life or from saving one's own is another case. One's fear of heights, for example, might prevent one from jumping into a net from a burning building even though if one had an appropriate pill, one would eliminate the desire not to jump and thereby survive.

Unlike the case of acting in IRE, acting out of IRE, when it produces harm, *is* likely to produce feelings of guilt or remorse as well as feelings of self-directed anger or shame. This is clearly true in the case in which one's irrational reaction to the threat to one's family results in harm that could have been avoided. But even if no one else is harmed, one's irrational reactions may well inspire guilt or remorse. Gambling or taking drugs on the basis of a desire out of IRE, for example, may result in guilt or remorse even if one only harms oneself. This would be particularly likely if one had been made painfully aware of the consequences by past experience and had vowed never to use drugs or to gamble again.

Although one's feelings of guilt or remorse would be natural in such a case, it is hard to see how they could be justified. In acting on a desire that is *out of IRE*, one is acting on one's desire that is motivationally strongest, even though one would not be motivated to keep it if one had the means available for its elimination. In this respect, one does not seem relevantly different from the compulsive. Of course, one would have acted differently if the desire on which one acted had had a different relative strength. But in this respect too the compulsive is no different, and we do not hold the compulsive responsible or ascribe blame to such an individual. Though one might be blamed for causing harm by one's irrational action and one might blame oneself, it is unclear what grounds the distinction between this case and the case in which ascriptions of responsibility and blame seem obviously unjustified.

Another possibility is that an action we are tempted to regard as irrational is the result of a cognitive rather than conative failure. Again, however, ascriptions of responsibility and blame seem to lack any justification. Suppose that one of one's actions appears irrational and worthy of blame but that one has lacked some crucial piece of information that would have altered one's decision to act. If at some earlier stage one irrationally declined to acquire the information, then one is, presumably, in some respect blameworthy. But in this case the question is simply pushed one step back. Since one failed to acquire the information because of a desire in IRE, a desire out of IRE, or some cognitive defect, the question of how one could be responsible and worthy of blame remains open. If, on the other hand, there was nothing blameworthy in the failure to acquire the information, it is not immediately apparent how there could be anything blameworthy in acting without having access to it. The same argument applies if one acts on the basis of a false belief.

Suppose, however, that one has all the relevant information but that under the pressure of stress, time constraints, or distractions one acts on the basis of an obviously bad inference. Here again, responsibility and blame for one's irrationality seem in place only if one found oneself in the situation as a result of some earlier irrational act.

If one were not to blame for being in the situation, how could one be blamed for the limitations on one's computational capacity?

Finally, consider cases in which one might be faulted for inattention, for insufficient effort, or simply for a slack performance. If one had known in advance that one was prone to such failures of performance and one was blameworthy in not preparing for such contingencies, then blame for the performance might be appropriate. If, however, one had had no prior warning of one's tendency toward inferior performances in the kinds of circumstances in question or no warning that such circumstances were likely to occur, then the justification for one's being blamed remains obscure.

5   Internal Justification and Rationality

Unless there is some solution to the puzzle about rationality, then whatever other role they play, ascriptions of rationality and irrationality will lack the practical force we ordinarily attribute to them. When we accuse someone of acting irrationally, what we do goes beyond stating that the person exhibits a particular psychological mechanism. We are not, for example, simply claiming that he or she possesses a certain set of desires or that he or she is prone to computational or performance failures. And it is not enough to add that by pointing to one or more of these facts, we may be warning others of their possibly detrimental effects. Not even the fact that such ascriptions may have beneficial consequences by deterring harmful behavior on the part of those to whom they are made is enough to capture their full force.

To have the full force that we ordinarily take such ascriptions to have, they must justify not only the adverse reactions of others toward our irrational actions but also our own attitudes of self-directed anger, shame, guilt, or remorse. To see how this is possible, recall that the notion of an ideal reflective equilibrium leads naturally to an internal conception of justification. A noninstrumental desire that is in IRE for a subject is justified for that subject by its coherence with, and hence its support by, that subject's other noninstrumental desires. But how could the blame that ascriptions of irrationality involve have an internal justification in this sense? And how would such an internal justification solve the puzzle of rationality?

Given this notion of internal justification, one of the claims that generates the puzzle of rationality can be stated as follows: there is no internal justification of self-directed anger, guilt, or remorse where actions stemming from desires in IRE are concerned. But if the notion of internal justification cannot help in the case of actions stemming from desires in IRE, it is difficult to see how it could help at all. In the case of actions stemming from desires out of IRE or from cognitive defects, the actions are not relevantly different from those of the compulsive or those of the person who is ignorant. Since we do not blame those who are ignorant or compulsive for their actions, we seem, even given the notion of internal justification, to be saddled with an arbitrary distinction. Another way of putting this is to say that if we are blamed when we are not relevantly different from those who are ignorant or those who are compulsive, we seem to have been blamed for our bad moral luck, and this seems clearly unacceptable.

Whether the dilemma regarding ascriptions of rationality, and more generally of responsibility, is really intractable, however, depends on whom we count as relevantly different from those who are compulsive or ignorant. Our ordinary assumption is that the distinction between those who are responsible and those who are not should depend only on properties that are intrinsic in the sense that they satisfy the following two conditions. First, they are determined by the psychology of the individual agent alone. For example, they are independent of facts about the utility of punishing the agent. Second, they are independent of the attitudes, values, commitments, and beliefs about responsibility that are held by the agent in question. Not even the fact that a person has a set of values as radically deviant as those of the psychopath is relevant to whether the person is genuinely responsible. Similarly irrelevant is whether the person lives in a society in which the medical model is the sole model of social deviance.[7] Even if in such a society the concepts of blame and punishment (as opposed to therapy or behavior modification) are held to be incoherent, the assumption is that the facts about responsibility and blame are independent of such facts about social practice. That is, either our social practices, including punishment, or the practices of those in the society where punishment is excluded get things right. The assumption is, in other words, that the social arrangements regarding who is punished and blamed and who receives therapy instead must answer to the facts about responsibility. The same is true of the attitudes and values of individuals that determine whether they are willing to accept blame and whether they regard guilt and remorse as justified. Thus such social and psychological facts cannot constitute the facts about responsibility. On this assumption, the claim that there is any relevant difference where responsibility is concerned between those who act compulsively or in ignorance and those who act out of IRE is difficult to support.

Corresponding to the assumption that the facts about responsibility depend only on the intrinsic properties of the agent is the following constraint. Any justification of our practices of ascribing responsibility and blame must be grounded in properties that are intrinsic in the sense described. Call this the *intrinsic-property constraint*. Suppose this constraint is unjustified. Suppose that whether we are responsible for an action depends on whether, if the action is harmful, we are justified in feeling guilt and remorse and in acquiescing in the suffering entailed by our being punished and blamed. And suppose that the justification in question is internal justification. Then whether we are responsible will depend on just those facts about our attitudes, values, and practices that the intrinsic-property constraint rules out as irrelevant. Now consider the claim that actions stemming from a desire out of IRE or from a cognitive failure are not relevantly different from compulsive actions or actions done out of ignorance. The reply would be that they *are* relevantly different. It is quite possible that for many cases of actions stemming from desires out of IRE, guilt and remorse would be justified, even though for many other such cases they would not be. In cases of weakness of the will, for example, we accept responsibility for the action that results when our strongest desire (in the motivational sense) is out of IRE. And we are apparently justified in doing so even though compulsive actions, for which we do not accept responsibility, are also ones that are caused when a desire out of IRE is the strongest. If we are in fact justified in accepting responsibility in such cases, then abandoning the intrinsic-property constraint and appealing to internal justification will provide a solution to the dilemma where ascriptions of responsibility are concerned.

To see what is involved in abandoning the intrinsic-property constraint, consider the following distinction between two kinds of compatibilism (cf. Glover 1983, 461–465). Let us say that *indirect-compatibilist theories* are those according to which punishment and blame are justified by appeal to one or more intermediate facts. These typically include the fact that the agent in question was responsible for what he or she did. This ascription of responsibility in turn is ordinarily justified by reference to the claim that in some sense the agent acted freely. And this claim itself is frequently supported by appeal to the alleged fact that in some relevant sense the agent could have done other than what he or she did. Compatibilist theories of this kind contrast with those that it is natural to call *direct-compatibilist theories*. According to these theories, punishment and blame are justified directly without reference to an independent notion of responsibility. Moreover, they are justified without appeal to the claim that the agent could have done otherwise. On a direct-compatibilist account, the agent is responsible for harm in virtue of the fact that the agent's being punished or blamed and the agent's feeling guilt or remorse are justified.

Dropping the intrinsic-property constraint means opting for a direct rather than indirect form of compatibilism. This is because dropping the constraint means giving up the assumption that for any person we might contemplate punishing, there is an intrinsic property in virtue of which punishment is justified, if it is justified at all. But such notions as an agent's having acted freely or having been able to do otherwise, as used by the indirect compatibilist, have clearly been intended to pick out just such intrinsic properties. Thus, dropping the intrinsic-property constraint means abandoning the attempt to provide the kind of justification of punishment that the indirect compatibilist envisages.

Direct compatibilists, of course, need not hold that the justification of punishment and blame is internal justification. P. F. Strawson (1974), Jonathan Glover (1983), and Daniel Dennett (1984a) are all direct compatibilists who differ in the accounts they offer of the justification of punishment and none of whose accounts is internalist in the sense I have sketched.[8] Among the direct-compatibilist accounts, however, the internalist version seems to do the least violence to our pretheoretical intuitions. Noninternalist versions either leave no room for guilt or remorse or provide no guarantee that if the punishment of some subject is justified, that subject's acquiescing in being blamed can be justified from his or her own point of view. Thus it is direct compatibilism in its internalist form that, I shall claim, provides a solution to the dilemma for ascriptions of responsibility and blame.

Such a solution to the dilemma regarding responsibility and thus to the dilemma with regard to rationality will be convincing, of course, only if it is possible to supply some content to the notion of an internal justification of our accepting blame and feeling guilt and remorse. But before we can see that such a justification might be possible, we must be clear about what it would entail. To be internally justified in accepting genuine blame or in accepting punishment or liability, one would have to be justified in doing so even when it could *not* be justified by reference to one's interests, including one's long-term interests. One would also have to be justified in accepting punishment or liability or feelings of guilt or remorse even when such acceptance could not be justified on utilitarian grounds. To be genuinely blamable, it is neither necessary nor sufficient that one be the most useful instrument of a social policy geared toward producing the best outcome. What is required is that one should be justified in accepting the blame (over some range of cases) for what one has *done*, regardless of the consequences of doing so. In order for the desire that one accept such blame to be internally justified, it must be part of one's IRE and hence must cohere with, and be supported by, the other desires in which that IRE consists. Moreover, we can assume that the IRE of any normal individual contains the desire that no one suffer unnecessarily and that that desire is unconditional. Since the desire to accept the blame (even when doing so will not produce the best consequences) may conflict with the desire that no one suffer unnecessarily, the former desire must also be unconditional. The question, then, is what other desires might exist that could support an unconditional desire of this kind.

The most promising way to approach this last question is to ask what would be lost to a person for whom, or a society for which, responsibility and blame were unintelligible. The answer, though complicated, seems to have two basic components. First, if one cannot be blamed for what one does, neither can one be credited. The desire, then, for authorship in the widest sense—the desire that one's creations, talents, and efforts be regarded as one's own and deserving of praise—is a desire that supports the desire to be blamable if one's actions cause harm.

Second, one's desire for a sphere in which one's own decisions carry authority and in which one cannot be second-guessed supports the desire to be blamable. Consider a society in which one could not be blamed for some class of actions because, for example, they were regarded as compulsive. In such a society one would lack an important type of internalized motivation to avoid such actions, and as a result, one would be less likely to do so. Also, in such a society one would lack any belief in one's ability to control the actions in question and would again be less likely to avoid them. In this case, however, it is difficult to see what grounds one could have for objecting to interventions by others when these were aimed at preventing such actions when they were likely to prove harmful. Consequently, one's desire for a sphere in which one has authority supports the desire that there be a class of actions for which one is blamable. Moreover, suppose one unconditionally desires not to harm others without justification. Then one's desire for a sphere in which one has authority supports the unconditional desire that one acquiesce in punishment and blame if an action for which one is blamable causes harm. This amounts to saying that if in IRE one desires *autonomy* (in one natural sense of the term), then one's desire to accept blame under some range of circumstances will be in IRE as well.

To say that the desire to accept blame for a certain range of actions would be supported in IRE is one thing. It is another thing to say what the principles would be like that distinguish the circumstances in which we could desire to accept blame from those in which we could not. We have already seen that the principles could not rest on intrinsic distinctions, but this tells us almost nothing positive about them. I am inclined, however, to think that there is room here for a great deal of variation. There seems to be nothing in the notion of an internal justification that rules out a society of super Sartreans who allow scarcely any excuses at all. The members of such a society could desire in IRE to accept blame for their actions under a far wider range of circumstances than we do. By the same token, there seems to be nothing to rule out a society in which even the man or woman on the street accepts as broad a range of excuses as would be accepted if most instances of deviance were understood in medical rather than judicial terms.

The solution to the dilemma regarding moral responsibility, then, lies in the fact that those who suffer may be internally justified in acquiescing in their suffering. Thus the solution justifies genuine punishment for those who act on desires out of IRE but not those who do not. It follows that we cannot genuinely blame the psychopath when his or her actions are motivated by desires in IRE, even if these actions result in serious harm. And this consequence raises two apparent difficulties. First, while we cannot blame the psychopath, it is essential to the account of the internal justification of blame that we can blame those who desire to be blamable. Furthermore, there is no reason why the psychopath should not desire to be blamable, in virtue of desiring the authorship of his or her creations. The conflict here, however, is merely apparent. To be blamable, there must be *some* class of actions for which the psychopath would be justified in feeling self-directed anger, guilt, or remorse. But these actions need not be the ones by which he or she knowingly and deliberately causes harm to others. They might instead be actions that because of the psychopath's motivational makeup, are weak-willed and thus not motivated by desires in IRE. The psychopath might be blamable, for example, for failing to act with sufficient ruthlessness in advancing his or her own interests. Thus there are two conditions for being justified in feeling guilt and remorse for one's actions and in acquiescing in the reactive attitudes, punishment, and blame that those actions elicit in others. The actions must belong to a class of actions for which one is blamable, and the actions must be performed on the basis of desires that are out of IRE. And whereas the actions of the psychopath that cause harm to others may well satisfy the first condition, they will not in general satisfy the second.

The second difficulty for this account of responsibility is that the consequence that we cannot punish the psychopath may seem to be in conflict with our pretheoretical intuitions. This may be the case despite the reservations about such punishment that many theorists have expressed on independent grounds. And the analogy between the psychopath and the person with normal moral commitments living among a tribe governed by superstitious taboos may not dispel the doubts concerning this consequence. But the fact that we cannot punish the psychopath for harming others will seem less implausible if we recognize that some of the consequences it may appear to have do not actually follow. As we have seen, the fact that punishment cannot be justified in these cases does not entail that we cannot protect ourselves from the psychopath. What does follow is that the justification of such protection will be of a different kind from the one that supports genuine punishment. The justification of punishment will involve notions like guilt and remorse and will appeal to the values of the subjects being punished and to the fact that these values justify their acquiescing in the suffering that their punishment entails. In contrast, we justify protecting ourselves from the psychopath on consequentialist grounds that need not involve the notion of desert. Just as we may quarantine a person without supposing that the person is responsible for his or her condition, so we may minimize our risk of being harmed by the psychopath without supposing that genuine blame is appropriate. In the case of the psychopath who is blamable for at least some actions, it is not even ruled out that we should enforce the full range of legal penalties on purely deterrent grounds. And in such a case all that would be missing is the connection between the enforcement of the penalties and any form of blame in which the person being penalized could acquiesce. This is sufficient, however, for saying that the penalities cannot constitute genuine punishment.

The account of rationality I have outlined is one according to which ascriptions of irrationality are a special case of ascriptions of responsibility and blame. Thus it is natural on such an account to address the dilemma where ascriptions of irrationality are concerned by appeal to this treatment of the dilemma regarding responsibility. The account of rationality, then, will involve the direct justification of ascriptions of irrationality and the ascriptions of blame that constitute them, and the justification will be an internal one. And as in the theory of responsibility, only those whose actions are out of IRE (or stem from ignorance or computational failures) will be open to genuine blame. Since we cannot genuinely blame those who are in IRE, it follows that those who are in IRE are not acting irrationally.

That this theory solves the puzzle about rationality (and it is difficult to see how a noninternalist theory could do so) is a strong point in its favor. But such an internalist approach to rationality has the consequence that we originally sought to establish. To say that SoHo indifference and future-Tuesday indifference might each be in equilibrium is to say that each might be part of a motivational makeup in IRE. And this is to say that such desires are not irrational. It was, after all, the desires out of IRE (as well as one's cognitive failings) for which one could be justified in accepting blame and feeling guilt or remorse. For the desires in IRE, this would not be possible. Hence, it is a consequence of an account of rationality, and an account supported on independent grounds, that the kind of indifference that I have called pathological need not be irrational.

By arguing for the rationality of future-Tuesday indifference, I have blocked the claim, strongly suggested by Parfit's discussion, that any theory with the consequence that future-Tuesday indifference is not irrational can be rejected for that reason. And this is, in fact, the only objection that Parfit offers to the present-aim theory. The possibility that future-Tuesday indifference is rational, however, is a consequence of a theory of rationality that is justified on independent grounds. Thus any argument that it must be irrational, if it is to be convincing, must be founded on an alternative treatment of rationality that we have at least as much reason to accept.

Acknowledgments

An earlier version of this paper was read to the Society for Philosophy and Public Affairs at the Eastern Division meeting of the American Philosophical Association, December 29, 1986. I am grateful to the commentators, Annette Baier and George Sher, for their discussion of these issues and to Amélie Rorty for her comments and suggestions.

Postscript

In chapter 9, I argue that punishment justified solely on utilitarian grounds does not satisfy our pretheoretical intuitions regarding justice and that it does not constitute *genuine* punishment. Only if the suffering entailed is suffering in which those who are punished can acquiesce does it constitute genuine punishment on this account. It may seem inconsistent, then, that I claim we can threaten to punish the psychopath and indeed carry out the threats on purely deterrent grounds.

The two claims, however, are consistent. Given the internalist direct account of responsibility, we can justify the punishment of those who act on desires that are not in IRE. And given substantive unconditional commitments to liberal and democratic ideals on the part of most of the members of society (see chapter 10), we can be assured that there will be sufficient compliance with social norms that the threat of punishment will be an effective deterrent where the nonpsychopathic members of the population are concerned. The question is whether in such a society the punishment of psychopaths would be justified.

But suppose that a law that would have this consequence were proposed. Not only normal subjects but psychopaths themselves would be rationally justified in supporting its passage. First, psychopaths might recognize that the alternative to being punishable would involve some form of preemptive isolation justified on the same grounds that justify a quarantine of those who carry dangerously contagious diseases. And certainly a rational psychopath could be justified in preferring to retain his or her freedom, even at the risk of being punished. The rational psychopath does, after all, consider himself or herself responsible in virtue of being justified in accepting blame for some actions (for example, those actions in which the psychopath fails to pursue his or her own interests as efficiently as possible). Thus a rational psychopath might very well desire that a law allowing the punishment of psychopaths exist and that he or she remain free to violate social norms whenever the chance of being caught and punished was small. Such a desire might have another source as well. The law that allowed the punishment of psychopaths would serve to protect each of them from the others. There is, of course, a sense in which the rational psychopath could *not* support the law. If he or she had violated some social norm and were about to be punished, the psychopath would not be justified in feeling guilt or remorse or in acquiescing in the punishment or blame. But the psychopath would be perfectly justified in supporting and hoping for the *passage* of such a law. And this suggests that the passage of such a law would not simply victimize those whose violations of social norms it was meant to deter.

To the charge of inconsistency, then, there is an apparently plausible reply. But does this reply undermine the argument against indirect-compatibilist theories of responsibility? The answer is no. The argument against indirect compatibilist accounts, as we have seen, involves a dilemma that trades on the following claim: any action that produces harm is performed on the basis of either a desire in IRE or a desire out of IRE; in the former case the agent does not seem relevantly different from the psychopath, and in the latter case the agent does not seem relevantly different from the compulsive. The solution to the dilemma is that from the perspective of an internalist-direct-compatibilist account, some of those who act on desires that are out of IRE *are* relevantly different from the compulsive. They may be internally justified in acquiescing in punishment and blame because of their desires for authorship and autonomy. And these considerations also apply to the psychopath who acts on desires that are out of IRE (for example, who is weak-willed in the pursuit of his or her own interests). Of course, as we have seen, the psychopath would *not* be rational in feeling guilt or remorse for violating a law or norm and causing harm as a result on the basis of desires *in IRE*. Thus the punishment for doing so will not be genuine punishment in my stipulative sense. It will be justified, however, and the possibility of such a justification is one that I neglected in chapter 7. But the justification will be parasitic on the fact that the psychopath is open to genuine blame.

This treatment of the psychopath, then, does nothing to undermine the dilemma for indirect-compatibilist theories. In chapter 8, however, I present a new argument (the "basic argument") for the internalist-direct-compatibilist account of responsibility that is independent of the argument that the discussion of the psychopath is meant to support. And just as the basic argument can be applied retroactively to the account of personal identity in chapter 5 (see the postscript to chapter 8), it can also be applied to the account of rationality in chapter 9. Just as we can ask in the context of moral responsibility why an interpretation of 'could have done otherwise' that licenses blame is the appropriate one (see chapter 8 and its postscript), so we can ask the same question regarding the blame associated with ascriptions of irrationality. Thus we can simply substitute the basic argument for the dilemma for indirect accounts of responsibility and derive the same account of rationality. Consequently, I have not attempted to expand the discussion of the psychopath significantly beyond its original scope.

PART V
Moral Theory

Chapter 10
Rawls and Ideal Reflective Equilibria

1 Introduction

The debate between John Rawls and his communitarian critics is at an impasse.[1] According to Rawls, the right is prior to the good.[2] Communitarians deny this claim.[3] I shall argue that the issue cannot be resolved in the absence of an explicit account of the moral psychology of commitment. Neither Rawls's position nor that of his critics has the support of any such account. I shall provide the outlines of a theory within the framework of which the conflicting positions regarding the priority of the right and the good can be clarified and assessed.

Let us say that the right is prior to the good in *the normative sense* if we are not justified in violating individual rights in order to maximize the good, however the good is understood. If we interpret the good as social welfare, for example, then rights are prior to the good in the normative sense just in case they provide side constraints on the legitimacy of attempts to maximize social welfare. In other words, they are prior to the good (construed as social welfare) in the normative sense just in case they are never weighed on the same scale as any of the components of social welfare, but they provide constraints on what counts as a legitimate weighing of those components.[4] Moreover, if the right is prior to the good in this sense, then we will not be justified in violating individuals' rights to maximize the good, even if minimizing the number of rights violations itself counts as part of that good. That is, we will not be justified in violating rights even when to do so would minimize the total number of rights violations.[5] And let us say that the right is prior to the good in *the sense of having greater generality* if principles of the right of the kind Rawls defends are compatible with a wide range of conceptions of the good, which are not themselves compatible with an equally wide range of principles of right.[6] Finally, let us say that the right is prior to the good in *the justificatory sense*[7] if our commitments where rights are concerned can be justified independently of our substantive commitments concerning the good.[8] Communitarians can agree with Rawls that the right is prior to the good in the normative sense and in the sense of having greater scope but disagree with Rawls's contention that it has priority in the justificatory sense.[9]

In what follows, I shall argue that Rawls's attempt to support the claim that the right is prior to the good in the justificatory sense faces insuperable difficulties. The support Rawls provides for this claim depends on two propositions: first, that certain liberal principles of justice[10] would be agreed upon by rational parties in a state of ignorance that included ignorance about their substantive conceptions of the good (i.e., would be agreed upon in the original position),[11] and second, that this fact could be used to justify our supporting these principles and their corresponding institutions in actual societies.[12] In section 2, I show why, among Rawls's arguments for the choice of his principles of justice in the original position, only what we might call the strains of commitment argument is compatible with the second proposition.[13] That is, only by imposing the procedural constraint that choices in the original position must be commitments can Rawls solve the problem (the problem of hypothetical contracts) of explaining how the fact that we would choose certain principles under hypothetical circumstances could justify our supporting those principles in our actual society. This leads to the following problem (the problem of commitment): since we can imagine in the original position having a conception of the good that turns out to be incompatible with Rawls's liberal principles (we might, for example, be religious fundamentalists), how could we rationally commit ourselves to such principles in ignorance of our conception of the good? Rawls's answer is that we have a highest-order interest in preserving the revisability of our conception of the good, whatever it turns out to be, and that only liberal principles of justice allow us to do so.[14] In other words, they constitute insurance for our possible future selves whose conception of the good is different from ours.

In sections 3 and 4, I provide an account of the moral psychology of commitment by reference to which I examine the rationality of sacrifices across a break in one's conception of the good. If such sacrifices were always rational, Rawls's response to the problem of commitment would be vindicated. I argue in sections 4 and 5, however, that across certain kinds of breaks in our unconditional commitments such sacrifices are *not* always rational. The fundamentalist, for example, would not necessarily be rational in supporting liberal principles for the sake of a possible future self who failed to share his or her commitment to fundamentalism. Thus Rawls's answer to the problem of commitment is inadequate. I shall call this problem for Rawls the *problem of unconditional commitment*.

In section 5, I argue that because of the problem of unconditional commitment Rawls faces a trilemma. First, it is possible (a) that unconditional commitments such as that of the fundamentalist are not irrational and (b) that given what we know in the original position, we must take seriously the possibility that we should turn out to have such a commitment. In this case we cannot commit ourselves to the liberal principles of justice in the original position. Second, it might be the case that unconditional commitments of the kind that the fundamentalist has *are* irrational (so that (a) is false). In this case Rawls can solve the problem of unconditional commitment but only at the expense of making rights irrelevant and thus undermining the argument for liberal principles that protect those rights. If all our commitments are conditional, then I argue that there is no point in making sacrifices to protect our possible future conceptions of the good. Third, it might be the case that given what we know in the original position, we could not turn out to have the kind of commitment that the fundamentalist has (so (b) is false). I argue that this could only be the case if we knew in the original position that we had a large set of unconditional and mutually supporting desires for the kind of freedom, autonomy, and responsibility that only liberal principles of justice could guarantee. But this possibility, though it is compatible with the priority of the right over the good in the normative sense and in the sense of having greater generality, is not compatible with the priority of the right in the justificatory sense. I argue that Rawls's claim for its priority in this latter sense cannot be sustained.

2   Hypothetical Contracts and Commitment

John Rawls's theory of justice as fairness, like any theory that invokes a hypothetical contract, raises the following question. Given that we *would* agree to a particular set of principles of justice under certain hypothetical circumstances, what justifies the claim that we have an *actual* obligation to support them and abide by them when no actual agreement has been made? And if we have no actual obligation to support them and abide by them, what could rationally motivate us to do so when there are other principles that we would find more advantageous? This question is particularly acute for Rawls, because in the hypothetical circumstances he specifies, the original position, we lack any knowledge of the conception of the good that actually motivates and justifies our actions. In Rawls's terminology, we choose the principles of justice by which we are to be bound behind a veil of ignorance.[15] Let us call the problem raised by this question *the problem of hypothetical contracts*.[16]

Rawls has an answer to this problem, which I shall call the *provisional reply*. According to Rawls, "the conditions embodied in the description of the original position are the ones we do in fact accept. . . . These constraints express what we are prepared to regard as limits on fair terms of social cooperation."[17] Let us assume with Rawls that we are *provisionally* inclined to accept these constraints as defining the limits on fair terms of social cooperation.[18] Then if the question arises as to why we should support the principles of justice that would be chosen in a merely hypothetical situation, we can reply that the constraints on the choice in that situation are fair. But whether this reply is adequate depends on the process of reasoning that results in the choice of these principles. Suppose, for example, that the lack of information in the original position about their conception of the good made it rational for self-interested parties to choose principles guaranteeing the highest average utility. In so choosing, they would be gambling on the outcome once the veil of ignorance was lifted. Now consider someone who is a member of an actual society that does provide the highest average utility, given the society's material circumstances, but whose own utility is low. Such a person might well ask why he or she should support the principles that govern the society. And in this case the provisional reply does *not* seem adequate. Given that there is no *actual* commitment to support the principles in question, such a person would seem to have no rational justification for doing so. Rather, the rational response for such a person would be to reconsider his or her provisional commitment to the constraints that define the original position. Therefore, the provisional reply *in isolation* is not an adequate response to the problem of hypothetical contracts. Whether it is in fact adequate depends on the kinds of rational considerations that would lead the parties in the original position to the principles that would be chosen. Thus the solution to the problem of hypothetical contracts depends in part on whether reasoning of the kind that would lead to the principles guaranteeing the highest average utility can be ruled out.

Rawls also has a response to this further problem inherent in the appeal to hypothetical contracts. Rawls requires that the agreement on the principles of justice made in the original position must be one to which the parties in the original position could *commit* themselves without knowing their conception of the good.[19] According to Rawls, for the agreement to be valid, "the parties must be able to honor it under all relevant and foreseeable circumstances."[20] (Rawls calls this the restriction on valid undertakings.[21]) In other words, the principles should be such that if in the original position the parties can foresee circumstances in which they would *not* be rationally motivated to support them (or in which they would be unable to support them given their desires, values, and other commitments), those circumstances must be ones that they would be rationally justified in dismissing as irrelevant. (The question of irrelevant circumstances will be treated in section 5.) It follows that the parties choosing the principles of justice behind the veil of ignorance cannot be allowed to gamble.[22] If gambling were allowed, the parties could choose principles that produced highly favorable outcomes for the majority in the society but unfavorable outcomes for a minority. However, they know that if it should turn out that they were in the minority, they would be unable to give the principles their rational support. Hence they will be unable to commit themselves to such principles in advance, and any such choice will be ruled out.

The constraint that the choice in the original position must allow commitment thus plays two roles. First, since the parties are not allowed to gamble, Rawls has an answer to the claim that they should choose whatever principles would ensure the highest average utility.[23] Because the choice of principles requires commitment, choosing to secure the highest average utility would be ruled out by the parties' recognition that when the veil of ignorance was lifted, they might find their actual position in society intolerable. They might, to take an exaggerated case, find that the high average utility was achieved through the toleration of slavery and that they were among the slaves.[24] Under such circumstances, support of the system on their part would not be rationally motivated (though, of course, they might lack the power to change it). Second, since the constraints on the hypothetical choice prevent gambling, Rawls has an answer to the problem of hypothetical contracts. If Rawls's constraint on the choice of principles is satisfied, this problem apparently never arises. If the principles selected are ones to which we would commit ourselves in complete ignorance of our actual circumstances, then whatever our situation is, we will be rationally motivated to support them.[25] Moreover, if some set of principles selected did not satisfy this constraint, then even if *we* were rationally motivated to support them once the veil of ignorance was lifted, we could not count on their eliciting the rational support of others. Hence if some set of principles satisfies this constraint, that fact provides a powerful argument for their acceptance in the original position.

Rawls does not claim, of course, that the restriction on valid undertakings alone determines the principles that would be chosen in the original position. For example, Rawls appeals to the maximin principle as part of his argument for the principles of justice that he himself favors.[26] But in the absence of an argument that some particular principles are ones to which we could commit ourselves, the claim that the maximin principle would justify the choice of these principles in the original position cannot justify our giving them our actual support. Conversely, if a set of principles satisfies the requirement that we could commit ourselves to them in the original position, then the argument that they satisfy the maximin principle is unnecessary.

To see this, suppose first that a proposed set of principles of justice satisfies the maximin principle. Suppose, however, that the principles allow outcomes in which individual subjects would not be rationally motivated to support the principles once the veil of ignorance were lifted. In this case, even if the maximin principle would justify the choice of principles in the original position, such principles could not be used to justify the social arrangements in an actual society. This is because given the hypothetical nature of the original position, it is open to anyone who finds his or her actual position in society rationally unacceptable to argue as follows: regardless of what choice *would have been made* if it had been necessary to make a choice in the original position, no commitment to any set of principles was *actually* undertaken.

Rawls explicitly recognizes this problem concerning hypothetical contracts in his discussion of the slaveholder's argument.[27] In Rawls's example, a slaveholder attempts to justify his position by arguing that the slave society provides the highest average utility and that the principle of highest average utility would be chosen in the original position. Of course, no such justification is possible. Thus Rawls acknowledges that considerations that would justify a choice behind the veil of ignorance may not justify it once the veil is lifted—and that unless considerations that have this feature can be prevented from determining the choice behind the veil of ignorance, there is no solution to the problem of hypothetical contracts. And without the restriction on valid undertakings, the maximin principle provides no guarantee that such considerations will not determine the choice.

This is not to claim that Rawls explicitly commits himself to a version of the restriction that requires that choices in the original position satisfy the following condition: for any of the possible outcomes once the veil of ignorance is lifted, those that are relevant and foreseeable are ones in which one would be *rationally motivated* to support the principles chosen. His discussion seems equally compatible with the apparently weaker restriction that all the possible outcomes that are relevant and foreseeable should be tolerable. But it is the stronger reading that is necessary to ensure the relevance of hypothetical agreements. Nothing in my main argument depends on the stronger reading, however, since, as we shall see, the possibility that one might be a religious fundamentalist prevents the choice of the two Rawlsian principles from satisfying the restriction on either reading.[28]

To see that the maximin principle is not necessary to justify a choice of principles in the original position, suppose that there are two sets of principles S_1 and S_2 whose worst outcomes are both tolerable. Suppose, however, that the worst outcome of S_1 is significantly better than the worst outcome of S_2. Then the restriction on valid undertakings (on the strong interpretation) will require the choice of S_1. For if one were to find oneself in the worst position allowed by S_2, one would be rationally motivated to work for the replacement of S_2 by S_1. Any appeal to the maximin principle, then, seems to be rendered superfluous by the restriction on valid undertakings, which, if I am correct, constitutes Rawls's solution to the problem of hypothetical agreements.

Rawls does appeal to considerations besides the maximin principle in his arguments against such specific candidates for the principles of justice as the principle of highest average utility. He claims, for example, that the best arguments for the latter principle involve an illegitimate appeal to the principle of insufficient reason.[29] But none of these arguments goes any way toward solving the problem of hypothetical contracts. Thus in considering the Rawlsian argument that relies on the restriction on valid undertakings, I am addressing the only argument capable of playing the role that Rawls's intended conclusions require.

On the face of it, however, the two principles of justice for which Rawls himself argues are no more successful in satisfying the restriction on valid undertakings than are the principles that guarantee highest average utility. That is, they seem no more successful in meeting the requirement that they should be principles to which the parties in the original position could commit themselves. As Rawls states the principles,

1. Each person is to have an equal right to the most extensive total system of equal basic liberties compatible with a similar system of liberty for all.[30]

2. Social and economic inequalities are to be arranged so that they are both (a) to the greatest benefit of the least advantaged and (b) attached to offices and positions open to all under conditions of fair equality of opportunity.[31]

But consider the possibility that when the veil of ignorance is lifted, one will find that one is a religious fundamentalist in a society in which like-minded fundamentalists make up an overwhelming majority. If one's highest values involve the establishment of a theocracy and this requires the suppression of religious dissent, could one be motivated to support the system of basic liberties required by the first Rawlsian principle?

Rawls's answer to this problem involves an appeal to what he calls our highest-order interests in developing and exercising the capacity for a sense of right and justice (that is, the capacity to honor fair terms of cooperation) and the capacity to decide upon, revise, and rationally pursue a conception of the good.[32] Let us call the first of these highest-order interests the *desire to be just* and the second the *desire for revisability*. (Since Rawls does not distinguish between interests, aims, and desires in a way that is relevant to the issues under discussion,[33] I shall use 'desire' in a sense broad enough to include any pro-attitude and speak interchangeably of higher-order and highest-order *interests* and higher-order and highest-order *desires*.) Rawls also mentions a higher-order interest in protecting and advancing our conception of the good as best we can, whatever it may be.[34] Let us call this the *desire for success*. Since the desire to be just is specified by reference to the notions of justice and fairness, it cannot play an essential role in the account of what justice and fairness consist in. Rather, the desire to be just must be understood (as must the desire for success) in a purely formal way. The desire to be just is the desire to develop and exercise a capacity to act from a sense of justice, whatever the content of that sense of justice might turn out to be.[35] Thus I shall focus my discussion on the desire for revisability and the desire for success.

In emphasizing the revisability of our conception of the good, Rawls suggests the following strategy for dealing with the example of the religious fundamentalist. What would motivate us as rational agents whose highest source of value was religious and theocratic to support the Rawlsian principles is the combination of the following desire and belief: the highest-order desire for revisability and the belief that the Rawlsian principles provide the best assurance that the desire will be satisfied. Alternatively, Rawls could appeal to the belief that at some time in the future we might have a radically different conception of the good and to the higher-order desire to protect our ability to pursue that conception effectively, i.e., to our desire for success.[36] In other words, our toleration of the religious views of others (and more generally our commitment to the most extensive total system of equal basic liberties compatible with a similar system of liberty for all) is motivated by the fact that it constitutes an insurance policy for our possible future selves.[37]

The strategy whereby our support of the Rawlsian principles of justice is secured by our desire to insure our possible future selves would, if it worked, justify that support in a special sense of 'justification'. The justification in question is *internal justification,* that is, justification in which there is a necessary connection between one's being justified in engaging in a certain kind of action and one's being rationally motivated to do so. Thus this reply of Rawls's adds a further feature to the circumstances of the original position. Parties in the original position must be able to commit themselves to the principles they would choose. But they consider such commitments in the light of the knowledge that they have a highest-order desire to ensure the revisability of their conception of the good and a higher-order desire to protect and advance that conception of the good whatever that conception turns out to be. And their being able to commit themselves to the Rawlsian principles under these conditions means that they must be able (rationally) to dismiss the possibility that when the veil of ignorance is lifted, they will be (rationally and) internally justified either in failing to support the principles or in working to undermine them. The desire for revisability will override their lower-order desires, even if they should prove to be of the fundamentalist sort. Thus the assumption that the parties in the original position have this desire is intended to make commitment possible in the face of the possibility of a fundamentalist conception of the good. And by making such commitment possible, the assumption is intended to ensure the superiority of the Rawlsian principles over those that guarantee the highest average utility.

This appeal to the possibility of commitment to the principles considered in the original position, however, raises a number of difficult questions in moral psychology. The fundamental problem involves the rationality of sacrifices for the benefit of future selves who are separated from us by a radical break in our conception of the good. In sections 3 and 4, I shall provide a general framework for discussing the rationality of concern in the face of anticipated changes of this kind. In the remaining sections I shall examine the implications of these results for Rawls's defense of his two principles of justice.

3 Ideal Reflective Equilibria and the Conative Core

Rawls's answer to the problem raised by the religious fundamentalist requires an account of the rationality of what we might call *identification across breaks in one's conception of the good.* That is, it requires an account of the conditions under which it is rational to make sacrifices now for the good of a future self whose conception of the good differs radically from the one that one currently holds.[38] Unless such sacrifices are sometimes rational, Rawls will be unable to appeal to the desire for revisability to support his first principle, since it is a desire to make such sacrifices. But an account of the rationality of identification across breaks in one's conception of the good presupposes an account of the distinction between desires whose satisfaction contributes to one's good and those whose satisfaction does not make such a contribution. Intuitively, it is clear that not all one's desires are on a par. Some desires are desires we desire not to have. And since it is not necessarily rational to satisfy such desires when they occur among one's present desires, it may be irrational to sacrifice one's present desires for the satisfaction of such desires in the future.

This issue is treated in the philosophical literature in the context of a number of different problems. One problem, characterized by Frankfurt, is that of distinguishing those desires with which a subject identifies and those that a subject regards as external to himself or herself.[39] One of the subject's desires, such as the desire for heroin, may be the subject's strongest desire in that it has the strongest tendency to influence the subject's actions. Such a desire may nonetheless be one on whose object the subject places a low or negative value. This raises the question of how to distinguish desires and values in the light of our "capacity for reflective self-evaluation."[40] Related to this is the problem of giving an account of internalist reasons. An account of internalist reasons is closely related to an account of internalist justification. It is an account of reasons that guarantees a noncontingent connection between what a subject has the strongest reason to do and what that subject is (in some sense) motivated to do.[41] And providing such an account raises a problem because what a subject thinks he or she has the strongest reason to do and what he or she is motivated to do apparently need not coincide. A third problem is one associated with weakness of the will. The weak-willed subject intentionally performs what he or she believes is not the best possible action, all things considered. The problem is to produce an account of what the distinction consists in between the subject's all-things-considered judgment and the desire that motivates his or her action.[42]

These three problems have a common component. Each case involves desires whose motivational strength is out of proportion with their evaluational strength. Given a clear account of the distinction between a desire's motivational strength and its evaluational strength, we can account for why some desires are external (in Frankfurt's sense), why some desires fail to provide reasons (in the internal sense), and why some actions are at odds with one's all-things-considered judgments. Hence, characterizing the distinction between evaluational and motivational strength is an essential step in determining when a radical change in a subject's desires has implications for the rationality of sacrifices across a break in one's conception of the good. The distinction between the motivational and evaluational strength of desires is characterized in part 4.[43] Here I shall simply describe the most important features of the account.

Imagine that we had complete control over our noninstrumental desires. Imagine, that is, that we had a pill that would allow us to eliminate noninstrumental desires when we preferred not to have them, to increase or decrease the strengths of those that remained, and to add those noninstrumental desires that we lacked and desired to have. The set of desires that would emerge, given that one is aware of the basic facts of one's motivational makeup, is one's *ideal reflective equilibrium* (IRE). And the requirement that one should be aware of the basic facts of one's motivational makeup is simply the requirement that one not be so caught up in any particular desire, for example, the desire to take some drug, that one could not reflect on the fact that the desire in question is in conflict with most of one's other desires. It is not required that one have any sort of sophisticated self-knowledge that would be unavailable to any normal subject under normal circumstances. And let us say that access to the pill described together with awareness of the basic facts of one's motivational makeup constitute *conditions of IRE*. The following are the most important consequences of the kind of control over our own motivational makeup that access to such a pill would provide.

- What motivates one to add or subtract desires or to increase or decrease their strengths must be one's other desires. The idea that one could step back from all one's desires simultaneously and choose which to keep is incoherent, since one would have no desires that could motivate one choice rather than another.
- One's decisions are motivated by the fact that there are relations of support among one's noninstrumental desires. One's desire to become a first-rate concert pianist supports and is supported by one's desire to be famous. This is not to say that one desires to be a concert pianist in order to be famous, or vice versa. But these desires, both of which are noninstrumental, support one another in a way in which the desire for a career of honest public service and the desire for great wealth that one earns oneself do not.[44] In eliminating one of the two latter desires and in adding desires that supported the one that re-

mained, one would be increasing the overall coherence of one's set of desires.

• To say that one's decisions increase the overall coherence of one's set of desires is not to say that they are motivated by a second-order desire to maximize the coherence of the set. Few people have any such desire, and those who do are likely to prefer many things over maximum coherence. What would motivate one to eliminate the desire (say) for heroin would be the other desires that the satisfaction of the desire for the drug would frustrate, for example, the desire for a healthy life, the desire for a successful career, the desire for normal human relationships, and so forth.

• One's ideal reflective equilibrium is relative to one's actual beliefs. Whether the desire for heroin supports and is supported by an otherwise normal set of desires depends on one's beliefs. If one mistakenly believes that one can satisfy the desire for heroin without frustrating one's other desires, there is no reason for one to eliminate the desire for the drug from one's IRE.

• The fact that if one's other desires were relatively normal, one would eliminate the desire for heroin shows that it is not the strength of the desire that determines whether it is eliminated. The desire for the drug might well be one's strongest desire in the sense that it has the greatest tendency to determine one's actions and would have this tendency even if it came into conflict with one's other desires. It will be eliminated, however, because of its lack of support among those other desires. Let us, then, distinguish a desire's *motivational strength*, which is its tendency to cause actions aimed at its satisfaction, and its *evaluational strength*, which is its tendency to remain under conditions of IRE. In a normal addict the desire for heroin would be eliminated under conditions of IRE, in spite of its high motivational strength, because its evaluational strength is low. For the person we might call the *integrated addict*, however, the desire for the drug coheres with his or her other desires. Hence it has a high evaluational strength and would be reinstated under conditions of IRE even if its strength began to wane.

• Just as the motivational strength of a desire is irrelevant to whether it is eliminated, so its content is irrelevant, except as it bears on its degree of support. In particular, the degree of generality of a desire has no direct bearing on whether it will remain. Very general desires may be eliminated because they lack support among more specific desires, and specific desires may be eliminated because they find no support among desires that are more general. In this respect, the formation of an ideal reflective equilibrium resembles the formation of Rawls's reflective equilibrium, which requires that one be ready to reject normative principles that fail to cohere with one's particular normative intuitions, and vice versa.

I shall now argue that by making use of the notion of a subject's IRE, we can solve the three problems mentioned earlier: Frankfurt's problem of characterizing those desires that are external and at odds with one's values, the problem of specifying the relation between one's desires and one's internal reasons, and the problem of accounting for one's all-things-considered judgments to which no motivationally effective desires correspond. Given that a desire survives in a subject's IRE, what can we conclude about its relation to the subject's values, the subject's reasons, and the subject's all-things-considered judgments? First of all, it would be too much to claim that such a desire necessarily represents one of the subject's values in any normal sense. Basic preferences, such as preferences for certain tastes and colors, are generally too trivial to count as values, but even the trivial desires that survive in IRE will not be in radical conflict with those things the subject does value. Furthermore, the motivational strength of such desires will be in proportion to their evaluational strength. If a basic preference becomes obsessive and threatens to frustrate one's desire not to spend inordinate amounts of time satisfying such preferences, and if this desire itself is well-supported, the obsessive preference will be decreased in strength or eliminated. And the desires that survive in IRE could not be external in Frankfurt's sense precisely because they cohere with the subject's other desires. The mark of such external desires is their failure to find an adequate source of support in the subject's other desires and values, but no such desire would remain under conditions of IRE.

Second, a desire that survives in IRE will be supported by reasons in the internalist sense. For it will be supported by desires that one would act on if one could act under conditions of IRE. The topic of internalist reasons is one that obviously requires more extensive discussion.[45] But even at this point we can see the intuitive difference between the desires that would survive in IRE and the desires that fail to provide internal reasons. Desires, if they provide reasons at all, provide internal reasons. And desires that survive in IRE are clearly unlike the typical examples of desires that do not provide a subject with reasons. Such desires lack the holistic support of a subject's other desires, and their motivational strength far exceeds whatever evaluational strength they may possess.

Finally, the desires that survive in IRE cannot conflict with one's all-things-considered judgments, at least to the extent that these judgments reflect one's internal reasons. Since the question of whether desires survive or fail to survive depends on their level of holistic support, there can be no counterpart of the weak-willed subject whose desire to take a drug is at odds with his or her judgment that, all things considered, it would be better to refrain.

Let us now return to the question of the rationality of identification across a break in one's conception of the good, which led to the notion of an IRE. Rawls must defend the first principle of justice against the objection that it could not be supported by a religious fundamentalist and that parties in the original position have no way of knowing that the fundamentalist's conception of the good is not theirs. Rawls's defense consists in the claim that even such fundamentalists would be rationally motivated to support such a principle as a form of insurance designed to protect their future selves, who might lack their fundamentalist convictions. This defense presupposes, however, that it is always rational to make significant sacrifices for the sake of one's future selves, even when their conception of the good is radically different from one's own. And the assessment of this defense requires that we have a reasonably clear account of what such a break might consist in.

The concept of an IRE provides one precise sense in which the notion of a break in one's conception of the good may be understood. Notice that two distinct IRE's are incommensurable in the sense that there is no rational path from one IRE to the other. At any rate, there is no *internal* reason (keeping one's beliefs fixed) for abandoning one IRE in favor of another. This is a trivial consequence of the definition of an IRE. Any consideration that would motivate a change in one's IRE would have done so already under the conditions of ideal reflective equilibrium. Since the IRE is the most coherent extension of one's actual noninstrumental desires that one could be motivated to produce, any reason that could be cited for abandoning one IRE and adopting another would necessarily lack motivational force for the subject in question.

In spite of the incommensurability of IREs, it would not be plausible to claim that the rationality of a sacrifice now for the satisfaction of desires in the future requires that one's present and future IREs be identical. Such a claim would make the rationality of sacrifice for the future depend on one's noninstrumental desires at the lowest level. That is, it would depend on one's most trivial and idiosyncratic tastes and preferences, such as the preference for tea over coffee. And although one could not be rationally motivated to bring about such a change in one's IRE, if one anticipated such a change's occurring, one would have the same motivation to make sacrifices in the present for the satisfaction of future desires that one would have if one anticipated the same IRE persisting unchanged. Thus in the first sense in which a change in one's IRE represents a break in one's conception of the good, the sense in which the change could not be rationally motivated, there is no reason to doubt that one could be rationally motivated to make sacrifices across the break.

For desires that are not mere tastes or isolated preferences, there is a stronger sense in which moving from one IRE to another, when it involves a change in such desires, represents a break in one's conception of the good. Two IRE's that differ with respect to such desires will be stable and discrete. There will be no path consisting of a sequence of gradual changes connecting one such IRE with another under conditions of IRE. Consider the case of Smith, who has well-supported desires both to become a prominent politician and an important artist. Both desires are supported from above by Smith's more general desires to make a lasting and important contribution in an area appropriate to his talents. Both are supported from below by specific desires to engage in specific kinds of artistic projects and to effect specific kinds of social reforms. Suppose, though, that Smith's desire to be a prominent politician is somewhat better supported than his desire to secure a place in the history of art. Given a number of empirical beliefs that Smith might plausibly hold, the desire to be a prominent artist may be eliminated under conditions of ideal reflective equilibrium. Smith might believe, for example, that there is no realistic possibility of satisfying both ambitions and that the unfulfilled ambition would be a constant source of frustration. If so, then since the desire to avoid needless frustration and its consequences is itself likely to be well supported, the elimination of the desire to make a major contribution in the arts would resolve the problem in a natural way.

Now suppose that Smith, having eliminated the artistic desires that conflicted with the predominantly political IRE, is suddenly inspired with the urge to put aside his political obligations and study the use of computer-generated graphics in experimental video projects. Prior to the change of his noninstrumental desires under conditions of IRE, the addition of these new desires on the artistic side might have been sufficient to produce an artistic IRE instead of a political one. Subsequent to the realization of the political IRE and the elimination of many of Smith's artistic desires, however, these new artistic desires will be relatively poorly supported and will be routinely eliminated under conditions of IRE. Only if the onset of these new artistic desires were accompanied by the spontaneous and simultaneous return of all the eliminated artistic desires would there be a change in IRE. And this, it is fair to say, would not be an evolution in Smith's conception of the good but an abrupt leap between two isolated centers of stability. That such a change would amount to a conversion of sorts gives us another sense in which the transition between two distinct IREs that differ over more than mere tastes represents a break. No merely local shift in a small number of noninstrumental desires will survive under conditions of IRE, and no set of such local shifts over time and under conditions of IRE can provide a gradual transition from one such IRE to another. Thus there is a second sense in which we might understand the notion of a break in one's conception of the good. One IRE might replace another, where the two differ with regard to more than tastes and isolated preferences.

Again, however, it is implausible to suggest that such a change could make the sacrifice of the satisfaction of one's present desires for the satisfaction of one's future desires irrational. If Smith did anticipate such a change taking place, either gradually because conditions of IRE did not obtain or as the result of a major shift in his desires and interests, there is no reason to suppose that he would be unmotivated to make sacrifices across the shift or that some form of irrationality would attach to his doing so. Thus in this second sense in which one's future conception of the good might represent a break with one's present conception, such a break provides no grounds for refusing to make significant present sacrifices for one's future.

But let us look at an example that does seem to call the rationality of such a sacrifice into question. Suppose that Brown is a committed follower of Nietzsche who is troubled from time to time by charitable feelings toward the weak of a more or less Christian sort. Such anomolous desires will, of course, be eliminated, as they occur, under conditions of IRE. And as in the earlier case, there will be no gradual transition from Nietzschean to Christian. Under conditions of IRE, only the simultaneous onslaught of a complete set of Christian desires at all levels, in greater numbers and more coherently related than their Nietzschean counterparts, could effect a conversion to a Christian IRE. In this case, however, in contrast to the previous case, there is a further sense in which the two possible IREs are incommensurable. Suppose Brown knows that at some time in the future she will undergo a radical IRE conversion from Nietzschean to Christian. If Brown is faced with the prospect of sacrificing some present Nietzschean desire for the satisfaction of some future Christian desire—a future desire that we can assume is far more important from the Christian point of view than the present desire is from the Nietzchean point of view—there would seem to be nothing irrational in her refusal to do so.

The situation is, in fact, more extreme than this claim suggests. Not only is it not clearly irrational of Brown to refuse to make such a sacrifice; it is difficult to see how making such a sacrifice *could* be rational. This is because there is no overarching value with reference to which the claim could be made that the future gain was greater than the present loss. That is, there is no higher value in terms of which trade-offs between Nietzschean and Christian values could be justified. In the internalist sense of 'reason', such a sacrifice on Brown's part could not be made on the basis of reasons.

The intelligibility of a subject's being unwilling to sacrifice Nietzschean desires for Christian desires stems from the possibility of a desire's being unconditional. Let us say that a desire is *unconditional* just in case it is a desire that the state of affairs that is its object should obtain whether or not one continues to desire that it obtain.[46] Consider one's desire that others flourish. This is a desire that, unfortunately, one might cease to hold in the future. A long run of traumatic disappointments and reversals might leave one permanently embittered and largely indifferent to the fate of others. But what one presently desires in desiring that others flourish does not make their flourishing conditional on the persistence of one's present concern. Certainly one desires now that one's present concern continue, but one also desires now that others should flourish even in its future absence. These same points apply normally in one's own case. Though a sufficiently severe depression might make one indifferent to one's own future, one desires now that it should go as well as possible, even in the event that in the future one should cease to have this desire.[47] Contrast these kinds of desires with the desire that one drink tea rather than coffee. One's desire now is that one drink tea only if one's desire to do so persists. Therefore, this desire is merely a conditional one.

For most of us, the range of desires that are unconditional in this sense is large and varied. One desires that one respect the rights of others whether or not one continues to want to do so. Of course, one would prefer that one refrained from violating others' rights out of a sense of the noninstrumental value of observing such restraint. Given the choice, however, one would prefer that one observed such restraint out of fear, habit, or self-interest than that one did not observe it at all. Hence the desire is unconditional.

The examples of unconditional desires that I have considered so far are normally held and normally held unconditionally. Desires for the realization of a variety of religious goals are almost invariably held unconditionally, if they are held, but for many, they are not held at all. And some desires, though held unconditionally by some, may be held conditionally or not at all by others. The desire that one make a contribution to the advancement of humanity (as opposed to the desire merely that humanity should advance) may be such a desire. The desire that one make more specific contributions, say of an intellectual or artistic kind, are even more likely to be held conditionally, though one can quite well imagine their being held unconditionally in particular cases. The same seems to be true of the desire that one uphold certain artistic or intellectual standards. The desire that one remain true to a particular cause or to a particular individual is also likely to fall into this category. Let us call the subset of desires in one's IRE that are unconditional the *conative core* of that IRE.

With the concept of a conative core in mind we can see more clearly what is involved in the different kinds of transitions between one IRE and another. Consider again the example of a change in taste. If one of one's basic preferences has survived in IRE, then one will, by definition, have no motivation to change it (as long as one's beliefs are kept fixed). But if one were to contemplate a switch in this preference induced from outside, one would have little reason to resist. The preference is a conditional one, and it is largely isolated from one's other conditional desires. Though it might be supported by a small number of other preferences, one could reach a new IRE with relatively minor adjustments. And the new IRE would be in no way inferior to the old one, even from the point of view of the old one.

If we assume that Smith's desire to make a political contribution is conditional, then the switch from the political IRE to the artistic one is equally unproblematic. Since the desire to make a political contribution supports and is supported by a large proportion of the set of Smith's noninstrumental desires, the change could only be brought about, under conditions of IRE, by a massive and simultaneous change in Smith's noninstrumental desires. But as long as the noninstrumental desires that are changed are conditional, the later IRE, as viewed from the perspective of the earlier one, will be no less acceptable.

Because desires for the realization of certain religious goals are often among the best examples of unconditional desires, the Nietzschean/ Christian case provides a contrast to the artist/politician case. A loss, of the kind involved in the Nietzschean/Christian case, of all or most of one's unconditional desires constitutes a *radical* break in one's conception of the good. Naturally, not any loss of one's unconditional desires has this consequence. One might, for example, lose most of one's unconditional religious desires as a result of losing one's belief in the existence of God. And if one's later doxastic state seemed clearly superior from *both* the earlier *and* the later perspective, the resulting change in one's desires would not be likely to raise worries about one's ability to identify across the break. In the Nietzschean/Christian case, however, we can imagine that the Christian beliefs seem completely unwarranted from the Nietzschean perspective and vice versa and that the beliefs are so disparate as to be incommensurable. Alternatively, we can imagine that the Nietzschean and Christian IREs involve the sensibilities, values, and commitments characteristic of the two positions but are unaccompanied by any of the specific beliefs in virtue of which the positions ordinarily differ. On either alternative, the transition from Nietzschean to Christian cannot be interpreted merely as doxastic improvement, and the question of the rationality of sacrificing present Nietzschean desires for future Christian desires becomes a pressing one.

The fact that such a sacrifice seems difficult to justify has an explanation in terms of the distinction between conditional and unconditional desires. Notice first that under conditions of IRE, unconditional desires will never be sacrificed for conditional desires. The reason is that in sacrificing conditional desires (regardless of how many there are and how well they support each other) in favor of unconditional desires, nothing is lost from the perspective of the subject who is to make the sacrifice. From this perspective the loss of any unconditional desires, however, would be extremely serious, regardless of how much more likely this would make the satisfaction of the subject's conditional desires.

Consider, for example, the unconditional desire to be honest even when dishonesty would work to one's advantage (in the long as well as the short term) and would be undetected. Suppose that this unconditional desire is supported by a few other unconditional desires, such as the desire to be like certain individuals who are known for their integrity and the desire to exhibit moral courage under difficult conditions. Suppose also that the overwhelming majority of one's desires are for a life of luxury and that though one has virtually no chance of achieving it honestly, one has a very good chance of achieving it through dishonest means that will almost certainly never be discovered. Given these desires and given the ability to change one's desires at will, one would eliminate the desires for luxury and replace them with desires compatible with the desire to remain honest. This decision would make it virtually certain that one will not lead the life of luxury that one desires. But this will involve no loss, since one will no longer desire it and the desires for luxury are conditional. The decision to eliminate the desire to remain honest, on the other hand, would involve one in a very significant loss. Though without the desire for honesty one would never *experience* the loss after the decision had been made, the future loss that would be involved is one that could be fully appreciated before the decision was made. Hence one would opt for the loss of the conditional desires.

The distinction between conditional and unconditional desires complicates somewhat the coherentist picture where the modification of one's motivational makeup is concerned. The structure of one's desires is two-tiered rather than strictly holistic. Coherentist considerations apply within each tier, but between the unconditional and conditional tiers the relation is like the one foundationalism postulates between basic and nonbasic propositions. Just as we never give up a basic proposition (according to the foundationalist) on the grounds that it fails to cohere with the nonbasic propositions we hold, so we never give up one of our unconditional desires for a conditional desire (or a set of conditional desires).

The last point is that although we may be forced to give up some unconditional desires because they fail to cohere with the other unconditional desires that we *hold simultaneously*, we will never give up one of our present unconditional desires because it fails to cohere with other unconditional desires that we *will hold* in the future. This again is explained by our perspective on the relative losses when we make the choice. From our point of view before we take the pill that defines an IRE, the loss of our present unconditional desire is a loss of major proportions and one for which we cannot be compensated by the acquisition of an unconditional desire we do not now possess. And the fact that the unconditional desire lost will not be missed and that the unconditional desire gained will in all likelihood be satisfied is irrelevant from our point of view before we take the pill.

Our intuitive response, then, that the Nietzschean would be irrational in sacrificing the satisfaction of present Nietzschean desires for the satisfaction of future Christian desires has a clear theoretical rationale. The promise of the future satisfaction of the Nietzschean's Christian desires is no compensation for the frustration of her present Nietzschean projects. Hence the sacrifice of the Nietzschean projects for the satisfactions available to the Christian is unjustified. Thus there is a sense in which identification across a break in one's conception of the good can be irrational. If the replacement of one IRE by another involves a change in the conative core, one may not be rationally motivated to sacrifice the satisfaction of desires in the first IRE for the satisfaction of desires in the second. In this sense, we do not *identify with the future desires*, whether or not we identify with the future self.

This analysis has implications for the question of whether the Christian is appropriately thought of as the same self as the Nietzschean. One of the major sources of the unity of the self over time—the willingness to make sacrifices in the present for satisfactions in the future—fails to carry across radical breaks in one's conception of the good. If the analysis were to stop here, then, we would have shown that there was some point to our speaking of distinct selves. To stop here, however, would be to stop short of showing that such talk is to be taken literally. The problem for any such claim is that despite her unwillingness to sacrifice her present for her future projects, the Nietzschean would be very likely to sacrifice her present desires to prevent the Christian self's experiencing serious pain. Moreover, she would be likely to make such trade-offs at a rate indicative of some special concern for the future Christian self. Such special concern for the future Christian person stages, coupled with the continuity of memory and possibly some basic personality traits, is likely to suggest that we are dealing with a single self, though admittedly one whose projects are severely dissociated over time.

Such an argument, however, depends on overlooking an important choice open to the Nietzschean *under conditions of IRE*. Though the fact that the Nietzschean is acting under the conditions of IRE now cannot prevent her future Christian conversion, there is another option open. She can eliminate that special concern that people ordinarily feel for their future selves. In particular, she can eliminate any desire she has now not to experience pain after the Christian conversion that goes beyond the general desire that people should not suffer pain unnecessarily. This is not, of course, to introduce any sort of self-destructive element into her present motivational makeup. It is simply to withdraw from the postconversion person stages that element of special concern that is at least a necessary condition for those later stages being stages of the earlier person.

This option would *not* be open if the Nietzschean held an unconditional desire which she would express as follows: none of the future person stages of my body that are continuous with my present person stages where memory is concerned should suffer pain if I can prevent it by making a less painful sacrifice now. (Even here, however, the issue is not completely straightforward. Since the Nietzschean desires are unconditional, the desire that embodies the Nietzschean's concern for the future person stages associated with her present body might be eliminated for its failure to cohere with them.) But such a desire need not be unconditional at all. And if it is not unconditional, there are good reasons why a Nietzschean would be justified in eliminating any disposition to make special sacrifices for the benefit of a Christian, even one with whom she was in some ways psychologically continuous. Without this desire she would have no more qualms about the effects that advancing her present Nietzschean projects would have on the future Christian person stages than she would have about their effects on any other Christian. In this case she would be free to pursue her present Nietzschean projects with a lack of inhibition that her knowledge of the future conversion would otherwise prevent. Thus her present desires and the fact that they are unconditional give her good reason to eliminate any special concern for the future person stages in question.

Once this last vestige of special concern for the Christian person stages is removed, however, the objection to talking about separate selves disappears. If the Nietzschean's indifference to her postconversion person stages is justified, we have established the following claim. There is no guarantee that selfhood carries across a sufficiently radical break in the structure of one's desires and one's conception of the good. In this sense it is plausible to say not only that the Christian fails to identify with her future Christian *desires* but also that she fails to identify with her future Christian *self*. Thus there are cases in which the irrationality of identification across a break in our conception of the good is the irrationality of *identification with our future selves*.

4   The Problem of Unconditional Commitment

With the concepts of an ideal reflective equilibrium and an unconditional desire in mind, let us reexamine the problem that the fundamentalist poses for Rawls. In the original position and behind the veil of ignorance, one considers whether one could commit oneself to Rawls's first principle of justice. One then entertains the possibility that when the veil of ignorance is lifted, one will find that one is a religious fundamentalist in a society in which fundamentalists make up the vast majority. The possibility also includes one's finding that one's strongest commitment is to the establishment of a theocracy. And let us assume that this is not an isolated desire. One finds when the veil is lifted that one believes that one's own salvation and the salvation of those one cares about most deeply depend on there being a widely and publicly shared sense of the sacred. One also believes that such a shared sense is impossible in a liberal, pluralistic, and secular society, perhaps because one believes that modern technology and its corresponding social relations have an inherent tendency to undermine the sort of sensibility one takes to be necessary for salvation. Only constant social intervention of a kind that would be impossible in a liberal, democratic, and secular society, one believes, would be sufficient to counteract this inherent tendency. (Of course, there could be radically different sources of a fundamentalist commitment. I have chosen this account because it involves no obviously absurd factual beliefs.)

As we have seen, Rawls's reply depends on his claim that we have a highest-order interest in ensuring the revisability of our conception of the good. Since we have called this desire the desire for revisability, let us call the thesis that we have such a desire the *revisability thesis*. According to this thesis, even when the veil of ignorance is lifted and one is fully aware of one's fundamentalist sympathies, one would be rationally motivated to sacrifice the satisfaction of one's actual religious desires in order to ensure that should one's desires change and one acquire a new conception of the good, one would be in no worse a position to pursue that alternative conception.

But suppose that one were to discover that one's religious desires were unconditional. And suppose that one would regard a secular conception of the good (or a religious conception fundamentally unlike one's own) in the way that the Nietzschean would regard the Christian's conception or vice versa. Then there is no reason why one should be rationally motivated to sacrifice one's actual religious desires to ensure the satisfaction of desires with which one does not identify, that is, desires one would prefer to frustrate. If the religious desires were unconditional, highly coherent, and mutually supporting, one might be rationally motivated to sacrifice the desire for revisability instead.

Thus the revisability thesis alone cannot guarantee that we would be rationally motivated to support the Rawlsian principles whatever our conception of the good should prove to be. And since we could imagine behind the veil of ignorance our having a fundamentalist conception of the good of the sort described, the revisability thesis is not sufficient to ensure that we would be in a position to commit ourselves to the Rawlsian principles of justice. Let us call this the *problem of unconditional commitment*.

The revisability thesis alone, then, is not an adequate response to the problem of unconditional commitment. Rawls has a further response, however, that again involves recourse to the thesis that we have a highest-order interest in maintaining the revisability of our conception of the good. In this case, though, the appeal is not to the claim that we have an interest in revisability but to the claim that the interest is one of our *highest-order* interests. Rawls does not, however, have any systematic account of what it is for an interest to be of higher- or highest-order. And as we have already seen, construing higher-order desires simply as desires that concern other desires does not result in their having any special status. Thus we must ask what would have to be true of a higher- or highest-order interest (or a higher- or highest-order desire) for the concept of such an interest or desire to provide a solution to the problem of unconditional commitment. And a solution to the problem of unconditional commitment requires that at least this much be true of higher-order desires: if desire *A* is of higher order than desire *B*, then for a rational agent, if *A* and *B* conflict, *A* must override *B* regardless of their content, their relative strengths, and their relative degrees of support (to the extent that the relative degrees of support can vary independently of the relative order of the desires).

Combined with the revisability thesis, this thesis about the order of our desires provides an answer to the problem of unconditional commitment. Let us call the desires that make up one's substantive conception of the good one's *substantive desires*. According to Rawls, one's substantive desires are of lower order than the desire for success, and the desire for success is of lower order than the desire to be just and the desire for revisability. Let us call these two latter, highest-order desires the *Rawlsian desires*. Then one's Rawlsian desires will override one's merely higher-order desire for success, and this desire will override one's substantive desires, regardless of their content. Let us call this thesis of Rawls's the *stratification thesis*. If the thesis is true, then the fundamentalist's concern with the revisability of his or her religious commitment will (if he or she is rational) override the desires that constitute the religious commitment itself. Hence the subject in the original position will be able to make a commitment to the Rawlsian principles of justice in spite of the possibility that when the veil of ignorance is lifted, his or her substantive desires will be those of the fundamentalist.

Although Rawls needs the stratification thesis, he provides no account of rationality and commitment that has it as a consequence. In the rest of this section I shall argue that the stratification thesis is incompatible with the analysis of commitment in terms of unconditional desires. But more important, I shall argue that Rawls faces a trilemma. And this trilemma counts against Rawls's position *whether or not* the analysis of commitment in terms of unconditional desires is accepted. The trilemma for Rawls's position is the following one.

Case 1 Let us assume first that the analysis of the rationality of commitment in terms of unconditional desires is largely correct. Then the best case for Rawls and for the stratification thesis is the one in which the two Rawlsian desires are unconditional. We are assuming that such unconditional commitments are not irrational and that the parties in the original position know that they have an unconditional desire for revisability. Thus they know that whatever their conception of the good is when the veil of ignorance is lifted, their desire for revisability will (as long as they are rational) override whatever conditional desires they turn out to have.

The problem in this case is that parties in the original position may turn out to have, and know they may turn out to have, other unconditional desires when the veil of ignorance is lifted. In particular, they know they may turn out to have precisely those unconditional desires that make up the fundamentalist's conception of the good. And unlike the desire for revisability, the fundamentalist's desire for a theocracy is not a single, isolated desire. Rather, it is part of a large and coherent set of unconditional desires, each one reinforced by the relations of mutual support in which they all stand. Thus when the veil is lifted and the unconditional fundamentalist desires are revealed, it is the desire for revisability that the subject will prefer to eliminate or frustrate. And since the subject knows this behind the veil of ignorance, he or she cannot make a commitment to the Rawlsian principles.

On the assumptions we have been making, the claim that the subject in question would prefer to frustrate or eliminate the desire for revisability once the veil of ignorance was lifted seems difficult to deny. But could such a subject, from the perspective of the original position, identify with those possible future selves that have fundamentalist convictions? Consider the analogy with the Nietzschean/Christian case. The Nietzschean may be fully committed to her Nietzschean projects even though she recognizes the empirical possibility that her desires, both conditional and unconditional, may at some time in the future become those of a Christian. Given, however, that she would not identify with such a future self, she need not be prepared to make present sacrifices from which she would intend such a future self to benefit. Nor need she be prepared to take *any* responsibility for the actions of such a future self. Thus it would be completely rational of her to regard this possibility as irrelevant where her commitment to her Nietzschean projects is concerned. Similarly, it might be argued, our knowledge in the original position that we have an unconditional desire for revisability prevents our identifying with a possible future self that, like the fundamentalist, will be motivated to frustrate or eliminate that desire. (This is a possible example of the case, mentioned in section 2, in which although we foresee in the original position circumstances in which we would not be rationally motivated to support the principles we had chosen, these circumstances are irrelevant to the question of whether we can commit ourselves to those principles.)

The question, however, is whether the single desire for revisability is analogous to the unconditional desires that make up the conative core of the Nietzschean. And the answer, I think, is no. It seems implausible to suppose that a single unsupported desire could give us the kind of stable foundation for our future choices provided by the desires in the Nietzschean's (or the Christian's) conative core. The coherence of the desires in such a conative core gives meaning and significance to the decisions based on them in a way in which no single, isolated desire could. In the case of the Nietzschean, there is nothing unintelligible about the failure to identify across the transition to a set of unconditional Christian desires. Imagine, by way of contrast, a heroin addict whose desires other than the desire for heroin were normal and provided no support for the desire to take the drug. Suppose, however, that none of the normal desires were unconditional. And suppose that the addict were faced with the prospect of a transition to a motivational makeup that lacked the desire for heroin and included a normal conative core of unconditional desires that were coherent and mutually supporting. If the addict claimed to be unable to identify across the transition on the grounds that the desire for heroin was his or her only unconditional desire, the intelligibility of the claim would be open to serious doubt. Thus it does not seem plausible to suppose that because of a single unsupported desire, unconditional though it might be, we would be rational in failing to identify with a future self in possession of a large number of unconditional desires that mutually support one another to form a coherent and meaningful set.

This suggests that it may in fact be irrational to hold a single unconditional desire. Alternatively, such a single unconditional desire may simply be insufficient to make the future prospect of a set of coherent and mutually supporting unconditional desires irrelevant to our present commitments. If either of these is the case, then in the original position we do have to take seriously the possibility that we will have desires like those of the fundamentalist when the veil of ignorance is lifted. And if we do, then we cannot commit ourselves to the Rawlsian principles of justice, which we could not rationally support if it turned out that such a conception of the good were ours. Thus in this case Rawls would have no answer to the problem of unconditional commitment.

It might be objected that this argument saddles Rawls with an analysis of his notion of highest-order interest for which his writings provide no support. The argument assumes, after all, that Rawls's highest-order interest or desire for revisability is to be understood as an unconditional desire, and this interpretation is one that Rawls has never endorsed. But the objection fails because the assumption that the desire for revisability is conditional can only make the difficulties for Rawls's position more apparent. Suppose the desire for revisability were merely conditional. Would a subject who had this desire behind the veil of ignorance fail to identify with a possible future self who would frustrate or eliminate it because he or she was a fundamentalist? To suppose that he or she would not identify with such a future self seems implausible. Of course, Rawls might claim that the desire for revisability would override all lower-order desires. Thus he might claim that the desire for revisability *would* override the desires that make up the fundamentalist's large and coherent set of unconditional desires. This is certainly an empirical possibility, but a person who discovered that he or she was a fundamentalist when the veil of ignorance was lifted and whose desire for revisability was both conditional and overriding would be irrational. Such a person would be even more like the normal heroin addict than was the fundamentalist whose single desire for revisability was *un*conditional. In this case both the fundamentalist and the ordinary heroin addict would have a single conditional desire that would override a large set of coherent and mutually supporting unconditional desires. And it seems unlikely that we could take the claim that the fundamentalist would be acting rationally in allowing this to happen any more seriously than we could take a similar claim on behalf of the addict.

Case 2   The argument in case 1 depends on the assumption that the notion of an unconditional desire is coherent and that such desires are not irrational. Suppose we drop this assumption. In this case there is an equally serious problem for Rawls. If unconditional desires are irrational, there is an argument that the subjects in the original position would not necessarily choose principles guaranteeing extensive individual liberties. Imagine a society governed by principles that guarantee very high average utility (together with a high minimum threshold). And imagine that this society has a significantly higher average level of utility and a higher minimum threshold than it would have if it were governed by the two Rawlsian principles. This, we can imagine, is because therapy is provided that allows the average level of utility to be maximized by changing subjects' substantive desires to bring them in line with the objective constraints on the available resources. This possibility might raise the average level of utility and the minimum threshold above what they would be if the society were governed by the Rawlsian principles for either or both of two reasons. First, the Rawlsian society might contain members who held their substantive desires unconditionally. These members of the society would not volunteer for therapy. And since their desires might be very difficult to satisfy with the available resources, their levels of utility would be significantly lower than they would be in the utilitarian society. Second, since the substantive goals of these members would not be coordinated in the most efficient way possible with those of the other members of the society, the resources available to everyone might be significantly reduced. In particular, the resources available for the therapy used to coordinate the goals of those who volunteered for it might be reduced, which would thereby significantly reduce the levels of utility generally.

Notice that we need not assume that the society that guarantees a very high average utility and a high minimum threshold is a utilitarian society. We can suppose that many of the possible ways of increasing average utility open to utilitarians would not be allowed in this society. Neither of the suggested ways of increasing the utility over what it would be under the Rawlsian principles, for example, requires that we decrease the utility of some in order to increase the utility of others (as long as we give no special weight to unconditional desires).

Suppose, then, that the desires of the subjects were all conditional or that they were prepared to disregard the possibility that they were unconditional, for example, on the grounds that it is irrational to hold one's desires unconditionally. Then there would be nothing to prevent such subjects from supporting one of these societies guaranteeing high average utility and a high minimum threshold if, once the veil of ignorance was lifted, the practical possibility of such a society were apparent. Such subjects would have no reason to make provisions for alternative conceptions of the good they might come to acquire in the future. They would be just as well off in having these alternative conceptions eliminated via some form of therapy if they were to prove inconvenient to satisfy. If the appropriate therapy were not available, of course, they might suffer, but they could insure against such suffering directly by ensuring themselves a high level of utility rather than by protecting all possible conceptions of the good they might come to hold. This means that given the possibility of a society that provided a very high average utility and a high threshold with the appropriate therapies available for changing desires, they would have no rational motivation to hold out for real rights and the Rawlsian principles at the expense of a sacrifice in utility for themselves or others. Since the parties in the original position could anticipate this possibility, they could not commit themselves to Rawls's first principle. Real rights (and the all-purpose nature of the primary goods) have a point if one intends to protect the *conceptions of the good* of one's possible future selves.[48] They are unnecessary, however, if all one is motivated to protect are the levels of utility of one's actual future self and if one is willing to eliminate any possible future selves whose utility would be low, given the resources available and the actual arrangements for their distribution. And if one's commitment to one's substantive desires is conditional, there is no reason to protect such possible conceptions of the good. Thus if the notion of an unconditional desire is incoherent or if unconditional desires are irrational, Rawls has no rationale for the importance that his first principle places on individual liberties or for the desire for revisability.[49]

Case 3   Suppose, finally, that we consider the following possibility. It is simply stipulated that in the original position we know that we will not be fundamentalists when the veil of ignorance is lifted. Given this knowledge, it might seem that we could commit ourselves to supporting liberal principles of justice. But notice first that there is nothing special about the unconditional desires of the fundamentalist. Any coherent set of unconditional desires raises the same potential problem. As long as it is allowed that subjects in the original position can have unconditional substantive desires, there is no way of guaranteeing that they will not experience conflicts between these desires and their desire for revisability. Regardless of their content, unconditional substantive desires can conflict with the desire for revisability and thus with liberal principles guaranteeing extensive personal liberties.[50] Suppose, for example, that one has a highly coherent set of unconditional desires concerning the advancement of science in addition to the unconditional desire for revisability. If one were then forced to choose between supporting a government based on liberal principles and supporting one that would devote far more resources to science, one could be rationally motivated to eliminate or frustrate the desire for revisability.

But might we not stipulate that whatever unconditional desires one will have when the veil of ignorance is lifted, they do not and will not conflict with the desire for revisability? The answer is that we cannot without rendering the notion of the original position superfluous. The original question to be settled was whether the right was prior to the good. And to stipulate that the unconditional desires of those in the original position will never in fact conflict with the desire for revisability (and thus with the motive for supporting liberal principles of right) is simply to render the concept of the original position irrelevant to the question it was originally intended to settle. If the Rawlsian argument that corresponds to the construction of the original position works only on the assumption that the right and the good never conflict, the argument cannot be called upon to *support* the claim that the right is prior to the good.

There is, of course, nothing to rule out the possibility that the desire for revisability involves more than a single isolated desire. The desire for revisability might itself be supported by a large and well-integrated set of unconditional desires. Such a set might consist of desires of the following sort: that one should arrive at one's conception of the good by oneself without undo influence from others, that one should be free to pursue one's conception of the good without interference as long as one refrains from interfering with others, that one should take responsibility for one's own mistakes, and so forth. In other words, the unconditional substantive desires can be guaranteed not to conflict with the desire for revisability just in case they form a coherent and self-supporting set of desires for precisely the kind of autonomy that the desire for revisability is designed to protect. Not only is it plausible to suppose that a subject might have such desires (in addition to an unconditional desire for revisability); it is also plausible to suppose that many or even most of the subjects to whom the Rawlsian arguments are addressed actually have them. Nonetheless, it would be useless to require of subjects in the original position that they have such desires and that they be aware that they do. Such a requirement would be no less self-defeating than the previous one. For if the argument for liberal principles of justice requires that we assume that subjects in the original position have, and know they have, such a set of unconditional substantive desires, then we are assuming these subjects know their conception of the good. Of course, such subjects do not know their conception of the good in complete detail. But this shows only that the right is prior to the good in the sense of having greater generality, and this Rawls's communitarian critics can easily concede. Moreover, the subjects we are currently imagining in the original position may (and, given the importance they attach to autonomy, are likely to) hold that rights provide side constraints on our attempts at maximization, whatever we might be tempted to maximize. Thus the right may be prior to the good in the normative sense as well. But if a subject in the original position must know that the desire for revisability (or more directly, a desire for a society governed by the conception of rights reflected in the first principle) is a part of his or her conative core in ideal reflective equilibrium, then it has been implicitly conceded that in the justificatory sense the good is prior to the right.

Can Rawls claim that what is meant by the priority of the right to the good is compatible with subjects in the original position knowing that their desire for revisability (or for a society governed by the first principle) is supported by a large set of coherent, mutually supporting, and unconditional desires for such things as autonomy, responsibility, and freedom? The answer is no. The argument for the first principle of justice that would result from such an understanding of the original position would be completely parasitic on the argument for the first principle that we could construct on the basis of an appeal to our reflective (or ideal reflective) equilibria. Suppose it is plausible that most people to whom the theory of justice is directed have the desire for revisability as part of their conative core. And suppose it is plausible that (given the other desires in their conative core) this would rationally motivate them to support the first Rawlsian principle, regardless of their circumstances. Then this would provide an argument for the first principle based on the nature of our reflective or ideal reflective equilibria that was independent of the construction of the original position. And if the argument that appeals to our reflective (or ideal reflective) equilibria is presupposed in its entirety in the construction of the original position, then the argument derived from that construction adds nothing by way of support to the original argument. Thus even if Rawls were willing to concede that the argument for the first principle requires very strong assumptions about our unconditional commitments, the resulting position has no place for the apparatus and arguments of the original position.

I conclude, then, on the basis of the trilemma, that Rawls cannot solve the problem of unconditional commitment.

6   Conclusion

The trilemma poses a fundamental problem for Rawls. Rawls's strategy is to make one's possible future selves go proxy for the other members of one's community in the sense that one's rational concern for one's possible future selves provides one's motivation to support liberal principles regarding the treatment of others. This attempt to exploit the analogy between one's possible future selves and others is one that runs through the work of Parfit and Nagel as well and finds its inspiration in Sidgwick.[51] This strategy works, however, only if rationality requires us to treat our future selves as the moral theory that it is being called upon to support claims we *ought* to treat others. But rationality requires no such thing. If our commitments are unconditional, we may be rationally motivated to frustrate our future selves that fail to share those commitments. If, alternatively, they are conditional, it will not be worth making sacrifices now to give our future conceptions of the good a reasonable chance of satisfaction. We will be content to ignore them and protect only our future levels of utility. And if the argument contained in the statement of the trilemma is correct, there is no way of arranging a combination of higher-order desires and ignorance of one's substantive desires to motivate an appropriate respect for the alternative conceptions of the good held by other parties.

The possibility of unconditional substantive desires presents the problem it does for Rawls because the transitions across differences in conceptions of the good of the kind that generate deep divisions in a pluralist society are not *rational* transitions. Indeed, Rawls recognizes this in his talk of conceptions of the good being incommensurable and in the example he chooses to illustrate this incommensurability. Rawls imagines a society divided between, roughly speaking, athletes, for whom meaning resides in "self-discipline" and "the risks and excitement of adventure achieved in competition and rivalry with others," and aesthetes, "who affirm certain aesthetic values and attitudes of contemplation toward nature, together with the virtues of gentleness and the beneficent stewardship of natural things."[52] This is, of course, just a somewhat milder version of the Nietzschean/Christian example. In neither case is it plausible to suppose that the differences in the conception of the good turn on differences in belief that could be settled, even in principle, by recourse to standards that would be neutral between the two views. And if this is not clear in the examples as described, they can easily be reconstructed to make this feature explicit.

Though Rawls recognizes this fact, at least implicitly, he does not recognize that it undermines a defense of his position that seems to play a crucial role in his recent work. In this work Rawls appeals to Allen Buchanan's argument that rationality requires that we ensure the revisability of our conception of the good.[53] Buchanan claims that rationality requires us to make sacrifices for our possible future conceptions of the good because our conception of the good is like any theory in being revisable.[54] According to Buchanan, our conception of the good may require revision if our values are inconsistent or if our beliefs are revised.[55] In my terminology, these revisions correspond to the changes that go into the formation of an IRE. However, Buchanan ignores two respects in which conceptions of the good are unlike scientific theories as he characterizes them. He ignores the possibility of incommensurable conceptions corresponding to which there are no further facts that could motivate the choice of one over the other. And Buchanan ignores the possibility that we might not care which internally coherent conception we held, as well as the possibility that we might be so committed to one that we would be willing to frustrate a future self who (for whatever reason) opted for the other. Thus it is not a requirement of rationality (as Buchanan has claimed) that one try to satisfy "the conditions necessary for critical revision" of one's conception of the good.[56] At least this is not a requirement if it means making significant sacrifices to ensure the realization of an incommensurable conception if that should happen to be held by a future self. Rawls's reliance on Buchanan's arguments fails to square with his evident desire to justify the sacrifices necessary to ensure toleration of others' conceptions of the good when these are genuinely incommensurate with our own. And these sacrifices cannot be justified merely by reference to the changes we might be rationally motivated to make in our own conception.

It might be objected to this that I have failed to observe the distinction between the political and personal realms, or worse, that I have ignored the warning that justice as fairness is political and not metaphysical.[57] In response to this there are two points to be made. The first point is that the materials from which I have constructed my criticisms are no more metaphysical than the materials from which Rawls has constructed his argument. Rawls's concern is to establish the motivational plausibility of justice as fairness and to appeal to its superiority in this respect to competing alternative conceptions. Rawls assumes that his theory need not address everyone and that the choices of the parties in the original position may be somewhat idealized.[58] And I have considered those relativizations and idealizations that seem compatible with Rawls's conclusions' retaining their interest. In fact, the conceptual apparatus that underlies Rawls's arguments and that which underlies my criticisms of the arguments is largely the same. The notion of the incommensurability of conceptions of the good is Rawls's, as is the idea of support among noninstrumental desires.[59] And the problem raised by religious commitment is a constant theme of Rawls's. Indeed, Rawls makes differences in religious belief stand in for differences in conceptions of the good generally.[60] Rawls does not define the notion of an ideal reflective equilibrium, but since he assumes that we have control over, and responsibility for, our own desires, he uses what amounts to the same notion, at least as far as substantive desires are concerned.[61] And although Rawls makes no use of the notion of an unconditional desire, the objections do not turn on the legitimacy of this notion. The dilemma for Rawls's position shows that the objections are as damaging for the design of the original position whether the notion of an unconditional desire is coherent or not.

The second point is that no less metaphysical conceptual apparatus will serve Rawls's purposes. Rawls wants his theory of justice to represent a *practical* solution to the problem of choosing principles to regulate the basic institutions of society. Thus the theory cannot rely on a merely *nominal* distinction between the political and the personal. To see the difficulty here, imagine the design that a utilitarian might propose for the separation of legislative and judicial functions. Proposed laws, the utilitarian might suggest, are to be judged by the contribution they make to utility. Judges, however, are to follow the law; their decisions should be independent of utility maximization.[62] This separation of functions would have a straightforward utilitarian justification if there were cases in which utility would be maximized by enforcing certain laws without regard to the maximization of utility in particular cases. By analogy, Rawls might propose that we can accept the two principles of justice in the context of the design of political institutions regardless of the content of our personal commitments.

The problem is that we have no explanation of how the decisions of a rational person concerning political issues could be insulated from his or her deepest and most fundamental substantive commitments. Consider, for example, the case of a utilitarian judge. For such a person, the question will arise as to why, when she can increase aggregate utility by ignoring the law, she should refrain from doing so. Since, by hypothesis, ignoring the law would have the best consequences, even if one takes into consideration all the effects on institutions and on her own reputation and character, this raises a serious problem for such a judge. If the rationale is to be practical and to provide rational motivation, it cannot simply appeal to the nominal distinction between judges and legislators. The perfectly rational reply to such a nominal distinction is, How can the fact that I am a judge give me a rational motive to refrain from maximizing utility in rendering my judgments, given that maximizing utility is my deepest substantive commitment? This problem of motivation is obviously a general problem for rule utilitarianism. If one's sole motive in adopting the rules is to maximize utility, then when following the rules would fail to maximize utility, one will have no motive to follow the rules. And the problem cannot be solved merely by reference to what the rules prescribe.

The result that these considerations point to is that we need more than a nominal distinction between the personal and the political. We need an account of the motivational structure that generates both our personal and our political behavior. And Rawls is committed to giving us just such an account. Rawls's aim is to show the congruence between a certain idealized conception of the self and his principles of justice. The principles of justice are principles that such an idealized self could be committed to supporting whatever his or her conception of the good turned out to be. If my arguments are correct, there are no such principles. As I have suggested, the problem is not that the original position yields a pair of determinate principles in virtue of an argument that begs the question against a large class of nonliberals. If I am right, on the assumption that unconditional desires are not irrational, the original position yields no determinate principles. (And it yields either no principles or the wrong principles if we assume that such desires are always irrational.) The original position, then, adds nothing to the method of reflective (or ideal reflective) equilibrium, which is already well suited to the task of systematizing and rendering more coherent our substantive moral and political commitments. Of course, the method of (ideal) reflective equilibrium is unsuited to justify the principles that result to those whose substantive commitments are significantly different. But as we have seen, this form of justification is not one that the original position and the corresponding arguments are capable of providing.

The upshot is not that we cannot be rationally motivated to respect the rights of others, that a society must be ruled by force, or that it must consist in members who share exactly the same conception of the good. The conclusion is that our commitments to the rights of others must have their support in our substantive desires, and thus that the right is *not*, in the justificatory sense, prior to the good. Such a substantive conception might involve an unconditional commitment to personal projects, personal ideals, and personal relations.[63] And these in turn might involve taking credit for one's achievements and responsibility for one's mistakes and the desire that the recognition of one's achievements should come from subjects who share a similar conception of responsibility and desert. In other words, because one's deepest commitments would be to projects and relations that were only possible on the basis of a shared sense of responsibility and mutual respect, one's actual substantive desires would motivate one's respect for the rights of others. Thus in the normative sense, the right may be prior to the good *for us*. Given unconditional desires such as these, we would not be motivated to violate the rights of others, either to maximize our own good or that of society as a whole.

This is, of course, only a sketch of a possible *substantive* motivation for liberal principles that embody respect for the rights of others. There is room for variation within this general conception, and there is no reason to suppose that there are not significant differences in the details of the more particular conceptions that would support the same liberal principles. In this sense, there is nothing to rule out Rawls's conception of an overlapping consensus in which the same principles of justice are supported by different detailed conceptions of the good.[64] But there is also no counterpart here of Rawls's claim that liberalism cannot be another sectarianism.[65] Such liberal principles discriminate against a wide range of conceptions of the good, not only the fundamentalist's conception but any conception that involves unconditional commitments to goals or ideals that might conflict with individual autonomy. And conceptions that contain no such ideals but which simply lack the liberal commitment to freedom, autonomy, and responsibility (including some utilitarian conceptions) will be ruled out as well. Clearly, some who hold such conceptions of the good will support liberal principles on strategic grounds because they believe that a liberal society is preferable to any alternative they might realistically expect. Their adherence, in other words, might represent a modus vivendi. Rawls, however, explicitly denies that this is how the principles are to be understood.[66] And this kind of support requires the subjects' detailed knowledge of their actual circumstances. Furthermore, such support would not survive the subjects' coming to believe that a society that was more to their taste but that failed to incorporate liberal principles was possible. Hence this kind of justification of liberal principles is unrelated to what the original position was expected to provide.

If there is no more to internal justification than the appeal to (ideal) reflective equilibria, this has obvious implications of a relativistic sort. But even if Rawls were willing to embrace these implications, the fact remains that the kind of relativism required cannot be made to square with the apparatus of the original position. If internal justification is by reference to our (ideal) reflective equilibria, then across radical differences in (ideal) reflective equilibria justification plays no role. Nothing in the design of the original position can change this fact, and if the design is modified to accommodate it, the construction becomes irrelevant to the task of justifying liberal principles to those whose ideal reflective equilibria resemble ours. To the extent that the claim for the priority of the right over the good is compatible with justification by appeal to (ideal) reflective equilibria alone, it is one that would be difficult to deny. But to the extent that the claim is captured only by reference to the original position, the Rawlsian thesis cannot be sustained.

Acknowledgments

I am grateful to David Brink, Joshua Cohen, Norman Daniels, Michael Hardiman, and Amélie Rorty for comments on earlier versions of this chapter.

Chapter 11

Utilitarianism, Realism, and Rights

1 Introduction

It is now widely assumed that consequentialist theories can overcome objections that were once thought to rule them out of serious consideration. The standard objections to consequentialism have had two sources. On the one hand, consequentialism has been thought to violate our most basic pretheoretical moral intuitions. Consequentialist theories, it has been held, imply that we would be required to punish or otherwise violate the rights of innocent people if such actions would have the best consequences overall. Even ideal consequentialist theories, which make the avoidance of rights violations an intrinsic good (that is, something to be valued apart from any further consequences it might have) would require that we violate some rights if this were necessary to prevent a large number of other rights violations. This implication has seemed to put consequentialist theories beyond the pale for those possessed of a normal moral sensibility.

On the other hand, consequentialism has been held to be self-defeating. Consequentialists, it has been claimed, cannot enjoy the benefits that accrue to those who can be counted on to tell the truth, keep their promises, punish those and only those who are guilty, and respect the rights of others, even when doing so is not expected to produce the best consequences. And this, it has been thought, is a conclusive objection to consequentialism on consequentialist grounds. If so, then it is an objection that requires no appeal to pretheoretical intuitions whose sources consequentialists have often tried to impugn.

The present confidence among consequentialists that these objections can be met rests on several recent developments, two of which are particularly significant. The first grows out of recent work on indirect forms of consequentialism. This includes arguments designed to show that, contrary to what had often been assumed, rule consequentialism does not collapse into act consequentialism. The importance of the distinction between rule and act consequentialism for those who are optimistic about the prospects for consequentialism has been emphasized by John Harsanyi. "If rule utilitarianism can really avoid the undesirable implications of act utilitarianism, then it may be possible after all to retain the intellectual and the practical advantages that utilitarianism seems to provide, without being forced to give up some of our deepest moral convictions and embrace a thoroughly distasteful super-Machiavellistic morality."[1] Moreover, there are forms of indirect consequentialism besides rule utilitarianism. And the variety of these forms, which include, for example, motive utilitarianism, has suggested that proponents of consequentialism enjoy far more freedom in framing a theory than their critics have supposed.

The second development that supports the present confidence among consequentialists is the denial that the success of consequentialism depends on its providing a moral decision procedure and a practical guide to action. It is now widely held that consequentialist theories should be regarded instead as providing the criterion for an action's being morally correct. Such a criterion, however, need not play any role in the psychological process by which we arrive at decisions about which actions to perform. Thus it has been open to consequentialists such as R. M. Hare to claim that decisions might be made (and that consequentialism might require that they be made) on the basis of motives, dispositions, and reasons that are nonconsequentialist or anticonsequentialist in character. This development has seemed to many to close the gap between consequentialist theories and their anticonsequentialist competitors.

Let us call the thesis that the theoretical resources available to the consequentialist are sufficient to secure any of the advantages that anticonsequentialist theories (in particular, rights-based theories) might enjoy the *rich resources thesis*. In what follows, I shall argue that this thesis is false. I shall in fact argue for two claims. The first claim is that consequentialist theories cannot provide real principles. Act-consequentialist theories, I shall argue, are unprincipled, and rule-consequentialist theories are pragmatically unprincipled. As a result, consequentialist theories cannot provide for real rights and promises and thus cannot do justice to our pretheoretical moral intuitions.

Second, consequentialist theories cannot provide for real rights and promises even in those cases in which the best consequences are produced by their provision. Consequentialism, whether it is act consequentialism, rule consequentialism, or some form of indirect consequentialism other than rule consequentialism, is in some contexts pragmatically self-defeating. Since rights-based theories are not self-defeating in the same contexts, this means that in spite of the resources available to consequentialists, the gap between consequentialist and anticonsequentialist theories cannot be closed.

The conclusion of these arguments is not that acting in accordance with a consequentialist theory is necessarily unjustified. Indeed, I shall suggest that under some circumstances, following such a theory would be justified for the members of some moral communities. The conclusion I am concerned to defend here, however, is that consequentialist theories and the kind of anticonsequentialist theories that provide for real rights and promises differ significantly in their basic structure. Though these differences are not readily apparent when the theories are considered only in extension, they will emerge when we consider how moral theories are to be embedded in an adequate moral psychology. It is only from the perspective of such a psychology that the most significant differences between consequentialist and anticonsequentialist theories can be appreciated.

Furthermore, I shall argue that the appeal to the distinction between consequentialism as a moral decision procedure and consequentialism as a criterion of moral rightness, even when the distinction is coupled with, or amounts to, a commitment to full-blown moral realism, cannot help the consequentialist. I shall argue that there are two versions of realism to be considered and that the appeal to realism creates a dilemma for the consequentialist. According to the first version of realism, a moral theory may be true even if no one is justified in holding the theory or in acting upon it. On this version, the truth of a moral theory is trivialized, and the fact of its truth is a merely anthropological fact. According to the second version of realism, the truth of a moral theory depends on whether moral agents would eventually converge on that theory under normal or reasonable circumstances. On this version of realism, however, the truth of consequentialism would be incompatible with our being disposed to respect the rights of others in cases where consequentialism and rights-based theories clearly conflict. Moreover, I shall argue that proponents of this version of realism have provided no good reasons for thinking that we will converge on consequentialism in the future. And I shall claim that there are a number of reasons for thinking we will not.

Thus neither version of realism answers the objection that consequentialism fails to satisfy our ordinary moral intuitions. These intuitions may, of course, fail to reflect our most basic values and commitments. But for those whose commitments are to real rights and promises, consequentialism will not provide an adequate moral theory.

2   Utilitarian Self-Defeat

Act consequentialism on the objective interpretation is the thesis that an action is right for an agent A at time t just in case its consequences would be at least as good as those of any other action open to A at t. And *act consequentialism on the subjective interpretation* is the thesis that an action is right for an agent A at time t just in case it is rational for A to believe at t that its consequences would be at least as good as those of any other action open to A at t. Unless otherwise specified, let us use 'act consequentialism' (AC) to pick out act consequentialism on the objective interpretation. We can say, then, that *act utilitarianism* (AU) is the version of act consequentialism according to which an action is right for an agent A at time t just in case it would make at least as great a contribution to aggregate utility as any other action open to A at t. Each theory prescribes that an agent should perform only those actions that are right for that agent. Although the results I intend to establish will apply to consequentialism generally, I shall often discuss utilitarianism when nothing turns on the distinction.

We can now define internal and external problems for a theory as follows.

> A situation S raises an *external problem* for a theory T if and only if what T prescribes in S violates our pretheoretical moral intuitions.

> A situation S raises an *internal problem* for a theory T if and only if there is at least one individual I in S such that I's being disposed to do what T prescribes causes results that are worse, evaluated according to T, than they would have been had I not been so disposed.[2]

And we can say that

> A theory T is *pragmatically self-defeating* if and only if
> (1) there are internal problems for T or
> (2) T is a consequentialist theory such that for some consequentialist theory T', there are internal problems for T' and the differences between T and T' are not such that a rational agent whose deepest commitment was to producing the best consequences would be motivated to follow T and not T' in every situation in which the internal problems for T' arose.

Now let us consider a number of examples that seem to raise either external or internal problems for AC. The present claim is merely that such examples raise prima facie problems for AC. Some of the examples are familiar, and some are variations of familiar examples. In the

following sections I shall consider the arguments that consequentialists have used to support the claim that these examples do not pose
actual problems for AC.

Hanging the innocent man   Imagine that the sheriff of an isolated town
can prevent the outbreak of riots in which dozens of innocent people
will be killed only by framing and executing an innocent man. Suppose
also that the sheriff predicts correctly that his framing this man will
never be discovered and that this action will have no other consequences relevant to its evaluation by reference to AC.[3]
   Let us stipulate that the sheriff's being disposed to perform the
action prescribed by AC (and by AU) does not result in this case in
worse consequences overall than would be possible if the sheriff were
not disposed to perform it. The problem, then, is an external one.
Because the conflict is between AC and our pretheoretical moral intuitions, it is open to the proponent of AC to argue that the example
undermines our intuitions, rather than the converse. This is the response J. J. C. Smart seems to favor in his discussion of the case.[4]
Such a response is not available in the present context, however, since
what is at issue is not the validity of AC but the capacity of AC to
accommodate our pretheoretical intuitions regarding rights. And the
example provides at least a prima facie objection to the claim that AC
can make such an accommodation. The rest of the examples I shall
consider raise either internal problems for AC or problems that are
both internal and external.

Nuclear deterrence   Suppose that as a known act-consequentialist (and
in particular a known act-utilitarian) leader of your country you face
the threat of a nuclear attack. And suppose that your best hope of
preventing the threat's being carried out lies in your ability to make a
credible threat to retaliate. Assume, however, that if most of your
country is destroyed in a first strike, you will prefer not to destroy the
rest of mankind by launching a counterattack. Your preferences, then,
are,

> Do not suffer an attack and do not retaliate >
> Suffer an attack and do not retaliate >
> Suffer an attack and retaliate,

where '>' is to be read 'is strictly preferred to'. If your preferences are
known, however, you will have no credible deterrent threat and hence
no strategy for securing the alternative you most prefer: that in which
you are not attacked.

This problem for AC arises because your reasons for threatening to retaliate are consequentialist (and utilitarian) in nature. You have, on the face of it, a consequentialist reason for threatening to retaliate, but you also have a conclusive consequentialist reason for refraining from retaliation if the threat is ignored. But since these facts are known, your threat will not be credible. As a result, there is no reason to make the threat in the first place. If, however, you had a nonconsequentialist reason for carrying out the threat (say that your honor required it) the threat would be credible and you would stand a good chance of realizing the alternative you most prefer. In this case, your being disposed to do what AC requires (together with the circumstances that make this fact known to potential aggressors) brings about consequences that are less good than would result if you were not so disposed. This, then, is an internal problem for AC.

The example of nuclear deterrence has seemed paradoxical to many, and there is no case in which the stakes are higher. If this were the only example that raised internal problems for AC, we might wonder whether this had any genuine significance for consequentialist theories. The examples that raise internal problems for such theories, however, need not be paradoxical and need not involve the highest possible stakes. What is crucial to the nuclear deterrence case is the fact that proponents of AC cannot make real promises and real voluntary commitments even when the best consequences would be brought about by doing so. By saying that they cannot make real promises and voluntary commitments, I mean that act-consequentialists cannot commit themselves at time t to perform an action a at $t + n$ which is such that (1) at t they know that a will not be the action that of all the actions available at $t + n$ has the best consequences and (2) they know at t that they will know at $t + n$ that a is not the action that, of all the actions available at $t + n$, has the best consequences. This is not to say that act-consequentialists cannot make promises in a wide range of circumstances. In many of these circumstances the long-term consequences of having a reputation for promise keeping and the long-term consequences of supporting and not undermining the social institution of promise keeping will outweigh the disadvantages of keeping the promise. But to say that act-consequentialists cannot make real promises and real commitments is to say that when the consequences of keeping a promise or commitment, including the consequences regarding their reputations and the institution of promise keeping, are not at least as good as the consequences of breaking the promise or commitment, act-consequentialists cannot bind themselves to perform the actions simply by making the promise or the commitment. The case of nuclear deterrence is one in which the consequences of an agent's keeping his or her commitment to retaliate are worse than the consequences (including the consequences for the agent's reputation and for social institutions) of breaking it, but the consequences are better if the agent is capable of making such a commitment. In addition, there are less dramatic cases.

The desert island promise   Imagine being stranded on a desert island with one other person who, as it happens, is the ruler of a powerful country. Although rescue is inevitable, the other person is seriously ill and does not expect to live until the rescuers arrive. This person has the power to make you her successor by giving you her ring, and as a proponent of AC (and in particular an act-utilitarian) you would welcome the opportunity to practice your principles on a world-historical scale. And since, as evaluated by your version of AC, your ruling the country in question would have far better consequences than any other alternative, you are in any case obligated to take advantage of such an opportunity. In fact, we can assume that your rule, as evaluated by AC, would have better consequences than anyone else's, even if you never violated the rights of others for the sake of utility. Unfortunately, your principles (or rather your lack of principles where the rights of others are concerned) are known to the current ruler. As a result, instead of giving you the ring, she throws it into the ocean.

Since the results as evaluated by AC are worse than they would have been if you had not been disposed to act as AC requires, this is another example of an internal problem. What is essential to this example is the lack of any external mechanism to secure the commitment that you have an act-consequentialist reason to make but no act-consequentialist reason to keep. In this case you as an act-consequentialist miss opportunities to cooperate with others that would have been available to an anticonsequentialist. In the nuclear deterrence case, however, there is the threat that you will be deliberately manipulated and exploited by others in virtue of your consequentialist dispositions. And this possibility as well is realized in less extreme cases.

Severe punishment   Imagine that you are a judge in a remote area with the responsibility for a group who, though they are under your jurisdiction, have never assimilated your culture. As a result of their traditions, these people engage in practices that, by the standards of AC, are highly antisocial. (Their traditional practices, for example, might be very destructive of the current environment.) But since you are known as an act-consequentialist (and more specifically as an act-utilitarian), these people believe that either you will not punish them for their practices or that if you do and they continue to engage in them, you will eventually relent. Thus they regard their best strategy as one in which they continue their practices and ignore any punishment you may impose, even if it is quite severe. You calculate that since the younger members of the group are leaving and the group is gradually dying out, the amount of suffering required to make them abandon their practices will be worse than the amount of damage the practices cause. Consequently, you are forced to ignore the practices. If, however, you could have made a credible threat (backed, say, by your personal honor) to impose a fairly severe punishment and to keep it up as long as the practices continued, the members of the group would have given up their practices, and the results, as evaluated by AC and AU, would have been much better.

The inability of act-consequentialists to make real commitments voluntarily as the occasion arises is not the only source of internal difficulties for AC. As we have seen, consequentialists have no standing commitment to justice or to the rights of others when these conflict with the production of the best consequences. And this fact, combined with the act-consequentialist's vulnerability to manipulation, produces another kind of problem internal to AC.

Blackmail   Imagine you are a senator being blackmailed by an organized crime syndicate. Suppose that a blackmail charge would be impossible to prove and that if you fail to meet the organization's demands, they will release information (which may or may not be true) that will result in your being removed from office. You correctly conclude that, as evaluated by AC (and in particular by AU), the consequences of your being removed are worse than the consequences of acceding to the demands. The political situation is in fact so desperate and the consequences of your removal so bad that you give in to demands that you violate the rights of innocent people and in some cases cause their deaths. If, however, you had been prepared to resist the demands whatever the consequences, the organization would not have attempted blackmail and a far better outcome would have resulted.

In the sections that follow, I shall discuss the arguments that have been and can be offered in favor of AC, given these apparent problems for the theory.

3   The Nominalist Fallacy

As we saw in section 1, it has been suggested that rule consequentialism could solve at least some of the problems for act consequentialism, especially those regarding our pretheoretical intuitions about rights and promises. In reply it has been argued that rule consequentialism cannot play this role, because rule consequentialism collapses into act consequentialism.[5] Claims of this latter kind, however, have not been formulated in a way that makes it possible to assess them conclusively. Let us then consider one way in which such a claim might be interpreted. Define *rule consequentialism* (RC) as the thesis that an act is right (for an agent at a time) just in case it is permitted by a set of rules, conformity to which by all (or most) members of some community would bring about consequences at least as good as those that would be brought about by conformity of all (or most) of the members of the community to any other set of rules. And define *rule utilitarianism* (RU) as the thesis that an act is right (for an agent at a time) just in case it is permitted by a set of rules, conformity to which by all (or most) members of some community would make at least as great a contribution to aggregate utility as would be made by conformity of all (or most) of the members of the community to any other set of rules. Then let us say that the extension of a moral theory is a function from possible situations consisting of contexts, agents, and possible actions of those agents to permissions, obligations, and prohibitions regarding those actions. We can then say that two moral theories are *extensionally equivalent* just in case they determine the same extensions.

If the claim that RC collapses into AC (or that rule utilitarianism collapses into act utilitarianism) is the claim that they are extensionally equivalent, then it is demonstrably false. Consider a classic prisoner's dilemma with the matrix in table 1, where the pairs of numbers represent years in prison for *A* and *B* respectively. Suppose that *A* and *B* both confess. Then both *A* and *B* will have satisfied AC, interpreted objectively (assuming that the consequences for the two parties involved are all the relevant consequences and that AC evaluates consequences in such a way that the less total time the two spend in prison the better). The reason is that taking what *B* did as given, *A* would have performed that action, of the two that were open, that

Table 1
The prisoner's dilemma

A	B		Do not confess
	Confess		
Confess	8	8	0 20
Do not confess	20	0	2 2

produced the best consequences. By confessing, A ensures that the total time spent in prison is sixteen years, whereas if he or she had not confessed, the total time spent in prison would have been twenty years. And exactly the same reasoning applies to B. But though A and B both satisfy AC if they both confess, neither one satisfies RC. This follows from the fact that in classic two-person one-shot prisoner's dilemmas, the best consequences are produced (assuming that the consequences for other people can be ignored) if everyone refrains from confessing. This means that according to RC, A should have refrained from confessing in spite of the fact that B confessed, because if everyone (or most people) confessed in these situations, that would produce the best results. The same reasoning applies to B. Hence, if they both confess, neither satisfies RC. Thus AC and RC are not extensionally equivalent.[6]

This argument answers one question about whether RC collapses into AC only to raise another, more interesting question. Given that AC and RC are not extensionally equivalent and that the distinction between them does not collapse in this sense, is there another sense in which the distinction does collapse? And the answer, I think, is yes. Consider the prisoner's dilemma again, and suppose that you believe correctly that the other person will fail to cooperate. (Assume for the sake of simplicity that the other person is simply maximizing his or her own utility and is acting on the desire that he or she spend as little time in prison as possible, regardless of the consequences for anyone else.) In this case, as we have seen, AC says that you should confess, whereas RC says that you should not confess, even though confessing produces the best consequences. Now suppose that you had originally been a proponent of AC and that your reason for adopting RC was your desire to produce the best consequences together with the recognition that in some contexts AC is self-defeating (in the sense that it is prone to internal problems). If you were then confronted with the prisoner's dilemma, what possible reason could you have not to confess? It is true that if everyone or nearly everyone refrained from confessing, better results would be produced than if more people confessed. But how could that fact provide *you* with a reason not to confess, given that confessing actually produces the best results in this case, and that it was the desire to produce the best results that led you to adopt RC in the first place? Of course, you might have some desire to follow RC for its own sake, quite apart from the consequences of doing so. But this desire would be completely unexplained by your original desire to produce the best consequences, and in this case it is in direct conflict with it. (I shall return to this issue in section 4.) And notice that the assumption that you were originally an act-consequentialist and adopted RC in order to bring about the best consequences is merely a heuristic device. All that the argument really requires is the assumption that your deepest commitment or ultimate concern is to bring about the best consequences and that you have no desires to follow any of the rules laid down by RC simply for their own sake. Thus there is a sense in which RC collapses into AC. A rational agent whose only noninstrumental desire is to bring about the best consequences and who recognizes the internal problems to which AC is prone will nonetheless follow AC rather than RC. Moreover, an attempt to adjust the extensional content of RC in order to sidestep this problem (and to do so whenever there is a conflict with AC) will be self-defeating, since it will eliminate the extensional difference that provides RC's advantage over AC.

Let us now consider the implications of this sense in which RC collapses into AC. Suppose that a consequentialist theory distinguishes two kinds of situations in extension. That is, suppose that there is a possible action in one situation that is mapped onto a permission, prohibition, or obligation and that there is a possible action in the other situation that is mapped onto a different value. And suppose there is no difference in the two situations in virtue of which a rational agent who knew all of the relevant facts about the consequences of each action and whose deepest commitment was to bring about the best consequences would be motivated to perform one action and not the other. Then I shall say that the theory makes a purely *nominal distinction*. And I shall say that theories that differ as a result of nominal distinctions alone differ in their *nominal content*. We can then define the *nominalist fallacy* as the assumption that either the internal or the external problems for AC depend only on its nominal content. Assume now for the moment that there is nothing that could rationally justify someone (whose ultimate concern was to produce the best consequences) in following the prescriptions of RC rather than AC in cases of conflict. Then the claim that RC could help solve either the external or the internal problems for AC is an instance of the nominalist fallacy.

To see the problem for proponents of RC, consider that in the case of blackmail described above, rule utilitarianism would require the person being blackmailed to resist the demands, since if everyone did so, such demands would cease. In the actual case described, however, it is stipulated that the highest aggregate utility is produced by yielding to the threats. Resistance to the threats would be unmotivated, then, for a rational agent, assuming that his or her only noninstrumental desire was to maximize aggregate utility. Thus an appeal to rule utilitarianism cannot solve the problems raised by cases of this kind. And since none of the essential features of this example are peculiar to utilitarianism, RC is no help in solving the internal problems for AC.

It might be objected at this stage, however, that the issue is irrelevant, since there are far more straightforward objections to RC. It has been argued, for example, that rule utilitarianism is open to the same problem regarding the punishment of the innocent as act utilitarianism.[7] The argument is that while rule utilitarianism may rule out some instances of punishing the innocent, it never rules out the possibility that a set of rules that allowed for unjust punishments would produce better consequences than any set that ruled them out completely. The same claim, moreover, might be made with regard to the other examples that raise problems for AC. That is, it might be claimed that although the switch to RC may solve some of the problems for AC, many or most of these problems will have counterparts that cause equally serious problems for RC. And if this claim is correct, detailed discussion of the nominalist fallacy may seem unnecessary.

Even if these standard objections to RC are correct, however, the objection that RC is only nominally distinct from AC, and thus open to all the problems that AC involves, is not without interest. The problems raised by the nominalist fallacy apply to a wide range of theories besides RC. Let us say that a theory T is a version of *indirect consequentialism* (IC) just in case T satisfies either of the following conditions.

1. There is some range R_1 of nonmoral properties such that according to T, for every property P in R_1 and for every action a, a is right if and only if

    i. for every property P' in R_1, the consequences of all actions that have P being performed are at least as good as the consequences of all actions that have P' being performed, and

    ii. a has property P.

2. There is some range R_2 of nonmoral properties such that according to T, for every property Q in R_2, Q's obtaining is justified if and only if for every property Q^* in R_2, the consequences of Q's obtaining are at least as good as the consequences of Q^*'s obtaining.[8]

My claim is that the strategy that appeals to the nominalist fallacy in criticizing RC is applicable to any form of indirect consequentialism and thus has an interest beyond its implications where RC is concerned. This is not to say that no version of indirect consequentialism differs from AC in more than nominal ways. Consider, for example, a version of motive consequentialism that says that an action is right just in case it stems from a motivational makeup such that if everyone had those motives, consequences at least as good would result as would result from any other set of shared motives. This theory clearly differs from AC in ways which are not merely nominal. Thus I shall not at this stage try to defend the general claim that the strategy behind the appeal to the nominalist fallacy can be applied to any form of indirect consequentialism. This general claim will be defended in section 5 after I consider the variety of anticonsequentialist motives that might be adopted on consequentialist grounds or incorporated into consequentialist theories. Here I shall discuss two versions of IC and show in each case how this critical strategy applies.

Nominal distinctions in the structure of theories and institutions
Consider H. L. A. Hart's answer to the question of why a utilitarian theory of punishment does not commit one to punishing the innocent when doing so would have the best consequences. Hart claims that the answer lies in our distinguishing two different kinds of questions: the question of how the practice of punishment is to be justified and the question of what justifies us in punishing a particular individual. Hart claims that something more than utilitarian considerations is required to answer the second question, because "a necessary condition for the just *application* of punishment to a particular individual includes the requirement that he has broken the law."[9] But he insists that the justification for the general practice of punishment is utilitarian and that no nonutilitarian principle is required.

Consider, then, a judge whose motivations are utilitarian and who is contemplating convicting and punishing a person she believes to be innocent. If she believes that punishing the person (or doing what would amount to punishing the person if the person's procedural rights were not violated) will make the greatest long-term contribution to aggregate utility, taking all the possible risks of damage to the legal institutions and to her own reputation into account, what source of rational motivation could there be to refrain? Of course, she can say to herself that the justification of the institution is one question and the justification for punishing a particular person is another, but if her most basic values and commitments are utilitarian, what could rationally motivate her treating these questions differently? This is an instance in which the theory that justifies punishment, both as an institution and in its particular applications, contains a nominal distinction to which there corresponds no difference in the behavior that would be justified for a rational and appropriately motivated agent.

In "Two Concepts of Rules" John Rawls appeals to a similar distinction between justifying the general practice of punishment and justifying its application in the case of a particular individual. Rawls claims that "utilitarian arguments are appropriate with regard to questions about practices, while retributive arguments fit the application of particular rules to particular cases." But Rawls goes on to emphasize, as Hart does not, the fact that the different questions correspond to different offices and institutions. "One distinguishes two offices, that of the judge and that of the legislator, and one distinguishes their different stations with respect to the system of rules which make up the law; and then one notes that the different sorts of considerations which would usually be offered as reasons for what is done under the cover of these offices can be paired off with the competing justifications of punishment. One reconciles the two views with the time-honored device of making them apply to different situations."[10] Does this pairing of the different questions with different offices and institutions solve the problem for utilitarianism, and does it do so in a way that avoids the nominalist fallacy? The answer in each case is no. Rawls is surely right in claiming later in the same paper that the creation of a public institution charged with punishing the innocent (when doing so would increase aggregate utility) would be very unlikely to find a utilitarian justification. But this claim is irrelevant to the original question of whether a utilitarian judge could be rationally motivated to refrain from punishing an innocent person when doing so would almost certainly make the greatest contribution to aggregate utility. Again imagine such a judge attempting to decide whether she should convict and punish the innocent person standing before her. If she is indeed contemplating violating the rights of such a person, how could her reminding herself that she is a judge and not a legislator provide a rational motive for ignoring the utilitarian argument in favor of administering the punishment? If the utilitarian argument in favor of the punishment is correct, then she will already have taken into account the possibility that she herself will be punished for failing to meet her obligations as a judge. And she will also have taken into account any special negative consequences that might flow from the public perception that a *judge* had victimized an innocent person to increase aggregate utility. Moreover, the argument that the distinctions in question are merely nominal, which raises a problem for rule utilitarianism, applies equally to any version of rule consequentialism. Thus the distinction between the judicial and legislative institutions, though sociologically real, is merely a nominal distinction where the internal and external problems for AC are concerned.[11]

4   Nonmaximizing Dispositions

Theorists in the grip of the nominalist fallacy assume that the problems for consequentialism can be solved by appeal to nominal distinctions alone. And such distinctions, as we have seen, have no motivational efficacy for those whose primary goal is to bring about the best consequences. This is because for someone who is rationally motivated to produce the best consequences, the significance of the fact that an individual action would violate a rule (or would be inappropriate to a particular social role) is exhausted by the consequences that the violation would produce. Thus, for such a person, if an individual action would produce the best consequences, its violation of a rule (or its inappropriateness for a particular social role) cannot provide that person with rational grounds to reject it.

But it might be objected that those theorists who have defended some form of indirect consequentialism never intended their defense to rely on nominal distinctions alone. Rather, it might be claimed that corresponding to the nominal distinctions there are real dispositions among the agents to whom the theories are addressed. Whether or not this claim is accurate for every theorist who has appealed to nominal distinctions, the appeal to the dispositions of agents does seem to be the most promising line for a defender of consequentialism to take. In this section, then, I shall consider whether such a reply, either combined with some appeal to nominal distinctions or taken independently, can succeed.

Let us consider what kind of psychological dispositions would be required to reinforce the distinction between (say) act and rule utilitarianism so as to give it more than merely nominal significance. Suppose one's ultimate goal is to make the greatest contribution to aggregate utility. A disposition that would give rule utilitarianism more than merely nominal significance would have to insulate one, in certain cases, from the motivational force of one's desire to maximize aggregate utility. The cases in question are those in which the desire is coupled with the argument that one could maximize aggregate utility by ignoring the rules endorsed by rule utilitarianism. It is natural to call a disposition capable of providing such insulation a nonmaximizing disposition. Let us say, as in chapter 7, d is a *nonmaximizing disposition* for a subject S between t and t' (where D is the set of S's desires at t and B is the set of S's beliefs at t) if and only if d prevents S's actions from maximizing the satisfaction of the desires in D (given the beliefs in B) even though D and B remain S's underlying beliefs and desires between t and t'. A nonmaximizing disposition might be the result of some of S's desires in D or beliefs in B becoming temporarily inaccessible or diminished in strength, or it might result from the temporary emergence of desires or beliefs that are not part of D or B or from the temporary increase in strength of some that are. Can an appeal to nonmaximizing dispositions solve the problems that the merely nominal distinctions between act and rule consequentialism raise? In particular cases the answer may be yes. But in many of the most important cases, the answer is no.

Consider again the case of nuclear deterrence. What kinds of dispositions would allow a utilitarian leader to make a credible threat to retaliate? The most obvious possibility would be a strong desire for revenge. Suppose, then, that one were such a leader. And imagine the most likely results if deterrence failed and one experienced an intense desire to retaliate. Suppose that one retains one's desires to maximize aggregate utility and one's beliefs supporting the conclusion that retaliating will *not* accomplish this, such as the belief that retaliation will bring about the end of human history. Suppose also that one retains one's knowledge that the disposition to feel an intense desire for revenge is no longer conducive to maximizing utility once deterrence has failed. One may also believe that the desire to retaliate will decrease in intensity over time. Will the desire to retaliate actually lead to retaliation under these circumstances?

For a number of reasons, a desire to retaliate that has this character is not likely to lead to retaliation with any reliability. First, if one retains one's desires to maximize utility, one will be motivated both to resist the desire to retaliate and to eliminate it if possible. Suppose the desire to retaliate is stronger than the desire not to retaliate in the sense that one could not hold out against the former desire indefinitely. It does not follow that one would be motivationally incapable of performing an action that would counteract the desire for retaliation. One might, for example, have access to a tranquilizer that would decrease the strength of the desire for revenge. Alternatively, one might have the means to make oneself unconscious. And the fact that the desire to retaliate was too strong to resist by one's own unaided efforts would not prevent one's acting so as to frustrate it.

Consider a parallel example. Imagine that you are standing on the roof of a six-story building which is on fire. The firemen below have a net and the chances of surviving if you jump are ninety percent. If you fail to jump, the chances of surviving are ten percent. Suppose, however, that your acrophobia makes it impossible to jump. In other words, your desire not to jump is overwhelmingly stronger than your desire to jump, despite your belief that jumping represents your best chance of survival. This fact would not necessarily prevent your accepting and taking a pill, if it were offered, that would rid you of your acrophobia with the foreseen consequence that you would jump. And this could easily be the case even though you were well aware when you accepted the pill that taking it would result in your jumping and even though your desire not to jump was (at the time you accepted the pill) overwhelmingly stronger than your desire to do so.

Of course, in the case of nuclear retaliation one might not have access to a pill that would rid one of the desire to retaliate or decrease its strength or to a drug one could use to make oneself unconscious. But in a case in which the stakes are as high as they are in this case, the possibility of suicide as an alternative to retaliation would have to be given serious consideration. Moreover, there are many other reasons why one might not retaliate in spite of the strength of one's desire for revenge. Since one retains one's utilitarian values and all of one's normal beliefs about the facts of the situation, one would be unable to justify one's desire to retaliate to one's aides or to anyone else whose cooperation was required to carry it out. Hence one might be forced by one's aides and advisors to take the tranquilizer, or one might be forcibly removed from the position of leadership or assassinated. Alternatively, those whose cooperation is required might simply refuse to obey orders. This would be especially likely if they expected one's desire for revenge to wear off with time. Furthermore, if one had this expectation oneself, it might make an otherwise irresistible desire resistible.

It may be objected, however, that the inadequacy of a nonmaximizing disposition in this case is a result of the fact that the desire to retaliate is not sufficiently consuming. Why should we assume, after all, that the desire to retaliate will weaken with time? And why should one assume that one would retain access to one's desire to maximize aggregate utility and to one's prior beliefs? The answer to the first question is that the desire for retaliation is modeled on the desire for revenge, and this desire does in many cases fade with time, especially when it conflicts with many other desires to which one is committed. But we need not think of desire for retaliation in these terms, and in many of the examples mentioned in which the desire to retaliate does not lead to successful action, the assumption that its strength will diminish in time plays no role.

The second question about one's continued access to one's desire to maximize utility and to the beliefs one held prior to the onset of the desire to retaliate raises more serious issues. Suppose that one does not retain access to this desire and these beliefs. Since we are currently examining the appeal to nonmaximizing dispositions, we can assume that, although one's desire to maximize aggregate utility is inaccessible, it does nonetheless still exist. This is because, by definition, when a nonmaximizing disposition is manifest, one *retains* one's earlier beliefs and desires. It is relative to these beliefs and desires that one is disposed, when the disposition is manifest, to perform actions that will not maximize the satisfaction of one's desires, given one's beliefs. On the other hand, the desire to maximize aggregate utility must be inaccessible in a very strong sense if this inaccessibility is to make the desire to retaliate efficacious. To see this, suppose that one retains conscious access to the desire to maximize utility or to any of the other desires that conflict with the desire to retaliate, for example, the desire not to kill innocent people, not to end human history, and so forth. Then if one has access to a drug such as the tranquilizer that will allow one to resist the desire to retaliate (or if one has access to the means of committing suicide), the desire to retaliate will not be efficacious. Since the disposition we are now considering is designed to overcome this difficulty, and since the desire for revenge is an isolated desire and one's other desires and beliefs support not retaliating, the desire for revenge and retaliation must fully occupy one's consciousness when the disposition is manifest. Let us call a nonmaximizing disposition of this kind a *rigid disposition*. Such a disposition is obviously unlike the emotional nonmaximizing dispositions with which we are familiar, such as anger or an ordinary desire for revenge. But this disposition is a logically possible one and hence deserves consideration.

The existence of rigid dispositions suggests that an appeal to such dispositions might solve the problem of utilitarian self-defeat. As an act-utilitarian leader with a *rigid* nonmaximizing disposition to retaliate, you would apparently have a credible deterrent threat. In reply to this suggestion there are a number of points to be made. First, the claim that utilitarianism is never self-defeating requires not only the logical possibility of rigid dispositions but also the logical impossibility of situations in which such a disposition or some adequate substitute is unavailable. Suppose again that one were an act-utilitarian leader, and suppose that one had no way of acquiring a rigid disposition to retaliate. And suppose that all the nonmaximizing dispositions that one had (or could acquire) were insufficient to ensure retaliation and that as a result one lacked a credible deterrent threat. Finally, suppose that because one lacked such a threat, the consequences as evaluated in utilitarian terms were worse than they would have been if one had not been disposed to maximize aggregate utility. Then there are cases in which utilitarianism is self-defeating precisely because in this case there is no disposition available that leads to retaliation, even though there is a *possible* (rigid) disposition that would.

This first point would not be of great interest, however, if in all the cases we might actually encounter, utilitarianism would not be self-defeating because there were nonmaximizing dispositions that satisfied the following two conditions: either we had a natural tendency to acquire them as we do emotional nonmaximizing dispositions, or they were dispositions that it would be feasible to cultivate and that would be useful in a broad range of situations. In many cases, however, neither condition would be satisfied. As we have seen, a deterrent threat may have to be backed by a rigid disposition if it is to be credible. But such a disposition would be extremely difficult to inculcate, if it could be inculcated at all, with anything like our present technology. Moreover, the disposition, because of its extreme inflexibility, would be relevant to a very narrow range of cases. A disposition that made one capable of retaliating in response to a nuclear attack is very different from a disposition that would allow one as a judge to punish criminal behavior even when doing so would not maximize aggregate utility. A disposition that made one capable of retaliating in response to a nuclear attack would simply be an internalized doomsday device and would involve many of the disadvantages of such a device; it would, for example, be of no use in unanticipated situations. Moreover, such a disposition would make it impossible for someone in its grip to justify his or her actions and decisions, and this would make it less likely that that person's orders would be obeyed. Finally, for many cases other than the case of nuclear deterrence, rigid dispositions do not even seem initially plausible as a solution to the problem. The case in which one is stranded on an island with a powerful ruler is a case of this kind. Indeed, any example in which one is required not to act as an act-consequentialist on an indefinite number of different kinds of occasions will be one in which rigid dispositions have no practical significance.[12] And unless such dispositions have practical significance, their theoretical availability is not an objection to the claim that there are circumstances in which AC is self-defeating.

The discussion so far has suggested that nonmaximizing dispositions will not help in countering the claim that AC is in some circumstances self-defeating. But we have, after all, examined only a few of the possible types of nonmaximizing dispositions: familiar emotional dispositions such as anger or a desire for revenge and rigid dispositions. There seems to be no guarantee, then, that there are not other kinds of nonmaximizing dispositions that can play the role for which these have proved inadequate. It is possible, however, to analyze nonmaximizing dispositions in more general terms than I have so far. Nonmaximizing dispositions work because relative to one's underlying set D of desires and B of beliefs, either they involve the loss or addition of a belief or desire, or they involve an increase or decrease in the strength of a belief or desire that one already has. We can classify nonmaximizing dispositions, then, according to whether they alter primarily one's beliefs or desires or both. Anger, for example, works primarily either by giving one a desire to harm someone that one did not have prior to believing that one had been harmed by that person or by increasing the strength of such a desire. (It may also have the secondary effect of putting one temporarily out of touch with some of one's beliefs, such as the belief that revenge is immoral or that it almost always creates more problems than it solves.)

There is another whole class of nonmaximizing dispositions, however, that involve primarily the addition, subtraction, strengthening, or weakening of some of one's beliefs. Self-deception is the most obvious example, but like emotional dispositions, self-deceptive dispositions are very little help in solving the problems for act consequentialism. Self-deception at its most extreme not only changes one's beliefs but also makes one relatively insensitive to evidence that would undermine the beliefs that one's deceiving oneself produces. This insensitivity, however, has its limits, and in high-stakes cases like that of nuclear deterrence, no amount of self-deception or denial is likely to succeed in insulating one, in the event that deterrence fails, from the recognition that there are conclusive reasons against retaliation. And if one were made the successor to the leader of a powerful country, it would also be unlikely to insulate one from the recognition of opportunities to maximize utility by violating the rights of others when the stakes were high. In each case it is plausible to suppose that even if the importance of the issues themselves were not enough to penetrate one's self-deception, some of those affected by the decision would likely find the means to do so. Again, of course, this would not be true of a rigid disposition. But as we have seen, rigid dispositions carry disadvantages that in many cases prevent them from providing an attractive solution to the problems for AC. And as we have also seen, there are a number of examples in which rigid dispositions simply cannot induce in act-consequentialists the behavior necessary to save act consequentialism from self-defeat.

We can classify nonmaximizing dispositions not only according to whether desires or beliefs are involved but also according to the kind of dissociation they produce between, on the one hand, one's desires and beliefs when the dispositions are manifest and, on the other, one's underlying desires and beliefs contained in the sets D and B. In particular, we can look at the conditions that trigger the dissociation and at the conditions that bring it to an end. Let us call the former the *entrance conditions* of the disposition and the latter the *exit conditions.* Emotional dispositions such as anger are usually triggered involuntarily by certain beliefs about our external circumstances, for example, that someone has deliberately caused us harm, and they fade with time. Nonmaximizing dispositions other than emotional dispositions may, of course, have quite different entrance and exit conditions. We can, however, still use the notion of exit conditions to generalize the argument that particular nonmaximizing dispositions such as the desire for revenge will not solve the problem of utilitarian self-defeat where deterrence is concerned. This is because for *any* nonmaximizing dispositions where nuclear deterrence is concerned, the stakes will be sufficiently high that the exit conditions of that disposition will almost certainly be met. The only exceptions to this generalization are rigid dispositions, and these, as we have seen, are of no use in a wide range of other cases of utilitarian self-defeat.

The reason that nonmaximizing dispositions cannot solve the problem of utilitarian self-defeat is that they leave intact one's deepest utilitarian values and commitments, as well as the beliefs that allow one to act rationally on those commitments. Such dispositions do, of course, put one out of touch in one way or another with the commitments or the beliefs or both. But as long as one's disposition is not rigid, there will be a range of conditions under which one will regain access to one's original commitments and beliefs. Furthermore, in cases like nuclear deterrence in which the stakes are extremely high, such conditions are almost certain to be realized.

Suppose in such a high-stakes case that we are committed to act utilitarianism. That is, suppose that maximizing aggregate utility is our ultimate value and that although our behavior is being governed by a nonmaximizing disposition, we have some access to the utilitarian commitment and to the beliefs we had prior to the nonmaximizing disposition's being manifest. (That is, whatever nonmaximizing disposition we have is nonrigid.) Then if we have some opportunity to rid ourselves of the nonmaximizing disposition or the desires that conflict with our act-utilitarian desires, we will do so. Moreover, in high-stakes cases we are very nearly certain to have such an opportunity.

We can recognize the plausibility of this conclusion if we consider once again the person contemplating jumping into the net from the roof of a burning six-story building. Regardless of how strong the person's desire not to jump is, such a person will, given the opportunity, rid himself or herself of the desire as a result of the value that such a person places on continued survival. As long as the fear of jumping is not so overwhelming that the person in question is unable to recognize the value he or she places on continuing to live, that person will take advantage of any opportunity to trigger the exit conditions of the nonmaximizing disposition not to jump—in this case by taking a pill that destroys the fear of jumping from a great height.

We can also use the analysis of nonmaximizing dispositions and exit conditions to explain why as utilitarians we cannot secure the advantages that accrue to antiutilitarians in the nuclear deterrence case simply by intending to retaliate. If we know in advance that when the time comes to perform a certain action we will have no rational reason to do so (and that we will continue to have access to this knowledge at every time up to and including the last moment at which we could perform the action), then there is a dilemma for anyone who claims that we could form the intention to perform the action in question. On the one hand, we could give ourselves a disposition that would lead to our retaliating under the conditions described. Such a disposition will not be an intention, however, because the disposition, to be effective, would have to be rigid. But any disposition we could give ourselves as the result of forming an intention is one we can give ourselves as the result of a basic act (forming the intention). And we have no capacity to give ourselves a rigid disposition as the result of a basic act alone. Indeed, even if we had such a capacity, the disposition in which it would result is so different from those produced as the result of our capacity to form intentions that there should be no temptation to assimilate the former capacity to the latter. On the other hand, we could fail to give ourselves any disposition we expect to be effective. In this case, since we cannot believe that we will retaliate, that we will try to retaliate, or even that we will have any reason or inclination to do so, and since in fact we can count on our *not* retaliating, we would again be in a state that we could hardly count as intending to retaliate.

This conclusion that a nonmaximizing (and nonrigid) disposition to perform an action is unlikely to result in that action's being performed if the stakes are sufficiently high is a plausible one. It is plausible because if the stakes are high enough, it is more likely that the exit conditions of the disposition will be triggered than that the action will be produced. But the argument for this conclusion presupposes that we know what it is for an agent's most fundamental values to be utilitarian. Thus the conclusion depends on distinguishing those desires that represent our values from those that do not, regardless of how much stronger these latter desires may be. In the case of jumping from the building, for example, we must distinguish between our desire to live, which is a desire for something we value, and our desire not to jump, which is not. And what is the connection between a desire's representing one of our values and its leading, under the circumstances we have been considering, to our being motivated to rid ourselves of desires with which it conflicts, regardless of their strength? Indeed, what is it for a desire to represent one of our values? It is to this question that I shall now turn.

5 Self-Supporting Dispositions

As we have seen, the fact that nonmaximizing dispositions to produce particular actions or kinds of actions are unreliable in high-stakes cases is tied to the fact that such dispositions are at odds with our real values. And this presupposes an account of why some desires and not others constitute such values. On the account most often given, for a noninstrumental desire to represent one of our values (or to be one of those desires with which we identify) is for it to be endorsed by a second-order desire that the first-order desire in question should be efficacious in determining our actions.[13] This account is open to a number of objections. First, such an account leads to an infinite regress. Suppose we want to know whether our first-order desire not to step on cracks represents one of our values or is one of the desires with which we identify. If we ask ourselves whether we want this desire to determine our actions, the answer is likely to be no—avoiding cracks is a meaningless bit of superstitious behavior.[14] We have, then, a second-order desire that this first-order desire not determine our actions. But the question then arises whether this second-order desire is one with which we identify, and this question generates the regress. This question also leads directly to the second problem: there is no necessary connection between a desire's being of higher order and its being a desire that we endorse or its being a desire for something that we value. Just as we may have a superstitious first-order desire not to step on cracks, so we may have an equally irrational second-order desire not to act on desires that we share with people we dislike. In a case of this kind we may be no more inclined to endorse the second-order desire than we are the first. And clearly this kind of problem can arise for desires of any order. A third problem for analyses of this type is that they fail to explain the apparent connection, in examples like that of the person whose strongest desire is not to jump from the six-story building and the political leader whose strongest desire is for revenge, between our failure to identify with some of our desires and our willingness to eliminate them when the opportunity arises.

There is an alternative account, however, of the distinction between the desires with which we identify and those from which we are alienated or on whose objects we place little or no value. Since I have presented this account in detail in part 4, I shall sketch only the main points here.[15]

Suppose that one had complete control over one's noninstrumental desires. Suppose, that is, that there were a pill that would allow one to eliminate noninstrumental desires one preferred not to have, to increase or decrease the strengths of those that remained, and to add those noninstrumental desires that one desired to have and lacked. The set of desires that would emerge, given that one was aware of the basic facts of one's motivational makeup, is one's *ideal reflective equilibrium* (IRE). And the requirement that one should be aware of the basic facts of one's motivational makeup is simply the requirement that one not be so caught up in any particular desire, for example, the desire to take some drug, that were that desire in conflict with most of one's other desires, one would be unable to reflect on that fact. It is not required that one have any form of sophisticated self-knowledge unavailable to a normal subject under normal circumstances. Let us say further that access to the pill described together with awareness of the basic facts of one's motivational makeup constitute *conditions of IRE*. The following are the most important features of the kind of control over our own motivational makeup that access to such a pill would provide.

- The motivation to add or subtract desires or to increase or decrease their strengths can only come from one's other desires. The idea that one could step back from all one's desires simultaneously and choose which to keep is incoherent, since one would have no desires that could motivate one choice rather than another.
- One's decisions would be motivated by the relations of support among one's noninstrumental desires. One's desire to conduct a major symphony orchestra supports and is supported by one's desire to be famous. This is not to say that one desires to conduct in order to be famous or vice versa. Rather, these desires, both of which are noninstrumental, support one another in a way in which the desire to spend one's life in the Peace Corps and the desire for great wealth that one earns oneself do not. In eliminating one of the two latter desires and in adding desires that supported the one that remained, one would be increasing the overall coherence of one's set of desires.
- To say that one's decisions would increase the overall coherence of one's set of desires is not to say that they are motivated by a second-order desire to maximize the coherence of the set.

Few people have any such desire, and those who do would be likely to prefer many things over maximum coherence. What would motivate one to eliminate the desire (say) for heroin would be the other desires that the satisfaction of the desire for the drug would frustrate, for example, the desire for a healthy life, the desire for a successful career, the desire for normal human relationships, and so forth.

• The fact that if one's other desires were relatively normal one would eliminate the desire for heroin shows that it is not the strength of the desire that determines whether it would be eliminated. The desire for the drug might well be one's strongest desire in the sense that it has the greatest tendency to determine one's actions and would have this tendency in any conflict with one's other desires. It would be eliminated, however, because of its lack of support among those other desires. We can distinguish, then, a desire's *motivational strength*, which is its tendency to cause actions aimed at its satisfaction, and its *evaluational strength*, which is its tendency to remain under conditions of IRE. In a normal addict the desire for heroin would be eliminated under conditions of IRE, in spite of its high motivational strength, because its evaluational strength is low. For the person we might call the integrated addict, however, the desire for the drug coheres with his or her other desires. Hence it has a high evaluational strength and would be reinstated under conditions of IRE even if its strength began to wane.

• Just as the motivational strength of a desire is irrelevant to whether it would be eliminated, so its content is irrelevant, except as it bears on its degree of support. In particular, the degree of generality of a desire has no direct bearing on whether it would remain. Very general desires could be eliminated because they lacked support among more specific desires, and specific desires could be eliminated because they found no support among more general desires. In this respect the formation of an ideal reflective equilibrium resembles the formation of Rawls's reflective equilibrium, which requires that one be ready to reject normative principles that fail to cohere with one's particular normative intuitions and vice versa.[16]

• One's ideal reflective equilibrium is relative to one's actual beliefs. Whether the desire for heroin supports and is supported by an otherwise normal set of desires depends on one's beliefs. If one mistakenly believed that one could satisfy the desire for heroin without frustrating one's other desires, there would be

no reason for one to eliminate the desire for the drug from one's IRE.
• There is one exception to the generalization that considerations of coherence determine which desires remain under conditions of IRE. Let us call desires for states of affairs that we want to obtain whether or not our desires for them continue to exist *unconditional desires*. Most people desire now that they continue to treat others honestly in the future, even if as the result of a series of traumatic experiences they no longer desire to do so. These contrast with conditional desires, such as the desire that one work at a certain job. Most people desire now that if in the future they no longer enjoy a certain kind of work, they will not continue to do it. And if there were a conflict under conditions of IRE between a conditional and an unconditional desire, it is the conditional desire that would be eliminated. This is because under normal circumstances the loss of a desire decreases the likelihood that the state of affairs it is the desire for will be realized. Thus from the point of view of a person choosing between a conditional and an unconditional desire, the loss of either desire would involve the loss of the object of the desire. But in the case of a conditional desire, the loss of the object and the loss of the desire cancel each other out, so if both are lost, there is no genuine loss to the subject. In contrast, to a subject contemplating the loss of an unconditional desire, the loss of the object of the desire is genuine, even if the desire itself will cease to exist.
• Finally, whereas none of one's desires in IRE are desires from which one is alienated, the unconditional desires represent one's deepest values and commitments. Thus we can appeal to the notions of ideal reflective equilibria and unconditional desires to characterize the distinction between mere desires and desires that constitute our values and commitments.

Recall now the motivation for seeking an analysis of the distinction between mere desires and values. The necessity of the analysis arose because we wanted a theoretical explanation of why nonmaximizing dispositions seemed incapable of playing the role for which some defenders of AC have them slated. In particular, we wanted an explanation of the connection between the following two facts: the act-consequentialist's deepest commitments are defined by AC, and being disposed to form a desire to act against AC, even if the desire one forms is one's strongest desire, does not provide a general solution to the problem of pragmatic self-defeat for AC. And we can explain this latter fact by appeal to the notion of an IRE.

By appealing to the distinction, defined in terms of conditions of IRE, between the motivational and evaluational strengths of desires, we can provide a general explanation of why nonmaximizing dispositions fail to solve the problem that AC is pragmatically self-defeating in high-stakes contexts. In acquiring a nonmaximizing disposition, one retains, by definition, one's act-consequentialist commitments. For example, if one is committed to act utilitarianism, the desire to bring about the highest aggregate utility will be the most basic desire in one's IRE. That is, it will be among the best supported, and it will be unconditional. By contrast, the desires that make up one's nonmaximizing dispositions will not belong to one's IRE and hence will be badly supported, if they are supported at all. In the nuclear deterrence case, for example, the desire to retaliate in the face of an attack will be completely unsupported by the desire to maximize aggregate utility, as well as by the desires that support this desire. Regardless of how strong the desire for revenge is, that is, regardless of how great the desire's motivational strength is, its evaluational strength will be extremely low once the attack has occurred. In other words, even though the disposition to experience an intense desire for revenge would remain under conditions of IRE before an attack had occurred, it would be immediately eliminated under conditions of IRE after such an attack.

The fact that a nonmaximizing disposition to retaliate would be eliminated under conditions of IRE before it produced a retaliatory response does not settle, of course, the issue as to whether such dispositions would be useful in providing a credible threat to retaliate. This is because we cannot assume that an act-utilitarian leader will be in conditions of IRE after such an attack. In fact, we can assume the opposite, since the pill in terms of which conditions of IRE are defined does not exist and is not likely to be available in the foreseeable future. However, the conclusion that nonmaximizing dispositions will not be efficacious in these contexts does not depend on the assumption that a person committed to act utilitarianism will be in conditions of IRE once the nonmaximizing disposition has been triggered. We can derive the same conclusion from the weaker assumption that in cases of this kind, once the disposition has been triggered (i.e., once the entry conditions of the disposition have been met), committed act-utilitarians will find themselves in a situation that *approximates* conditions of IRE. This is because, although once the disposition is triggered such subjects will not have the perfect control over their motivational makeup that they would have under conditions of IRE, in high-stakes situations the means of eliminating the unsupported desires that make up the nonmaximizing disposition will almost always exist. As we have seen in the discussion of nuclear deterrence, tranquilizers might reduce the strength of the desire for revenge to the point where it could be resisted. But if this were not sufficient, act-utilitarian leaders have access either to a drug that would render them unconscious during the period in which the decision had to be made or, in the most dramatic cases, to suicide. And although these methods for dealing with the desire for revenge are extremely crude compared to the pill that defines conditions of IRE, in high-stakes cases such methods would almost always be available and effective.

Of course, this argument does not work for rigid nonmaximizing dispositions. And not all the situations in which the pragmatic self-defeat of AC is an issue will be high-stakes situations. But as we have already seen, rigid, nonmaximizing dispositions are badly suited to situations, such as that of desert island promise, that call for flexible and intelligent responses over an indefinite period of time. And in such situations one is very likely to succeed in working out over time some set of strategies for dealing with one's desires that are out of IRE, even if they cannot be eliminated altogether. If the stakes are significant, there are precautions one can take in advance to prevent oneself from acting on the desires that are out of IRE. For example, one can arrange to have therapy, one can undergo conditioning, or one can arrange to have oneself hypnotized. One can also make side bets so that the motivational strength of one's desire not to act on the desires that are out of IRE and with which one does not identify is greater than the motivational strength of those desires themselves. One can also delegate one's responsibilities to others when one seems most likely to act on the desires with which one does not identify or authorize others not to accede to one's orders when one seems to be acting on such desires. And we should bear in mind that it is not being argued that nonmaximizing dispositions are never efficacious. The thesis is merely that in a wide range of circumstances, the appeal to nonmaximizing dispositions cannot save AC from pragmatic self-defeat.

These criticisms of the appeal to nonmaximizing dispositions may suggest to the proponents of AC the following defense. Suppose that one finds oneself in circumstances in which the disposition to maximize utility would lead one to make a smaller contribution to aggregate utility than one would make if one were not so disposed. Why, then, should one not give oneself a disposition to refrain from maximizing utility that consists not of desires out of IRE but of desires in IRE with which one identifies? Why, in other words, could one not make a sufficiently drastic change in one's motivational makeup so that after the change had taken place, the desire not to maximize aggregate utility would be, or be the result of, one of one's fundamental values? Let us call the disposition to act on such a desire in the appropriate circumstances a *self-supporting disposition*. The question is, then, can the appeal to self-supporting dispositions solve the problem of pragmatic self-defeat for AC?

Let us begin by imagining what this suggestion would look like in the case of nuclear deterrence. To give oneself a self-supporting disposition to retaliate if attacked would be to change one's desires in a sufficiently radical way that if the disposition to retaliate failed to deter potential aggressors and an attack was launched, one would prefer in IRE to retaliate, even if that meant destroying the rest of humanity. This means that a desire for revenge, to preserve one's honor, or to carry out some conception of justice that would motivate a retaliatory strike would have to be well supported by a wide range of other desires. The desire for honor or for justice of the appropriate kind would have to play a central part in a highly coherent and well-articulated worldview in which human welfare and even the preservation of the human race was of comparatively little importance. Such a view would seem to us bizarre, but it is also clearly not logically impossible.

If we switch from the example of nuclear deterrence to the desert island example, the case for the proponent of AC looks even better. In this example all one need give oneself is a coherent set of mutually supporting and unconditional desires to respect the rights of others, even when doing so prevents one from maximizing aggregate utility. And this is a set of desires that is in no way bizarre or difficult to understand.

Let us grant that such self-supporting dispositions are logically possible and put aside the question of whether we have or are likely to acquire the technology to produce them. Does the possibility of (say) an act-utilitarian acquiring such a disposition help to solve the problem of pragmatic self-defeat for AU in particular and for AC generally? If this is the only response that the proponent of AU can make to the problem, then on the face of it, it is difficult to see why this should count for AU rather than against it. If the only options act-utilitarians have in dealing with the problems of AU surrounding pragmatic self-defeat is to cease, on act-utilitarian grounds, to be act-utilitarians, why is this not conclusive confirmation of the self-defeating tendencies of AU? We should not be mislead, in examples of this kind, into supposing that if the self-supporting disposition is adopted on act-utilitarian grounds, then the act-utilitarian commitments are still in some sense ultimately in control. An argument to this effect could well be made in the case of an act-utilitarian who has or adopts some set of nonmaximizing dispositions. But it is precisely because the act-utilitarian remains in touch (to varying degrees) with his or her act-utilitarian commitments that act-utilitarians with such dispositions often produce no more utility than act-utilitarians without them, even though nonutilitarians do. In contrast, in adopting a self-supporting disposition to act in antiutilitarian ways, the utilitarian adopts a motivational makeup from which there is no route back to the utilitarian commitments. Even if the change should prove to be disasterous from a utilitarian point of view and should turn out to produce far less utility than the utilitarian could have produced without undergoing the change, once the utilitarian has made the change there will be no rational motivation to reverse it. The goal of maximizing utility will cease to exercise any rational influence on such a subject, except possibly as constrained by the more fundamental considerations of rights, honor, justice, or the like.

There may, of course, be a *non*rational route back to utilitarianism. One might, against one's deepest wishes, lose one's commitments to rights and regain one's original utilitarian commitments in virtue of some causal process over which one had no control. To be effective, however, such a process would in many cases have to consist in a complete and unforeseen conversion. If such a conversion were foreseen, one would be rationally motivated to take measures, either to prevent it or to neutralize its worst effects. And if one reacquired the utilitarian desires one at a time, then since each one would fail to cohere with one's desires to respect rights, one would be rationally motivated to eliminate each desire as it arose. Thus in circumstances in which one had even moderately effective control over one's own motivations, only the very improbable event of a complete and unforseen conversion would provide even a nonrational route back to one's original utilitarian commitments.

The conclusion that self-supporting dispositions cannot help the utilitarian is reinforced if we imagine an extreme example in which all utilitarians make themselves, on utilitarian grounds, into antiutilitarians. Let us suppose that they do this by giving themselves self-supporting dispositions to respect the rights of others. And let us assume that their most basic commitments to rights are unconditional and that none of the agents have false beliefs that have a significant bearing on their moral commitments. Then if having a rational motivation requires that one reason on the basis of one's actual beliefs and one's deepest commitments concerning values, no such agent could be rationally motivated to maximize aggregate utility (when doing so would conflict with respecting rights).

This fact reveals an asymmetry between consequentialism and rights-based theories. Whereas one can be rationally motivated on consequentialist grounds to produce a commitment in oneself to respect rights, one cannot be rationally motivated to move in the other direction. That is, given that one is committed to respecting rights and that this commitment is unconditional, one cannot be rationally motivated to give oneself a disposition to produce the best consequences in cases where this would involve rights violations. Though there is a rational route from consequentialism to rights-based theories, there is no rational route in the other direction.

The conclusion, then, is not only that AC and those versions of consequentialism (such as RC) that are only nominally distinct from AC are pragmatically self-defeating. The conclusion applies to indirect consequentialism generally. Consider the version of motive-utilitarianism that says that an action is right just in case it is motivated by a psychological makeup that is such that if everyone's actions were motivated by that psychology, aggregate utility would be maximized. Now ask whether the psychological makeup consists in nonmaximizing or self-supporting dispositions. If it consists in nonmaximizing dispositions, there will be contexts in which the version of utilitarianism in question is pragmatically self-defeating. And if it consists in self-supporting dispositions, we have seen no reason to suppose that the fact that such a theory solves the problem of self-defeat for AU counts in favor of utilitarianism.

Furthermore, suppose we have a theory that satisfies the second clause of the definition of indirect consequentialism and thus evaluates things other than actions. The theory might say, for example, that an institution is justified just in case the existence of that institution produces at least as much utility as would be produced by any alternative institution. But if this theory is to be more than nominally distinct from AU, the specification of the institution must include some psychological disposition in virtue of which agents are motivated to comply with the norms of the institution when they could produce more utility by violating them. Thus again the question arises as to whether we are dealing with a nonmaximizing or self-supporting disposition. And as we have just seen, neither alternative seems to answer the objection that the theory in question is self-defeating.

To suppose that the possibility of self-supporting dispositions could count in favor of AU would be to make the truth of moral theories completely independent of the conditions under which agents could be rationally motivated to act on them. It is no accident, then, that many proponents of AU have appealed to moral realism in their defense of the theory. That is, they have appealed to the claim that a criterion of the moral correctness of actions is not a decision procedure for action. In sections 6 and 7, I shall examine the appeal to realism as a defense of AU and of consequentialism generally.

6 Realism without Convergence

As we have seen, the only response that the consequentialist has to the problem of pragmatic self-defeat for AC consists in the claim that an act-consequentialist can, on act-consequentialist grounds, adopt an anticonsequentialist disposition that is self-supporting. In so doing, act-consequentialists turn themselves into agents for whom consequentialist considerations, when they conflict with those agents' anticonsequentialist dispositions, can provide no rational motivation.

Let us consider such a group of consequentialists, in particular, a group of act-utilitarians, who have given themselves self-supporting commitments to a rights-based theory. If with respect to such a group of agents act utilitarianism is still true, then the conditions under which a moral theory can be true for a group of agents must be independent of the conditions under which such agents can be rationally motivated to act on it. And the appeal to realism in support of utilitarianism is designed to support just such a divorce between a criterion of moral rightness and a decision procedure on which agents can be rationally motivated to act.

The appeal to realism in support of utilitarianism raises the following question, however: What would the truth of a moral theory on which no agents could be rationally motivated to act *consist in*? In the most extreme case in which all utilitarians have given themselves antiutilitarian dispositions and are no longer rationally motivated to fulfill AU, what kind of fact would nonetheless still make utilitarianism *true*? In this section I shall examine three suggestions as to the kinds of facts that might play this role.

Consider the following proposal. Utilitarianism is true in virtue of the meanings of such moral terms as 'good' and 'right'. This suggestion, of course, has until recently not seemed promising. Ever since Moore, the attempt to define 'goodness' in terms of happiness (or more generally, utility) has confronted the objection that it is always an open question whether happiness or utility are in fact good.[17] Since the question makes sense, and since analogous questions make sense for any other naturalistic account of goodness that might be proposed, the conclusion has been that no such account could give the meaning of 'goodness'. Similar considerations apply to other moral terms, such as 'rightness'.

As a result of the influence of the various causal and historical theories of reference, however, Moore's objections to the proposal that 'goodness' might pick out a naturalistic property have come to seem less pressing. According to these theories, the reference relation has some or all of the following features:

- Singular terms such as 'Aristotle' have no analytic definitions. Moreover, speakers who use such terms may fail to associate with them any descriptive content sufficient to individuate the referent. Suppose, for example, that our use of the term 'Jonah' is a consequence of the fact that as originally used, the term referred to an actual person, about whom a myth grew up that had no significant basis in fact. Thus if the only description any of us now associates with the term 'Jonah' is 'the Biblical figure swallowed by a whale', then the only description we associate with 'Jonah' is true of no one. Nonetheless, according to the causal-historical theories of reference, 'Jonah' refers to the person it was originally used to designate if our current usage is causally connected in the right kind of way with the term's original use. If, for example, the term 'Jonah' was attached to a particular individual in an initial baptism, and if the term was passed from one person to another, each of whom intended to use it in the same way in which it was used by others in the community, then in spite of the false beliefs of the later speakers and in spite of their lack of individuating beliefs, they continue to refer to the original person.
- In addition to the thesis that proper names cannot be defined, causal theorists hold the more controversial thesis that many predicates have no analytic definitions. Water is H_2O, even though we might discover other chemical combinations that produce all of the observable properties of water. Thus water cannot be defined as 'a colorless, odorless liquid that . . .' (where the description is nonindexical and is couched in terms of observable properties of water), since there could be other liquids that satisfied any such description without their being water. What determines the necessary and sufficient conditions for being water is not the set of descriptions speakers of the language associate with the word 'water' but empirical research that establishes the scientific nature of the substance to which we have been referring. Thus, to be water is to be similar in appropriate ways to given samples of liquid. And this similarity

relation is the province of experts and may be inaccessible to ordinary speakers. Moreover, the existence of experts in a linguistic community gives rise to a division of linguistic labor. As the result of the ability of experts to describe and identify such natural kinds as molybdenum or titanium, ordinary speakers, who cannot do either, nonetheless refer to the same items the experts do.

• On causal-historical theories of reference, not only can a speaker refer to an item in cases in which that item has no analytical definition and the speaker knows no description that would provide necessary and sufficient conditions for being that item. It is also possible to refer even in cases in which there *are* analytically necessary conditions for being the object in question and the speaker is mistaken about some of these conditions. A speaker who is unaware, for example, that arthritis is necessarily a condition of the joints and who utters the sentence 'I have arthritis of the thigh' is saying that he or she has arthritis and not some more general rheumatoid condition.

Given this causal-historical conception of meaning and reference, it is possible to frame a reply to Moore's argument that moral terms cannot pick out naturalistic properties. According to this reply, the claim that 'good' picks out a natural property is compatible with its not being true a priori that the property's obtaining is good. On the causal-historical theory of reference, what 'good' picks out may be discoverable only through empirical research and not by appeal to the linguistic intuitions of speakers. Thus 'water' refers to H_2O, even though it would have made perfect sense to question the identity of water and H_2O before this empirical fact was established. Similarly, it might turn out that 'goodness' refers to happiness or utility (and thus that goodness *is* happiness or utility) even though it makes sense now to ask whether instances of happiness or utility are good.

It is possible, then, that the answer to the question of what would make utilitarianism true even when no one was rationally motivated to accept it lies in the meanings of such moral terms as 'right' and 'good'. Consider the following examples of ways in which this might be the case if the causal-historical theorists are right.

Original baptism   Imagine that at some time in the past our ancestors were all act-utilitarians. Suppose that as a result the term 'goodness' was explicitly used to refer to utility, and 'rightness' picked out the property that certain actions have of making the greatest contribution, of all the actions open to the agent, to maximizing aggregate utility. Think of this as the period of initial baptism in which the moral vocabulary originally acquires its meaning. This is analogous, for example, to the initial baptism in which Jonah acquires his name. Imagine, then, that our ancestors encounter some of the problems of pragmatic self-defeat to which act utilitarianism is prone. Consequently, they acquire false beliefs that allow them to solve many of these problems without giving up their commitment to utilitarianism. They believe, among other things, that it is rational to follow moral rules, although the prescriptions of the moral rules conflict with the prescriptions of act utilitarianism and although they retain their commitments to maximize aggregate utility. We can suppose, in particular, that these rules require that they respect certain rights, even at the expense of aggregate utility. This is possible if we suppose that they reason on the basis of distinctions that, though merely nominal, do provide them with motives to respect the rights of others, even though their deepest commitments are to maximizing utility. In other words, they reason irrationally. And we can imagine that this in turn is possible if we suppose that their beliefs about rationality are sufficiently complicated and difficult to disentangle that they might plausibly function as a source of mystification. We can also suppose that their problems are never sufficiently serious that they are forced to confront this incoherence in their scheme of commitments and beliefs. For this reason also, then, we can suppose that these inherently unstable beliefs persist. The upshot is that most of the members of the community in question affirm such statements as 'An action may be wrong even though it makes the greatest contribution to aggregate utility' and 'Goodness is not the same as utility'. This is analogous to the stage at which the myths about Jonah take hold. Now let us suppose that although we are currently divided between commitment to utilitarianism and commitment to rights-based theories, some such set of historical developments explains our current use of moral terms. We can also suppose that most people have retained their ancestors' basic commitment to utilitarianism, though many are no longer in the grip of the mystifying beliefs about rationality. If the meanings of our moral terms in such a case are analysed on the analogy of the causal-historical analysis of 'Jonah', then it is plausible to claim that the meanings of the moral terms are determined by their original use, in spite of the misconceptions that have grown up around what they originally designated. Thus in such a society, 'goodness' would mean utility, and 'right' would mean utility maximizing.

Natural kinds   In this case, imagine a society for which moral concepts are natural-kind concepts. This might be in virtue of a relatively explicit convention concerning moral concepts. Alternatively, it might be that all concepts, unless there is some strong reason not to, are treated as we treat 'water' according to the causal-historical analysis. (A concept's being a logical concept or its being a concept defined by an explicit, stipulative definition or its being a concept intended to pick out artifacts, for example, would provide a strong reason not to treat it as a natural-kind concept.) And let us suppose that utility can be understood as being sufficiently like a natural kind that if the meanings of moral terms are explicated by reference to utility, these moral terms will count as natural-kind terms for the purposes of the convention in question. Suppose, for example, that human beings count, for the purposes of the convention, as a natural kind or that they belong to some wider class of creatures that does. And suppose that as a result, natural human needs and the satisfaction of natural human needs count as sufficiently close to natural kinds that notions of utility defined in terms of them count as natural-kind concepts. Suppose also that construing moral terms as natural-kind terms not only coheres well with the conventions already established but makes possible the systematic presentation of a number of empirical laws connecting moral facts with nonmoral circumstances. Finally, suppose that no way of construing moral terms as having the meanings they seem to have for proponents of rights-based theories would allow them to be construed as natural-kind terms, even on the very liberal understanding of natural-kind terms we have been considering. Then in this case again moral terms would have their meanings defined by reference to utility.

Conventional usage   Suppose that in some linguistic and moral community most of the individuals are utilitarians, and most use 'goodness' and 'right' as though they were synonymous with 'utility' and 'utility maximizing'. Although it is not an explicit convention in this community that 'goodness' and 'right' have these meanings, most community members are unmoved by the claim that even when they know that some state of affairs involves a great deal of utility, it is an open question whether it is good. But we can imagine that there is a significant minority who hold rights-based moral theories and for whom Moore's open question argument seems to refute decisively the claim that 'goodness' and 'right' have definitions in terms of utility. On an account analogous to the one many proponents of causal-historical theories favor for arthritis, not only would the linguistic behavior of the majority justify assigning utilitarian meanings to their uses of moral terms; it would also justify assigning utilitarian meanings to those terms as they are used by the minority as well. Thus 'goodness' and 'right' would have utilitarian meanings in the society as a whole and not merely as they are used by the majority.

Let us suppose that in each of the societies described, there is a significant minority of individuals who are fully committed to a rights-based morality, where full commitment means that their desires to acknowledge the rights of others are unconditional desires in IRE. Would such subjects be motivated to embrace utilitarian ideals or policies in any of the societies in question? The answer, of course, is no. Given that such subjects have an unconditional commitment to a rights-based theory, their embracing utilitarianism would represent a loss for them for which there could be no compensation. This would be the case even if such subjects could take a pill that would give them, instantaneously, a new IRE in which utilitarian ideals were unconditionally supported. This is because of the asymmetry we have seen in section 5 between utilitarian and rights-based theories. From a utilitarian perspective there is no objection to one's making oneself into an antiutilitarian if it has the best consequences, whereas from the rights-based perspective, good consequences are strictly secondary to the requirement that one not violate the rights of others.[18] This fact was noted in section 5 when we saw that there is no rationally motivated route back to utilitarianism from commitment to a rights-based theory.

How, then, would subjects unconditionally committed to a rights-based theory in any of the societies described respond to the discovery that moral terms had utilitarian meanings in their society? The answer is that such subjects would come to recognize that these so-called moral terms were incapable of playing the role genuine moral terms are required to play. Such terms could not be used by the proponents of the rights-based theories to recommend goals or to evaluate goals or actions because to say that a goal was good or that an action was right or ought to be performed would be to say that the goal involved a certain amount of utility or that the action maximized utility and it would therefore be to say something irrelevant. Nor could such terms be used in policy debates with utilitarians. For the proponents of rights-based theories to use them in such contexts would be to allow their utilitarian opponents to beg the most important questions and to ignore their principled opposition to utilitarian assumptions. In the light of this recognition, those committed to rights-based theories would simply coin new terms to serve the functions for which the existing moral terms were unsuited.

Let us call the facts reported in reporting what the terms 'goodness' and 'right' mean in the societies described *anthropological facts*. Then the first argument against the appeal to moral realism to support utilitarianism is this: if utilitarianism is true in virtue of the fact that 'goodness' and 'right' mean utility and utility maximizing and if this fact is supported by the kinds of reasons that a proponent of the causal-historical theory of reference might cite, then the truth of utilitarianism (or more generally, consequentialism) is a merely anthropological fact. Let us call this the *mere-facts* objection.[19] The upshot is that if the appeal to moral realism is to be any help in answering the objections to utilitarianism, the facts that make true moral theories true cannot be merely anthropological facts. If the truth of utilitarianism, for example, were to consist in such facts, then its truth would not be the truth of a theory whose terms had the function of our moral terms. If this were the only sense in which utilitarianism were true, the opponents of utilitarianism could cheerfully admit its truth, as well as the truth of the claims that utility is the ultimate good and that it is right to maximize utility. Such opponents of utilitarianism would simply insist (correctly) that such facts were of no interest to them, and they would coin new terms (say 'good*' and 'right*') with which to express such claims as 'Utility is not the ultimate good*' and 'It is wrong* to maximize utility when this involves violating the rights of others'. Thus if the truth of utilitarianism were a merely anthropological fact, then its truth would be of no interest in discussions of serious moral controversies. It is difficult, then, to see how the appeal to its truth thus understood could solve the problems raised by utilitarian self-defeat.

In the two sections that follow, I shall consider alternative proposals as to what kinds of facts might make utilitarianism true.

7   Convergent Realism

It might be objected that the three examples of causal accounts of the meanings of moral terms fail to capture what is crucial to the realist's thesis that utilitarianism is true and that 'goodness' means utility and that 'right' means utility maximizing. What the realist assumes, it might be claimed, is not simply that there is some causal or historical connection between our use of moral terms and utilitarianism. In particular, it is not sufficient for the realist that there be a causal connection that has genuine analogies to the connection between 'Jonah' and Jonah or 'water' and H_2O or 'arthritis' and arthritis. Such a connection, as we have seen, is compatible with the existence of at least a substantial segment of the population for whom there is no rational motivation to embrace the requirements of utilitarianism. And it is this feature of the appeal to a causal or historical connection alone that leads to the mere-facts objection and the conclusion that the truth of utilitarianism could not consist in such facts. According to the present objection, however, the realist is making a stronger claim, and it is a claim that is incompatible with utilitarianism's having no rational appeal to a major portion of the population.[20] According to this objection, the realist's claim is not only that there is a causal or historical connection between considerations of utility and moral considerations but also that moral properties such as that of an action's maximizing utility *regulate* moral terms such as 'right'. Richard Boyd, for example, characterizes the reference relation as follows: "*Roughly,* and for non-degenerate cases, a term *t* refers to a kind (property, relation, etc.) *k* just in case there exist causal mechanisms whose tendency is to bring it about, over time, that what is predicated of the term *t* will be approximately true of *k* (excuse the blurring of the use-mention distinction)."[21] And the claim that 'goodness' refers to utility according to this characterization of reference goes well beyond the claim that the meanings of moral terms are determined in ways analogous to those in which the meanings of natural-kind terms are determined. On a natural interpretation, the passage suggests that if the defense of utilitarianism by appeal to moral realism works, moral agents will eventually *converge* on utilitarian beliefs. That is, they will converge in thinking that goodness is utility and that those actions are right that maximize utility. The suggestion, then, is that if moral terms such as 'goodness' and 'rightness' refer to utilitarian properties such as utility and the maximization of utility, there are causal mechanisms such that over time, what we say of moral properties will be true of utilitarian properties. And it seems plausible to suppose that this would be true only if it were true for more than a segment of the population and only if the truth were more than a merely anthropological fact.

On a natural interpretation of Boyd's characterization of moral semantics, then, for moral terms to refer to natural properties, the uses of the terms must be regulated by the properties. And implicit in the notion of regulation seems to be the idea that people will converge toward the recognition of those properties as the properties that their terms pick out. This interpretation is borne out when we consider Boyd's account of how such regulation is likely to work. Boyd's account is given on the assumption that the true moral theory is a version of consequentialism that he calls "homeostatic consequentialism." According to this theory, the things that are morally good are things that satisfy fundamental human needs. These consist in physical, medical, psychological, and social needs and include the need for love and friendship, the need to engage in cooperative efforts, the need to exercise control over one's own life, the need for intellectual and artistic appreciation and expression, and the need for physical recreation (p. 203). Furthermore, the goods are homeostatically clustered in the sense that the presence of some goods tends (under appropriate conditions) to favor the presence of others or there are underlying mechanisms or processes that tend to maintain the presence of these goods or both (p. 197). In particular, this homeostatic clustering of moral goods has two sources, on Boyd's view. First, "these goods themselves are—when present in balance or moderation—mutually supporting" (p. 203). Second, there are psychological and social mechanisms—including cultivated attitudes of mutual respect, political democracy, egalitarian social relations, various rituals, customs, and rules of courtesy, and ready access to education and information—that contribute to the homeostasis (p. 203).

Although Boyd does not say that actions are right just in case they make the greatest contribution to the aggregate good, he does say that justice and obligation are derivative concepts (p. 205), as, of course, they would be on any ordinary understanding of consequentialism and as they would not be on any theory that took rights as side constraints. Moreover, Boyd insists that the satisfaction of the fundamental human needs of one individual tends to be conducive to their satisfaction for others and that his definition of good involves the homeostatic unity of human need satisfaction in the society generally (p. 204 fn.). In other words, the rightness of an action is a function of its contribution to the aggregate good. Boyd seems to refrain from calling this utilitarianism only because the good is defined in largely objective terms rather than in terms of pleasure, happiness, or the satisfaction of desires. In spite of Boyd's reluctance to use the term, however, the theory seems to be a version of (ideal) utilitarianism.

Having defined a notion of moral goodness, Boyd goes on to suggest that understood in this sense, moral goodness regulates our use of the term 'good' (in moral contexts). Boyd argues first that we are fitted by nature to acquire moral knowledge of the good. This is because given Boyd's definition of 'good' in terms of the satisfaction of fundamental human needs, evolution favored those who were disposed to acquire such knowledge quickly and efficiently. As a result, we begin with an approximation to knowledge of the good. Second, there is a process of reflective equilibrium that involves observation of empirical facts, naturally occurring social and political experiments, moral intuitions (which are taken to be analogous to the intuitions of researchers in the sciences), and moral theory. Our moral reasoning, according to Boyd, involves the interplay of these elements as we engage in "trade-offs" between these categories of moral belief in order to achieve a harmonious "equilibrium" (p. 185). Boyd calls this the "realist conception of reflective equilibrium" (p. 210). Assuming that we start with an approximation to moral knowledge of the good, this process by which we arrive at reflective equilibrium allows us to make successively better approximations over time. There is thus a general tendency toward the growth of moral knowledge and for what we say about the good to be true of the homeostatic cluster of fundamental human goods. Hence the homeostatic cluster regulates the term 'good' (p. 210).

That it is implicit in this account of regulation that we will converge on the answer to moral questions is suggested by Boyd's claim that we all start with an approximation to the truth and there is a mechanism that produces increasingly accurate approximations. Moreover, on Boyd's account, there are no insurmountable obstacles to convergence on moral issues, given that the conditions under which the development of our moral knowledge takes place are not unreasonable. This is made clear in Boyd's explanation of the current diversity of moral opinion. On Boyd's account, such diversity is the result of several factors. First, the homeostatic cluster of properties that make up the moral good are only contingently related. It is possible, then, for some of the properties to occur in the absence of others. And when this is the case, the applicability of the moral vocabulary defined by reference to the homeostatic cluster will be indeterminate. Certain moral disputes, then, will be the result of a failure of bivalence where the application of moral predicates is concerned. Second, although we start with an approximation to moral truth, people in different cultures are likely to start with different approximations and to develop them at different rates. Thus there is no guarantee that a moral dispute between two different moral traditions will be capable of resolution "within the theoretical and methodological framework which the two traditions *currently* have in common" (p. 213). Third, the improvement of the initial approximation is difficult and has certain social and economic prerequisites. Boyd suggests that an appreciation of certain moral goods may be possible only in relatively democratic societies and an appreciation of other goods may require favorable economic conditions. Hence progress toward moral agreement is subject to forces of "social distortion" (p. 212). Thus although convergence is not guaranteed, the obstacles to convergence in moral opinion are no different from the obstacles to convergence in scientific opinion.

Boyd's assumption that on his account of morality human beings will converge in their moral opinions under reasonable conditions is also implicit in his discussion of the most likely way in which his account could turn out to be wrong. According to Boyd, this would be a situation in which the fundamental moral goods lack the described homeostatic unity and in which there are two or more stable ways of achieving homeostasis between these goods, each of which slights some goods in currently unacceptable ways. In other words, there would be no psychologically and socially stable way of reconciling the conflicts between the fundamental human goods that would be satisfactory by reasonable current standards (p. 224). And it seems to be the impossibility, in such a situation, of convergence of moral opinion under the best circumstances that makes this example one in which Boyd's account breaks down. Furthermore, the centrality of convergence is made virtually explicit in Boyd's claim that "agreement on nonmoral issues would eliminate *almost all* disagreement about the sorts of moral issues which arise in ordinary moral practice" (p. 213).

The importance of convergence in Boyd's account is no accident. Convergence is exactly what the proponent of a realist view such as Boyd's needs to counter the mere-facts objection. Recall that the problem posed by the mere-facts objection arose because the truth of the claim that 'goodness' meant utility and that 'right' meant utility maximizing in some society was not in itself sufficient to establish any fact of moral or evaluative significance. It is quite possible, given causal and historical theories of meaning, that the (so-called) moral terms might have utilitarian meanings in some society, even though a substantial portion of the community was fully committed to one or more rights-based theories of morality. For such a subcommunity, the terms alleged to be moral terms would simply fail to carry any evaluative significance, and the members of the subcommunity would be rationally motivated to coin new terms with which to carry on their evaluative discourse. And the relation between such a subcommunity and the community as a whole would then be like the relation between the communities that realize different moral traditions in the case Boyd describes in which his realist conception of morality would fail.

If, however, such communities and subcommunities will always converge under reasonable conditions, this kind of case is ruled out. In communities in which such convergence has occurred or will occur, the fact that moral terms have utilitarian meanings cannot be a merely anthropological fact. That is, it cannot be a fact that has no rational motivational significance for a substantial portion of the community. If the moral beliefs of all the members of the community are destined to converge eventually, then the fact that utility regulates the conception of the good for members of the community cannot be a matter of indifference to any of them.

What makes moral realism significant, then, cannot be merely the application of causal and historical theories of reference to moral terms. What gives this application significance is the assumption of convergence in moral opinion. Moral realism coupled with any weaker assumption allows, as we have seen, for the existence of subcommunities for whose members the moral facts as construed by the realist have no rational motivational force. Thus without the assumption of convergence, moral realism is open to the mere-facts objection.

The assumption of moral convergence does not, however, provide a solution to the problems for utilitarianism that the appeal to realism was designed to solve. The appeal to moral realism coupled with the assumption of moral convergence raises two sorts of problems if they are intended to support utilitarianism. First, there is no good reason to suppose that convergence to any form of utilitarianism is likely. (I shall say more about this in section 8.) Second, it was the apparent falsity of the assumption that led to the appeal to moral realism in the first place. Recall first that act utilitarianism cannot capture the extensional content of rights-based theories. And recall that this is the case even if we allow the nonviolation of rights to count as either one significant part of the good to be maximized or the only part of that good. This, of course, raises the question of why a utilitarian should care about an extensional gap between act utilitarianism and rights-based theories. The answer is that rights-based theories are more in line with our pretheoretical intuitions (a fact that may or may not move the utilitarian) and that rights-based theories may, as we have seen, provide more utility than act utilitarianism (a fact to which the utilitarian must give serious consideration). In other words, there is the problem of pragmatic self-defeat for utilitarianism.

Switching to rule utilitarianism does allow us to close the gap between utilitarianism and rights-based theories. We can simply take a version of rule utilitarianism whose rules specify the same obligations and permissions as whatever rights-based theory is in question. But closing the extensional gap between utilitarianism and rights-based theories simply opens a pragmatic gap between them. Those motivated to move from act utilitarianism to such a version of rule utilitarianism by the consideration that some rights-based theory provides more utility in some contexts will be unmotivated to follow the prescriptions that the appropriate version of rule utilitarianism yields when these conflict with the prescriptions of act utilitarianism. Moreover, as we have seen, the appeal to nonmaximizing dispositions cannot solve the problem of pragmatic self-defeat for utilitarianism. And finally, an appeal to self-supporting dispositions cancels any commitment to utilitarianism in favor of a commitment to a rights-based theory. And unless there is some sense in which utilitarianism is true in spite of our being rationally motivated to follow a rights-based theory, this move is not an answer to the claim that utilitarianism is self-defeating but a confirmation of it. This problem led to the appeal to realism to find a sense in which the truth of utilitarianism might be independent of the motives of actual agents in ideal reflective equilibrium. But to the extent that we can attach such a sense to realism, any appeal to realism is open to the mere-facts objection. And to the extent that this objection is met, it is met by a claim like Boyd's that in reflective equilibrium human beings under reasonably auspicious circumstances converge in their moral beliefs. But since those committed to rights-based theories as a result of utilitarian self-defeat will not converge to a believe in the truth of utilitarianism (except in the mere-facts sense), we need the truth of realism to block objections stemming from our apparent nonconvergence to utilitarianism, and we need convergence to utilitarianism to support the truth of realism in more than the merely anthropological sense.

Thus the appeal to realism involves a dilemma for the utilitarian. Either the realism in question requires convergence in moral opinion or it does not. If it does not—or if the convergence in moral opinion amounts to no more than the truth of realism in the anthropological sense—then the utilitarian realist faces the mere-facts objection. If realism requires convergence in more than the anthropological sense, that is, if it requires convergence in the prescriptions that rational agents are rationally motivated to follow, then the appeal to realism will not answer the objection that utilitarianism cannot provide real rights.

We are now in a position to review the whole argument for this last claim. To begin, recall that utilitarianism and rights-based theories do not converge. This claim is supported by three further claims. First, as we have seen, AU and rights-based theories give different prescriptions over a range of examples in which utility is maximized by violating rights. These include examples in which more utility (or as much utility) would be produced in a community of moral agents, some of whom are disposed to violate rights, than in a community in which no agents are so disposed, and examples in which this is not the case and in which AU is pragmatically self-defeating. The fact that AU is pragmatically self-defeating in contexts in which rights-based theories are not shows that there are significant structural differences between the two sorts of theories in precisely those contexts in which the theories' commitments to rights are at issue. Second, as we have also seen, rule utilitarianism and act utilitarianism are only nominally distinct. Third, indirect forms of utilitarianism that rely on nonmaximizing dispositions collapse into act utilitarianism in contexts in which the stakes are sufficiently high. Only if our commitment to respect the rights of others is in virtue of a self-supporting disposition, i.e., only if we are committed in IRE to some form of rights-based theory, can the claim that our commitment is to real rights be sustained.

At this point the utilitarian realist may claim that AU can be true even if what we are internally motivated to follow are the prescriptions of some rights-based theory. But we have now seen that in order to avoid the mere-facts objection to AU, utilitarian realists must suppose that we are in the process of convergence toward commitment to AU. Therefore, the claim that AU could provide real rights requires that we could be committed to a rights-based theory in IRE while utilitarianism was nonetheless true. On the other hand, the truth of AU (if it is not to be a merely anthropological fact) requires that we be committed to AU in IRE (or at least that we be converging toward such a commitment). Thus if utilitarianism is true and this fact is more than a merely anthropological one, we cannot have a stable and lasting commitment to real rights.

8   The Prospects for Convergence

As the preceding summary of the overall argument makes clear, the conclusion is not that utilitarianism is false or that it is unjustified. It is that utilitarianism (and AC generally) cannot provide real rights, in spite of the allegedly rich resources that are thought to allow these theories to mimic any of the advantages of their rights-based competitors. To this it might be replied, however, that we are in fact generally converging toward commitment to AU. If such a convergence were indeed underway, then it might be argued that the lack of real rights would not be a serious drawback. In a society of individuals committed to utilitarianism, rights would inevitably have less significance than they currently have, and something less than real rights might be quite sufficient. A disposition on the part of members of the society not to violate rights except when doing so would have unquestionably better consequences than respecting them might, for example, provide committed utilitarians as much personal security as our real rights, such as they are, currently provide us. Similarly it might be argued that the problem of self-defeat will not be sufficiently important, under the circumstances we are actually likely to face, to prevent our convergence to AU.

Is the claim of the utilitarian realist that we are converging toward commitment to AU plausible? The legitimacy of this question is, of course, open to doubt if it is construed as one to be settled on largely a priori grounds. But there should be no objection to an appeal to a priori considerations when these are intended to counter a priori arguments that the utilitarian realist's claim is true. And there are several reasons for thinking that the utilitarian realist is unlikely to make a convincing case for this claim.

First, there is no direct evidence that our present moral commitments are utilitarian in character, and there is a good deal of evidence to the contrary. Our institutions seem strongly antiutilitarian in many cases in which AU and rights-based theories conflict. Moreover, many of our desires to respect the rights of others look like the kind that would survive in our IREs. If this is the case, then, as we have seen, there is at least no rational route from our present commitments to commitment to any version of utilitarianism.

If we suppose that utilitarian self-defeat will not be a serious problem in the future, however, the following argument for convergence to utilitarianism might seem attractive. Assume that a community whose members were committed utilitarians would enjoy the highest level of utility that the members of any community in similar circumstances could achieve. In other words, assume that near universal commitment to utilitarianism is optimal where the production of aggregate utility is concerned. This assumption is hard to fault, given that utilitarian self-defeat is assumed to be negligible. The claim is, then, that because such commitment to utilitarianism is optimal, we will over time find the means to bring about a utilitarian society.

There are two problems, however, that any argument of this kind faces. The first is that it ignores the depth that our commitments to antiutilitarian, rights-based theories may have. If these commitments are ones we have in IRE, they will constitute barriers to our bringing about a utilitarian society. Suppose, though, that our commitment to rights is not this deep. A further problem for this argument lies in the fact that it assumes that an optimal outcome will be realized without suggesting any process describable in microfoundational terms by which such an optimum might be brought about. That is to say, there is no description of a process in terms of actions that individual agents could be rationally motivated to perform that would result in the end state being predicted. And we are now sufficiently familiar with the many ways in which what is collectively optimal may fail to be optimal for any of the individuals concerned to suppose that this gap in the utilitarian realist's argument will be easily filled. Although it might be to everyone's advantage if everyone were a utilitarian (putting aside his or her commitment to rights), it does not follow that it would be to anyone's advantage to convert unilaterally to utilitarianism or to raise his or her children as utilitarians.[22]

There is, moreover, a further objection to the claim that we will converge to AU. The best explanation of our apparent commitment to rights is that it represents a solution to the problem of egoistic self-defeat. And egoistic self-defeat, as opposed to utilitarian self-defeat, is a problem whose practical significance no one would be likely to deny. Many-person prisoner's dilemmas are a pervasive feature of social existence, and egoists collectively do worse than nonegoists as a result. Moreover, these problems cannot be solved simply by making cooperation compulsory. This is because the social cooperation required by the system of norms and sanctions that such a solution to this form of the prisoner's dilemma presupposes is itself subject to many-person dilemmas of the same kind. As a result, a disposition to respect the rights of others in at least some instances would give us a collective advantage over rational egoists and would, in many contexts, give each of us an individual advantage.[23] And our present commitment to rights is likely to reflect this fact.

If this is a plausible explanation of our commitment to respect rights, the commitment is likely to be a deep one and not one that we could easily shed. Many-person prisoner's dilemmas in which rights are at stake often involve scarce resources and in some instances are matters of life and death. Thus only a disposition that would work in high-stakes cases is likely to solve the problem of egoistic self-defeat. And as we have seen, a self-supporting disposition is far more likely to be effective in high-stakes cases than one that is merely nonmaximizing. And as we have also seen, this is because in high-stakes cases only a disposition that is very well supported and hence has no exit conditions will persist. Since this means that the disposition to respect rights *will* be in IRE (and is likely to be unconditional because the desire to prevent unnecessary suffering that would motivate rights violations is also likely to be unconditional), we know that there will be no rational route to utilitarianism in any form.

The argument that our disposition to respect rights is an unconditional commitment in IRE does not show, of course, that there is no *irrational* route to a commitment to utilitarianism. Since we are not in conditions of IRE, small changes in our motivational makeup can accumulate. And over time a sequence of small changes could provide a path from one IRE to another, significantly different one. This process is indeed irrational, since each of the changes is one we would be rationally motivated to prevent, if this were possible, and to reverse, if we had the means to do so. Such a process might be called *moral drift*. And as we have seen, the distinction between individual and collective rationality suggests that there is no reason to expect, and some reason not to expect, that moral drift will result in a utilitarian society. It is true, nonetheless, that none of the considerations we have examined rules out the possibility of our acquiring a commitment to utilitarianism as the result of such a process. But in the absence of an argument as to why moral drift should take exactly this direction, the prospects for our conversion to utilitarianism do not seem promising.

Postscript

In response to the argument that our commitment to individual rights precludes our converging toward utilitarianism, the following reply might be made. Rationality, it might be held, requires that distinctions concerning norms or values reflect objective distinctions. But this suggestion has two possible interpretations. On the first, the suggestion is that our norms or values *should* reflect objective distinctions, where the force of this normative claim is somehow grounded in our rationality and not in any of our more substantive moral commitments. There is an alternative, however, to this normative interpretation. The claim might instead be an empirical one to the effect that our norms and values *do* (or will eventually) converge toward a set whose distinctions mirror objective distinctions. And these two readings of the claim clearly require different responses.

Call the claim that distinctions concerning norms and values *should* reflect objective distinctions the *normative-objectivity requirement*. Those who make the claim in this form would seem to ignore the issue of internal justification. That is, they ignore the basic argument according to which metaphysical and semantic considerations alone cannot settle questions about how we are justified in acting if that justification is to have any relevance to our actual choices. This argument is developed in the context of moral responsibility, but it applies as well to personal identity, rationality, the distinction between consciousness and self-consciousness, and the discussions of moral theory. There are also two further arguments that are clearly related to the basic argument and that support the same conclusion. One is Shoemaker's argument, which I endorse in chapter 3, against the application of the Putnam-Kripke approach to reference to determine the meaning of 'pain'. Shoemaker claims that if the referent of 'pain' is determined by the expression 'whatever it is *in us* that realizes the best functional characterization of pain', then the semantics of the term will yield answers to important philosophical questions that can only be regarded as question begging. This approach to the semantics of 'pain', for example, yields a completely trivial answer to the question of whether creatures who were functionally indistinguishable from humans but whose neurophysiologies were radically different could feel pain. The triviality of the negative answer that follows from this account of pain is especially apparent if we imagine asking the question in a practical context. If our concern is to determine whether we would be justified in doing to the creatures things that would cause pain to humans, can we really suppose that the issue would be settled when we learned that on the Putnam-Kripke account of the semantics of 'pain' the term has no application to the creatures in question?

This argument appears again in another guise in the mere-facts objection. As we have seen, the upshot of the objection is that facts about which moral theory is true or about what we ought to do, if they are independent of what we are internally justified in doing, are merely anthropological facts in the following sense. They are facts that we could acknowledge in our role as anthropological observers of our own society without their having any interest for us in our role as agents concerned to choose among the actions open to us. This is obvious in cases where the facts are established on semantic grounds of the kind mentioned in the Shoemaker argument. But the point applies generally to all those cases in which the facts are established on grounds that could not provide internal justifications for action.

Suppose the basic argument and its variants are correct. Then in the absence of some connection between the normative-objectivity requirement and what we are internally justified in doing, the requirement is vulnerable to the objection that it is question begging and irrelevant. Moreover, there are a number of cases, some of which we have seen, in which the requirement actually conflicts with considerations of internal justification. The most extreme examples, of course, are cases of pathologically indifferent subjects (chapter 9). In these cases extremely important distinctions in the subjects' patterns of concern have no counterparts in the subjects' objective conceptions of the world. The subject who is future-Tuesday-indifferent, for example, has no false beliefs that would lead him to place any objective significance in the distinction between Tuesdays and other days of the week.

Although future-Tuesday indifference is a particularly vivid violation of the normative-objectivity requirement, it is by no means the only example. We have seen in chapter 10 that the fundamentalist may be unprepared to show concern for a future person who is psychologically and physically continuous with him or her, given that the future person has a different conception of the good. And in chapter 10, I describe an even more extreme case (the Nietzschean/Christian case) in which a subject is prepared deliberately to withdraw concern from such a future person. Furthermore, I argue in chapter 5 that whether bodily continuity is required for personal identity cannot be settled by reference to objective considerations alone but depends in part on the norms and values of the society for which the question arises. Thus a wide range of possible cases provide counterexamples to the normative-objectivity requirement.

The claim, however, is not merely that if we construe norms and values in terms of internal justification we can imagine exceptions to the normative-objectivity requirement. It is rather that such exceptions are ineliminable in principle. Consider that although we can stipulate senses in which normal subjects are free to choose among possible actions (and although our norms require that we do so), from an objective point of view (if we assume the truth of determinism) the future is no more open than the past. Of course, there is a distinction between what we can and cannot *know* regarding future events. But this distinction could hardly count as *objective*. And a conception of the future in which this distinction is ignored is not one on which it is possible to act; to see all features of the future as equally fixed and thus to see the future as we see the past would reduce us to a completely helpless passivity.

The normative-objectivity requirement, then, is one that we are not justified in accepting and that in any case we cannot fully accept and remain human agents. Thus we are not forced down a slippery slope from concern for ourselves to impartial concern for all the future person stages with which we are physically and psychologically continuous (perhaps discounted by the degree to which such person stages resemble us psychologically) and from there to impartial benevolence in general. Hence, given the connection (for which I argue in chapter 9) between rationality and internal justification, there are no grounds for the claim that if we are rational, our values should reflect our objective conception of the world.

It might be claimed, however, that where our values are concerned, rationality requires objectivity independently of whether such objectivity is internally justified for us or not. This is analogous to the claim that a moral theory (for example utilitarianism) could be true even though no one would be internally justified in following its prescriptions. In chapter 11, I review the grounds for this claim where utilitarianism is concerned, and I argue that were this claim true, it would be a merely anthropological fact. Exactly analogous considerations would show that if the claim regarding rationality were true, it would also lack the significance it purports to have.

The best interpretation of the objectivity requirement, however, may not be the normative one. Let us call the claim that for rational creatures, distinctions among norms and values will inevitably come to reflect objective distinctions the *empirical-objectivity requirement*. Of course, it will have to be conceded that our seeing ourselves as agents and our taking responsibility for our actions imposes some limitations on the requirement. But it might be maintained that for a broad range of moral values our departures from objectivity can be expected to diminish with time.

This suggestion seems to ignore two facts. First, where individual rights are concerned, what we are internally justified in doing seems to violate the objectivity requirement. This is because, as we have seen, it is plausible to suppose that we would be internally justified in upholding such rights even if we could produce more utility (either individually or collectively) by ceasing to do so. Second, what we are internally justified in doing is what we are in fact actually disposed to do, at least under suitably idealized circumstances. Thus it seems we are disposed, under some appropriate range of circumstances, to uphold rights, even if we could produce more utility by violating them.

A sophisticated version of the suggestion, however, would accommodate these facts. We do not, after all, have complete control over our own motivational makeup, nor do we always or even usually act under ideal circumstances. In its sophisticated version, then, the suggestion would be that since our motivations are largely outside our control, there will be a general tendency for our individual and social values to converge toward those that maximize aggregate utility. Hence the empirical-objectivity requirement will be satisfied.

That the requirement will be satisfied is, of course, an empirical claim, and no a priori argument alone can establish its falsity. But it is worth noting that there is no mechanism that could plausibly be thought to ensure this result. As I argue in chapter 11, the existence and pervasiveness of many-person prisoner's dilemmas shows that individual rationality fails to guarantee that arrangements that would be to everyone's advantage will be realized. Indeed, the existence of these dilemmas shows that individual rationality may itself prevent the realization of such arrangements. Moreover, most of the changes required to maximize aggregate utility would not make everyone better off; rather, they would make some better off at the expense of others. And there is no mechanism that could reasonably be supposed to connect individual rationality (at least among those who are not already committed as individuals to impartial benevolence) with the inevitability of such redistributions. Of course, it is true that if individually we were converging toward a commitment to impartial benevolence, this would provide a connection between individual rationality and norms, values, and institutions that would tend to maximize aggregate utility. But as I claim in chapter 11, we have no reason to suppose that at the individual level any such convergence is underway. Thus the prospects for either version of the objectivity requirement do not seem promising.

We have, then, what appears to be a relativistic conclusion. Utilitarianism would be justified for a group whose commitments in IRE were to impartial benevolence and who had few if any commitments to autonomy or authorship of the kind that would ground desires for individual rights. Since this pattern of commitments is almost certainly not ours, it is far more likely that some form of rights-based theory is justified for us.

There may, however, be another possibility that captures the most attractive features of both relativism and realism. Notice first that the motivational makeup that would make a commitment to utilitarian principles possible, that is, an extreme and impartial form of altruism, seems relatively improbable on evolutionary grounds. Genetic evolution alone would be unlikely to produce altruism in the extreme form required to support a commitment to utilitarianism. Moreover, the addition of cultural evolution to genetic evolution does not make such altruism much more probable. In subjects whose innate tendencies toward altruism were limited, there would be little incentive to make their children extremely and impartially benevolent through education. Of course, everyone might be better off if everyone supported such an educational program for children. But the collective benefits of such a program could not provide individuals with an incentive to cooperate, because, regardless of what others did, each would be better off if his or her children remained less than perfectly impartial in their benevolence. In other words, the attempt to initiate such a program would involve one more example of the many-person prisoner's dilemma.

The difficulty in imagining an evolutionary route to utilitarianism might be overlooked if there were no other account of how we avoid the problems raised by the self-defeating nature of egoism. Suppose, however, as I suggest in chapter 11, that our commitment to rights provides an alternative account. If, as it seems reasonable to assume, the development of the psychological basis of such a commitment is not as unlikely on evolutionary grounds as the development of an extreme and impartial altruism, then the following claim may be plausible. Under most normal conditions, the process of evolution will produce subjects whose psychologies make them better suited to acquire nonutilitarian than utilitarian commitments. Such subjects may be best suited to acquiring norms and commitments that constrain the kinds of interventions allowed in others' affairs but that require only limited sacrifices where benefits to strangers are concerned. That is, such subjects may be best suited to acquire norms that most closely resemble those of rights-based, rather than utilitarian, moral theories.

If this line of thought is correct, then it seems that *if* a commitment to a moral theory with significant structural similarities to rights-based theories would evolve under normal circumstances, the dichotomy between realism and relativism will have proved to be seriously misleading. The position I am suggesting, then, has the following features:

1. Utilitarianism and rights-based moral theories are structurally distinct and do not converge.
2. Rational individuals whose motivations we would find perfectly intelligible (though in some cases unnaturally saintly, in others distinctly ruthless, and in some cases both) would be justified in following the prescriptions of utilitarianism, whereas we are justified in following a rights-based theory.

These would seem to give the relativist all or most of what he or she could reasonably want. However, the position also has the following additional features:

3. Virtually all actual subjects are justified in following one *kind* of moral theory: a theory with significant structural similarities to rights-based theories.
4. Any group of rational subjects who had evolved under normal circumstances *would* be justified in following this kind of theory.
5. This form of moral theory explains our pretheoretical moral intuitions as well as what we say about moral issues.

And this would seem to give the realist at least most of what he or she has wanted as well.

It is possible, though, that this last claim is too strong. It may be that the realist would get only part of what was wanted from a position according to which different groups would be justified in following significantly different antiutilitarian theories. It does seem, nonetheless, that if any account of our moral commitments like the one I have sketched is true (and I have certainly not provided an argument that would establish such a claim), the distinction between realism and relativism may be less significant than has generally been assumed.

Notes

Introduction

1. Roderick Chisholm, *The First Person: An Essay on Reference and Intentionality* (Minneapolis: University of Minnesota Press, 1981), p. 87.
2. This is apparently Nagel's view in Nagel 1979c.
3. See Rawls 1971, pp. 26–27.

Chapter 1

1. Hilary Putnam, "Is Semantics Possible?" in his *Mind, Language and Reality,* vol. 2 of *Philosophical Papers* (Cambridge: Cambridge University Press, 1975), pp. 139–152; "Explanation and Reference," *Mind, Language, and Reality,* pp. 196–214; "The Meaning of 'Meaning'," *Mind, Language, and Reality,* pp. 215–271; "Meaning and Reference," *Journal of Philosophy* 70 (1973): 699–711.
2. Stephen Stich, "Do Animals Have Beliefs?" *Australasian Journal of Philosophy* 57 (1979): 15–28; "Autonomous Psychology and the Belief-Desire Thesis," *Monist* 61 (1978): 573–591; "On the Ascription of Content," in Andrew Woodfield, ed., *Thought and Object* (New York: Oxford University Press, 1982), pp. 153–206. Tyler Burge, "Individualism and the Mental," in Peter French, Theodore Uehling, and Howard Wettstein, eds., *Midwest Studies in Philosophy,* vol. 4, *Studies in Metaphysics* (Minneapolis: University of Minnesota Press, 1979).
3. Stich, "Autonomous Psychology and the Belief-Desire Thesis," pp. 575–578.
4. Stich takes belief tokens to be states of a person. States are taken to be the instantiation of properties by objects during time intervals. Two belief states (token beliefs) are of the same type if they instantiate the same property, and they are of different types if they instantiate different properties. If two people believe that power corrupts, then the property they both instantiate is *believing that power corrupts.*
5. Putnam, "The Meaning of 'Meaning'," pp. 223–227.
6. Stich, "Autonomous Psychology and the Belief-Desire Thesis," pp. 585–586.
7. Putnam, "The Meaning of 'Meaning'," p. 269.
8. "The Meaning of 'Meaning'," p. 234.
9. David Kaplan, "Demonstratives," in Joseph Almog, John Perry, and Howard Wettstein, eds., *Themes from Kaplan* (New York: Oxford University Press, 1989).
10. This is a slight oversimplification. For Kaplan, an intension is not *identical* to the corresponding content; it merely *represents* that content. Similarly the function from contexts of utterance to contents *represents* the character. I shall continue to ignore this distinction, since Kaplan himself ignores it in most contexts and since it is irrelevant to the points made in this paper.
11. John Perry, "Frege on Demonstratives," *Philosophical Review* 86 (1977): 494.

12. Saul Kripke, *Naming and Necessity* (Cambridge: Harvard University Press, 1980), pp. 23–24.
13. Hartry Field, "Conventionalism and Instrumentalism in Semantics," *Noûs* 9 (1975), 375–405. "Quine and the Correspondence Theory," *Philosophical Review* 83 (1974): 200–228.
14. Philip Kitcher, "Theories, Theorists, and Theoretical Change," *Philosophical Review* 87 (1978): 519–547.
15. Hartry Field, "Mental Representation," *Erkenntnis* 13 (1978).

Chapter 2

1. "Demonstratives," in Joseph Almog, John Perry, and Howard Wettstein, eds., *Themes from Kaplan* (New York: Oxford University Press, 1989).
2. See "The Meaning of 'Meaning'," in Putnam, *Mind, Language, and Reality*, vol. 2 of *Philosophical Papers* (New York: Cambridge University Press, 1975).
3. See Tyler Burge, "Individualism and the Mental," in Peter French, Theodore Uehling, and Howard Wettstein, eds., *Midwest Studies in Philosophy*, vol. 4, *Studies in Metaphysics* (Minneapolis: University of Minnesota Press, 1979).
4. Robert Stalnaker, "On What's in the Head," in James E. Tomberlin, ed., *Philosophical Perspectives*, vol. 3, *Philosophy of Mind and Action Theory* (Atascadero, Calif.: Ridgeview, 1989).
5. In *Psychosemantics* (Cambridge: MIT Press, 1987), chapter 2.
6. "On What's in the Head," pp. 295–296. Stalnaker has said in conversation that he is here presupposing a notion of absolute space.
7. Daniel Dennett, "Beyond Belief," in Andrew Woodfield, ed., *Thought and Object* (New York: Oxford University Press, 1982).
8. Dennett, "Beyond Belief," p. 42.
9. "On What's in the Head," p. 304.
10. Dennett mentions the Magoo example but not the problem that it raises for the characterization of a notional world. See "Beyond Belief," p. 48.
11. The following objections are similar to ones proposed by Ned Block.
12. *Australasian Journal of Philosophy* 50 (1972), pp. 249–258.
13. In his *Philosophical Papers*, vol. 1 (New York: Oxford University Press, 1983).
14. For a more detailed treatment, see chapter 7.
15. "Radical Interpretation," p. 110. Lewis does say (p. 110) that he leaves it open whether the truth condition of a sentence should specify the actual truth value of the sentence, what the truth value would be in various counterfactual situations not too remote from actuality, or the truth value at all possible worlds. Although this characterization of truth conditions allows for a number of different possibilities, it does not seem designed to allow for narrow content.
16. "Radical Interpretation," p. 113.
17. This version of the example is due to Brian Loar. See "Social Content and Psychological Content," in D. Merrill and R. Grimm, eds., *Contents of Thought* (Tucson: University of Arizona Press, 1986), p. 103. For the original example, see Kripke, "A Puzzle about Belief," in Avishai Margalit, ed., *Meaning and Use* (Dordrecht: Reidel, 1979).
18. Loar makes a similar point about this example. See "Social Content and Psychological Content," p. 103.
19. See Davidson, "Belief and the Basis of Meaning," in his *Inquiries into Truth and Interpretation* (New York: Oxford University Press, 1984).

Chapter 3

1. Shoemaker 1975, 1981, 1982, and Block 1980. The term 'physicalist-functionalism' is unlikely to please either Shoemaker or Block. Shoemaker regards himself as defending functionalism, at least where qualia are concerned, rather than offering an alternative theory. Block, on the other hand, has little sympathy for functionalism, and even the category of physicalist-functionalism that I shall sketch might seem objectionable. Nonetheless, I think this term is appropriate. As in every question of terminology, we can distinguish two components. There is, first of all, the question of where to divide the space of possible positions. Since I shall claim that both Shoemaker's position and Block's are vulnerable to the same set of arguments and that this is a vulnerability that functionalism does not share, the distinction between functionalism and physicalist-functionalism is not only motivated but is dictated by my substantive position. The second question is how the subspaces of the space of possible positions should be labeled. On this point Shoemaker can argue that his position bears a stronger similarity to the positions historically associated with the term 'functionalism' than the position for which I am using the term. If this were the case, it might be more appropriate to call what I call 'functionalism' and 'orthodox functionalism' by another name. Such a claim, however, does not seem to me to be supported by the evidence. Shoemaker's claim that particular qualia are not functionally definable rules out functionalism as a *complete* theory of mind. And this is sufficiently at odds with the spirit in which functionalism was advanced to justify treating Shoemaker's position as an alternative to functionalism as it is ordinarily understood. Moreover, since I shall argue that what I call 'functionalism' is the only viable descendant of the original theory, it seems reasonable to reserve for it the shorter and simpler term.

The case of Block is more complicated, since if we compromise the functionalist principle that the nature of the realization of a functional system is irrelevant to the psychological properties of that system, it is hard to know where to draw the line between physicalist-functionalism and (type-type) physicalism. Fortunately, for the purposes at hand we can stipulate that (type-type) physicalism is to count as a version of physicalist-functionalism. The difficulties that arise for physicalist-functionalism over qualia are difficulties for physicalism as well. The choice of terminology is further complicated by the fact that if the nature of the realization of functional states is relevant to mentality, then mentality may depend on more than physical facts. Functionalism has always left open the possibility in principle of nonphysical realizations of functional systems. If for the physicalist-functionalist it is the nature of the functional realization that matters, then physicalist-functionalism should leave open this possibility as well. Hence at least some versions of Cartesian dualism could count as versions of physicalist-functionalism. I shall ignore this qualification in most of what follows.

2. Besides those mentioned above, see Armstrong 1968, pp. 73–125, Lewis 1983a, Rey 1980, Searle 1980, 1981, Churchland and Churchland 1981, and Putnam 1981, pp. 75–102.

3. See Harman 1982. See also Dennett 1978d, Kitcher 1979, and Lycan 1981. Dennett's claim that all instantiations of a flowchart theory of pain might feel pain suggests that where qualia are concerned, Dennett's functionalism is orthodox. However, his idea that pain might be identified with a "natural kind" (p. 228) points in the other direction. Lycan's criticisms of Block make it clear that orthodox functionalism is the correct category, but his skepticism about the functional/physical distinction necessarily blurs the line between orthodox and physicalist-functionalism. And Kitcher's

more recent article (1982) makes it clear that she is an agnostic where the merits of orthodox as opposed to physicalist-functionalism are concerned. In what follows, I shall sometimes use the term 'functionalism' for 'orthodox functionalism' where there is no chance of confusion.

4. This, of course, is an oversimplification. The correct functional description of the subject's inputs and outputs is a matter of long-standing debate. For an argument that inputs and outputs must themselves be described relationally, see White 1982a, chap. 1.

5. See Nagel 1979c. The term 'transcendentalism' is intended to suggest the affinities between Nagel's criticism of Cartesian (substance) dualism and those of Kant and Husserl. See also Kant 1965, A341–A405, B399–B432, and Husserl 1973, pp. 18–26.

6. Nagel 1979c, p. 201.

7. The argument, strictly speaking, is not that absent qualia are impossible but that absent qualia raise insurmountable obstacles for any *nontranscendental* theory.

8. Goldman 1976.

9. The notion of functional definability that occurs in the definiens of Shoemaker's definitions is strong definability. In other words, a state is functionally definable in the strong sense if and only if it has a definition in which no mental terms occur in the definiens. A mental state is functionally definable in the weak sense if it has a functional definition, given that we allow in the definiens terms that are not themselves strongly functionally definable.

10. To see that the negation of AQT-2 is equivalent to the negation of thesis (1), suppose that qualitative states are only weakly functionally definable. Then whether a subject has qualitative states will depend on whether that subject has nonqualitative states that themselves are not (strongly) functionally definable. Let us suppose that such a subject is functionally equivalent to a normal subject. In spite of the equivalence, such a subject may lack some of the nonqualitative states of the normal subject that are not functionally definable, and hence may lack qualitative states. If qualitative states are strongly functionally definable, this possibility is ruled out. Hence the negation of AQT-2 is equivalent to the negation of thesis (1).

11. Shoemaker's claim that qualitative states are weakly definable, however, is compatible with the claim, which he also makes, that two subjects who are functional duplicates may *differ* in the particular character of their qualitative experience. (Shoemaker's thesis that inverted qualia are possible is merely a special instance of this latter claim.) These two claims are compatible because, as we have seen, Shoemaker does not regard it as essential to ordinary qualitative states such as pain that they feel like what we have when we experience them. All that is essential to pain, besides its functional role, is that it involve some kind of qualitative experience. The same is true for all the qualitative states picked out by our normal vocabulary of mental terms. Thus Shoemaker can hold that as long as absent qualia are impossible, our ordinary terms for qualitative states are weakly functionally definable. We could, however, artificially define qualitative states whose *particular* qualitative character would be essential to their identity. We might, for example, define 'pain$_S$' as any state that feels exactly like the last headache of some particular subject S. Such artificial qualitative states do not fall within the scope of Shoemaker's claim that qualitative states are weakly functionally definable.

It follows that Shoemaker uses 'qualitative states' in two senses. When in the statement of the negation of AQT-2 (see table 1) he says that qualitative states are weakly definable, he means *ordinary* qualitative states, such as pain. When in the definition of functional definability in the weak sense he uses the expression 'nonqualitative mental states', this contrasts not only with *ordinary* qualitative states but also with such artificially defined states as pain$_S$. In particular contexts it is usually clear which sense Shoemaker has in mind.

12. The term 'ersatz pain' is due to Lawrence Davis. See Block 1980, p. 253.
13. The term 'imitation man' is Keith Campbell's. See Campbell 1970, p. 100.
14. See Putnam 1975c and Kripke 1980.
15. In correspondence.
16. This claim is defended in the context of a more detailed discussion of the distinction between beliefs narrowly and widely construed and an argument that functionalism is a theory of narrow belief in chapters 1 and 2.
17. Even if some version of the symmetry argument did yield the conclusion that is needed, Shoemaker has failed to notice that this argument would prove too much. We could use the same argument to show that the Martians, who are functionally but not neurophysiologically equivalent to us, not only have pains but have pains that feel exactly like ours. Suppose, for example, the hypothesis is that Martian pains differ from ours in that theirs are never "shooting" pains. Since they are functionally equivalent to us, they will *claim* to have shooting pains under exactly the same circumstances that we claim to have them. If the difference between the Martians' neurophysiology and ours is irrelevant to their claims to have pain, it is equally irrelevant to their claims to have shooting pains. Hence any argument that supports their claim to have pains will support their claim to have pains with *any* qualitative characteristics we attribute to ours. Of course, it is possible to object that the feelings the Martians experience when they experience pain may be unlike the feelings we experience, though they describe their pains in exactly the same ways. If this were possible, however, there would be no argument from the symmetry between what Martians and humans could sincerely say about what they feel to any symmetry between their actual feelings and ours. Hence either the symmetry argument proves that qualia differences between Martians and humans are impossible, and thereby undermines Shoemaker's version of physicalist-functionalism, or it fails to prove that absent qualia are impossible. Thus Shoemaker's argument for the symmetry of the Martian and human claims to experience pain undermines his own version of physicalist-functionalism.
18. Shoemaker has made this argument explicit in correspondence.
19. The distinction between expressions that are synonymous or that have the same sense and expressions that are coreferential a priori is meant to accommodate the kinds of cases that are familiar in mathematics. Two mathematical expressions may be coreferential a priori, and this fact may be sufficiently far from obvious, even to a fully competent speaker, that we would not want to call them synonymous.
20. See Smart 1971, p. 59. As the statement of the general principle suggests, the crucial distinction for this argument is not between synonymous expressions and non-synonymous expressions but between expressions that are coreferential a priori and expressions that are coreferential a posteriori. Nonsynonymy is not sufficient to generate a duality of properties, since the nonsynonymy of two expressions that pick out the same referent does not require that the referent have *logically distinct* features in virtue of which the two expressions pick it out.
21. Smart does not provide a topic-neutral translation of 'the experience of having pain'. What I have provided is one natural analogue of his translation of 'the experience of seeing an afterimage'. 'And so forth' should be taken to stand in for a long list of typical causes of pain, since the description is intended as a description of pain and not of the particular kind of pain associated with pin pricks. Needless to say, the merits of neither this nor any other particular topic-neutral translation is at issue here.

22. As the argument suggests, the existence of a physicalist or a topic-neutral description that picks out the same event as the mentalistic expression 'Smith's pain at *t*' is irrelevant so long as no such description is coreferential a priori with the mentalistic expression. This is true regardless of whether the physicalistic or topic-neutral description is rigid or nonrigid. (Skeptics about the existence of a rigid reading of such a description may take the term derived from the original description by the addition of Kaplan's operator 'Dthat'. The operator transforms the description into a term that rigidly designates the object *actually* satisfying the description. See Kaplan 1989.) Any such description *not* coreferential a priori with the mentalistic expression refers to Smith's pain in virtue of a property different from that in virtue of which the mentalistic expression picks it out. If, for example, the topic-neutral and nonrigid description 'the state of Smith at *t* of the type that typically causes him to say "ow" ' picks out Smith's pain at *t*, it does so in virtue of a topic-neutral property that Smith's pain has at the actual world but lacks at those possible worlds where Smith says "damn" when in pain and "ow" when mildly embarrassed (assuming that 'Smith's pain at *t*' is rigid). If we give the topic-neutral description a rigid reading, then it picks out Smith's pain at *t* at every possible world. Unless the mentalistic expression is coreferential a priori with this topic-neutral description, however, it will still pick out Smith's pain in virtue of a *different* property from the topic neutral one, and the problem of property dualism will remain.

It might be objected with reference to this last case that the topic-neutral property corresponding to the rigid topic-neutral description 'Dthat the state of Smith at *t* of the type that typically causes him to say "ow"' is identical with the mental property corresponding to the mentalistic description 'Smith's pain at *t*' on the grounds that they have the same extension. I am not committed, however, to the thesis that if two descriptions are not coreferential a priori, then the properties expressed by those descriptions can be shown to be distinct by the fact that they have different extensions. Consider the descriptions 'Dthat the first Postmaster General' and 'Dthat the inventor of bifocals'. These are not coreferential a priori, but they are satisfied by the same individual at each possible world, namely Franklin. And if there are rigid properties expressed by these two rigid descriptions, then these properties have the same extension at every possible world. What I claim is that *there are* two properties in virtue of which these descriptions pick out Franklin and that they can be shown to be distinct because they *do* differ in their extension. These are the property of being the first Postmaster General and the property of being the inventor of bifocals. It is these properties that provide the two routes to Franklin in virtue of which he is picked out by descriptions that are not coreferential a priori.

This argument assumes that the mentalistic and topic-neutral descriptions pick out a *token* physical state. A topic-neutral description might purport to pick out a *type* of physical state instead of a token. For a topic-neutral description, however, this will not be the case unless the description is rigid and contains an explicit reference to a particular species. This is because no one seriously disputes the assumption that the topic-neutral properties associated with pain might be realized in different physical-state types in different actual species or in the same species at different possible worlds. Suppose that it *is* claimed that our actual use of 'pain' is such that we can fix the reference of 'pain' to a type of physical state by the use of a rigid, topic-neutral description coextensive with 'pain' a priori. Call the topic-neutral properties of pain the 'causal role of pain'. Such a claim might be made for the description 'the state (type) that realizes the causal role of pain in humans' on a rigid reading. This would not raise the problem of property dualism, since, by hypothesis, both the topic-neutral expression and the expression 'pain' share the same route to the referent. This suggestion, however, merely restates the parochial view of the meaning of mental terms, whose inadequacy Shoemaker points out (1981, p. 595). The parochial view *trivializes* physicalist-functionalism by making the claim that there could be subjects who were functionally equivalent to us and who felt no pain true as a matter of linguistic convention. If 'pain' did have the meaning suggested, we would be forced to coin a new term to which it would be stipulated that the parochial theory did not apply and that would be true of a state just in case it had the same phenomenal quality as one of our pains. The philosophically interesting question would then become whether subjects who were functionally equivalent to us could lack the states thus defined.

23. This argument that we are forced to postulate irreducibly mentalistic properties unless 'pain' has a topic-neutral translation is similar to Smart's argument for the same conclusion. (How far the similarity goes will depend on a number of issues in the interpretation of Smart's position, which cannot be settled here.) I have recast Smart's talk of contingent-identity statements in terms of identity statements known a posteriori.

Richard Rorty has claimed (1970, p. 400) that there are three possible responses to Smart's argument for property dualism: (1) Formulate adequate topic-neutral translations. (2) Drop the principle that properties are identical only if the terms referring to them are synonymous. (3) Adopt the principle that two things can be identical in some sense even if they do not share all and only the same properties. Rorty's second proposal is obviously no help to the physicalist-functionalist, since the criteria of property identity have already been fixed by the theoretical role that properties have to play in explaining the fact that 'pain' and the relevant neurophysiological description are coreferential despite the fact that they are not coreferential a priori. I discuss the first proposal below in the context of the orthodox-functionalist approach to qualia. The third proposal does not provide a genuine alternative to the transcendental-property-dualist position, which I claim is a consequence of Shoemaker's and Block's antifunctionalist intuitions.

24. It was because of this formal analogy that I claimed in note 1 that some versions of Cartesian dualism—those that emphasize the causal role of mental substance—could be counted as instances of physicalist-functionalism.

25. On Shoemaker's view, ordinary qualitative states such as pain present no problem, because he is committed to the possibility of giving *them* a topic-neutral analysis. As we saw in note 11, however, if we define 'pain$_S$' as any state that feels like some particular individual's last headache, such an expression will *not*, according to Shoemaker, have even a weak functional definition. Thus it will not have a topic-neutral translation. Hence it will raise the same problems for Shoemaker that 'pain' raises for Block. Notice that the issue is not whether functionalism must provide an analysis of such artificial terms as 'pain$_S$' as well as of our ordinary mentalistic vocabulary. The problem for Shoemaker is not that he fails to provide a *functionalist* account of terms such as 'pain$_S$'. The problem is that since such terms are definable, Shoemaker must provide *some* account of their meaning, and the account he does provide has, as does every physicalist-functionalist account, two unacceptable consequences. The first, as we have seen, is the existence of transcendental properties; the second, as we shall see, is the lack of a principled distinction between those physical facts that are relevant to a subject's qualitative experiences and those that are not.

26. After completing this paper, I discovered that this last point against Shoemaker is also made in Seager 1983. Seager's point occurs in the context of a different assessment of functionalism, which, unfortunately, I cannot discuss here.

Chapter 4

1. I have argued in chapter 3 that only transcendental theories provide a viable alternative to functionalism where an account of qualitative states such as pain is concerned. In that earlier paper I left open the question of whether one should prefer a transcendental or a functionalist account. Thus, in arguing that transcendental dualism does not provide a convincing account of qualia, I am completing the argument begun in the earlier paper that the functionalist account, contrary to what is generally assumed, is an attractive one.

2. Thomas Nagel, "Subjective and Objective," in his *Mortal Questions* (New York: Cambridge University Press, 1979), 201.

3. I shall use 'state' and 'event' interchangeably since the distinctions that might be made between them are irrelevant to the issues at hand. For a discussion of the possible distinctions, see Jaegwon Kim, "Events as Property Exemplifications," in Myles Brand and Douglas Walton, eds., *Action Theory* (Dordrecht: Reidel, 1976), 159–160.

4. I shall assume that one and the same particular event will have a number of different properties. This assumption, or some analogue of it, seems to be required to account for the fact that an event typically has, among others, the property of being caused by some prior event or events and the property of causing some number of events subsequent to it.

5. See Nagel, "Subjective and Objective" and "The Limits of Objectivity," the latter in *The Tanner Lectures on Human Values* (Salt Lake City: University of Utah Press, 1980), 77–139.

6. That this Cartesian conception of the mental, according to which mental states interact causally with physical states, does not mesh easily with the privileged epistemological role Descartes himself intended subjective experience to play is argued forcefully by Gilbert Ryle. See *The Concept of Mind* (Harmondsworth, England: Penguin Books, 1963), chap. 1.

7. Nagel makes this point with regard to substance dualism when he says that "the question of how one can include in the objective world a mental substance having subjective properties is as acute as the question how a physical substance can have subjective properties." See "Subjective and Objective," p. 201. The point, however, applies to any version of interactionist dualism.

8. Immanuel Kant, *Critique of Pure Reason* (New York: St. Martin's Press, 1965), A341–A405, B399–B432; Edmund Husserl, *Cartesian Meditations* (The Hague: Martinus Nijhoff, 1973), 18–26; Ludwig Wittgenstein, *Tractatus Logico-Philosophicus* (London: Routledge and Kegan Paul, 1961), 5.631–5.641 and *Notebooks, 1914–1916* (New York: Harper and Row, 1961), 80–86.

9. In what follows I shall be concerned for the most part with privileged access regarding our own qualitative states. The claim that we have privileged access to the content of our own conscious beliefs raises issues that go beyond the scope of the paper.

10. See especially section 4.

11. David Armstrong, "Is Introspective Knowledge Incorrigible?" *Philosophical Review* 72 (1963): 417–432 and *A Materialist Theory of the Mind* (New York: Humanities Press, 1968), 100–113.

12. See chapter 3.

13. For arguments against treating 'pain' as a natural-kind term, see Sydney Shoemaker, "Absent Qualia Are Impossible—A Reply to Block," *Philosophical Review* 90 (1981): 581–599 and chapter 3, this volume.

14. For similar objections to this argument, see Frank Jackson, "Is There a Good Argument against the Incorrigibility Thesis?" *Australasian Journal of Philosophy* 51 (1973): 61; John Pollock, *Knowledge and Justification* (Princeton: Princeton University Press, 1974), 31–32 and 77–78; and Keith Lehrer, *Knowledge* (New York: Oxford University Press, 1974), 91–95. Armstrong has a number of other arguments against the existence of privileged access. Jackson criticizes these in "Is There a Good Argument against the Incorrigibility Thesis?"

15. Lehrer, pp. 80–100.

16. Tyler Burge, "Individualism and the Mental," in Peter French, Theodore Uehling, and Howard Wettstein, eds., *Midwest Studies in Philosophy*, vol. 4, *Studies in Metaphysics* (Minneapolis: University of Minnesota Press, 1979), 73–121.

17. See Hilary Putnam, "The Meaning of 'Meaning' " in his *Mind, Language, and Reality*, vol. 2 of *Philosophical Papers* (New York: Cambridge University Press, 1975), 215–271, and Saul Kripke, *Naming and Necessity* (Cambridge: Harvard University Press, 1980).

18. Chapter 1.

19. Having appealed to the distinction between privileged access and weakly privileged access to answer Lehrer's argument, I shall proceed to ignore it in what follows.

20. Moritz Schlick, "Positivism and Realism," in A. J. Ayer, ed., *Logical Positivism* (New York: Free Press, 1959), 93.

21. David Lewis, "Postscript to 'Mad Pain and Martian Pain'," in his *Philosophical Papers*, vol. 1 (New York: Oxford University Press, 1983), 131.

22. Laurence Nemirow, "Functionalism and the Subjective Quality of Experience" (Ph.D. dissertation, Stanford University, 1979), chap. 2.

23. For the notion of a singular proposition, see David Kaplan, "Dthat," in Peter French, Theodore Uehling, and Howard Wettstein, eds., *Contemporary Perspectives in the Philosophy of Language* (Minneapolis: University of Minnesota Press, 1979), 383–400.

24. See Ludwig Wittgenstein, *Philosophical Investigations* (New York: Macmillan, 1968), secs. 242–363; Saul Kripke, *Wittgenstein on Rules and Private Language* (Cambridge: Harvard University Press, 1982); and G. Baker and P. M. S. Hacker, *Scepticism, Rules, and Language* (Oxford: Blackwell, 1984). For arguments that the private language argument cannot accomplish what it purports to, see Robert Fogelin, *Wittgenstein* (London: Routledge and Kegan Paul, 1976), chaps. 12 and 13, and Simon Blackburn, "The Individual Strikes Back," *Synthese* 58 (1984): 281–301.

25. Lehrer, p. 100.

26. David Lewis, "Psychophysical and Theoretical Identifications," *Australasian Journal of Philosophy* 50 (1972): 256.

27. Lewis, "Psychophysical and Theoretical Identifications," p. 258.

28. Lewis, "Psychophysical and Theoretical Identifications," p. 258.

29. The intrinsic similarity between pain and pain belief that the dispositional strategy is meant to secure is, of course, the similarity between two sets of dispositions or functional properties and not necessarily a similarity in the way these dispositions or functional properties are realized. Nonetheless, the requirement that there be a high degree of privileged access ensures that if a pain occurs, something very much like a pain belief occurs. This is true in the only sense in which similarity is relevant, given an objective, dispositional analysis of the mental. Thus it rules out the objection to the relational strategy that even if psychologically privileged access is guaranteed, it is possible to have a state exactly like pain and a state exactly like the belief that no pain exists, except that the first state does not cause a pain belief and the second state is not caused by a state in which nothing resembling pain is present.

30. See Lehrer, p. 96.

31. It might be suggested that a hybrid theory could combine the relational strategy and the dispositional strategy in the following way. Take the case of pains. Since the state of believing that one is in pain must include a disposition, such a belief state must have objective properties essentially. Thus in order to apply the dispositional strategy, the state of being in pain must itself have most of these objective properties essentially. (That is, it must be necessary that it have most of these objective properties. If it did not have them necessarily, then pain could occur without them and hence without there being anything very similar to pain belief. Thus there would be no guarantee of a high degree of transparent access.) And in order for the account to have a significant transcendental component, pain must have transcendental or subjective properties essentially. So in order to guarantee a high degree of incorrigible access, pain belief must have most of these transcendental properties essentially. In other words, we could try to guarantee a high degree of transparent and incorrigible access in a hybrid theory by making some objective properties essential to pain and some subjective properties essential to pain belief.

The problem with this approach emerges if we consider one of the subjective properties of the state of being in pain, for example, the property of hurting. This property must have objective properties that are essential to it if we want to guarantee transparent access to it. But then even the transcendental or subjective properties of the state of pain will have aspects that are not completely given from the first-person, subjective point of view. And this seems to contradict the claim that they are subjective properties and to defeat the point of a transcendental account.
32. For an argument that there is a principled distinction to be drawn, see chapter 3.

Chapter 5

1. *Reasons and Persons* (New York: Oxford, 1984), pp. 210–211.
2. *Mortal Questions* (New York: Cambridge, 1979).
3. "The Self and the Future," in his *Problems of the Self* (New York: Cambridge University Press, 1973), pp. 46–52.
4. *Identity and Spatio-temporal Continuity* (New York: Blackwell, 1967), p. 53.
5. For a notion of supervenience that fits Parfit's remarks very closely, see Terence Horgan, "Supervenience and Cosmic Hermeneutics," *Southern Journal of Philosophy* 22 supplement (1983): 19–38.
6. This principle, which underlies a number of Williams's arguments, is formulated by Parfit, p. 267. For an explicit formulation of principle 1 by Williams, see "Cosmic Philosopher," *New York Review of Books* 29, no. 2 (February 29, 1982): 33. The review is of Robert Nozick, *Philosophical Explanations* (Cambridge: Harvard University Press, 1981).
7. Parfit considers a number of similar cases but does not seem to recognize their full force. See *Reasons and Persons*, pp. 229–230.
8. There is an alternative for dealing with the apparent counterexamples to principles 1 and 2 that does not have the consequence that relations to other people must be included among the facts upon which identity and survival supervene. On this alternative, whether identity or what matters are preserved depends not on the *actual* relations to others of the subject in question but on what relations he or she *thinks* obtain and has internalized. The facts about identity and survival, then, supervene on the physical and psychological facts about the subject, the future person, and any competitors. But this suggestion is not one in which Williams, Parfit, or Nozick could take any comfort. Even if this alternative were to prove attractive, it would be extremely implausible to claim that whether *S* survives as *P*

depends only on the intrinsic relations between S and P, or between S on the one hand and P and P's competitors on the other. On any ordinary interpretation, the requirement that the relations must be intrinsic would rule out S's beliefs about the social practices in his community, just as it rules out facts about the practices themselves. Thus if principle 2 and Nozick's position are not regarded as false on this alternative, they will be very different claims from what was apparently intended.

9. Others have objected to the narrowness of the set of facts considered relevant to questions of identity and survival by most of the parties to the current debate. They include Norman Daniels, "Moral Theory and the Plasticity of Persons," *Monist* 62 (1979): 265–288; Peter McInerny, "My Future, Right or Wrong," *Philosophical Studies* 44 (1983): 235–245; and Amélie Rorty, *The Identities of Persons* (Berkeley: California University Press, 1976), pp. 3–4, and "Persons and Personae" in her *Mind and Action* (Boston: Beacon, 1988).

10. Sydney Shoemaker makes a similar point in Shoemaker and Richard Swinburne, *Personal Identity* (Oxford: Blackwell, 1984), p. 132.

Chapter 6

1. Georges Rey, "A Reason for Doubting the Existence of Consciousness," in Richard Davidson, Gary Schwartz, and David Shapiro, eds., *Consciousness and Self-Regulation* vol. 3 (New York: Plenum, 1983), pp. 1–39.

2. D. M. Armstrong, "What Is Consciousness?" in his *Nature of Mind* (Ithaca, N.Y.: Cornell University Press, 1981), pp. 61 and 65–66.

3. Bernard Baars, "Conscious Contents Provide the Nervous System with Coherent, Global Information," in Davidson, Schwartz, and Shapiro, pp. 41–79.

4. Rey, p. 12.

5. Rey, p. 11.

6. Daniel Dennett, "Why the Law of Effect Will Not Go Away" and "Artificial Intelligence as Philosophy and as Psychology," in his *Brainstorms* (Montgomery, Vt.: Bradford Books, 1978), and William Lycan, "Form, Function, and Feel," *Journal of Philosophy* 77 (1981): 24–50.

7. Dennett, "Why the Law of Effect Will Not Go Away," p. 80.

8. Rey, pp. 4–5 and 21–28.

9. Rey, pp. 14–15.

10. Kaplan, "On the Logic of Demonstratives," in Peter French, Theodore Uehling, and Howard Wettstein, eds., *Contemporary Perspectives in the Philosophy of Language* (Minneapolis: University of Minnesota Press, 1979), pp. 402–404.

11. See Hilary Putnam, "The Meaning of 'Meaning'," in his *Mind, Language, and Reality*, vol. 2 of *Philosophical Papers* (New York: Cambridge University Press, 1975), pp. 215–271; Saul Kripke, *Naming and Necessity* (Cambridge: Harvard University Press, 1980); Tyler Burge, "Individualism and the Mental," in Peter French, Theodore Uehling, and Howard Wettstein, eds., *Midwest Studies in Philosophy*, vol. 4, *Studies in Metaphysics* (Minneapolis: University of Minnesota Press, 1979), pp. 73–121.

12. See David Wiggins, *Sameness and Substance* (New York: Oxford University Press, 1980), p. 172.

13. This example was suggested to me by Edward Stein.

14. In responding to this example, which was suggested by Ned Block, I am not attempting to settle any important questions about personal identity. To the extent that the example raises traditional questions about the identity of persons over time, it is irrelevant to the issues at hand. Neither the original group fusion example nor

any of the examples of sophisticated subsystems involve the special connection that history might establish between a person and a particular physical realization of that person's psychology. I discuss these latter questions in chapter 5.

15. See John Perry, "The Problem of the Essential Indexical," *Noûs* 13 (1979): 3–21.

16. John Rawls, *A Theory of Justice* (Cambridge: Harvard University Press, 1971), pp. 12, 19, and 505.

17. See, for example, Immanuel Kant, *Critique of Pure Reason* (New York: St. Martin's Press, 1965), B131–B140, and the discussion in Jonathan Bennett, *Kant's Analytic* (New York: Cambridge University Press, 1966), secs. 28–31.

18. See Thomas Nagel, "Subjective and Objective," in his *Mortal Questions* (New York: Cambridge University Press, 1979), pp. 196–213.

19. Ned Block, "Troubles with Functionalism," in C. Wade Savage, ed., *Perception and Cognition: Issues in the Foundations of Psychology*, vol. 9, *Minnesota Studies in the Philosophy of Science* (Minneapolis: University of Minnesota Press, 1978), pp. 279–281.

20. Derek Parfit, *Reasons and Persons* (New York: Oxford University Press, 1984), pp. 246–248.

21. In chapter 3, I argue that only the functional features are relevant.

Chapter 7

1. This is a stipulative definition. The question of whether there are cases that we would describe as self-deception (if we had access to all the facts) but that do not fall under this definition is one I shall leave open. What distinguishes this case is its theoretical simplicity, the fact that it is likely to figure in the analysis of at least some more complex cases, and the fact that it is the most difficult case. For some of the difficulties of giving necessary and sufficient conditions for our actual use of the term, see Jennifer Radden, "Defining Self-Deception," *Dialogue* 23 (1984): 103–120.

2. See F. A. Siegler, "Demos on Lying to Oneself," *Journal of Philosophy* 59 (1962): 469–475; J. V. Canfield and D. F. Gustafson, "Self-Deception," *Analysis* 23 (1962): 32–36; T. Penelhum, "Pleasure and Falsity," *American Philosophical Quarterly* 1 (1964): 81–91.

3. Roy Schafer, *A New Language for Psychoanalysis* (New Haven: Yale Univ. Press, 1976), p. 234.

4. See Daniel Dennett, "Why the Law of Effect Will Not Go Away" and "Artificial Intelligence as Philosophy and as Psychology," both in his *Brainstorms* (Montgomery, Vt.: Bradford Books, 1978), pp. 71–89 and 109–126, and William Lycan, "Form, Function, and Feel," *Journal of Philosophy* 78 (1981): 24–50.

5. See chapter 2, section 5, for some brief remarks on homuncular models and rationality.

6. For a number of objections to homuncular theories, see Ronald de Sousa, "Rational Homunculi," in *The Identities of Persons*, ed. Amélie Rorty (Berkeley: Univ. of California Press, 1976), pp. 217–238. De Sousa's objections, however, depend on his assumption that weakness of the will provides the strongest case for homuncular analyses. I would agree that if weakness of the will provides the strongest case, then such analyses seem misguided. But self-deception provides a far stronger case for homuncular analyses than the one de Sousa criticizes.

7. For a discussion that emphasizes the self-deceiver's responsibility, see Herbert Fingarette, *Self-Deception* (London: Routledge and Kegan Paul, 1969), chap. 2.

8. I shall not discuss determinism in what follows. However, it will make the motivation for the position I defend clearer if I make explicit my assumption that any justification of our practices of assigning punishment and blame should apply in what is, as it

were, the worst-case scenario for responsibility. This may be a case in which determinism is true, a case in which some combination of determinism and indeterminism holds, or a case in which some alternative is realized. My own view is that any coherent possibility is a worst-case scenario. But to defend this would require an argument that goes beyond the scope of the chapter.

9. Robert M. Adams, "Involuntary Sins," *Philosophical Review* 94 (1985): 3–31; Thomas Nagel, "Moral Luck," in his *Mortal Questions* (New York: Cambridge Univ. Press, 1979), p. 28; Joel Feinberg, "Problematic Responsibility in Law and Morals," in his *Doing and Deserving* (Princeton: Princeton Univ. Press, 1970), p. 35.

10. Thomas Nagel, "Moral Luck"; Joel Feinberg, "Problematic Responsibility"; Bernard Williams, "Moral Luck," in his *Moral Luck* (New York: Cambridge Univ. Press, 1981), pp. 20–39.

11. J. L. Mackie, *Ethics: Inventing Right and Wrong* (New York: Penguin Books, 1977), pp. 203–226; Holly Smith, "Culpable Ignorance," *Philosophical Review* 92 (1983): 543–571.

12. I use the expressions 'intrinsic desire' and 'noninstrumental desire' interchangeably, but I avoid the term 'intrinsic desire' in order to prevent confusion. Having the intrinsic desires one has is not one of one's intrinsic properties, since it involves one's values and commitments. And it provides the basis not for an intrinsic justification but for an internal justification (i.e., a justification that necessarily provides motivation) for a set of practices regarding responsibility.

13. This point is also made by Stephen Darwall; see *Impartial Reason* (Ithaca: Cornell Univ. Press, 1983), p. 109. I further develop the notion of an equilibrium with respect to one's noninstrumental desires in chapters 7 through 11.

14. Nothing depends on the assumption that the IRE for a particular subject at a given time will be determined uniquely (without appeal to the subject's ability to make arbitrary choices). Nonetheless, the assumption that in normal cases there will be significantly different possible equilibria is likely to stem from a misunderstanding of the concept. It should be emphasized that the addition and subtraction of desires is not motivated by an abstract commitment to coherence. What would motivate the heroin addict to eliminate the desire for heroin are competing desires, such as the desire for success in a conventional career, the desire for fulfilling relationships with nonaddicts, and the desire for a long and healthy life—desires that are systematically frustrated by the desire for heroin. Thus there would be no temptation to maximize coherence by eliminating all but one desire (and hence no necessity of choosing among the many ways of doing this). Given that one starts with a wide variety of noninstrumental desires, the desire to maximize coherence by eliminating all but one would itself be eliminated by its failure to cohere with a significant number of other desires.

Furthermore, the idea that a single desire would make up a maximally coherent set is mistaken. Though we may increase the chances that a set of beliefs is *consistent* by eliminating most of the beliefs in the set, we will not ordinarily increase its *coherence*. Though in a normal set of beliefs there is always the possibility of conflict, the various beliefs also support one another in virtue (at least in part) of the explanatory relations between them. Similarly, given a set consisting of a very small number of desires, though the potential for conflict would be minimized, the set would not be highly coherent. Such desires would be unsupported by other desires and hence would be arbitrary: if such a desire were to fade there would be no motivation to replace it. But desires that are mutually supporting may give one another significance that they would not have in isolation. (Gilbert Harman speaks of adopting ends in order to give significance to ends one has previously had and unity to one's life as a whole. I would not understand this, however, as Harman seems to, solely in terms of the means-end relation. See his "Practical Reasoning," *Review of Metaphysics* 29 [1976]: 461–463.)

Thus coherence among noninstrumental desires is maximized in a way that is motivated by the desires one already has: one eliminates those desires that are a source of serious conflict, adds desires that could help resolve existing conflicts (say by adding noninstrumental desires to do things that are required by one's other noninstrumental desires), and adjusts the strength of one's desires to maximize their joint satisfaction. The fact that this procedure still allows the possibility of a significant area of indeterminacy for particular agents will not affect the points I go on to make.

15. On the distinction between conditional and unconditional desires, see Derek Parfit, *Reasons and Persons* (New York: Oxford Univ. Press, 1984), pp. 151–154. For related distinctions among desires, see Stephen Schiffer, "A Paradox of Desire," *American Philosophical Quarterly* 13 (1976): 197–199; Thomas Nagel, *The Possibility of Altruism* (New York: Oxford Univ. Press, 1970), pp. 29–30; and Bernard Williams, "The Makropulos Case: Reflections on the Tedium of Immortality," in his *Problems of the Self* (New York: Cambridge Univ. Press, 1973), pp. 85–87.

16. The desires in one's IRE are endorsed at least to the extent that they would not be eliminated. The desires in one's conative core, however, represent commitments of a kind that it seems appropriate to identify as one's most fundamental values. Thus the notion of a conative core plays a role similar to the role played by Harry Frankfurt's notion of the first-order desires with which one identifies in virtue of one's second-order desires. (See his "Freedom of the Will and the Concept of a Person," *Journal of Philosophy* 68 (1971): 5–20. By switching from a foundationalist to a coherentist approach, however, I avoid the obvious problem for Frankfurt of an infinite regress to increasingly higher-order desires. More important, I avoid the problem that there is no necessary connection between a desire's being of higher order and its being a desire with which one identifies.

17. See Vinit Haksar, "Aristotle and the Punishment of Psychopaths," *Philosophy* 39 (1964): 323–340; Herbert Fingarette, *On Responsibility* (New York: Basic Books, 1967), chap. 2; Joel Feinberg, "Crime, Clutchability, and Individual Treatment," in his *Doing and Deserving* (Princeton: Princeton Univ. Press, 1970), pp. 252–271; J. G. Murphy, "Moral Death: A Kantian Essay on Psychopathy," *Ethics* 82 (1972): 284–298.

18. I shall be assuming throughout that justification is necessarily motivating. The assumption is defended below in this section.

19. The requirement is not arbitrary that any justification of our practice of ascribing responsibility, punishment, and blame must show how those made to suffer could be justified in acquiescing in the suffering and in feeling guilt and remorse. The requirement stems from the problem of distinguishing genuine punishment and blame from mere manipulation. As I shall argue in section 3, this distinction is firmly entrenched in our actual practices concerning responsibility, and no weaker requirement seems capable of capturing it.

There is another reason, however, for the requirement that a theory preserve this distinction. In the context of a defense of a homuncular view of self-deception, the problem is to justify, in the ascription of responsibility, a distinction between self-deception and other-deception that has no intrinsic justification. This problem only arises on the assumption that genuine punishment and blame involve more than manipulation to produce some desired result (and that there is more to justifying such distinctions in ascribing responsibility than such a consequentialist approach allows). The reason that the problem only arises on this assumption is that the consequences of blaming people for self-deception and for being deceived by others clearly differ in socially significant ways. Self-deception is far more likely to work to one's own advantage and to the disadvantage of others than is one's being deceived by another. Hence there are far stronger consequentialist considerations in favor of blaming the former than the latter. Thus, on a consequentialist approach to responsibility, the original problem for homuncular models of self-deception never arises.

Given the distinction between punishment and manipulation, the claim that *punishment* requires reachability does not imply, of course, that the *manipulation* of those who are unreachable is never justified. And we are surely justified in protecting ourselves against those who fall outside our practice of responsibility, punishment, and blame, just as we protect ourselves from the criminally insane. But the justification of such practices will differ from the justification of genuine punishment. For those who are unreachable, pain and suffering in excess of what is required to prevent greater pain and suffering would almost certainly be unjustified, though it is often justified for those who are reachable. On the other hand, measures that minimize suffering but would violate the autonomy of those who are reachable might well be justified for those who are not.

20. Given that neither consequentialist nor retributivist theories can justify the punishment of psychopaths, it would be useless to appeal to hybrid theories of punishment. If social utility cannot justify such punishment and retributivist theories fail, then the position that claims that punishment is justified because it is a part of an institution that maximizes social utility and that the institution provides constraints that prevent punishing the innocent is equally inadequate. If neither the utilitarian nor the retributivist justification is cogent on its own, then requiring that they both apply cannot solve the problem.

21. P. F. Strawson, "Freedom and Resentment," in his *Freedom and Resentment* (London: Methuen, 1974), pp. 1–25.

22. Strawson, "Freedom and Resentment," p. 22.

23. Notice that this account reverses the normal order of justification where responsibility is concerned. On the usual account, the metaphysical and value-neutral fact that a subject could have done otherwise (together with other value-neutral facts) grounds the ascription of responsibility that justifies the imposition of punishment or blame. On my account, the ascription of responsibility is grounded in our acceptance of the suffering that punishment and blame involve, our possession of the appropriate reactive attitudes toward the subject in question, and a certain kind of justification (to be described in section 5) of that acceptance and those attitudes. If there is any sense in which one could have done anything other than one did, it is to be understood in terms of the notion of one's being responsible and not vice versa. For an argument against the idea that one's ability to have done other than one did should be analyzed in terms that are ultimately normative, see Bernard Berofsky, "The Irrelevance of Morality to Freedom," in *Action and Responsibility*, ed. the Faculty of the Department of Philosophy, Bowling Green State University (Bowling Green, Ohio: Applied Philosophy Program, Bowling Green State Univ., 1980), pp. 38–47.

24. See Parfit, *Reasons and Persons*, pp. 12–23.

25. To interpret Strawson in this way is in effect to regard his position as a species of motive utilitarianism. (See Robert M. Adams, "Motive Utilitarianism," *Journal of Philosophy* 73 [1976]: 467–481.) To understand Strawson in this way is to suppose that the good to which the reactive attitudes contribute and that would justify our keeping them if we had the technology to bring about their elimination is independent of the attitudes themselves. Call this the *thin interpretation* of Strawson. On the

thick interpretation, Strawson would deny this. On the thick interpretation, Strawson's position would be much closer to the one I outline in sections 4 and 5. Strawson, however, does not develop the conceptual apparatus necessary to clarify the distinction between the positions corresponding to the thick and thin interpretations. Nor does he discuss the relativistic implications, which I discuss in section 5, of the position corresponding to the thick interpretation.

26. See, for example, Karl Menninger, *The Crime of Punishment* (New York: Viking, 1968); B. F. Skinner, *Beyond Freedom and Dignity* (New York: Alfred A. Knopf, 1971); and Barbara Wootton, *Crime and the Criminal Law* (London: Stevens and Sons, 1963) and *Social Science and Social Pathology* (London: Allen and Unwin, 1959), part 2.

27. These social conditions faced by the act-consequentialist will be part of the argument (in section 5) that our self-supporting dispositions concerning responsibility have an act-consequentialist rationale. But is it necessary, for cooperation, to require that subjects have an *internalized* disposition to keep promises even at great cost? If it is not, if some social mechanism of enforcement would secure the benefits, then the legitimacy of justifying a self-supporting disposition by reference to such a requirement is open to dispute. The question, then, is whether the requirements that motivate the acquisition of a self-supporting disposition to keep promises are realistic.

   The answer, I think, is yes. The institution of a *social* mechanism for enforcing contracts and promises itself presupposes self-supporting dispositions of the sort described. Even the practices of enforcement that we associate with organized criminal activity presuppose self-supporting dispositions to uphold contracts regardless of the consequences, at least on the part of the enforcers. Hence the reference to social mechanisms of enforcement postpones rather than solves the difficulties inherent in securing the benefits of cooperation.

28. The act-consequentialist might, of course, acquire an *indirect disposition* to support the institution of punishment in the lottery society. She might do so by acquiring a self-supporting disposition to keep her word and then promise to support the institution. Because the disposition is indirect, however, it would not provide the grounds for her acquiescing in the punishment of others in the sense of her being justified in feeling resentment or moral indignation. Nor would it justify her feeling guilt or remorse in her own case. Moreover, her disposition to support the institution in question is clearly parasitic on her self-supporting disposition to keep her promises come what may. And this latter disposition is precisely the kind that an account of responsibility should explain. Thus this possibility is one we can ignore where the justification of punishment and blame are concerned.

   There is another alternative to an indirect disposition, and that is an alienated disposition. Recall that the argument against Strawson's appeal to nonmaximizing dispositions to support our institution of punishment depended on a number of specific features of the social context in which it occurs: that judicial procedures are lengthy, impersonal, open to scrutiny, and subject to criticism and appeal and that particular decisions and not just the institutions themselves must be explained and defended. This means that there is room for a number of practices in some ways like punishment but based on nonmaximizing rather than self-supporting dispositions.

   Consider again the act-consequentialist who wants to join the society in which punishment is distributed by lottery. We have seen that given a perfect technology for acquiring and extinguishing dispositions, she cannot form the direct disposition to support the practice of punishment come what may. Suppose, however, we consider the case of imperfect technology. Let us define a *noncrisis period* as one in which a nonmaximizing disposition is supported on consequentialist grounds and a *crisis period* as one in which it is not. For the act-consequentialist, a noncrisis period is any period in which she calculates that the chances of her or a loved one's being chosen for punishment are outweighed by the advantages of living in the lottery society. In such a period it is to her advantage to join the society if she can and support its practices. And she is disposed to do so. If against all odds the act-consequentialist or a loved one is chosen as one of the people to be sacrificed, she enters a crisis period. It will then be to her advantage (and she will be disposed) to thwart the society's practices if she can and to eliminate any dispositions of hers that would prevent her doing so.

It is the possibility of such crisis periods that keeps the act-consequentialist from joining the society (or allows her to join only on the basis of an indirect disposition, the possibility of which is irrelevant for our purposes). Acquisition of a self-supporting disposition to uphold the society's practices would eliminate the possibility, since unlike nonmaximizing dispositions, self-supporting dispositions are always supported for the subject who has them. For the act-consequentialist, however, there is no direct self-supporting disposition to support the punishment lottery that involves no false beliefs.

Suppose that the technology for eliminating dispositions were, however, imperfect. The act-consequentialist might then join the society on the following terms. Assume that she could induce a disposition to support the practice of punishment and that, although not inextinguishable, could not be eliminated (for technological reasons) during the time span of any crisis period likely to occur. (The wheels of justice might move faster than any form of therapy or conditioning that could remove the disposition.) Such a disposition exists. All that is required is a desire whose motivational strength is great enough. In the absence of perfect technology, its lack of support among other desires is no impediment to its survival, and its strength ensures that it will be acted upon. From the point of view of the members of the lottery society, such a disposition to support the society's institutions would be a perfectly adequate alternative to one that was self-supporting.

From the point of view of the act-consequentialist, however, this disposition differs significantly from a self-supporting disposition. Let us call this non-self-supporting disposition an *alienated disposition*. The terminology is appropriate because for the act-consequentialist to act on this disposition would be for her to act against her best judgment. Her action would be analogous to that of a drug addict succumbing to a desire that he or she would destroy if the possibility were open.

Thus an alienated disposition to support the institution of punishment, like an indirect disposition, is not a disposition to acquiesce in the punishment of oneself or others, to recognize that punishment as appropriate, or to be justified in feeling resentment, indignation, guilt, or remorse. Hence the claim stands that unless our practice of ascribing responsibility and blame for self-deception has an internal justification, we cannot acquiesce in the suffering that such practices entail.

29. There is further support for the plausibility of this claim in Stephen Darwall's discussion of self-deception and autonomy in "Self-Deception, Autonomy, and Moral Constitution," chap. 19 in McLaughlin and Rorty, eds., *Perspectives on Self-Deception* (1988).

Chapter 8

1. Albert Spaggiari, *Fric-Frac: The Great Riviera Bank Robbery* (Boston: Houghton Mifflin, 1979).

2. That I take this claim for granted is meant to suggest not that the details are easy to spell out but merely that they are irrelevant to the issues at hand. See John Earman, *A Primer on Determinism* (Dordrecht: Reidel, 1986).

3. G. E. Moore, *Ethics* (New York: Oxford University Press, 1965), pp. 84–95.

4. Thomas Hobbes, *Leviathan, Parts I and II* (New York: Bobbs-Merrill, 1958), part 2, chap. 21; John Locke, *Essay Concerning Human Understanding* (New York: Oxford University Press, 1975), book 2, chap. 21, sec. 21; David Hume, *An Enquiry Concerning Human Understanding* (Indianapolis: Hackett, 1983), sec. 8; Moore 1965, pp. 84–95; A. J. Ayer, "Freedom and Necessity," in his *Philosophical Essays* (London: Macmillan, 1954), p. 282.

5. I am using 'classical compatibilism' in roughly the sense in which it is used by David Shatz. See "Free Will and the Structure of Motivation," in Peter French, Theodore Uehling, and Howard Wettstein, eds., *Midwest Studies in Philosophy*, vol. 10, *Studies in the Philosophy of Mind* (Minneapolis: University of Minnesota Press, 1985).

6. The problem might be circumvented, however, by appeal to an analysis of free action in terms of our behavior's being caused by our desires, wants, or preferences. This is a point to which I shall return in the discussion of hierarchical theories.

7. This kind of example is due to Harry Frankfurt. See "Alternate Possibilities and Moral Responsibility," *Journal of Philosophy* 66 (1969): 834–836.

8. This principle is discussed by John Martin Fischer in his *Moral Responsibility* (Ithaca: Cornell University Press, 1986), p. 19.

9. Frankfurt, "Freedom of the Will and the Concept of a Person," *Journal of Philosophy* 68 (1971): 15–19.

10. Frankfurt suggests in one passage (1971, p. 19) that moral responsibility requires only that *either* one does what one wants to do *or* that one's will is the result of a second-order volition. The rest of Frankfurt's discussion, however, suggests that both conditions must be met.

11. Frankfurt 1971, pp. 19–20.

12. See Irving Thalberg, "Hierarchical Analyses of Unfree Action," *Canadian Journal of Philosophy* 8 (1978): 211–226; David Shatz, "Free Will and the Structure of Motivation"; Gary Watson, "Free Agency," *Journal of Philosophy* 72 (1975): 217–219.

13. Fischer makes this claim, the possibility of which was anticipated by Watson. Moreover, Fischer agrees with Watson that this claim does not remove the difficulties for Frankfurt's position. See Fischer 1986, pp. 48–49.

14. Watson 1975, p. 220.

15. Watson 1975, p. 215.

16. Watson 1975, p. 215.

17. Watson, "Skepticism about Weakness of the Will," *Philosophical Review* 86 (1977): 331–332.

18. Watson 1977, p. 332.

19. *Journal of Philosophy* 81 (1984): 553–565.

20. Moritz Schlick, *Problems of Ethics* (New York: Prentice-Hall, 1939), chap. 7; P. H. Nowell-Smith, *Ethics* (Harmondsworth, England: Penguin Books, 1954), pp. 291–306; Daniel Dennett, *Elbow Room* (Cambridge: MIT Press, 1984) and "I Could Not Have Done Otherwise—So What?" *Journal of Philosophy* 81 (1984): 553–565.

21. P. F. Strawson, "Freedom and Resentment," in his *Freedom and Resentment* (London: Methuen, 1974), p. 4.

22. Strawson 1974, p. 23.

23. Strawson 1974, p. 23.

24. See, for example, Karl Menninger, *The Crime of Punishment* (New York: Viking, 1968); B. F. Skinner, *Beyond Freedom and Dignity* (New York: Alfred A. Knopf, 1971); and

Barbara Wootton, *Crime and the Criminal Law* (London: Stevens and Sons, 1963) and *Social Science and Social Pathology* (London: Allen and Unwin, 1959), part 2.
25. The account is summarized in chapters 9 and 11 and extended in chapter 10.
26. Quoted in Jonathan Culler, *Structuralist Poetics* (Ithaca: Cornell University Press, 1975), p. 156.
27. John Rawls, *A Theory of Justice* (Cambridge: Harvard University Press, 1971), pp. 19–21.
28. Frankfurt 1971, p. 12.
29. Jorge Luis Borges, "Borges and I," in *Labyrinths* (New York: New Directions, 1962).
30. Spaggiari 1979, p. 137.
31. I develop these remarks further in chapter 5.
32. See chapter 9.

Chapter 9

1. The example of SoHo indifference was suggested by Jerrold Katz.
2. This is not to say that there are not other ways of explaining how making oneself a multiple personality subject might constitute a rational response to the anticipation of unavoidable pain. For example, by making it the case that the different parts of one's future are not psychologically continuous with each other, one could anticipate now a *part* of one's future in which one would not anticipate the pain and suffering that one now anticipates. This seems, however, to be a much less powerful strategy for dealing with unavoidable pain than the one that involves withdrawing one's concern for those person stages that undergo the pain.
3. The role intended for the unconditional desires that survive in one's IRE is analogous to the role played by Harry Frankfurt's higher-order desires (1971). Both the notion of a desire's being unconditional and in one's IRE and Frankfurt's notion of a desire's being appropriately endorsed by a desire of second (or higher) order are intended to capture the intuitive idea of a desire's being one with which one identifies. And the desires with which one identifies are the ones that represent one's deepest values and commitments. I discuss these issues in more detail in chapter 7. The notion of an unconditional desire in IRE, however, is designed to sidestep the most obvious problem with Frankfurt's analysis: the fact that one's higher-order desires may be as alien to one as one's first-order desires and that the analysis therefore leads to an infinite regress.
4. The dichotomy that results if we put aside cases of ignorance is in one respect seriously oversimplified. (This was pointed out to me by Annette Baier.) Consider the case of genuine moral dilemmas. Suppose, for example, that before one has access to the pill that allows one to realize one's IRE, one has an unconditional desire not to betray one's friend, come what may, and an unconditional desire not to betray one's country under any circumstances. It seems at least conceivable that both desires might be well supported and that in forming one's IRE, one might opt to keep both. Moreover, one could opt to keep one's desires to accept blame and to feel guilt and remorse if one were to act in such a way that either desire were unfulfilled. And it seems conceivable that one could do this knowing full well that it would have the following result. There would be possible circumstances (those in which not betraying one's country would mean betraying one's friend and vice versa) in which one would be motivated to acquiesce in punishment or blame and in feelings of guilt and remorse regardless of what one's choice under those circumstances turned out to be. Suppose such an IRE is not inconceivable. Then it will *not* be the case either that we act in IRE without remorse (or without remorse that would survive in IRE)

and are not relevantly different from the psychopath or that we act out of IRE on the basis of a desire that we prefer not to have and are not relevantly different from the compulsive. We may act in IRE and still feel remorse that is itself fully supported in IRE. Such a possibility, however, contributes nothing toward the solution of the dilemma for ascriptions of responsibility and blame. The possibility of such an IRE simply makes the dilemma a trilemma. Suppose that one actually faced the situation in which one was forced either to betray one's friend or one's country. And suppose that in fact one betrayed one's friend. In this case one would be motivated in IRE to accept any blame ascribed by others in addition to one's own guilt and remorse. But it is even less obvious how one could be justified in doing so in this case than it is in the case in which one acts on a desire out of IRE.

5. P. F. Strawson makes the connection between genuine punishment and the appropriateness of these attitudes (which he calls other-reactive and self-reactive attitudes) when he says, "So the preparedness to acquiesce in that infliction of suffering on the offender which is an essential part of punishment is all of a piece with this whole range of attitudes of which I have been speaking. It is not only moral reactive attitudes towards the offender which are in question here. We must mention also the self-reactive attitudes of offenders themselves. Just as the other-reactive attitudes are associated with a readiness to acquiesce in the infliction of suffering on an offender, within the 'institution' of punishment, so the self-reactive attitudes are associated with a readiness on the part of the offender to acquiesce in such infliction *without* developing the reactions (e.g., of resentment) which he would normally develop to the infliction of injury upon him; i.e., with a readiness, as we say, to accept punishment as 'his due' or as 'just' " (1974, 22).

6. The similarities between the puzzle about responsibility and the puzzle about rationality, however, raise the following question. The puzzle about responsibility was generated by our taking as basic the problem of justifying our practice of blaming those who cause harm for which we regard them as responsible. The problem is generated, that is, by our taking as basic the problem of justifying such reactive attitudes as resentment and indignation where others are concerned and guilt and remorse in our own case and the suffering they entail. Similarly, the problem of rationality is generated by our taking as basic the problem of justifying a similar set of reactive attitudes toward those who cause harm by acting in ways we consider irrational. How, then, can we distinguish within this framework between irrationality and immorality?

It seems implausible to suppose that immorality and irrationality can be distinguished by a special set of reactive attitudes specific to each. It seems perfectly possible, for example, to feel guilt and remorse for one's actions that are irrational as well as those that are immoral. This seems especially true when an irrational action causes serious harm. It also seems implausible to claim that morality rather than rationality is involved if the interests of others are at stake. One can easily cause harm to others, as well as to oneself, by actions that are irrational but not immoral. Consider, however, a clear case of irrationality. Someone performs an action that leaves a whole group of people (including himself or herself) far less well off than some other action would have that was readily available. If we assume that the agent bears the others no ill will but rather has a genuine interest in their welfare, this seems to be a case of irrationality but not immorality. On the other hand, someone willing to gain an advantage by causing harm to others will ordinarily count as immoral. In what follows, I shall not try to refine this distinction any further, since it is sufficiently clear in the paradigm cases, and nothing I shall say turns on a more precise formulation.

7. For proposals that treat social deviance in medical terms, see Menninger 1968 and Wootton 1959, part 2; 1963.
8. In Strawson's case the need to justify our reactive attitudes is apparently denied, though some of Strawson's remarks might point in the direction of a theory like the one I suggest. For Dennett, the justification is a consequentialist one, and such a justification makes it difficult, as I have argued, to capture the distinction between punishment and blame on the one hand and manipulation and the exercise of power on the other. Glover suggests that we interpret our reactive attitudes as aesthetic attitudes. But our aesthetic attitudes may themselves fail to cohere with our desire not to cause others to suffer by blaming them for their actions when we have no justification for doing so. As a result, Glover seems to fall back on what is a consequentialist (and essentially utilitarian) justification of our reactive attitudes. Thus the possibility of an alternative approach to the justification of these attitudes is worth exploring.

Chapter 10

1. John Rawls, *A Theory of Justice* (Cambridge: Harvard University Press, 1971); "Kantian Constructivism in Moral Theory: The Dewey Lectures, 1980," *Journal of Philosophy* 77 (1980): 515–571; "Social Unity and Primary Goods," in Amartya Sen and Bernard Williams, eds., *Utilitarianism and Beyond* (New York: Cambridge University Press, 1982), pp. 159–185; "Justice as Fairness: Political, Not Metaphysical," *Philosophy and Public Affairs* 14 (1985): 223–251. Works by communitarians include Michael Sandel, *Liberalism and the Limits of Justice* (New York: Cambridge University Press, 1982); Alasdair MacIntyre, *After Virtue* (Notre Dame: Notre Dame University Press, 1981); Charles Taylor, "Atomism," in his *Philosophy and the Human Sciences: Philosophical Papers*, vol. 2 (New York: Cambridge University Press, 1985), pp. 187–210.
2. Rawls 1971, pp. 28, 31, and 449.
3. Sandel 1982, p. 14.
4. For Rawls's claim that the right is prior to the good in the normative sense, see Rawls 1971, pp. 3–4, 28, 31, 450, 563, and 574–575.
5. For a discussion of the priority of rights that makes this implication clear, see Robert Nozick, *Anarchy, State, and Utopia* (New York: Basic Books, 1974), pp. 28–30.
6. For the claim that the right is prior to the good in the sense of having greater generality, see Rawls 1971, pp. 260 and 447–448.
7. For the claim that the right is prior to the good in the justificatory sense, see Rawls 1971, pp. 211, 560, and 574–575.
8. The distinction between the normative and the justificatory senses of the priority of the right is similar to Sandel's distinction between the moral and the foundational senses. However, Sandel does not distinguish the priority of the right in the sense of its having greater generality from the other two. Sandel 1982, pp. 2–7.
9. Communitarians can accept the priority of the right in the sense of its having greater generality, since they allow for some variations in conceptions of the good, though not always at the same points at which their liberal opponents do. For a sketch of how a communitarian (or at least someone who denies the priority of the right in the justificatory sense) might come to accept the priority of the right in the normative sense, see section 6.
10. For the first principle, see Rawls 1971, p. 250. For the second, see p. 83.
11. Rawls 1971, sec. 4 and chap 3.
12. Rawls discusses hypothetical contracts and their justificatory force in 1971, pp. 21, 167–168, and 587, and in 1985, pp. 236–237.

13. For Rawls's discussion of the strains of commitment and the role it plays in the choice of principles in the original position, see 1971, p. 145, sec. 29, and p. 423.
14. Rawls 1982, p. 164.
15. Rawls 1971, sec. 24.
16. The problem of hypothetical contracts is discussed by Thomas Nagel in "Rawls on Justice," *Philosophical Review* 82 (1973): 220–234, and by Ronald Dworkin in "Justice and Rights" in his *Taking Rights Seriously* (Cambridge: Harvard University Press, 1977), pp. 150–183. Nagel claims that the problem would be solved by assigning a more modest role to the original position than the one it is required to play in a *Theory of Justice*. According to Nagel, the original position serves to *model* rather than to *justify* Rawls's version of liberalism. This suggests that although the original position and the corresponding arguments could not justify Rawls's liberalism to someone whose conception of the good could not be realized in a liberal society, the original position *could* play the following role. For subjects whose conception of the good would *not* be frustrated in a liberal society, it could guide the choice of specific principles that would govern such a society. Moreover, in guiding their choice of principles, it could play a role in systematizing and rendering more coherent the substantive moral intuitions of such subjects, thereby playing a role in justifying those intuitions *for them*. I shall go on to argue, however, that the original position cannot play even this modest role. The problem is not that the original position yields the two Rawlsian principles in virtue of an argument that begs the question against nonliberals. The problem is rather that the original position cannot be made to yield the two principles.
17. Rawls 1971, p. 21.
18. On the provisional acceptance of constraints, see Rawls 1971, sec. 4, especially p. 20, and sec. 87, especially pp. 578–579.
19. Rawls discusses commitment in 1971, p. 145 and sec. 29.
20. Rawls 1971, p. 175.
21. Rawls 1971, p. 183.
22. Rawls 1971, p. 166, sec. 28, and pp. 175–177.
23. For Rawls's discussion of principles guaranteeing highest average utility, see 1971, secs. 27–28.
24. For Rawls's discussion of slavery, see 1971, pp. 158–160, 167–168, and 248.
25. There is one complication in this line of argument. As I shall argue in section 4, one need not be rationally motivated by one's future concerns if they result from a sufficiently different conception of the good from one's present conception. But this means that one could commit oneself to a set of principles now (say the Rawlsian principles) even though one recognized that there were possible circumstances in which one would not be rationally motivated to support the principles (that is, those circumstances in which one's conception of the good was sufficiently different from one's present conception). Thus it might seem that the Rawlsian constraint requiring commitment is not sufficient to solve the problem of hypothetical contracts. And if this were the case, then even if we could commit ourselves to the Rawlsian principles in the original position, the principles could not serve as an appropriate source of appeal in either justifying or criticizing actual societies.

This conclusion, however, would be too quick. If we *could* commit ourselves to the Rawlsian principles in the original position, then the only *actual* people for whom the principles could not play a justificatory role would be those whose *actual* values and circumstances prevent their being rationally motivated to support the Rawlsian principles. And though the Rawlsian principles would not then play a justificatory role for every rational person regardless of his or her circumstances, they would not thereby cease to be of interest. The problem, as I shall argue in sections 5 and 6, is that in the original position we can imagine possible circumstances in which we would not be motivated to support the Rawlsian principles, the possibility of which *does* prevent us from committing ourselves to the Rawlsian principles in the original position. The problem stems from the fact that we do not have access in the original position to our substantive conception of the good. Thus we have no basis for discounting any of the substantive conceptions of the good that we might turn out to have when the veil of ignorance is lifted and that might be incompatible with the Rawlsian principles. (This argument is spelled out in detail in section 5.) Thus I shall be arguing not that the Rawlsian constraint is too weak but that it cannot be satisfied by the Rawlsian principles.

26. For the discussion of the maximin principle, see Rawls 1971, pp. 152–157 and 175.
27. Rawls 1971, p. 167.
28. Rawls does suggest the stronger reading when he says, "the parties cannot agree to a conception of justice if the consequences of applying it may lead to self-reproach should the least happy possibilities be realized. They should strive to be free from such regrets. And the principles of justice as fairness seem to meet this requirement better than other conceptions, as we can see from the earlier discussion of the strains of commitment (Sec. 29)" (1971, p. 423).
29. Rawls 1971, p. 169.
30. Rawls 1971, p. 250.
31. Rawls 1971, p. 83.
32. Rawls 1980, p. 525, and 1982, p. 164.
33. See 1971, p. 560, where Rawls makes it clear that our nature is independent of our aims and ends, just as it is independent of our desires. Interests do have a special status for Rawls, but this must be due to their being of higher-order than our other desires, rather than to their differing from desires in not being motivational states. For Rawls, our higher-order and highest-order interests could not, for example, be those things that we *ought* to desire, since we have access to these interests in the original position, where we lack any access to our substantive moral beliefs.
34. Rawls 1980, p. 525.
35. Rawls 1971, p. 145, where Rawls makes it clear that the capacity for a sense of justice is a capacity "to understand and act in accordance with whatever principles are finally agreed to."
36. See Rawls 1980, p. 526, where Rawls suggests the first reply and where he refers to Allen Buchanan, "Revisability and Rational Choice," *Canadian Journal of Philosophy* 3 (1975): 395–408, who suggests the second one.
37. For Rawls's use of the insurance metaphor, see 1971, p. 176.
38. The notion of identification has two components: one's ability to identify with one's future desires and one's ability to identify with the future self that has those desires. These two components will not be distinguished until the end of section 4.
39. Harry Frankfurt, "Identification and Externality," in Amélie Rorty, ed., *The Identities of Persons* (Berkeley: University of California Press, 1976), pp. 239–251, and "Freedom of the Will and the Concept of a Person," *Journal of Philosophy* 68 (1971): 5–20.
40. Frankfurt 1971, p. 7.
41. On internal reasons, see William Frankena, "Obligation and Motivation in Recent Moral Philosophy," in A. I. Melden, ed., *Essays in Moral Philosophy* (Seattle: University of Washington Press, 1958), pp. 40–81; Bernard Williams, "Internal and External Reasons," in his *Moral Luck* (Cambridge: Cambridge University Press, 1981), pp. 101–113; and Michael Smith, "The Humean Theory of Motivation," *Mind* 96 (1987): 36–61.

42. Gary Watson, "Free Agency," *Journal of Philosophy* 72 (1975): 205–220, and Wright Neely, "Freedom and Desire," *Philosophical Review* 83 (1974): 32–54.
43. I first make the distinction in chapter 7 and summarize it in chapters 9 and 11. The most complete account of the distinction occurs in chapter 8.
44. For Rawls's brief remarks about a relation of support among desires similar to the one I sketch, see Rawls 1971, p. 211. See also Stephen Darwall, *Impartial Reason* (Ithaca: Cornell University Press, 1983), p. 85.
45. I discuss some of the relevant issues in chapter 7.
46. For the distinction between conditional and unconditional desires, see Derek Parfit, *Reasons and Persons* (New York: Oxford University Press, 1984), pp. 151–154. Related distinctions have been made by Stephen Schiffer, "A Paradox of Desire," *American Philosophical Quarterly* 13 (1976): 197–199; Thomas Nagel, *The Possibility of Altruism* (New York: Oxford University Press, 1970), pp. 29–30; and Bernard Williams, "The Makropulas Case: Reflections on the Tedium of Immortality," in his *Problems of the Self* (New York: Cambridge University Press, 1973), pp. 85–87.
47. One would not, of course, want resources wasted on oneself if they could not make a difference and if they might make a significant difference to someone else. But good fortune might bring one out of one's depression, even if one did not care about being brought out.
48. On primary goods, see Rawls 1971, secs. 11, 15, 25, 40, and 60.
49. If unconditional desires were merely irrational and not incoherent, then although subjects in the original position would know that they might have such desires when the veil of ignorance was lifted, this alone would not prevent their committing themselves to (for example) the Rawlsian principles. They would be no less capable of commitment than would the Nietzschean whose commitments are not undermined by her recognition that she might in the future come to have Christian desires as a result of some process outside her control.
50. For a discussion of the relation between perfectionism and liberal principles of justice, see T. M. Scanlan, "Rawls' Theory of Justice," in Daniels 1975.
51. Henry Sidgwick, *The Methods of Ethics* (London: Macmillan, 1907); Parfit, *Reasons and Persons*; Nagel, *The Possibility of Altruism.*
52. Rawls 1982, p. 179.
53. Rawls 1980, p. 526; 1982, p. 165. The references are to Buchanan, "Revisability and Rational Choice."
54. Buchanan 1975, pp. 398–405.
55. Buchanan 1975, pp. 399–400.
56. Buchanan 1975, p. 401.
57. See Rawls 1985; Amy Gutmann, "Communitarian Critics of Liberalism," *Philosophy and Public Affairs* 14 (1985): 308–322; and Charles Larmore, Review of *Liberalism and the Limits of Justice, Journal of Philosophy* 81 (1984): 336–343, and *Patterns of Moral Complexity* (New York: Cambridge University Press, 1987), pp. 118–130.
58. Rawls 1982, p. 169.
59. Rawls 1982, p. 211.
60. For Rawls's use of religious differences as an analogy in clarifying the notion of incommensurable conceptions of the good generally, see 1980, pp. 539–540.
61. For Rawls's assumption that we have control over, and responsibility for, our substantive desires, see 1982, p. 169.
62. This scheme is very similar to one that Rawls has actually suggested. See "Two Concepts of Rules," *Philosophical Review* 64 (1955): 3–32.

63. The personal ideals and projects need not, of course, be private or idiosyncratic. That they are personal does not rule out their being the products of shared understandings imparted by the traditions of a particular culture.

64. For Rawls's reference to an overlapping consensus, see 1985, pp. 225–226.

65. For the claim that liberalism is not just another sectarianism, see Rawls 1985, p. 246.

66. For the claim that support of the principles involves more than a modus vivendi, see Rawls 1985, p. 250. Charles Larmore criticizes this claim in *Patterns of Moral Complexity*, pp. 123–125.

Chapter 11

1. John Harsanyi, "Rule Utilitarianism and Decision Theory," in Hans Gottinger and Werner Leinfellner, eds., *Decision Theory and Social Ethics* (Dordrecht: Reidel, 1978), p. 11.

2. If there is an internal problem for a theory, then in Derek Parfit's terms the theory is indirectly individually self-defeating. See his *Reasons and Persons* (New York: Oxford University Press, 1984), pp. 5–7.

3. The example is J. J. C. Smart's. See J. J. C. Smart and Bernard Williams, *Utilitarianism: For and Against* (New York: Cambridge University Press, 1973), pp. 69–70.

4. Smart and Williams 1973, pp. 69–72.

5. See Smart and Williams 1973, pp. 11–12, and David Lyons, *The Forms and Limits of Utilitarianism* (New York: Oxford University Press, 1965), chap. 3.

6. Allan Gibbard, "Rule-Utilitarianism: Merely an Illusory Alternative?" *Australasian Journal of Philosophy* 43 (1965): 211–220; G. Ezorsky, "A Defense of Rule Utilitarianism against David Lyons," *Journal of Philosophy* 65 (1968): 533–544; Donald Regan, *Utilitarianism and Co-operation* (New York: Oxford University Press, 1980), pp. 18–19.

7. This point is made by McCloskey (1963) and discussed by Smart in Smart and Williams 1973, p. 70.

8. The application of condition (1) to rule utilitarianism is as follows. Let $R_1 = \{P_1, P_2, \ldots\}$. Let P_1 = the property of an action's being prescribed by set S_1 of rules, let P_2 = the property of an action's being prescribed by set S_2 of rules, etc. According to rule utilitarianism, for every property P in R_1 and every action a, an action is right if and only if (i) the consequences of all actions that have P being performed are at least as good as the consequences of all actions being performed that have any other property in R_1 and (ii) a has property P.

Condition (2) has the following application to one version of motive utilitarianism. Let $R_2 = \{Q_1, Q_2, \ldots\}$. Let Q_1 = the property of everyone's having motivational makeup M_1, let Q_2 = the property of everyone's having motivational makeup M_2, etc. According to (one version of) motive utilitarianism, for every property Q in R_2, everyone's having the motivational makeup associated with Q is justified if and only if the consequences of everyone's having that motivational makeup are at least as good as the consequences of everyone's having the motivational makeup associated with any other property in R_2.

Obviously, many theories that are not intuitively versions of indirect consequentialism will count as versions according to this characterization. For example, theories for which either R_1 or R_2 contains only one element will fall into this category. For purposes at hand, however, that the characterization counts too many theories as versions of indirect compatibilism is not a serious drawback. It may be potentially confusing, however, that act utilitarianism is extensionally equivalent to a theory that satisfies the first clause of this characterization if we let R be the set whose only member is the property of being a particular action of an agent at a time such that the action makes at least as great a contribution to aggregate utility as any other action open to that agent at that time. We can, if we like, eliminate this example by stipulation.

9. H. L. A. Hart, "Murder and the Principles of Punishment: England and the United States," in his *Punishment and Responsibility* (New York: Oxford University Press, 1968), p. 80.

10. John Rawls, "Two Concepts of Rules," *Philosophical Review* 64 (1955): 3–32.

11. Similar criticisms of RC and of Rawls's suggestion in "Two Concepts of Rules" have been made by David Lyons. See his "Utility and Rights," in J. Pennock and J. Chapman, eds., *Ethics, Economics, and the Law* (New York: New York University Press, 1982). Lyons, however, does not frame the issue in terms of the motivation that a rational agent whose deepest commitment was to bring about the best consequences would have to comply with the theories in question.

12. It might be suggested that this problem could be solved by appeal to a rigid disposition to keep one's promises. Although this suggestion might solve the problem in certain situations, it has two drawbacks that prevent its being anything like a general solution. First, a rigid disposition would prevent the kind of flexibility in interpreting the spirit of a promise that is required in many situations. Second, a rigid disposition, if it were a disposition to satisfy a condition that could only be realized gradually over time, would leave one incapable of carrying out any other activities until the condition was fully realized.

13. See Harry Frankfurt, "Freedom of the Will and the Concept of a Person," *Journal of Philosophy* 68 (1971): 5–20.

14. The issue is somewhat more complicated than this suggests. We might think of the desire not to step on cracks as irrational and one that is in no sense a desire for something we value. But we might nonetheless recognize that although we would be better off without the desire, given that we have no effective way of eliminating it, it is less costly, and thus better, to satisfy it than to frustrate it systematically. In this case, however, it is open to proponents of this type of view to say that the desire that we want to determine our actions is not the desire not to step on cracks but the desire that those first-order desires that are less costly to satisfy than to frustrate should be satisfied.

15. This is the account that I outline in chapters 7 and 9. I provide further details in chapter 8, and I extend the account in chapter 10.

16. See Rawls, *A Theory of Justice* (Cambridge: Harvard University Press, 1971), p. 20.

17. G. E. Moore, *Principia Ethica* (New York: Cambridge University Press, 1903).

18. One could not be motivated to convert to act utilitarianism by, for example, the belief that if one did not convert, a powerful figure would ensure that more rights violations would occur than would be brought about by one's conversion. Rights-based theories that take rights as side constraints require not that one do whatever is necessary to minimize the number of rights violations but that one refrain from violating rights. And in turning oneself into a utilitarian, one is either ensuring that one will violate others' rights or at least making it far more likely that that will occur. Suppose, however, that one knew with near certainty that if one made oneself into an act-utilitarian, one would not violate anyone's rights and would make a much greater contribution to aggregate utility than one would make if one remained a proponent of a rights-based theory. In this case, it seems, the conversion would not be ruled out by all rights-based theories according to which rights are side constraints. Any such theory should, however, rule out one's violating rights now in order to make oneself less prone to do so in the future.

19. Although the mere-facts objection is related to John Mackie's argument from queerness (*Ethics: Inventing Right and Wrong*, pp. 38–42), the conclusion is significantly weaker than Mackie's. Whereas Mackie argues that the facts in virtue of which a moral theory is true would have to be intrinsically motivating, my claim is simply that the facts in virtue of which a moral theory is true, if the appeal to moral realism is to support utilitarianism, cannot be the kinds of facts in virtue of which 'Utility is good' and 'Maximizing aggregate utility is right' are true in the initial-baptism, natural-kinds, and conventional-usage examples.

20. At least it is incompatible with utilitarianism's lack of appeal for a significant segment of the population in the absence of a widescale conversion of that part of the population to a rights-based theory to avoid the problems of pragmatic self-defeat for utilitarianism. In other words, convergence to utilitarianism might be followed by conversion to some form of antiutilitarian theory as a result of utilitarian self-defeat. I discuss the possibility of such a conversion and its implications at the end of this section.

21. Richard Boyd, "How to Be a Moral Realist," in Geoffrey Sayre-McCord, ed., *Essays on Moral Realism* (Ithaca: Cornell University Press, 1988), p. 195. (All parenthetical page references are to this article.)

22. For a discussion of these issues in a somewhat different context, see Jon Elster, "Marxism, Functionalism, and Game Theory," *Theory and Society* 11 (1982): 453–482.

23. On the obstacles to social cooperation among rational egoists posed by many-person prisoner's dilemmas, see David Braybrooke, "The Insoluble Problem of the Social Contract," *Dialogue* 15 (1976): 3–37, and Russell Hardin, "Individual Sanctions, Collective Benefits," in Richmond Campbell and Lanning Sowden, eds., *Paradoxes of Rationality and Cooperation* (Vancouver: University of British Columbia Press, 1985). In contrast to rational egoists, those who are disposed to respect the rights of others will solve at least some of the many-person prisoner's dilemmas that make social cooperation difficult to sustain. Imagine a group of such people who can recognize each other with some degree of reliability in competition with people whose pursuit of their own self-interest is not similarly constrained. People in the former group could be expected to flourish, since their ability to trust one another would allow them to engage in cooperative behavior for mutual benefit in a variety of contexts in which people in the latter group could not. David Gauthier discusses some of the advantages open to those disposed to constrain the pursuit of their own self-interest in "Morality and Advantage," *Philosophical Review* 76 (1967): 460–475, and in *Morals by Agreement* (New York: Oxford University Press, 1986), chap. 6. But Gauthier does not discuss the kinds of psychological dispositions that could produce nonmaximizing behavior, especially in high-stakes cases.

Bibliography

Adams, R. M. 1976. "Motive Utilitarianism." *Journal of Philosophy* 73:467–481.

Adams, R. M. 1985. "Involuntary Sins." *Philosophical Review* 94:3–31.

Armstrong, D. M. 1963. "Is Introspective Knowledge Incorrigible?" *Philosophical Review* 72:417–432.

Armstrong, D. M. 1968. *A Materialist Theory of the Mind*. New York: Humanities Press.

Armstrong, D. M. 1981. "What Is Consciousness?" In his *Nature of Mind*. Ithaca: Cornell University Press.

Ayer, A. J. 1954. "Freedom and Necessity." In his *Philosophical Essays*. London: Macmillan.

Baars, B. 1983. "Conscious Contents Provide the Nervous System with Coherent, Global Information." In Davidson, Schwartz, and Shapiro 1983.

Baker, G., and Hacker, P. M. S. 1984. *Scepticism, Rules, and Language*. Oxford: Blackwell.

Bennett, J. 1966. *Kant's Analytic*. New York: Cambridge University Press.

Berofsky, B. 1980. "The Irrelevance of Morality to Freedom." In *Action and Responsibility*, ed. the Faculty of the Department of Philosophy, Bowling Green State University. Bowling Green, Ohio: Applied Philosophy Program, Bowling Green State University.

Blackburn, S. 1984. "The Individual Strikes Back." *Synthese* 58:281–301.

Block, N. 1978. "Troubles with Functionalism." In C. W. Savage, ed., *Perception and Cognition: Issues in the Foundations of Psychology*, Minnesota Studies in the Philosophy of Science, vol. 9. Minneapolis: University of Minnesota Press.

Block, N. 1980. "Are Absent Qualia Impossible?" *Philosophical Review* 89:257–274.

Borges, J. L. 1962. "Borges and I." In J. L. Borges, *Labyrinths*. New York: New Directions.

Boyd, R. 1988. "How to Be a Moral Realist." In G. Sayre-McCord, ed., *Essays on Moral Realism*. Ithaca: Cornell University Press.

Bratman, M. 1987. *Intention, Plans, and Practical Reason*. Cambridge: Harvard University Press.

Braybrooke, D. 1976. "The Insoluble Problem of the Social Contract." *Dialogue* 15:3–37.

Buchanan, A. 1975. "Revisability and Rational Choice." *Canadian Journal of Philosophy* 3:395–408.

Burge, T. 1979. "Individualism and the Mental." In P. French, T. Uehling, and H. Wettstein, eds., *Midwest Studies in Philosophy*, vol. 4, *Studies in Metaphysics*. Minneapolis: University of Minnesota Press.

Campbell, K. 1970. *Body and Mind*. Garden City, N.Y.: Doubleday.

Canfield, J. V., and Gustafson, D. F. 1962. "Self-Deception." *Analysis* 23:32–36.

Chisholm, R. 1981. *The First Person*. Minneapolis: University of Minnesota Press.

Churchland, P. M., and Churchland, P. S. 1981. "Functionalism, Psychology, and the Philosophy of Mind." *Philosophical Topics* 12:121–146.

Culler, J. 1975. *Structuralist Poetics*. Ithaca: Cornell University Press.

Daniels, N. 1979. "Moral Theory and the Plasticity of Persons." *Monist* 62:265–288.

Darwall, S. 1983. *Impartial Reason*. Ithaca: Cornell University Press.

Darwall, S. 1988. "Self-Deception, Autonomy, and Moral Constitution." In McLaughlin and Rorty 1988.

Davidson, D. 1984a. "Belief and the Basis of Meaning." In Davidson 1984b.

Davidson, D. 1984b. *Inquiries into Truth and Interpretation*. New York: Oxford University Press.

Davidson, R., Schwartz, G., and Shapiro, D., eds. 1983. *Consciousness and Self-Regulation*, vol. 3. New York: Plenum.

Dennett, D. C. 1978a. "Artificial Intelligence as Philosophy and as Psychology." In Dennett 1978b.

Dennett, D. C. 1978b. *Brainstorms*. Montgomery, Vt.: Bradford Books.

Dennett, D. C. 1978c. "Why the Law of Effect Will Not Go Away." In Dennett 1978b.

Dennett, D. C. 1978d. "Why You Can't Make a Computer That Feels Pain." In Dennett 1978b.

Dennett, D. C. 1982. "Beyond Belief." In Andrew Woodfield, ed., *Thought and Object*. New York: Oxford University Press.

Dennett, D. C. 1984a. *Elbow Room*. Cambridge: MIT Press.

Dennett, D. C. 1984b. "I Could Not Have Done Otherwise—So What?" *Journal of Philosophy* 81:553–565.

De Sousa, R. 1976. "Rational Homunculi." In A. Rorty 1976.

Dworkin, G. 1970. "Acting Freely." *Noûs* 4:367–383.

Dworkin, R. 1977. "Justice and Rights." In his *Taking Rights Seriously*. Cambridge: Harvard University Press.

Earman, J. 1986. *A Primer on Determinism*. Dordrecht: Reidel.

Elster, J. 1982. "Marxism, Functionalism, and Game Theory." *Theory and Society* 11:453–482.

Ezorsky, G. 1968. "A Defense of Rule Utilitarianism against David Lyons." *Journal of Philosophy* 65:533–544.

Feinberg, J. 1970a. "Crime, Clutchability, and Individual Treatment." In Feinberg 1970b.

Feinberg, J. 1970b. *Doing and Deserving*. Princeton: Princeton University Press.

Feinberg, J. 1970c. "Problematic Responsibility in Law and Morals." In Feinberg 1970b.

Field, H. 1974. "Quine and the Correspondence Theory." *Philosophical Review* 83:200–228.

Field, H. 1975. "Conventionalism and Instrumentalism in Semantics." *Noûs* 9:375–405.

Field, H. 1978. "Mental Representation." *Erkenntnis* 13:9–61.

Fingarette, H. 1967. *On Responsibility*. New York: Basic Books.

Fingarette, H. 1969. *Self-Deception*. London: Routledge and Kegan Paul.

Fischer, J. M. 1986. *Moral Responsibility*. Ithaca: Cornell University Press.

Fodor, J. 1987. *Psychosemantics*. Cambridge: MIT Press.

Fogelin, R. 1976. *Wittgenstein*. London: Routledge and Kegan Paul.

Frankena, W. 1958. "Obligation and Motivation in Recent Moral Philosophy." In A. I. Melden, ed., *Essays in Moral Philosophy*. Seattle: University of Washington Press.

Frankfurt, H. 1969. "Alternate Possibilities and Moral Responsibility." *Journal of Philosophy* 66:829–839.

Frankfurt, H. 1971. "Freedom of the Will and the Concept of a Person." *Journal of Philosophy* 68:5–20.

Frankfurt, H. 1976. "Identification and Externality." In A. Rorty 1976.

French, P., Uehling, T., and Wettstein, H., eds. 1979. *Contemporary Perspectives in the Philosophy of Language*. Minneapolis: University of Minnesota Press.

Gauthier, D. 1967. "Morality and Advantage." *Philosophical Review* 76:460–475.

Gauthier, D. 1986. *Morals by Agreement*. New York: Oxford University Press.

Gibbard, A. 1965. "Rule-Utilitarianism: Merely an Illusory Alternative?" *Australasian Journal of Philosophy* 43:211–220.

Glover, J. 1983. "Self-Creation." *Proceedings of the British Academy* 69:445–471.

Goldman, A. 1976. "Discrimination and Perceptual Knowledge." *Journal of Philosophy* 73:771–791.

Gutmann, A. 1985. "Communitarian Critics of Liberalism." *Philosophy and Public Affairs* 14:308–322.

Haksar, V. 1964. "Aristotle and the Punishment of Psychopaths." *Philosophy* 39:323–340.

Haksar, V. 1965. "The Responsibility of Psychopaths." *Philosophical Quarterly* 15:135–145.

Hardin, R. 1985. "Individual Sanctions, Collective Benefits." In Richmond Campbell and Lanning Sowden, eds., *Paradoxes of Rationality and Cooperation*. Vancouver: University of British Columbia Press.

Harman, G. 1976. "Practical Reasoning." *Review of Metaphysics* 29:431–463.

Harman, G. 1982. "Conceptual Role Semantics." *Notre Dame Journal of Formal Logic* 23:242–246.

Harsanyi, J. 1978. "Rule Utilitarianism and Decision Theory." In H. Gottinger and W. Leinfellner, eds., *Decision Theory and Social Ethics*. Dordrecht: Reidel.

Hart, H. L. A. 1968. "Murder and the Principles of Punishment: England and the United States." In his *Punishment and Responsibility*. New York: Oxford University Press.

Hobbes, T. 1958. *Leviathan, Parts I and II*. New York: Bobbs-Merrill.

Horgan, T. 1983. "Supervenience and Cosmic Hermeneutics." *Southern Journal of Philosophy* 22, supplement: 19–38.

Hume, D. 1983. *An Enquiry Concerning Human Understanding*. Indianapolis: Hackett.

Husserl, E. 1973. *Cartesian Meditations*. The Hague: Martinus Nijhoff.

Jackson, F. 1973. "Is There a Good Argument against the Incorrigibility Thesis?" *Australasian Journal of Philosophy* 51:51–62.

Kant, I. 1965. *Critique of Pure Reason*. New York: St. Martin's Press.

Kaplan, D. 1979a. "Dthat." In French, Uehling, and Wettstein 1979.

Kaplan, D. 1979b. "On the Logic of Demonstratives." In French, Uehling, and Wettstein 1979.

Kaplan, D. 1989. "Demonstratives." In J. Almog, J. Perry, and H. Wettstein, eds., *Themes from Kaplan*. New York: Oxford University Press.

Kim, J. 1976. "Events as Property Exemplifications." In M. Brand and D. Walton, eds., *Action Theory*. Dordrecht: Reidel.

Kitcher, P. 1978. "Theories, Theorists, and Theoretical Change." *Philosophical Review* 87:519–547.

Kitcher, P. 1979. "Phenomenal Qualities." *American Philosophical Quarterly* 16:123–129.

Kitcher, P. 1982. "Two Versions of the Identity Theory." *Erkenntnis* 17:213–228.

Kripke, S. 1979. "A Puzzle about Belief." In Avishai Margalit, ed., *Meaning and Use*. Dordrecht: Reidel.

Kripke, S. 1980. *Naming and Necessity*. Cambridge: Harvard University Press.

Kripke, S. 1982. *Wittgenstein on Rules and Private Language*. Cambridge: Harvard University Press.

Larmore, C. 1984. Review of *Liberalism and the Limits of Justice*. *Journal of Philosophy* 81:336–343.

Larmore, C. 1987. *Patterns of Moral Complexity*. New York: Cambridge University Press.

Lehrer, K. 1974. *Knowledge*. New York: Oxford University Press.

Lewis, D. 1972. "Psychophysical and Theoretical Identifications." *Australasian Journal of Philosophy* 50:249–258.

Lewis, D. 1983a. "Mad Pain and Martian Pain." In Lewis 1983b.

Lewis, D. 1983b. *Philosophical Papers*, vol. 1. New York: Oxford University Press.

Lewis, D. 1983c. "Postscript to Mad Pain and Martian Pain." In Lewis 1983b.

Lewis, D. 1983d. "Radical Interpretation." In Lewis 1983b.

Loar, B. 1986. "Social Content and Psychological Content." In D. Merrill and R. Grimm, eds., *Contents of Thought*. Tucson: University of Arizona Press.

Locke, J. 1975. *Essay Concerning Human Understanding*. New York: Oxford University Press.

Lycan, W. 1981. "Form, Function, and Feel." *Journal of Philosophy* 78:24–50.

Lyons, D. 1965. *The Forms and Limits of Utilitarianism*. New York: Oxford University Press.

Lyons, D. 1982. "Utility and Rights." In J. Pennock and J. Chapman, eds., *Ethics, Economics, and the Law*. New York: New York University Press.

McCloskey, H. J. 1963. "A Note on Utilitarian Punishment." *Mind* 72:599.

McInerny, P. 1983. "My Future, Right or Wrong." *Philosophical Studies* 44:235–245.

MacIntyre, A. 1981. *After Virtue*. Notre Dame: Notre Dame University Press.

Mackie, J. L. 1977. *Ethics: Inventing Right and Wrong*. New York: Penguin Books.

McLaughlin, B., and Rorty, A., eds. 1988. *Perspectives on Self-Deception*. Berkeley: University of California Press.

Menninger, K. 1968. *The Crime of Punishment*. New York: Viking.

Moore, G. E. 1903. *Principia Ethica*. New York: Cambridge University Press.

Moore, G. E. 1965. *Ethics*. New York: Oxford University Press.

Murphy, J. G. 1972. "Moral Death: A Kantian Essay on Psychopathy." *Ethics* 82:284–298.

Nagel, T. 1970. *The Possibility of Altruism*. New York: Oxford University Press.

Nagel, T. 1973. "Rawls on Justice." *Philosophical Review* 82:220–234.

Nagel, T. 1979a. "Moral Luck." In Nagel 1979b.

Nagel, T. 1979b. *Mortal Questions*. New York: Cambridge University Press.

Nagel, T. 1979c. "Subjective and Objective." In Nagel 1979b.

Nagel, T. 1980. "The Limits of Objectivity." In *The Tanner Lectures on Human Values*. Salt Lake City: University of Utah Press.

Neely, W. 1974. "Freedom and Desire." *Philosophical Review* 83:32–54.

Nemirow, L. 1979. "Functionalism and the Subjective Quality of Experience." Dissertation, Stanford University.

Nowell-Smith, P. H. 1954. *Ethics*. Harmondsworth, England: Penguin Books.

Nozick, R. 1974. *Anarchy, State, and Utopia*. New York: Basic Books.

Nozick, R. 1981. *Philosophical Explanations*. Cambridge: Harvard University Press.

Parfit, D. 1984. *Reasons and Persons*. New York: Oxford University Press.

Penelhum, T. 1964. "Pleasure and Falsity." *American Philosophical Quarterly* 1:81–91.

Perry, J. 1977. "Frege on Demonstratives." *Philosophical Review* 86:474–497.

Perry, J. 1979. "The Problem of the Essential Indexical." *Noûs* 13:3–21.

Pollock, J. 1974. *Knowledge and Justification*. Princeton: Princeton University Press.

Putnam, H. 1973. "Meaning and Reference." *Journal of Philosophy* 70:699–711.

Putnam, H. 1975a. "Explanation and Reference." In Putnam 1975d.

Putnam, H. 1975b. "Is Semantics Possible?" In Putnam 1975d.

Putnam, H. 1975c. "The Meaning of 'Meaning'." In Putnam 1975d.

Putnam, H. 1975d. *Mind, Language, and Reality*. Vol. 2 of *Philosophical Papers*. New York: Cambridge University Press.

Putnam, H. 1981. *Reason, Truth, and History*. New York: Cambridge University Press.

Radden, J. 1984. "Defining Self-Deception." *Dialogue* 23:103–120.

Rawls, J. 1955. "Two Concepts of Rules." *Philosophical Review* 64:3–32.

Rawls, J. 1971. *A Theory of Justice.* Cambridge: Harvard University Press.

Rawls, J. 1980. "Kantian Constructivism in Moral Theory: The Dewey Lectures, 1980." *Journal of Philosophy* 77:515–571.

Rawls, J. 1982. "Social Unity and Primary Goods." In A. Sen and B. Williams, eds., *Utilitarianism and Beyond.* New York: Cambridge University Press.

Rawls, J. 1985. "Justice as Fairness: Political, Not Metaphysical." *Philosophy and Public Affairs* 14:223–251.

Regan, D. 1980. *Utilitarianism and Co-operation.* New York: Oxford University Press.

Rey, G. 1980. "Functionalism and the Emotions." In A. Rorty, ed., *Explaining the Emotions.* Berkeley: University of California Press.

Rey, G. 1983. "A Reason for Doubting the Existence of Consciousness." In Davidson, Schwartz, and Shapiro 1983.

Rorty, A., ed. 1976. *The Identities of Persons.* Berkeley: University of California Press.

Rorty, A. 1988. "Persons and Personae." In her *Mind in Action.* Boston: Beacon.

Rorty, R. 1970. "Incorrigibility as the Mark of the Mental." *Journal of Philosophy* 68:399–424.

Ryle, G. 1963. *The Concept of Mind.* Harmondsworth, England: Penguin Books.

Sandel, M. 1982. *Liberalism and the Limits of Justice.* New York: Cambridge University Press.

Scanlan, T. M. 1975. "Rawls' Theory of Justice." In N. Daniels, ed., *Reading Rawls.* New York: Basic Books.

Schafer, R. 1976. *A New Language for Psychoanalysis.* New Haven: Yale University Press.

Schiffer, S. 1976. "A Paradox of Desire." *American Philosophical Quarterly* 13:195–203.

Schlick, M. 1939. *Problems of Ethics.* New York: Prentice-Hall.

Schlick, M. 1959. "Positivism and Realism." In A. J. Ayer, ed., *Logical Positivism.* New York: Free Press.

Seager, W. 1983. "Functionalism, Qualia, and Causation." *Mind* 92:174–188.

Searle, J. 1980. "Minds, Brains, and Programs." *Behavioral and Brain Sciences* 3:417–457.

Searle, J. 1981. "Analytic Philosophy and Mental Phenomena." In P. French, T. Uehling, and H. Wettstein, eds., *Midwest Studies in Philosophy,* vol. 6, *Foundations of Analytic Philosophy.* Minneapolis: University of Minnesota Press.

Shatz, D. 1985. "Free Will and the Structure of Motivation." In P. French, T. Uehling, and H. Wettstein, eds., *Midwest Studies in Philosophy,* vol. 10, *Studies in the Philosophy of Mind.* Minneapolis: University of Minnesota Press.

Shoemaker, S. 1975. "Functionalism and Qualia." *Philosophical Studies* 27:291–315.

Shoemaker, S. 1981. "Absent Qualia Are Impossible—A Reply to Block." *Philosophical Review* 90:581–599.

Shoemaker, S. 1982. "The Inverted Spectrum." *Journal of Philosophy* 79:357–381.

Shoemaker, S., and Swinburne, R. 1984. *Personal Identity.* Oxford: Blackwell.

Sidgwick, H. 1907. *The Methods of Ethics.* London: Macmillan.

Siegler, F. A. 1962. "Demos on Lying to Oneself." *Journal of Philosophy* 59:469–475.

Skinner, B. F. 1971. *Beyond Freedom and Dignity.* New York: Alfred A. Knopf.

Smart, J. J. C. 1971. "Sensations and Brain Processes." In D. Rosenthal, ed., *Materialism and the Mind-Body Problem.* Englewood Cliffs, N.J.: Prentice-Hall.

Smart, J. J. C., and Williams, Bernard. 1973. *Utilitarianism: For and Against.* New York: Cambridge University Press.

Smith, H. 1983. "Culpable Ignorance." *Philosophical Review* 92:543–571.

Smith, M. 1987. "The Humean Theory of Motivation." *Mind* 96:36–61.

Spaggiari, Albert. 1979. *Fric-Frac: The Great Riviera Bank Robbery*. Boston: Houghton Mifflin.

Stalnaker, R. 1989. "On What's in the Head." In J. Tomberlin, ed., *Philosophical Perspectives*, vol. 3, *Philosophy of Mind and Action Theory*. Atascadero, Calif.: Ridgeview.

Stich, S. 1978. "Autonomous Psychology and the Belief-Desire Thesis." *Monist* 61:573–591.

Stich, S. 1979. "Do Animals Have Beliefs?" *Australasian Journal of Philosophy* 57:15–28.

Stich, S. 1982. "On the Ascription of Content." In A. Woodfield, ed., *Thought and Content*. New York: Oxford University Press.

Strawson, P. F. 1974. "Freedom and Resentment." In his *Freedom and Resentment*. London: Methuen.

Taylor, C. 1985. "Atomism." In his *Philosophy and the Human Sciences*, vol. 2 of *Philosophical Papers*. New York: Cambridge University Press.

Thalberg, I. 1978. "Hierarchical Analyses of Unfree Action." *Canadian Journal of Philosophy* 8:211–226.

Watson, G. 1975. "Free Agency." *Journal of Philosophy* 72:205–220.

Watson, G. 1977. "Skepticism about Weakness of the Will." *Philosophical Review* 86:316–339.

White, S. L. 1982a. "Functionalism and Propositional Content." Dissertation, University of California, Berkeley.

White, S. L. 1982b. "Partial Character and the Language of Thought." *Pacific Philosophical Quarterly* 63:347–365. Reprinted as chapter 1 of this volume.

White, S. L. 1986. "Curse of the Qualia." *Synthese* 68:333–368. Reprinted as chapter 3 of this volume.

White, S. L. 1987. "What Is It Like to Be an Homunculus?" *Pacific Philosophical Quarterly* 68:148–174. Reprinted as chapter 6 of this volume.

White, S. L. 1988. "Self-Deception and Responsibility for the Self." In McLaughlin and Rorty 1988. Reprinted as chapter 7 of this volume.

White, S. L. 1989. "Metapyschological Relativism and the Self." *Journal of Philosophy* 86:298–323. Reprinted as chapter 5 of this volume.

White, S. L. 1990. "Rationality, Responsibility, and Pathological Indifference." In O. Flanagan and A. Rorty, eds., *Identity, Character, and Morality: Essays in Moral Psychology*. Cambridge: MIT Press. Reprinted as chapter 9 of this volume.

Wiggins, D. 1967. *Identity and Spatio-temporal Continuity*. Oxford: Blackwell.

Wiggins, D. 1980. *Sameness and Substance*. New York: Oxford University Press.

Williams, B. 1973a. "The Makropulos Case: Reflections on the Tedium of Immortality." In Williams 1973b.

Williams, B. 1973b. *Problems of the Self*. New York: Cambridge University Press.

Williams, B. 1973c. "The Self and the Future." In Williams 1973b.

Williams, B. 1981a. "Internal and External Reasons." In Williams 1981b.

Williams, B. 1981b. *Moral Luck*. New York: Cambridge University Press.

Williams, B. 1981c. "Moral Luck." In Williams 1981b.

Williams, B. 1982. "Cosmic Philosopher." *New York Review of Books* 29, no. 2, February 29.

Wittgenstein, L. 1961a. *Notebooks, 1914–1916*. New York: Harper and Row.

Wittgenstein, L. 1961b. *Tractatus Logico-Philosophicus*. London: Routledge and Kegan Paul.

Wittgenstein, L. 1968. *Philosophical Investigations*. New York: Macmillan.

Wootton, B. 1959. *Social Science and Social Pathology*. London: Allen and Unwin.

Wootton, B. 1963. *Crime and the Criminal Law*. London: Stevens and Sons.

Index